AS-Level
Geography

The Revision Guide

Editors:

Dominic Hall, Gemma Hallam, Kate Houghton, Simon Little, Becky May,
Kate Redmond, Jennifer Underwood.

Contributors:

Sheila Ambury, Margaret Collinson, Chris Critchlow, Peter Goddard,
Rebecca Rider, Dennis Watts, Pamela Watts, Eileen Worthington BSc hons.

Proofreaders:

Roger Best, Jamie Campbell, Edward Robinson, Eileen Worthington.

Published by Coordination Group Publications Ltd.

This book is suitable for:

AQA A, AQA B, Edexcel A, Edexcel B and OCR A.

There are notes at the tops of double pages to tell
you if there's a bit you can ignore for your syllabus.

ISBN: 1 84146 973 4
Groovy website: www.cgpbooks.co.uk
Jolly bits of clipart from CorelDRAW
Printed by Elanders Hindson, Newcastle upon Tyne.

Contents

The Hydrological Cycle

What better way to start off a lovely new Geography book than with some nice rivers...
*These pages are for **Edexcel A**, **Edexcel B**, **AQA A**, **AQA B** and **OCR A**.*

The **Atmosphere**, **Hydrosphere** and **Biosphere** Make Up a **Hydrological Cycle**

The global hydrological system is a **closed system**. This means that water doesn't come into planet Earth, and doesn't leave planet Earth. Earth's water goes round and round the **hydrological cycle**.

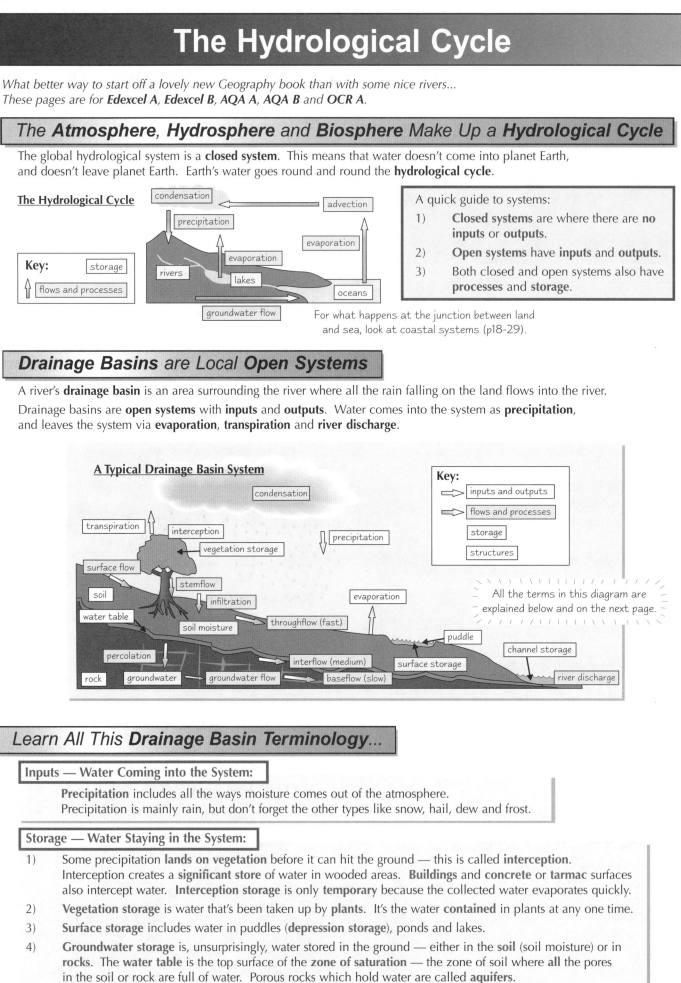

For what happens at the junction between land and sea, look at coastal systems (p18-29).

A quick guide to systems:

1) **Closed systems** are where there are **no inputs** or **outputs**.

2) **Open systems** have **inputs** and **outputs**.

3) Both closed and open systems also have **processes** and **storage**.

Drainage Basins are Local **Open Systems**

A river's **drainage basin** is an area surrounding the river where all the rain falling on the land flows into the river.

Drainage basins are **open systems** with **inputs** and **outputs**. Water comes into the system as **precipitation**, and leaves the system via **evaporation**, **transpiration** and **river discharge**.

Learn All This **Drainage Basin Terminology**...

Inputs — Water Coming into the System:

Precipitation includes all the ways moisture comes out of the atmosphere.
Precipitation is mainly rain, but don't forget the other types like snow, hail, dew and frost.

Storage — Water Staying in the System:

1) Some precipitation **lands on vegetation** before it can hit the ground — this is called **interception**. Interception creates a **significant store** of water in wooded areas. **Buildings** and **concrete** or **tarmac** surfaces also intercept water. **Interception storage** is only **temporary** because the collected water evaporates quickly.

2) **Vegetation storage** is water that's been taken up by **plants**. It's the water **contained** in plants at any one time.

3) **Surface storage** includes water in puddles (**depression storage**), ponds and lakes.

4) **Groundwater storage** is, unsurprisingly, water stored in the ground — either in the **soil** (soil moisture) or in **rocks**. The **water table** is the top surface of the **zone of saturation** — the zone of soil where **all** the pores in the soil or rock are full of water. Porous rocks which hold water are called **aquifers**.

5) **Channel storage** is so obvious that it's often overlooked — a river or stream almost always has some water in its channel.

The Hydrological Cycle

...and Learn All This **Drainage Basin Terminology** As Well...

Flows — Water Moving From One Place To Another:

1) **Overland flow** (or surface runoff) is water flowing over the land (duh...). It can flow over the whole surface or in little channels. Overland flow is common in **arid areas** where torrential rain falls on hard baked land.

2) **Throughfall** is water dripping from one leaf to another.

3) **Stemflow** is water running down a plant **stem.**

4) **Throughflow** is water moving slowly downhill through the soil. Throughflow is faster through "**pipes**" — things like **cracks in soil** or along **plant roots** or **animal burrows**.

5) **Infiltration** is water soaking into the soil. Infiltration rates are influenced by soil type, soil structure and how much water's already in the soil. In a heavy storm, water can't infiltrate away fast enough, so it flows over the surface.

6) **Percolation** is water seeping down through soil **into the water table.**

7) **Interflow** is like **groundwater flow** — water flowing **downhill** through **permeable rock** below the water table.

8) **Groundwater flow** is water flowing **slowly** below the water table through **permeable rock**. Water flows very slowly through most rocks but some rocks with lots of **joints** (gaps that water can get through), e.g. limestone, can have faster groundwater flow. Groundwater flow feeds into rivers through river banks and river beds — this is called **baseflow.**

9) **Channel flow** is the water flowing along in the river itself. This is also called the river's **discharge.**

Outputs — Water Leaving the System:

1) **Evaporation** is water turning into water vapour — going from a liquid to a gas.

2) **Transpiration** is a process carried out by plants. Plants and trees take up water through their roots and transport it to their leaves where it is transferred to the atmosphere by evaporation.

3) Evaporation and transpiration together are called **evapotranspiration.**

4) **River discharge**, or river flow, also takes water out of the system.

There are **Different Types** of **Rainfall**

For precipitation to happen, you need **clouds**. Clouds are formed when air rises — the water vapour in the air cools and condenses into tiny droplets. When tiny water droplets clump together to form big droplets, you have rain.

1) **Convectional rainfall** happens when convection (the **upward movement** of **warm air**) causes clouds to form. This happens when a chunk of land or sea surface is hotter than the areas around it. The air above it gets **hotter** and **less dense**, and **rises**. The air **cools** as it rises, and the water vapour it contains **condenses** to make tiny water droplets — a **cloud**.

2) **Orographic rainfall** is also called **relief rainfall**. It happens when the **air** moves towards a **hill** or **mountain**. The **slope** of the hill **forces** the air to **rise**. As it rises up into cooler air, it **cools** enough so that the water vapour it contains **condenses** to form a cloud. For relief rainfall, you need a steep enough slope to force air upwards.

3) **Frontal rain** happens at a **weather front**, where **two air masses** meet. Where **warm air** meets **cold air**, the warm air rises over the cold air and cools to form a cloud. There's plenty more about fronts on pages 48-49, by the way.

Practice Questions

Q1　List five ways in which water is stored in the hydrological cycle.

Q2　What's the correct term for water "soaking" into the soil?

Q3　Plants give off water vapour from their leaves. What is this process called?

Q4　Explain how "orographic rainfall" is formed.

Exam Questions

Q1　What difference does a permeable rock make to the flows of water in the water cycle of a drainage basin?　(4 marks)

Q2　How might seasons affect the amount of water reaching a river?　(4 marks)

Yeah, maybe it's a little large to wash your hands in...

There are two parts to this. First, you've got the global hydrological cycle with rain and evaporation and flowing water and all that. Then you've got the components of a drainage basin, and the processes going on in the basin. There's a mighty huge lot of processes and stores to learn, and unfortunately you do have to know them, otherwise the rest of the section will be El Tricky.

River Discharge

Some of this might be familiar from GCSE Geography, but some of it's bound to be new.
*These pages are for **Edexcel A**, **Edexcel B**, **AQA A**, **AQA B** and **OCR A**.*

River Discharge *is the* Amount *of* Water *Flowing* — *in* m³/s *or* cumecs

A "popular" Geography fieldwork task is to measure river discharge. To do this, you stand in the river, time the **channel velocity** by timing how long something that floats takes to pass between two points, and take measurements of the river's **width** and **depth**. You take these measurements at several points, and use them to make drawings of the river's **cross section**. Then you can calculate the amount of **cubic metres** of water that are flowing in the river **per second**.

River discharge is measured in **cubic metres per second** — this is a bit of a mouthful, so geographers usually shorten it to **cumecs**.

Doing river discharge measurements in UK rivers is a really good way to get absolutely FREEZING cold and wet.

1) **More precipitation** means more **discharge**.

2) **Hot weather** means a faster rate of evaporation, so **less discharge**.

3) People take water out of the river for various uses — this is called **abstraction**. This **reduces** the **discharge**.

Hydrographs *Show* River Discharge *Over a Period of* Time

Hydrographs are graphs of river discharge over time. **Storm hydrographs** show river discharge after a storm event. **Annual hydrographs** show river discharge over a whole year. The diagram below shows a really lovely **storm hydrograph**.

1) There's a **lag time** (delay) between the **peak rainfall** shown in the rainfall bar graph and the **peak discharge** shown for the river. This delay happens because it takes **time** for rainwater to **seep** into the soil and **flow** into the river.

2) The **rising limb** is the time when the discharge is increasing **quickly** after the storm event.

3) The **falling limb** is the time when discharge is **decreasing**.

4) The **exact shape** of the hydrograph varies with each **river drainage basin** — and each individual **storm event**.

5) A basin with **rapid runoff** and not much **storage** capacity gives a hydrograph with a **short lag time** and **high peak**. This is called a **"flashy"** hydrograph — as in "flash floods".

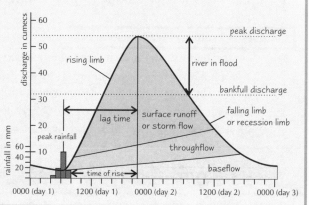

Drainage Basin Factors Affect the Storm Hydrograph

1) A **larger drainage basin** means more discharge — it catches a lot of precipitation. **Small** basins tend to be flashy.

2) **Steep sided** drainage basins have **shorter lag times** — because water flows **quickly** downhill into the river.

3) **Long, narrow** basins drain **slowly** over a long time — they have **longer lag times**. **Round** basins drain **quickly**, and have **shorter lag times**.

4) Basins with high **"stream density"** (lots of streams) drain **quickly**, and have **shorter lag times**.

Other Physical Factors Affect the Storm Hydrograph

1) **Weather** affects peak discharge. **Intense** storms usually give the most dramatic hydrographs. Weather also affects lag time — e.g. snow that's fallen in **winter** can **melt** and flow into the river in **spring**.

2) **Climate** affects peak discharge. Hot, dry climates have little precipitation and lots of evaporation.

3) **Rock type** affects lag time. **Impermeable** rocks don't store water — water has to flow through the **soil** (throughflow) and over the **surface** (runoff/overland flow) — this makes for a short lag time and steep rising limb.

4) The **type of soil** is a factor. Sand drains well, but clay gets saturated quickly. When soil's saturated, water has to flow over the **surface**. **Overland (surface) runoff** is much **faster** than **throughflow** and **baseflow** through soil and rock.

5) **Vegetation** affects **interception**, the amount of water **stored in** plants and the amount of **transpiration**.

6) The **amount** of water **already present** in the drainage basin (geography boffins call this **"antecedent moisture"**) affects discharge. If the ground's already **waterlogged**, water will flow quickly over the surface into the river, giving a short lag time and steep rising limb.

Storm Event Case Study — Lynmouth, 1952
See p13 for more on the Lynmouth flood disaster.

Heavy rain fell on **saturated** ground (there was a record rainfall of **300 mm** in the two weeks preceding the storm) — peak discharge was very high (above the maximum discharge that the river could keep in its banks). Runoff is **fast** in the **steep valleys** (some with a **1:4 gradient**) of the River Lyn drainage basin. The local geology of impermeable **Devonian sandstone** and **slate** increased runoff. The storm hydrograph for this event had a **short lag time** and a **steep rising limb**. The resulting flood was very severe.

River Discharge

Human Activity Also Affects the Hydrograph

1) In urban areas, the soil is covered with man-made **impermeable** materials like **concrete**. This increases **surface run off** — water flows quickly back into the river before it's had a chance to **evaporate** or **infiltrate** into the soil. This makes the lag time short — giving a **flashy** hydrograph with a risk of flooding.

2) Also, man-made **drainage systems** affect the hydrograph in a similar way. Water flows down drains into the river before it can **evaporate** or **infiltrate** into the soil — again giving a **flashy** hydrograph with short lag time.

The River Regime is the Annual Variation in Discharge

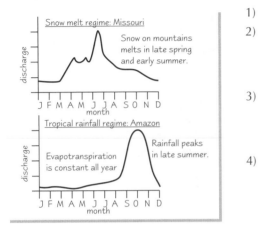

1) River regimes describe a river's flow through the year.

2) Most river regimes have some variation caused by climate. **Simple regimes** have one period of high discharge and one period of low discharge. They're influenced by **climate** — the **amount** and **timing** of **precipitation**, and the **rate** of **evapotranspiration**.

3) **Complex regimes** have more peaks and troughs in discharge. They're not just affected by climate, but also by characteristics of the basin itself, like variations in **rock type** and the **steepness** of the hills in the basin.

4) Complex river regimes are also affected by **human activities** — for example, management of a river to **provide water**, to carry away **waste**, to make the river **navigable**, and to prevent flooding. **Dams** tend to make the river regime **less variable**. Water stored in reservoirs is released into the river when needed.

5) **Small** drainage basins are likely to have **complex regimes**. In **large** river basins (e.g. the Amazon, the Missouri) the different variables tend to cancel each other out and leave you with just the effect of climate.

Soil Moisture Budgets Show How Much Water is Going Into and Out of the Soil

Soil moisture budgets are worked out from inputs and outputs.

1) In wet seasons, there's more **input** of water.

2) In warmer, drier seasons, there's more **output** — there's a lot of **evaporation** and a lot of **transpiration** from growing vegetation. This removes moisture from the soil.

3) At the end of a dry season, there's a **deficit** (shortage) of water in the soil. This has to be paid back in the next wet season. This payback is called **soil moisture recharge**.

4) **Field capacity** is where the soil has regained enough moisture for plants to use without becoming waterlogged.

Soil moisture budgets are just for Edexcel B people.

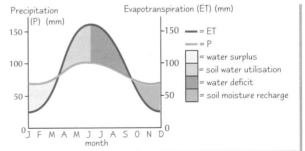

Practice Questions

Q1 What's the unit of measurement for river discharge?
Q2 What term is used for the amount of water the ground can hold without becoming waterlogged?
Q3 Why do some large basins have long lag times, while others have short lag times?
Q4 What is a "river regime"?

Exam Questions

Q1 Describe the human factors that can affect river discharge. (4 marks)

Q2 Explain how vegetation can affect a river's lag time. (4 marks)

You aren't discharged from learning all this rivers malarkey, yet...

Three different sorts of diagram on two pages must seem somewhat unfair. No need to get them mixed up, though. Storm hydrographs have lots of information for one graph, but they're not so bad once you learn them. River regimes are straightforward — discharge over the year. Soil moisture budgets show how much water the soil gets from rain compared to how much it loses.

River Processes

*All the rivers work you did in your earlier school Geography is coming back to haunt you now... It's unlikely that you'll remember it all, so read all this — including the easy bits. These pages are for **Edexcel A**, **Edexcel B**, **AQA A** and **AQA B**.*

Erosion of River Beds and Banks is an Important River Process

1) **Vertical erosion** deepens river channels. A large load of coarse material is needed to erode the river bed.
2) **Lateral erosion** makes the river wider. This happens in the middle and lower stages of the river.
3) **Headward erosion** makes the river longer. This happens up near the source of the river.

There are five types of river erosion:

1) **Hydraulic action** is the pressure of water breaking rock particles away from the bed and banks. It's strongest in rapids and at waterfalls, or during floods.
2) **Air bubbles** in turbulent stretches of water can **implode** and form a **vacuum**, **sucking** pieces of rock off the banks. This is called **cavitation**.
3) **Corrasion** (abrasion) is when the eroded pieces of rock **scrape** against the bed and banks, and remove more material. Most erosion of river beds and banks happens by corrasion.
4) **Solution** (corrosion) is the dissolving of rock by chemical processes. Carbon dioxide dissolves in water to form a **weak acid**, which reacts with rocks like **limestone** and **chalk**.
5) **Attrition** happens as eroded rocks smash into each other and shatter into smaller fragments. Their edges also get rounded off as they rub together. Attrition **doesn't erode** the bed and banks — it just makes the particles of rock in the river smaller and more rounded.

> Carrying **eroded material** helps the river **erode more**.
> **Clear water** isn't as good at eroding as water with **pebbles** and **sand** in it.

Transport is the Process of Carrying Eroded Bits of Rock along in the River

The **energy** of the river flowing downhill causes erosion and also provides the force needed to **transport eroded material**. The eroded material carried in a river is called its **load** or **sediment**.

1) **Most** material is carried by **suspension** — fine material is swooshed up by turbulence and carried along in the water above the river bed. Suspended material tends to colour the water and make it look dull and muddy.
2) Substances which can **dissolve** in water are carried in **solution**.
3) Large particles are too heavy to be carried in suspension. They can be **bounced** along the river bed, which is called **saltation**. Very large particles are **dragged** along the river bed by the force of the water. This is called **traction**.

Hippos — saltation, solution, suspension or traction?

The **amount** and **type** of sediment transport depends on these factors:

1) What the **bed and banks** of the river are like — a river flowing through smooth rock will carry less sediment than a river flowing over a loose bed of mud and sand.
2) Whether the river is flowing **fast** or **slowly**. The bigger the particle, the faster the river has to flow in order to transport it.
3) Whether **human intervention** has done anything drastic to the river, e.g. building a dam which would trap lots of sediment behind it.

Deposition is the Process of Dropping the Eroded Material

Deposition happens when the river **loses energy** so that it no longer has enough energy to carry its load of eroded material.

These are the main causes of energy reduction:

1) **Reduced rainfall** causes lower discharge, which means the river has less energy.
2) **Increased evaporation** or **abstraction** (taking water out of the river for human use) also causes lower discharge.
3) **Friction** in **shallow** areas of the river and close to the **banks** also uses up some of the energy of the river.
4) The river loses energy when it **slows down**, e.g. on the inside bend of a meander.
5) Finally, a lot of energy is **absorbed** when the river meets the **sea**.

River Processes

Each River has a Limit to the Load and the Size of Particles it can Carry

1) The **capacity** of a river is the **total load** being transported by the river.

2) The **competence** is the **largest size of particle** that the river can carry.

3) As **velocity increases**, larger and larger particles are transported. The **Hjulström** graph in the diagram shows the relationship between velocity and particle size.

4) As **velocity falls**, particles are dropped in **order of size**, largest first.

A **sediment budget** is the **balance** between sediment load **added** to a river and sediment load **dropped** by the river.

Since the Aswan Dam was built, the **River Nile** has a **deficit** in its sediment budget — the dam traps sediment behind it, so the **sediment input** in the river has decreased.

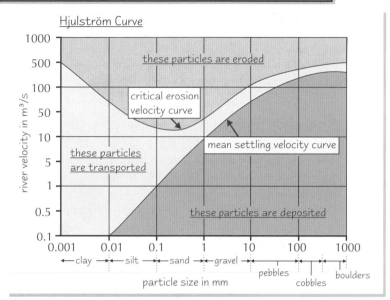

The Shape of a River Channel Affects its Transport Efficiency

1) The **more efficient** the river, the **more energy** it has available for erosion and transport.

2) **Channel efficiency** is measured by **hydraulic radius**. A really efficient river has a high hydraulic radius.

3) The hydraulic radius is the channel's **cross section area** divided by the length of its **wetted perimeter**. (The wetted perimeter is the banks and bottom of the river that are in contact with the water.)

A   cross section = 10m²
      wetted perimeter = 9m
      hydraulic radius = 1.1m

B   cross section = 14m²
      wetted perimeter = 11m
      hydraulic radius = 1.3m

River B is more efficient than river A

As you go Downstream, the River Channel Changes

These things get **bigger** as you go downstream from source to sea:

- **Velocity**
- **Discharge**
- **Width** and **depth**
- Channel **efficiency**
- **Amount** of load

These things get **smaller** as you go downstream:

- **Friction**
- **Turbulence**
- **Roughness** of channel
- **Size** of sediment particles
- **Gradient**

Practice Questions

Q1 What is "corrasion"?

Q2 How are very large particles carried by a river?

Q3 Give two examples of factors which can cause a river to deposit sediment.

Q4 What does the Hjulström Curve show?

Exam Questions

Q1 What does the hydraulic radius tell you about a river and how is it calculated?   (3 marks)

Q2 Explain why the mean particle diameter of sediment in a river decreases with distance from the river's source.   (3 marks)

Hjulström curve — sounds more like something you'd see in IKEA...

OK, apart from that scary-looking diagram, this is in fact pretty simple. Bits of river beds and river sides get knocked, sucked or scraped into the river. That's erosion. The river carries them along in its water, and then drops them when it slows down. That's transport and deposition. The faster the river is going, and the more water there is, the more stuff it can carry. See — not too bad.

River Landforms

You need to know about the **long profiles**, **cross profiles** (of either the **valley** or the **channel**) and the different **landforms** of rivers. These pages are for **Edexcel A**, **Edexcel B**, **AQA A** and **AQA B**.

If this slope is a smooth curve, it's called a graded profile.

The **Long Profile** is the **River's Slope** from its Source to the Sea

A long profile tells you what a 'side view' of a river from its **source** to its **mouth** looks like. Near the source there is lots of **erosion** and the profile is **steep**. At the mouth there isn't much erosion, but there is lots of **transport** and **deposition** and the river's **gradient** is very **gentle**.

These features affect a river's long profile:

1) **Waterfalls** are steps in the long profile. They form where hard rock resists erosion.

2) **Rapids** are mini-waterfalls with turbulent flow where there are several bands of rock of varying resistance.

3) **Potholes** can form when water is flowing quickly — they're made by pebbles whirling round in little holes in rocks.

4) **New land** can be created (e.g. **by falling sea levels**). If this happens, the river will erode into the new land and extend the long profile of the river. A waterfall (known as a **knickpoint**) will form and mark the junction between the old long profile and the newly created one.

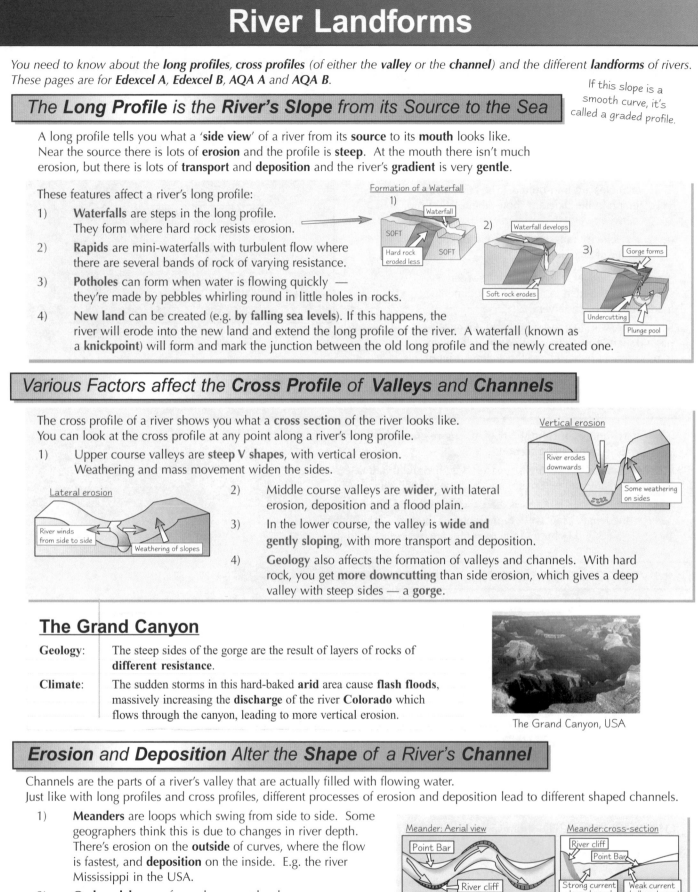

Various Factors affect the **Cross Profile** of **Valleys** and **Channels**

The cross profile of a river shows you what a **cross section** of the river looks like. You can look at the cross profile at any point along a river's long profile.

1) Upper course valleys are **steep V shapes**, with vertical erosion. Weathering and mass movement widen the sides.

2) Middle course valleys are **wider**, with lateral erosion, deposition and a flood plain.

3) In the lower course, the valley is **wide and gently sloping**, with more transport and deposition.

4) **Geology** also affects the formation of valleys and channels. With hard rock, you get **more downcutting** than side erosion, which gives a deep valley with steep sides — a **gorge**.

The Grand Canyon

Geology: The steep sides of the gorge are the result of layers of rocks of **different resistance**.

Climate: The sudden storms in this hard-baked **arid** area cause **flash floods**, massively increasing the **discharge** of the river **Colorado** which flows through the canyon, leading to more vertical erosion.

The Grand Canyon, USA

Erosion and Deposition Alter the Shape of a River's Channel

Channels are the parts of a river's valley that are actually filled with flowing water. Just like with long profiles and cross profiles, different processes of erosion and deposition lead to different shaped channels.

1) **Meanders** are loops which swing from side to side. Some geographers think this is due to changes in river depth. There's erosion on the **outside** of curves, where the flow is fastest, and **deposition** on the inside. E.g. the river Mississippi in the USA.

2) **Ox-bow lakes** are formed as meanders become more **eroded** until the **neck** of the loop is broken through, often during flooding. The loop is left as an oxbow lake, and **deposition** dams off the lake from the river.

3) **Braiding** happens when streams carry vast amounts of **eroded sediment** (e.g. in meltwater or in deltas). Sediment is **deposited** as **islands** in the channel, causing the river to **split up** into many small, winding channels.

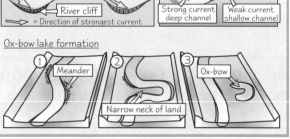

River Landforms

Flood Plains, Levees and Deltas are caused by Deposition

Flood plains get covered in deposited sediment

1) Deposition happens most where the river has a **flood plain** — a flat area of land on either side of a river that floods frequently.

2) Flood plains are formed as **meanders** go further and further **downstream**. The flood plain is covered by deposition when the river floods. The deposited material is called **alluvium**.

Levees are embankments

1) Levees are **embankments** formed by the river overflowing its banks. As the water spreads onto the flood plain, **friction increases** because the river is flowing over a much larger wetted perimeter. Some of the river's energy is absorbed, so the river drops some of its coarser load onto the flood plain surface at the top of its banks.

2) Levees can also be **man-made** (to stop flooding) and it can be hard to tell the difference.

Deltas are formed when the river reaches the sea (or a lake)

1) When a river reaches the sea (or lake) the **slow moving water** in the sea or lake **absorbs** the **energy** of the **river**.

2) This means that the river has to **drop its load** of material. These deposits build up on the sea bed. Eventually the alluvium rises above sea level, and **blocks** the mouth of the river. The river has to **braid** into several **distributaries** in order to reach the sea.

The **River Nile** has a huge **arcuate (fan shaped) delta** where it enters the Mediterranean Sea. The Mediterranean doesn't have **strong currents**, and has only a small **tidal range**. This means that large amounts of **alluvium** have built up.

The Nile used to flood **every year**, so a large area was covered with deposits each year. Since the **Aswan Dam** was built, the Nile no longer floods every year. The dam traps a lot of the alluvium that would have made the delta even bigger.

Arcuate delta

Digitate delta

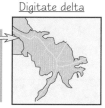

The Mississippi delta is a **bird's foot** or **digitate** delta.

It's formed where the sea is particularly **still**, allowing the distributaries to form long **undisturbed fingers** of deposits. This is similar to the formation of **levees**.

Extreme Events Have an Impact on River Landforms

Floods can change the shape of river channels — flood water breaks through meanders.

Lava flows can **dam** and divert rivers. See p 41 for more on lava flows.

Earthquakes can raise and lower ground level.

Practice Questions

Q1 Describe how waterfalls are formed.

Q2 Name a feature formed by vertical erosion that causes circular hollows in the river bed.

Q3 Which landform occurs along river banks?

Exam Questions

Q1 What are braided channels? Under what conditions do they form? (4 marks)

Q2 The R. Nile has been prevented from regularly flooding the flood plains in its lower reaches by dam construction. From your knowledge of rivers generally, what effects will this have on the river? (4 marks)

I drove my Chevy to the levee — and it was a boring old riverbank....

Some of this is covered in GCSE, so you may feel like you've seen it all before. Thing is, they take a slightly different tack at AS level — instead of treating rivers like they're all the same, with upper stage features, lower stage features and nice neat V-shaped valleys, they like you to be able to say how the river and the rock it's flowing through affect the shape of its lovely landforms.

Ecosystems in a River Environment

*These two pages are for **Edexcel B**. There's more about ecosystems in section 6, by the way, but for Edexcel B, you only need to know this river ecosystem gubbins and some coastal ecosystems in section 2 — not the section 6 stuff.*

Hydroseres show *Succession* (Changes) in *Fresh Water Environments*

1) Areas like **ox-bow lakes** which have **no vegetation** are **gradually colonised** by plants.

2) As years pass, seeds of **different species** can grow as **conditions improve** — the **soil** gets **deeper**, the lake **silts up**, and **decay** of dead **organic matter** provides more **nutrients**.

3) The **name** for this chain of events, from clear water to the fullest development of plants that's possible, is the **plant succession**. In **fresh water**, the precise name for the succession is a **hydrosere**.

The first plants to grow in the water are "pioneer species", such as algae.

alder

These are the later stages of the hydrosere.

bulrush

iris

reeds

*You Can **Describe** the **Structure** of a Hydrosere Ecosystem*

An **ecosystem** is a **community** (an interacting group) of plants (flora) and animals (fauna) that live together in a particular **environment**. In **wet** areas like river banks and ponds, the plants that grow are the ones that can **cope** with the wet conditions, e.g. **reeds**, **willow trees** and **irises**. These plants support many animals, e.g. **frogs**, **dragonflies**, **birds** and **beetles**.

If you're describing the structure, you refer to what's there, i.e. what you can see.

1) There are the living things — flora and fauna. These are also called the **biotic components**. The mass of all the living things is called the **biomass**.

2) Also there's **decaying organic matter** from excretion and from dead plants and animals.

3) The **physical arrangement** of the plants into layers of different heights is also part of the structure.

4) You could also describe **where** different species live — the **habitats** of different plants and animals.

5) There are important **non-living** things or **abiotic components** — air, water, rocks and nutrients.

*You Can **Describe** the **Functioning** of a Hydrosere Ecosystem — How It Works*

In an ecosystem, there are different **processes** such as photosynthesis and respiration.
There are **inputs**, **flows** and **outputs** of **energy**. **Nutrients** cycle around the ecosystem.

1) The **input** of the **Sun's energy** allows plants to produce **food** in the process of **photosynthesis**. Plants produce the food for all living things, so this process is also called **primary production**.

> Photosynthesis: carbon dioxide + water + sunlight = glucose + oxygen

> Respiration: glucose + oxygen = carbon dioxide + water + energy

2) Living things (plants and animals) convert food to energy using **oxygen**, in the process of **respiration**.

3) The Sun's energy **flows** through an ecosystem as food is **eaten**. Plants, herbivores, carnivores, and decomposers belong to different stages called **trophic levels** in the food chain. Animals eat organisms in the **trophic level below** them, and take on **energy**.

Not all the energy in each trophic level passes to the next level up — some is used up by movement and growth. Also, not all the plants or animals in each trophic level are eaten by the consumers in the next level up, so the energy they contain doesn't move up through the ecosystem.

4) **Nutrients**, e.g. nitrogen, are taken from air, water and soil by plants. They are passed along the food chain or web, and eventually returned and recycled during the **decay** of tissues or waste matter.

5) Most hydroseres are **high productivity** systems — they produce lots of biomass. Plants **grow quickly** because they have plenty of sunlight, **CO$_2$**, **warmth**, **water** and **nutrients**.

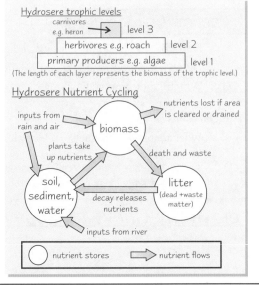

Hydrosere trophic levels

carnivores e.g. heron → level 3

herbivores e.g. roach — level 2

primary producers e.g. algae — level 1

(The length of each layer represents the biomass of the trophic level.)

Hydrosere Nutrient Cycling

inputs from rain and air

biomass

nutrients lost if area is cleared or drained

plants take up nutrients

death and waste

soil, sediment, water

litter (dead + waste matter)

decay releases nutrients

inputs from river

○ nutrient stores ⇨ nutrient flows

Ecosystems in a River Environment

There are Many Different Aquatic Ecosystems in a River Basin

1) **Lakes**, **ox-bow lakes** and **ponds**, e.g. on the edges of Coniston Water, Cumbria.
2) **Fen marshes**, e.g. Norfolk Broads.
3) **Peat bogs**, e.g. Highlands of Scotland.
4) **Riverbank** zones and **washlands** (wet areas in floodplains which store floodwaters), e.g. along River Thames.

The wetlands in river basins are important habitats for a variety of plants and wildlife. The banks, floodplains and lakes often have unusual or rare wildlife, which all adds to the **biodiversity** (the variety of ecosystems) in an area.

Hydroseres are often Under Threat

Wetlands are threatened now that more and more **rivers** are being **managed**. For example, **flood control schemes** may turn the banks into **concrete walls**, where **nothing** can grow and live. There are other threats too:

1) Wetlands are also under threat from eutrophication, e.g. marshes in Norfolk. Eutrophication is when water becomes **too rich** in **nutrients** (e.g. because fertiliser leaches into rivers from nearby fields) — plants grow too much, and when they die, their **decay uses up so much oxygen** that other organisms **can't survive**.
2) Pollution from agriculture, industry, boating and sewage can seriously harm ecosystems, e.g. parts of the R. Trent.
3) Wetland habitats are often drained and reclaimed for farming and housing, e.g. the Somerset Levels.
4) Peat bog habitats, e.g. in Ireland, are destroyed by digging up peat for fuel or for garden use.

Many wetlands are now **protected** because their wildlife is **unusual** (e.g. otters, newts, dragonflies) or **rare** (e.g. sundew plants in peat bogs). These wetlands are now **conservation areas** — e.g. **SSSIs** or **Ramsar** sites.

Wetlands are also important "**flood buffer zones**" which **allow** rivers to **overflow** without threatening areas where people live, and allow **flood water** to **infiltrate** and **refill underground water supplies**.

SSSI stands for Site of Special Scientific Interest. Ramsar sites are protected by the "Ramsar convention" on wetlands — an international treaty on wetland conservation.

Practice Questions

Q1 What is a "hydrosere"?
Q2 Define "pioneer species", naming an example from a hydrosere.
Q3 Name two abiotic components of a hydrosere.
Q4 Define "trophic level".

Exam Questions

Q1 Study the diagram of the Coniston Water hydrosere.

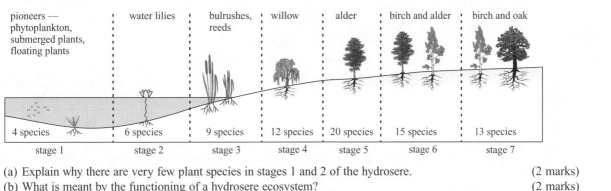

| pioneers — phytoplankton, submerged plants, floating plants | water lilies | bulrushes, reeds | willow | alder | birch and alder | birch and oak |

| 4 species | 6 species | 9 species | 12 species | 20 species | 15 species | 13 species |
| stage 1 | stage 2 | stage 3 | stage 4 | stage 5 | stage 6 | stage 7 |

(a) Explain why there are very few plant species in stages 1 and 2 of the hydrosere. (2 marks)
(b) What is meant by the functioning of a hydrosere ecosystem? (2 marks)

Q2 Explain two ways in which wetland habitats are under threat from humans. (4 marks)

No need to be so weird about it — we've all seen a pond before...

Don't get too bogged down with the special terms on these pages — you just have to learn them. Practise drawing the diagrams too, and draw some food chains and webs while you're at it. It's a slight bummer that these pages kind of repeat what's in Section 6, but then Section 6 contains a whole load of content that you just plain don't have to bother with for Edexcel B.

Flooding as a Hazard

*Flooding can be a really nasty problem — there are serious floods pretty much every single year in the UK, or so it seems. These pages are for **AQA A**, **Edexcel A** and **Edexcel B**.*

Floods put *Lives*, *Property* and *Activities* at *Risk*

1) Flooding occurs when the **discharge** of the river (the flow in cumecs or cubic metres per second) is so high that the river over-tops the banks, spilling over onto the floodplain.

2) When people's **lives** and **property** are threatened by this, flooding becomes a **hazard**. People living near a river are often aware of the risk — they know that there may be a danger from flooding.

3) Floods of a **large magnitude** don't happen very often. They're called **extreme events**. Small floods can happen quite frequently. By keeping records over many years, people can predict how **often** a flood of a certain size (magnitude) may occur – this is called the **Recurrence Interval** (RI). A **small flood** may have a Recurrence Interval of only **1 or 2 years**. The **Lynmouth flood** of **1952** was a huge, **freak** event, with a recurrence interval of **50 000 years**.

Negative impacts of flooding

1) **People** and **animals** lose their **lives**.

2) Homes, farms and businesses are **inundated** (under water) and **damaged**. ⟵

3) **Transport** and **power supplies** are affected.

4) Rescue work and **repairs** are costly. Insurance premiums go up after floods.

It's not just getting wet that's the problem. During a flood, sewers often contaminate flood water. A flooded house can be thigh-deep in, well, other people's waste matter. Very yucky.

Positive impacts of flooding

1) Rivers in flood have **higher discharges** and transport more **sediment**. This is deposited as fertile **silt** on the **floodplain**, or carried to the mouth to form **estuaries** (e.g. Severn) and **deltas** (e.g. Ganges, Bangladesh).

2) Flooding creates **wetlands**, e.g. marshes and ponds, where special **hydrosere ecosystems** develop (see p10-11).

3) The **infiltration** of floodwater into the floodplain **recharges underground water supplies**.

There are **Natural Causes** *of Flooding*

1) One of the main causes is **rainfall**, especially **intense rain** and **long duration** rain. If the ground becomes **saturated** (all air spaces full of water) then runoff and flooding are even worse.

2) **Melting snow** and **ice** are also important causes of flooding.

3) Other **physical characteristics** of drainage basins increase the risk of flooding:

Sparse vegetation or deciduous trees	⟹ **Less interception**, more **runoff**
Steep slopes	⟹ **Rapid runoff to main channel**
High **drainage density** (lots of streams per unit area)	⟹ **Rapid runoff to main channel**
Large drainage basin area	⟹ **Larger catchment area** for rain or snow leads to **high discharges**
Impermeable areas e.g. **clay soils**, and rocks such as **granite** or **shale**	⟹ **Infiltration** is **low**, runoff is **high**

Deciduous trees, which are bare in winter, give poorer protection from flooding than coniferous trees which are green all year.

All these factors lead to a steep rising limb and short lag time, meaning a flood is likely.

Porous rocks like chalk let water soak in. Permeable rocks like limestone allow infiltration into joints, so flooding is less likely unless they become saturated.

There are **Human Causes** *of Flooding*

People can often make floods more **frequent** and more **severe** by **changing things** around the **drainage basin**.

1) **Urbanisation** can make flooding worse. **Towns** have large areas of **impermeable tarmac** and **concrete**, so when it rains, **runoff is very rapid**. There are **fewer areas** of **soil** and **vegetation** which would allow slow **interception** and **infiltration**. Also **gutters** and **drains** quickly take runoff to the rivers.

2) **Agriculture** can increase the risk of flooding. **Ploughing** and **overgrazing** can leave areas **bare**. **Runoff increases**. The runoff can also pick up **soil** and carry it into the rivers, which makes them **overflow more**.

3) **Deforestation** increases the risk of flooding. Clearing trees and plants **decreases interception**, **transpiration** and **infiltration**, and **increases runoff** and **soil erosion**.

4) **River management schemes** (see p14–17) can actually end up making flooding **worse** — e.g. when dams and levees fail, they release massive waves of flood water all at once.

Flooding as a Hazard

Flooding Hazards Exist in Both MEDCs and LEDCs

Remember — an MEDC is a More Economically Developed Country and an LEDC is, yep you guessed it, a Less Economically Developed Country.

Millions of people live in flood risk areas — floodplains are actually very **attractive** areas for **settlement**, **farming** and **routeways**. **Alluvium** deposited on floodplains makes lovely **fertile soil** for agriculture. Rivers are handy sources of **irrigation**, and useful for **transport**.

- Examples of inhabited floodplains in MEDCs include the **Severn** plain in the UK and along the **Mississippi** in the USA.
- Examples of inhabited floodplains in LEDCs include the **Ganges** in Bangladesh and the **Yangtse** in China.

Flooding in the UK — Lynmouth, 1952

A more recent UK example is the floods in Boscastle, Cornwall, on 16th August 2004. The village was devastated by a 10 foot wall of water flowing at 40 miles per hour, after 2 inches of rain fell in just 2 hours during storms. Buildings were destroyed and cars swept away. Nobody was killed, but many villagers had to be airlifted to safety.

Lynmouth Flood, North Devon, 1952

Effects: 15th August 1952. After heavy rain, the East and West Lyn rivers suddenly rose and carried huge amounts of water and boulders down to Lynmouth, destroying houses and bridges. 34 people were killed. 38 buildings were destroyed, and 55 more were so badly damaged that they had to be demolished. Over 100 cars were swept away.

Natural causes: There was **extremely heavy rain** on already **saturated** ground. The valleys are **steep**, and runoff is fast. Floods are frequent. All the water from a large, wet, moorland drainage basin meets at Lynmouth. Also, the rivers at Lynmouth flow through narrow valleys, so water levels rose quickly.

Human causes: Building development diverted rivers from their natural flood courses and confined them in **narrow channels**. Fallen trees from a previous storm hadn't been cleared — they dammed up bridges so that water from smaller floods was held back until it burst out in one go, along with the runoff from the August 15th storm.

Reasons for impact: The flood happened in the **middle of the night** — there were no warnings, and it was **too dark** for people to see how bad it really was. Residents expected moderate floods, so they didn't evacuate. It was the middle of summer — there were lots of **tourists** in holiday accommodation close to the rivers — this increased the death toll.

Response: A **flood warning** system has been installed. Building on flood plains has been restricted. River channels and bridges have been widened. The river channel has been re-shaped so that flood water would mostly spill out away from the main settlement.

Flooding in a large basin in an LEDC — Bangladesh

Flooding from the Ganges/Brahmaputra/Meghna basin, Bangladesh, 1998

Effects: Three major rivers, the Brahmaputra, Ganges and Meghna were above their flood levels through August and September. **Two thirds** of Bangladesh was flooded for **nine weeks**. Flood waters reached **roof level** on houses. **30 million** people were left **homeless**.

Causes: Large areas of Bangladesh are on the **natural floodplain**. There's **intense, long duration rainfall** every year in the Monsoon rains, and there's **snowmelt** — in 1998 there were also **September storms**. Sea level in the Bay of Bengal was **very high**, so water couldn't flow out to the sea fast enough. **Urbanisation** and **deforestation** increased runoff.

Reasons for impact: Bangladesh is a very **poor** country and can't afford **flood defences** or **flood warning systems**. Vulnerable floodplain areas are inhabited by poor farmers without the resources to **evacuate**. Lack of **clean water** meant diseases like **cholera** and **dysentery** spread. **Rice crop failed** so **food aid** was needed.

Response: **Flood shelters** on stilts were built. People were educated about **water safety**. Flood Action Plan has global funding.

Practice Questions

Q1 Name three natural causes of flooding.
Q2 Describe the hydrograph shape that suggests flooding is likely.
Q3 Give two examples of inhabited floodplains — one in an LEDC and one in an MEDC.

Exam Questions

Q1 Describe two arguments in favour of letting floods happen. (2 marks)

Q2 Explain two ways in which urban areas increase the risk of flooding. (4 marks)

If only the "getting wet" part of flooding were the worst part...

It's normal for most rivers to overflow sometimes, but people have made it more of a problem. You need to learn all the causes of flooding. Boring old list-making will help — a list of causes under two headings (natural and human), and a list of things people can do to reduce the impact of a flood. Unfortunately, there's nothing you can do to completely stop floods from happening.

Drainage Basin Management

Management is about the strategies that people use to tackle problems and issues in drainage basins.
*It's needed because so many people live and work near rivers. These pages are for **Edexcel A**, **Edexcel B** and **AQA A**.*

The **River's Natural Processes** often cause **Management Problems**

1) **Flooding** causes deaths, destroys crops and causes damage to homes and industry.

2) During **high discharges**, rivers transport large loads of **sediment**. When they deposit the sediment, it silts up **navigation channels** and **reservoirs**, which then need to be cleared. (Sediment isn't all bad, though. It helps to build deltas and beaches and it adds nutrients to floodplains. If sediment flows are altered, **coastal erosion** can increase.)

> Don't forget that "discharge" means the volume of water flowing per unit time (in cumecs). It doesn't mean pollution or sediment.

3) **Meanders** make river transport routes **longer** and **slower**, e.g. on the Mississippi.

4) **Meandering** channels form **ox-bow lakes**, which affect **farmland.** **Shifting** and **braided** channels affect **farming** and **river transport**.

5) Some rivers have **seasonal regimes** (**low discharges** in summer when there's less rain, more **evapotranspiration**, and more **abstraction**). This causes **water shortages** and increased concentrations of **pollution**, killing **fish** and **plants**.

> Abstraction means people taking water for irrigation and home and industry use.

6) **Groundwater levels** can fall in **aquifers** (stores of water in porous rock underground). Water shortages can lead to **hosepipe bans**, e.g. in SE England during summer.

7) **Hydro-electric power generation** needs regular, constant discharges of water.

Human Activities Also Lead to Management Problems

1) Building of **urban areas** increases runoff, decreases infiltration and increases the chance of flooding.

2) **Deforestation** increases runoff and decreases interception and evaporation, increasing flooding and soil erosion.

3) **Agriculture** can lead to **soil erosion** (e.g. through ploughing and cultivation), bringing more sediment to the river.

4) **Agriculture** can also cause **pollution** and **eutrophication** in the river (e.g. through leaching of fertilisers).

5) **Global warming** may increase flooding, as **rainfall patterns** and **storm frequencies** change.

> Human actions in **one country** can affect the **same river** in **another country** — e.g. **deforestation** in **Nepal** can cause flooding further down the River Ganges in **Bangladesh**. This becomes a **political issue** — countries have to decide **who** should deal with it.

Some drainage basins are easier to manage than others.

River Management Has Several Aims

- reduce flooding
- produce regular, clean water supplies
- generate hydro-electric power
- control pollution from fertilisers, sewage, industry and boats
- provide recreation — e.g. fishing, canoeing, narrowboating
- provide transport for people and goods
- conserve wetland ecosystems

All these need **money** and **technical expertise**. Schemes in MEDCs can cover more of these aims than schemes in LEDCs.

There are Different Approaches to Basin Management

1) In the **past**, the main aim was **flood control**, using structures like dams and embankments.

2) Now people realise that it's better to **understand** the whole basin and its processes, and try to **work with** the natural processes in the basin. People study rainfall, geology, relief, ecosystems and land use, measure river discharges and draw hydrographs to learn what the river's up to so they can work with it. This is called an **integrated** or **holistic** approach.

3) **Sustainable basin management** aims to use the river today but also **conserve** it for the future.

4) In England, the **Environment Agency** helps manage river basins. They work with **decision makers** such as local **councils** and **water companies** to put together integrated plans for English river basins.

5) Decision makers have to weigh up the **costs** and **benefits** of different kinds of river management, and they have to try to meet all the **aims** in the orange box above — this can be a bit of a **balancing act**. Decision makers need to look at the **social** and **political** costs and benefits as well as the **economic** (money) costs and benefits.

Drainage Basin Management

Hard Engineering Schemes use Man-Made Structures

Strategy	Benefits	Examples
1) **Dams** and **reservoirs**	• Discharge is **regulated** to make **floods less likely** • Water supply is more **even** • **HEP** generation attracts industry • improved **irrigation** • improved **navigation** and **tourism**	Mississippi (USA) Nile (Aswan Dam, Egypt) 3 Gorges Project, Yangtse River (China)
2) **Channelisation** • Channel **widened/deepened** (dredging) ⇨ river **flows faster** and **holds more water** • Channel **straightened** ⇨ river **flows faster** • Sides and bed **concreted** ⇨ more stable banks, **less erosion** • **Levees** built ⇨ **contain high discharges** without flooding		San Gabriel River (Los Angeles, California) Rhône (France) Trent (UK)

There are many Disadvantages with Hard Engineering Schemes

1) They're **ugly** and **unnatural**. **Channelisation** in particular really reduces the **recreation value** of the river — it makes it harder for people to have a nice time on or by the river, boating, fishing etc.

2) They're **costly** to **build** and **maintain**, and need **technical skill**. **LEDCs** often **can't afford** these schemes.

3) **Wildlife** and **wetland habitats** are **destroyed**.

4) Less flooding means less **infiltration** into **groundwater supplies** — this means droughts become more likely.

5) Floods may be **less frequent**, but may actually be **more hazardous** when they do happen e.g. Mississippi, 1993 — when the **levees** were finally **breached**, a **huge** amount of water burst onto the land very quickly.

6) **Processes** are **altered** — e.g. **sediment** is deposited in reservoirs.

Soft Engineering Schemes Work With, not Against, the Basin Processes

Strategy	Benefits	Problems	Examples
Afforestation	• increased interception • less runoff • increased lag times	• some areas are not suitable for trees • expensive	R. Severn Catchment (UK) Upper Ganges (Nepal)
Terracing of slopes	• slows down runoff • increased lag times	• time consuming • expensive	Mississippi (USA) Nepal
Floodplain zoning New buildings not allowed on areas prone to flooding	• buildings not damaged • water infiltrates, so less runoff	• no use in areas which are already urbanised	Shrewsbury (UK)

Restoration schemes return areas to **natural wetland**. Some parts of the floodplain are allowed to **flood naturally**, to allow infiltration and development of **wetland ecosystems** — e.g. River **Kissimmee**, Florida (see p17).

Practice Questions

Q1   What is "hard engineering"?

Q2   What is "channelisation"?

Q3   Describe one way of reducing runoff on slopes.

Q4   Define "sustainable basin management".

Exam Questions

Q1   Choose one river management strategy and explain how it affects river processes and ecosystems.   (3 marks)

Q2   Identify two problems that are caused by low river flows.   (2 marks)

Maybe it'd be easier to ask the clouds to please not rain...

River management seems like an impossible problem to solve. You've got a river and its drainage basin, you've got some rain, and you've got a bunch of people who want exactly the right amount of water for their general household, farming and business needs. Oh, and they definitely don't want any floods. And if they could have picnics on the riverbank, that'd be just spiffy.

Drainage Basin Management

*An important aim of many management schemes is to reduce the flood hazard. You'll need to learn case studies like these for your exam. These are for **AQA A**, **Edexcel A** and **Edexcel B**. The Colne and Kissimmee studies are just for **Edexcel B**.*

Case Study 1 — Hard Engineering on the Rhône, France (MEDC)

Causes of Flooding

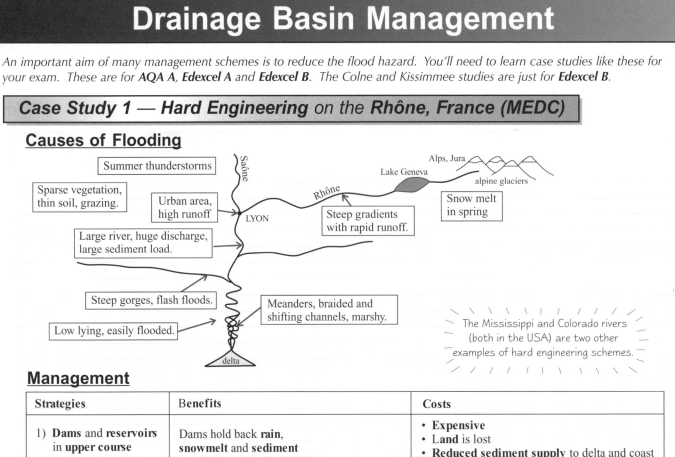

Summer thunderstorms

Sparse vegetation, thin soil, grazing.

Urban area, high runoff

Large river, huge discharge, large sediment load.

Steep gradients with rapid runoff.

Snow melt in spring

Steep gorges, flash floods.

Low lying, easily flooded.

Meanders, braided and shifting channels, marshy.

Saône · Rhône · LYON · Lake Geneva · Alps, Jura · alpine glaciers · delta

The Mississippi and Colorado rivers (both in the USA) are two other examples of hard engineering schemes.

Management

Strategies	Benefits	Costs
1) **Dams** and **reservoirs** in **upper course**	Dams hold back **rain**, **snowmelt** and **sediment**	• **Expensive** • **L**and is lost • **Reduced sediment supply** to delta and coast
2) **Dams** and **reservoirs** in **lower Rhône**	• Dams **regulate flow** • **Hydroelectric power** • **I**rrigation	• **Expensive** • **Habitats** are lost
3) **Channelisation**	• Improved **navigation** • Water held in by **levees** • Straight concrete channel is more **efficient**.	• **Expensive** • Loss of **recreation** value • **Habitats** are lost

Case Study 2 — Flood Management in Bangladesh (LEDC)

Background: Bangladesh has vast annual floods to deal with, and food crops are destroyed by flooding every year. There's a large and growing population. The country is poor.

Basin: **Huge catchment area** over 175 million km². Basin is **low lying**.

Precipitation: High **rainfall** mostly from wet Monsoon June-Sept. — causes massive discharges. **Himalayan snowmelt** in spring and summer adds to discharges.

Channels: Large sediment loads carried and deposited, forming **braided**, **shifting channels**.

Weather: **Coastal floods** from **cyclones** raise river levels near the sea.

Other factors: **Deforestation**, **farming** and **urbanisation** increase the flood risk.

Management: It's particularly difficult to manage a huge low lying area made mostly of clays. Bangladesh can't afford to spend much on basin management.

River Nile, Egypt is another good LEDC case study. It's a multi-purpose scheme — you might well have studied it for GCSE.

Strategies	Benefits	Costs
1) Flood action Plan built **levees**	**Crops** protected, **cities** protected	• Sudden breaches make flooding **worse**. • **Debt** — millions of £ borrowed to pay for levees. • **Stagnant water** in levees increases **disease**.
2) Plans to build **large drainage canals**	**Flood water** would be **drained** into river	**Expensive**
3) **Soft engineering** — **allow** flooding but improve **warnings**. Build **new houses** on **raised areas**.	• fishing protected • fertile sediment deposited • ground water recharged	**Flood hazard** still **remains**.

Drainage Basin Management

Before management	Hard engineering (1962-1971)		Restoration scheme (1999 onwards)
• River meandering and braided • Severe flooding • Important wetland ecosystems	**Channelisation** (straightened river, levees, storage reservoirs, locks)		Main **aim** is to **restore river** and **ecosystems** • **Canal blocked off, levees removed** except around towns • **Flooding allowed** on **meadows**
	<u>Impacts</u> **Environmental costs**	• **loss of hydroseres** • water became **stagnant** • less water **infiltrated** to **groundwater**	**Environmental success** — hooray!
	Economic cost — very expensive		**Cost** about **$450 million**

In the UK, the **River Colne** (tributary of Thames) restoration project has brought back **meanders**, **ox-bow lakes** and **wetland marshes**, and improved the flow of a 2 km long stagnant **channelised** section.

River Basins are Managed for Water Supplies

1) Water is removed from **rivers** for **homes**, **industry** and **irrigation** (this is called **abstraction**). Water can also be taken from **groundwater**.

2) A related issue is **pollution**. Pollutants, e.g. nitrates from fertiliser, sewage and chemicals like lead, are monitored in the UK by the Environment Agency.

Over-abstraction can cause:

- low **river discharges**, and drying out of **hydroseres**.
- **subsidence** because **ground dries out** (especially where houses are built on clay soil).
- seepage of **seawater** into **rocks** near the **coast**.
- water shortages in areas that rely on **irrigation**.

Problems: Jordan has **low annual rainfall**, averaging less than 250 mm per year (it's a desert/semi desert climate). There are **high temperatures** and high **evaporation**. Jordan's **growing population** increases the demand for water.

Strategies:
1) **Buy** and **transfer** water from **another country** (by sea or pipeline).
   For: This helps with supplies.
   Against: It's **costly**. And there are **political** issues (Jordan must **stay on good terms** with the country selling the water.)

2) Build **waste water recycling plants**, or **de-salinisation** plants (to remove salt from sea water so it's drinkable).
   For: This helps with supplies.
   Against: It's costly.

3) Increase the present use of **storage tanks** to collect rainfall.
   For: It's **cheap** and **sustainable**. Hooray!

Practice Questions

Q1 List four physical causes of flooding on the Rhône.

Q2 Give one example of hard engineering and one example of soft engineering in Bangladesh.

Q3 Compare the success of hard engineering to the success of soft engineering on the River Kissimmee, Florida.

Q4 What are the costs and benefits to Jordan of developing de-salinisation plants?

Exam Questions

Q1 Describe a river management strategy in a named MEDC, and state its economic and environmental impacts. (5 marks)

Q2 With an example, describe some of the environmental, social and economic impacts of river restoration. (5 marks)

There's something to be said for and against all these schemes...

Often, exam questions on river management are about the impacts of a river management scheme. Make sure you can separate them into economic, social, environmental, and political impacts. Political impacts are easy to forget about — every big decision made affects people, and they can make a fuss about it. Don't forget to cover both sides — the costs and the benefits.

Introduction to Coastal Environments

*The coastal zone contains a wide variety of landscapes and ecosystems. Coasts are affected by marine, land and atmospheric processes. This section is for **Edexcel A**, **Edexcel B** and **AQA B (Option Q)**.*

Beaches are Divided into Zones

A beach has **four zones** — **offshore**, **nearshore**, **foreshore** and **backshore**.

1) The **backshore** doesn't normally get hit by waves, except during severe storms.
2) The **foreshore** is the area between high tide and low tide.
3) The **nearshore** is where breaking waves form.
4) The **offshore** is out past the breaking waves.

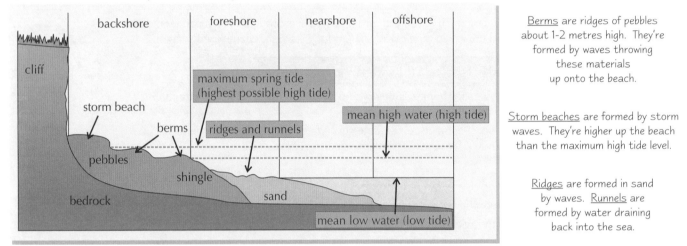

Berms are ridges of pebbles about 1-2 metres high. They're formed by waves throwing these materials up onto the beach.

Storm beaches are formed by storm waves. They're higher up the beach than the maximum high tide level.

Ridges are formed in sand by waves. *Runnels* are formed by water draining back into the sea.

The Coastal System Consists of Inputs, Processes and Outputs

1) **Inputs** include **river sediment** coming in from a delta or estuary, or sediment from **eroded cliffs** or from further out to sea.
2) There are lots of **processes** in the beach system. There's wave action, tidal movement, erosion, deposition etc.
3) **Outputs** include **sediment** being **lost** to the sea **further out**, or to another bit of beach further along the coast.
4) As with any dynamic (continually changing) system, the processes in the system are working to reach **equilibrium**. If one element changes because of an outside influence, it **upsets the equilibrium** and changes the other components. E.g. a **higher rate** of **erosion** followed by **deposition** puts **more material** on the beach — this **slows down** the rate of erosion as it protects the coastline. This is **negative feedback** (this means when a system responds to reverse a change).

This explains what happens when a river meets the sea:

1) Where a **river** enters the coastal system there is a **mixed zone** of sea and river water action where the effects of both systems become **integrated**.
2) Lots of **sediment** from the river flows out into the sea. Some of this may settle to form a **delta**. The rest gets **carried out to sea** and becomes part of the sea system.
3) Each river mouth is different because of differing local conditions of **climate**, **currents** and **tides**.

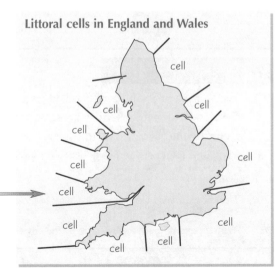

Littoral cells in England and Wales

Coastal sediment cells or **littoral cells** are lengths of coastline which are pretty much entirely **self contained** for the movement of shingle and sediment. That means that **processes** going on in **one cell** don't affect the movement of beach material in **another** cell. Coastal cells are therefore **regional** level systems.

Storms (especially tropical hurricanes and cyclones) can change a shoreline in a very short space of time. The strong winds and seas associated with severe storm events can **flood low-lying coastal areas**, e.g. Bangladesh, or can **wash away** large sections of **dunes** or **cliffs**, e.g. along the West African coastline and along the littoral zone of California.

Introduction to Coastal Environments

Beach Processes — *Waves* are Responsible for **Erosion** and **Deposition**

1) **Waves** are created by the **wind** blowing over the surface of the sea. The **friction** between the wind and the surface of the sea gives the water a **circular motion**.

2) The effect of a wave depends on its **height** and **fetch**. The **fetch** is the distance over which the waves are built up. The height of a wave depends on the wind speed.

3) As waves approach the shore they **break**. Friction with the sea bed makes the wave motion more elliptical (squashed and oval-shaped). The **crest** of the wave rises up and then **collapses** onto the beach.

4) Water breaking onto the beach is called the **swash**. Water washing back towards the sea is called the **backwash**.

5) There are two types of wave. **Surfing** breakers have a short wavelength, and are high and steep. They are **destructive** — they pound onto the beach and **remove** material from it. **Surging** breakers have a long wavelength, and are low and gentle. They are **constructive** — they carry material up the beach.

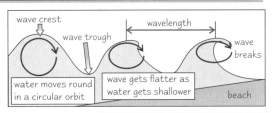

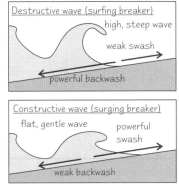

Beach Processes — *Currents* Transport **Sediment** and **Shingle**

1) Currents are the general flow of water in one direction. They can be small scale (e.g. in a river channel) or large scale (e.g. in an ocean).

2) Currents move material landwards and along the coast — this is called longshore drift.

3) Swash (blue arrows in the diagram) carries sediment (e.g. shingle, pebbles) up the beach, parallel to the prevailing wind. Backwash (orange arrows) carries sediment back down the beach, at right angles to the shore line.

4) When there's an angle between the prevailing wind and the shore line, a few rounds of swash and backwash move the sediment along the shore line.

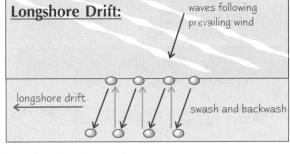

Beach Processes — *Tides* are Another Important Factor

The area of land between **maximum high tide** and **minimum low tide** is where landforms are **created** and **destroyed**.

Practice Questions

Q1   Outline the main processes which shape coastal zones.
Q2   Draw a table to show the main inputs, processes and outputs of a coastal system you have studied.
Q3   How do coastal processes work to try to maintain equilibrium on a coastline?
Q4   Sketch a diagram to show how longshore drift works.

Exam Questions

Q1   Explain how storm beaches and berms are formed. What is the difference between a storm beach and a berm?   (3 marks)

Q2   Name and describe the two different kinds of waves.   (4 marks)

What did the sea say to the beach — nothing, it just waved...

Not another thing that they insist you learn as a "system" with "inputs, outputs, processes and flows". Fraid so. They're mad to pieces on this system thing. Still, it does help for the rest of the section to have a good idea of where beach sediment comes from, and how it gets added to beaches and taken away. Learn the wave terms like "swash" and "backwash" — they're useful.

Coastal Landforms

*Coastal processes constantly change coastal landforms. These pages are for **Edexcel A**, **Edexcel B** and **AQA B** (**Option Q**).*

On the *Coast*, there's *Attack* from *Weathering* and from *Wave Action*

1) Repeated **wetting and drying** in the **splash zone** (the area where waves hit) causes rock to **expand** and **contract**, producing **cracks**. These cracks are **weak spots** which are vulnerable to **weathering** and **erosion**.

2) **Salt crystals** form in the **splash zone** when splashes of seawater evaporate. These crystals grow in cracks in the rock, putting **pressure** on the rock and **cracking** it apart.

3) There's less risk of **frost shattering** (where water **expands** as it **freezes** and puts pressure on rocks) rock than there is **inland** — the coast tends to have smaller **variations** in temperature than inland. But some rocks, like **chalk**, are **weak enough** to be weathered by the limited frosts on the beach.

Weathering, wind action and mass movement are called sub-aerial processes.

Waves carry a great deal of energy, and are responsible for a lot of erosion.

1) The energy of a wave as it breaks against a cliff is enough to detach bits of rock — this is **quarrying**. Bubbles of air can be forced into cracks to loosen rock — this is called **cavitation**.

2) Bits of rock and sediment transported by the waves can smash and grind against rocks and cliffs, breaking bits off and smoothing surfaces. This is called **abrasion** or **corrasion**.

3) Bits of rock in the water smash against each other and break into smaller bits. This is **attrition**.

4) **Soluble** rocks (e.g. limestone, chalk) get gradually **dissolved** by the seawater. This is **solution**.

5) **Hydraulic action** — air in cracks in cliffs is **compressed** when waves crash in, and expands explosively when waves retreat. This breaks off rock pieces.

Some *Coastal Landforms* are caused by *Erosion*

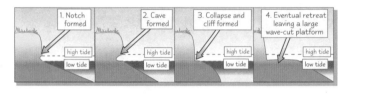

1. Notch formed — high tide / low tide
2. Cave formed — high tide / low tide
3. Collapse and cliff formed — high tide / low tide
4. Eventual retreat leaving a large wave-cut platform — high tide / low tide

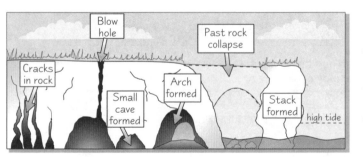

Blow hole — Past rock collapse — Cracks in rock — Arch formed — Small cave formed — Stack formed — high tide

1) **Cliffs** are a common coastal landform. They're formed by the action of **waves** and **weathering**. **Resistant** rock makes **high** cliffs.

2) **Wave-cut platforms** are **flat surfaces** left behind when a cliff is eroded back.

3) **Bands** of alternating **soft rock** and **hard rock** form alternating **bays** and **headlands**. When weaker rock is uncovered, it erodes quickly, to form a bay. Harder rock is left as a headland.

4) **Erosion processes** take advantage of weak spots (e.g. joints) in rock to form **caves**.

5) Caves on the opposite sides of a narrow headland eventually join up to form an **arch**.

6) When an **arch** collapses, it forms a **stack**.

7) Stacks become worn down to form **stumps** — these are only visible at low tide.

Some *Coastal Landforms* are caused by *Deposition*

1) Beaches are "**landforms from deposition**" — they're formed when **constructive** waves dump a heap of **sediment** on the shore.

2) **Bars** are formed by **waves breaking offshore**. The waves gradually deposit sediment (picked up from the sea bed further out to sea). Bars can build up until they're visible **above sea level**. There are a lot of offshore bars off the **North Norfolk coast** — e.g. **Scolt Head Island**, a bar covered in vegetation with marshland behind it.

3) A **spit** is a bank of **sand** or **shingle** that sticks out into the sea, like **Spurn Head** or **Hurst Castle Spit**. **Longshore drift** (see p19) is the process responsible for forming spits.

4) A spit or bar that connects an island to the mainland is called a **tombolo**. **Chesil Beach** in Dorset is a top example of a tombolo.

5) **Cuspate forelands** are **triangular** shaped bits of land sticking out into the sea. They form by longshore drift, from waves coming from different directions. **Dungeness** in Kent is a cuspate foreland.

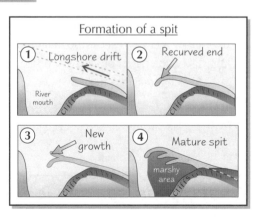

Formation of a spit
1. Longshore drift — River mouth
2. Recurved end
3. New growth
4. Mature spit — marshy area

Coastal Landforms

Geology affects the Formation of Coastal Landforms

1) Rocks that have **strong crystalline bonds**, e.g. most metamorphic and igneous rock, are **resistant** to erosion. Strongly bonded sedimentary rocks, e.g. chalk, carboniferous limestone and old red sandstone, are also resistant. These are all called "**coherent**" **rocks**. They make **high**, **steeply angled** cliffs.

2) Rocks with **weak bonds** and **weak structures** such as conglomerates (rocks made of pebbles stuck together, basically), sands and clays are easy to erode. These are called "**incoherent**" rocks. Their cliffs tend to get undercut at the base. Slumping and rotational slip (see p44) erode them to make **unstable**, **stepped** cliffs.

3) Low lying coasts with **incoherent** rocks have **sand dunes**, **coastal marshes** and **estuaries**.

4) Water can soak through porous rocks, which weakens junctions between porous and impermeable rock.

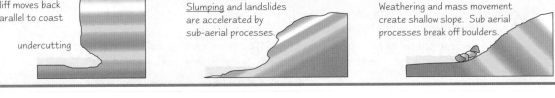

The **alignment** of **rock strata** can also affect the form of the coastline.

Horizontal strata: Cliff moves back parallel to coast — undercutting

Strata sloping into the sea: Slumping and landslides are accelerated by sub-aerial processes.

Strata sloping into the land: Weathering and mass movement create shallow slope. Sub aerial processes break off boulders.

Wave Direction Affects Beach Formation

1) **Swash aligned beaches** are built when waves break parallel to the shore. Sediment moves up and down the beach, but not along it. You get **crescent shaped** beaches in bays and **linear** beaches on straight coasts.

2) **Drift aligned beaches** are built when waves break at an angle to the shore. They often have **spits** with **recurved laterals** — the end of the spit curves back in on itself (see page 20).

Sediment size also affects wave action and beach formation.

Shingle beaches are **steep** and **narrow**, made up of **larger** particles which pile up at steep angles.

Sand beaches (smaller particles) are **longer** and **flatter**, with a stronger swash.

Wave Refraction also Affects Coastal Processes

1) Erosion and deposition are affected by the process of **wave refraction**. When the coast is **curved** or **indented**, wave fronts **curve** and **distort** as they approach the coast.

2) Where waves **diverge**, they **lose power**. They drop their load of sediment — there's **deposition**.

3) Where waves **converge**, they **increase in power**, and **erosion** takes place.

— = Wave front
— = Wave energy
= Hard rock
= Soft rock
= Beach
waves diverging
waves converging

Practice Questions

Q1 Name four landforms of coastal erosion and four landforms of coastal deposition.

Q2 What are incoherent rocks? Name two examples.

Q3 Why are shingle beaches short and steep, while sandy beaches are long and shallow?

Exam Questions

Q1 Name the natural processes involved in shaping coastlines. (3 marks)

Q2 How does the geology and alignment of rock strata affect coastline shape? (3 marks)

Q3 Give an account of the role that waves play in the development of coastal landforms. (5 marks)

Oh, we do like to be beside the seaside...

At AS level, the landforms you have to know are pretty much the same ones you have to know for GCSE (not much help if you didn't do GCSE, I know, but then they're not that hard to learn anyway). You need to know more about the factors that affect how they form — they're quite hot on asking you about the effects of geology and waves and sediment size, and all that.

Changing Coastal Ecosystems

Changes in coastal ecosystems come from natural changes and from human activity.
*Changing ecosystems have an effect on **landforms**, too. These pages are for **Edexcel B** and **AQA B** (**Option Q**).*

Sand Dunes are Formed by the Wind Blowing Sand About

All dunes need four conditions to form and grow: 1) A **good supply** of **sand**.   2) **Prevailing onshore winds**.
3) Shallow offshore zone with a large **gentle beach** exposed at low tide.   4) A large **backshore** area to accumulate dunes.

Plant Succession Changes Sand Dunes

Plants help to **anchor** and **stabilise** dunes. They reduce wind speed and movement of sand.   Plant succession on sand dunes
is a process which starts off with plants growing on bare sand, and ends up with proper soil and mature shrubs and trees.

Sand dunes are a very harsh environment for plants.

- Sand dunes are very **dry** — they hardly hold any water.
- They're also constantly being **moved** by the **wind** — it's hard for plants
  to get a foothold. Strong winds blow **salt** onto the dunes.
- Plants need **organic matter** in the soil to grow well. They don't get this in sand.

Plant succession on sand dunes is called a psammosere. There's more about succession in section 6.

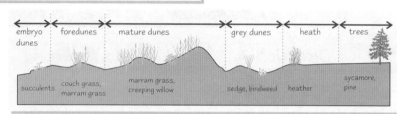

1) Sand particles blow along the beach. They're **trapped** by **debris**, and form **small mounds** called **embryo dunes**.

2) **Salt-tolerant** succulent plants grow on the embryo dunes once they're above high tide level. These first species to colonise are called the **pioneer species**. **Dead leaves** add **organic** material to the sand. More organic material is blown in by the wind and trapped by plants. This organic material provides **nutrients**.

3) Drought resistant **couch grass** grows on the embryo dunes. It has **long roots** which reach down for water, and also help **anchor** the dunes. The embryo dunes get bigger and develop into **fore-dunes** and then **mature dunes** as couch grass and marram grass trap more sand. **Marram grass** is the most common plant on mature **dunes**.

New embryo dunes form in front of the older dunes.

4) Between the dunes there are dips called **dune slacks**. These flood after heavy rain, so wetland species like **creeping willow** and **sedge** grow in the slacks.

5) Further back, on the **grey dunes** there's enough organic material to make a greyish soil that suits **heather**. Eventually, the soil is rich enough to support shrubs and **trees**.

Strong winds cause blow-outs — plants and soil get blown out of the sand dune, and the sand is then quickly eroded.

Human Activity Changes Sand Dunes

Human activity **exposes the sand** and encourages **erosion**.

1) Sand dune areas are pretty, and popular with tourists. Tourists' feet trample down vegetation and erode fragile sand dune soil. Once plants are gone, the sand can be very easily blown away. People who ride **bikes** and drive **4×4s** and **quad bikes** over sand dunes cause **massive erosion**.

2) In the past, sand was **extracted** for **building**.

3) Dunes can be **managed** to help prevent erosion. Dunes on nature reserves have fenced off areas where people can't go. They have clearly marked paths, often with wooden matting or a boardwalk to prevent erosion from trampling.

Plant Succession and Human Activity Change Salt Marshes

Tides and currents deposit **sediment** on the coast. The sediment is **sorted** so the **finest mud** is deposited in the intertidal zone. **Mudflats** build up, and they are **colonised** by plants. Plants help to **slow** the movement of water, and their **roots** help **stabilise** the marsh.

Plant succession in a salt water environment is called a halosere.

1) Salt marsh plants have to be adapted to **wet**, **salty** conditions.

2) The **pioneer species** (first to colonise) include **grasses** with **long roots** to trap sediment.

3) **Reeds** and sedge grow on the higher marshes which are less salty.

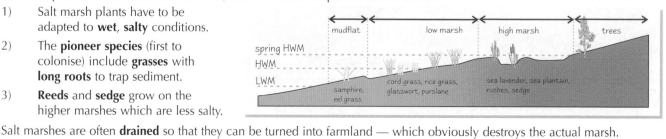

Salt marshes are often **drained** so that they can be turned into farmland — which obviously destroys the actual marsh.
Sea walls keep the sea water out of the salt marsh, which damages the salt-loving plant ecosystem.

Changing Coastal Ecosystems

Coral Reefs are Another Coastal Ecosystem

1) Coral is a **living organism** with a hard **calcium carbonate exoskeleton**. **Coral reefs** are **colonies** of hundreds of thousands of coral **polyps**.

2) Coral only grows in **tropical** waters, so coral reefs are found between **30° N** and **30° S**, where the sea temperature is **between 16°C** and **31°C**.

3) Coral grows well in **oxygenated** water. It tends to be found on the **windward** side of land, where the **breaking waves** are — breaking waves are all frothy and aerated (full of bubbles).

4) Coral has **blue-green algae** living inside it. These algae are the **producers** of the ecosystem. The algae need sunlight to make food, so the coral reef can only grow in **shallow** water, where sunlight gets through.

5) Coral **feeds** on the **blue green algae** and on **plankton**.

6) Lots of species of **fish** live in the crevices in a coral reef.

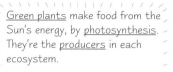

Green plants make food from the Sun's energy, by photosynthesis. They're the producers in each ecosystem.
Herbivores eat plants. They're primary consumers.
Carnivores eat animals. They're secondary consumers.
Energy moves from the bottom to the top of the food chain.
See p60 for more detail.

Coral Reefs Build Up Over Time

A lagoon is a body of water that separates a piece of land from a coral reef.

Coral reefs are built up by **layers of coral** growing on the **skeletons** left by **previous generations**.

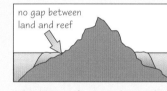

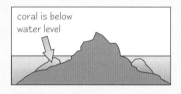

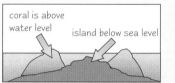

no gap between land and reef

coral is below water level

coral is above water level   island below sea level

1) **Fringing reefs** extend straight out from the land.

2) **Barrier reefs** are separated from land by a lagoon or channel.

3) **Atolls** are **coral islands** with a ring of reef around a lagoon.

Charles Darwin suggested a theory of atoll formation:

1) **Lava** from **underwater volcanic eruptions** forms a cone that eventually pops up above the water as an island.

2) **Coral** grows in the warm shallow water around the island, forming a **fringing reef**.

3) After a long time, the volcano becomes extinct, and it starts to **wear down**. Sea water gets in between the coral reef and the island to make a **barrier reef**.

4) When the volcano **erodes** below the sea, or when the **sea level rises** to cover it, the coral carries on growing to form an **atoll**.

Another theory says that when sea levels fall, coral reefs and islands get worn down by **erosion**, and then the coral slowly builds up again.

Practice Questions

Q1 How are sand dunes formed?

Q2 Describe the zonation of plants on a sand dune.

Q3 Describe the conditions needed for coral to grow.

Exam Questions

Q1 State the ideal conditions for a dune system to become established and stabilised. (4 marks)

Q2 There is more species diversity on fixed mature dunes than on mobile fore-dunes. Explain why this is. (4 marks)

Q3 Describe Darwin's theory of the formation of coral atolls. (5 marks)

If you were a plant, would you want to live on a bare sand dune...

Thought not. I wonder what on earth possesses these couch grasses to go and live by the sea where it's so dry, and your whole sand dune can be blown away before you know it. Must be lack of competition, I suppose. Once these ecosystems get going, they generate their own soil. Clever. Coral is weird, but luckily all you need to know for the exam is on this page.

Coastal Processes and People

*Coastal areas contain some of the most fertile farmland, are major centres of industry and trade, provide recreation and are areas of settlement. These areas are all under threat from coastal processes, both in the short term (years and decades) and in the long term (thousands of years). These pages are for **Edexcel A**, **Edexcel B** and **AQA B** (**Option Q**).*

Erosion can be an Immediate *Threat* to *Coastal Land*

1) The **Holderness** coast near Hull in Eastern England is the fastest eroding coastline in Europe.

2) The coastline is **retreating**. Farmland and houses are at risk of **falling** into the sea.

3) The cliffs are made up of **glacial deposits** of **clay**, which is easily washed away.

4) Large areas of **low lying land** have been used for farming, industry and housing. **500 000** people live in the area, most of them less than **2 m** above sea level.

5) **Coastal defences** have been built to protect the land — see p28 and p29 for more about coastal management.

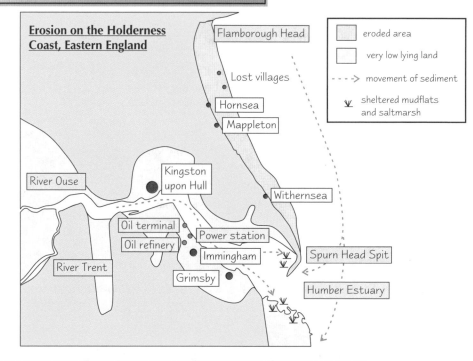

Erosion on the Holderness Coast, Eastern England

- Flamborough Head
- Lost villages
- Hornsea
- Mappleton
- River Ouse
- Kingston upon Hull
- Withernsea
- Oil terminal
- Oil refinery
- Power station
- Immingham
- Spurn Head Spit
- River Trent
- Grimsby
- Humber Estuary

Legend:
- eroded area
- very low lying land
- - - -> movement of sediment
- ﹀ sheltered mudflats and saltmarsh

In the Short Term, **Deposition Patterns** *and* **Features** *can* **Change**

Changing patterns of deposition can alter the equilibrium between deposition and erosion.

1) **Barrier islands** are formed from an **offshore bar** (see p20), with beach on the offshore side and marshland on the bay side. They're constantly being **eroded** on the **offshore** side and **building** up on the **bay** side, e.g. East coast of the USA.

2) Usually there's an equilibrium between erosion and deposition. If the deposition patterns are altered, the equilibrium is disturbed, and the barrier island can be **eroded**. This puts any settlements on the barrier island at risk.

3) Dredging **rivers** and **estuaries** on the **mainland** or on the **island** disrupts the equilibrium by **removing sediment** that would be deposited at sea.

Delta Environments can *Change* in the *Short Term*

Deltas are formed from deposition of river sediment (see p9). Changes upriver affect the delta.

1) Millions of people live on the **Nile delta**, which is only a tiny bit above river and sea level. The **land** is **sinking**, and the **sea level** is **rising** as well. The land is also getting **more salty**, and **less fertile**.

2) The **Aswan Dam** has had **positive** and **negative** effects. On one hand, it's increased the amount of **cultivable land** and it's **improved navigation** on the Nile. But...

3) The dam **traps** the millions of tons of **silt** washed down from the Ethiopian highlands every year. This used to **enrich** the Nile delta, but it now clogs up the dam instead. As a result, the delta is **sinking** and becoming more **saline** (salty) because of the intrusion of sea water. The **silt-less water** is **eroding** the delta, and there's no more **silt** to replace it.

In the Short Term, Coastal Floods can *Threaten Coastal Land*

Case study —Towyn Floods, Wales, 1990

There's more about floods in general on p12-13.

Background:	Average ground level 4 m above sea level. Protected by sea wall. Sewage pumped out to sea.
Event:	On the 26th Feb. 1990 there was a severe storm with high winds. There was a storm surge (a very, very high wave) which combined with high winds and high tide to have devastating effects. The sea wall was breached. Many people were trapped in their houses. Electricity failed, which meant that sewage could not be pumped out, and flood water became contaminated with sewage.
Response:	Over 5000 people were evacuated and placed in emergency accommodation. The sea wall was repaired. Water was pumped out of houses, and contaminated furniture removed from houses with help from the council and the military.

Coastal Processes and People

Changes in *Sea Level* Happen over the *Long Term* — i.e. Thousands of Years

1) Changes in local sea level may be caused by **eustatic movements**, i.e. fluctuations in the **worldwide sea level**.

2) They can also be caused by **isostatic movements**, i.e. **land** rising or sinking on a local scale.

3) These changes can cause coastlines to become **submerged** underwater or to **emerge** from below sea level.

4) When the coastline is **submerged** due to rising sea levels or sinking land levels, **estuaries** are **drowned** to form **rias**. There are **rias** on the **south west coast**, at Fowey, Plymouth, Salcombe and Dartmouth.

5) **Fjords** are a lot like rias, but they're **drowned glacial valleys** rather than drowned estuaries. There are lots of fjords in Norway, and there are some in New Zealand, Alaska and on the west coast of Canada.

6) **Submerged forests** give evidence of rising sea levels. There are some off the coast at Hartlepool (North East England).

7) **Raised beaches** occur where land is rising (geographers call them "**coastlines of emergence**"). There are raised beaches in Applecross Bay on the North West coast of Scotland. They show where the **land rose** faster than the sea after the **Ice Age**, once the weight of ice was gone.

8) The **former cliffs** (also called **abandoned cliffs**) of raised beaches are no longer eroded by the sea. They get slowly covered by **vegetation**.

In the *Long Term*, *Global Warming* May Cause a *Slow Rise* in Sea Level

Sea levels have **fallen** and **risen** in response to the formation and melting of **glacial ice** — the more water there is in **glaciers** and **polar ice sheets**, the less there is in the **sea**. The formation and melting of glacial ice depends on **global temperatures**, which seem to be changing more rapidly than before.

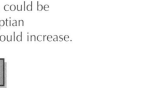

1) In the 20th century, average global temperatures rose by **0.6° C**.

2) Sea levels have risen by **10-25 cm** in the last 100 years.

3) By 2100 temperatures could rise by up to **4° C**. This depends on whether temperature keeps on rising as fast as it has been doing recently, or not. By 2100 sea levels could rise by **50 cm**. Again, this all depends on whether the temperature keeps rising quickly or not.

4) **100 million people** live in low-lying coastal areas. If the sea level does rise by 50 cm, then low lying coral islands and atolls such as the **Maldives** and **Bahamas** could be completely submerged.

5) **Poorer** people are going to be the most affected by a big rise in sea level. **25% of Bangladesh** could be submerged. **30% of Egypt's arable land** could be under water. Important sites of Ancient Egyptian civilisation would be lost, too. Rising sea levels in areas like Bangladesh mean that erosion would increase.

Salt Marsh and Mangrove Swamps Adjust to Rising Sea Levels

1) Sea level change usually happens slowly so some environments have time to **adjust**. **Salt marshes** such as those around the Thames, Humber and Severn estuaries, and in the Florida Everglades are naturally tolerant of salt water. Subtropical **mangrove swamps**, e.g. in Bangladesh, the Philippines, and New Guinea, are also tolerant of salt water.

2) **Saline tolerant ecosystems** can remain in **equilibrium** with sea levels.

3) However... these areas are being reduced by **land reclamation**. Areas of the Florida Everglades are being drained for housing and tourism.

Practice Questions

Q1 What is a storm surge?

Q2 What is the difference between isostatic and eustatic movement?

Q3 Give two examples of landforms that show there must have been a rise in sea levels.

Q4 Why would global warming make the sea level rise?

Exam Questions

Q1 With reference to a named case study, explain how erosion and flooding are threatening coastal settlements. (6 marks)

Q2 Describe the possible outcomes of a global rise in sea levels caused by global warming. (4 marks)

I'd start moving up onto high ground now...

For these pages, you need to be able to give examples for erosion, deposition, coastal floods and changing sea level. The examples here are nice ones, but if your teacher has given you detailed examples in class, and told you to use those, then use them. In the exam, you might get maps and photos and you'd have to spot the difference before and after some big change.

Human Use of Coastal Areas

*Coasts are some of the most populated areas in the world, and the interaction between humans and the environment often throws the natural coastal system out of equilibrium. Governments are increasingly encouraging the sustainable use of coasts. These pages are for **Edexcel A** and **Edexcel B**.*

Coastal Land Uses can cause Land Use Conflicts

1) Until recently, the coastal zone in the UK was thinly occupied — only people whose livelihoods were concerned with the sea lived next to the sea.

2) Over the last 200 years or so, the amount of **coastal development** has rapidly **increased**. Ports have expanded to meet the demands of **industrialisation**. There's been an extensive spread of **settlement** and tourism along the coastal zone.

3) There are many different **demands** on the coastal land, and natural processes can put human activity at risk.

50% of people in LEDCs live less than 60 km from the coast. By 2025 more people will live near the coast than were alive in 1990. Whoah.

Case Study — Norfolk Coast

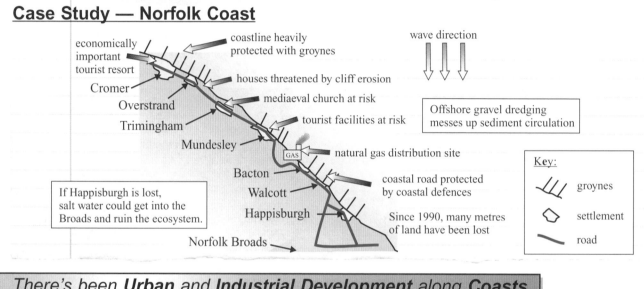

There's been Urban and Industrial Development along Coasts

Human use of coastal areas can easily **muck up natural coast processes**.

(1)
- Most coastal cities are **ports**. Building big artificial harbours interferes with natural sediment drift processes.
- Large settlements create a lot of **pollution**. It's tempting to chuck waste straight into the sea, but that'd be bad for **water quality**. MEDCs can afford to **treat sewage** before pumping it to sea. LEDCs, not so much.

(2)
- Coastal land was traditionally used for **heavy industry** in MEDCs — e.g. **coal mining, iron works** and **chemicals** in NE England. Today, there are alternative industries like **fish farming** in MEDC coastal areas.
- In **LEDCs** the coast is also used for heavy industry and a range of more temporary industries such as **ship breaking**. **Traditional fishing** is still a big part of the coastal economy in many LEDCs.

(3)
- The coastal zone is invariably rich in **hydrocarbon** reserves.
- Oil rigs and pipelines cause **degradation** of the coastal zone — e.g. on the coastline of **Nigeria**.

(4)
- **Coastal sand** and **gravel** is quarried and **dredged** for **building**.
- This interrupts the **sediment cell circulation** and causes **beach depletion**. For example, the Baie d'Audierne, Brittany has **retreated 50 m** in **50 years** because of offshore gravel dredging. Dredging shingle from Start Bay, Devon to build Devonport dockyard in Plymouth made the beaches more vulnerable to erosion. The coastal village of **Hallsands** on Start Bay fell into the sea during a severe storm in 1917.

Case study — ASSBY (Alang Sosiya Ship Breaking Yard), India

Background: Situated near Alang, Gujarat, India. ASSBY's unique geographical combination of high tidal range and a wide continental shelf allows ships to breach easily at high tide. With 182 plots and some 35 000 labourers, it's one of the world's biggest ship breaking yards.

The problem: Massive coastal urbanisation — lots of migrant workers coming in.
Coastal pollution and environment degradation caused by the processes employed to destroy the ships.

The future: Without tight regulatory control by the Indian Government the coast of Gujarat will be destroyed.

Human Use of Coastal Areas

Tourism and Recreation are Important Uses of Coastal Land

1) **Tourism** is one industry that could be **sustainable** — as long as it's **managed properly**.

2) Many coastal sites are poorly managed. This leads to **degradation** of the coastline, which makes them **less attractive** as tourist destinations and results in **economic decline**. Spain's Costa Del Sol is an example of this.

3) Coastal management has to leave the coast looking nice and pretty if it's going to be used for tourism.

4) Tourist facilities such as **golf courses**, **campsites** and **marinas** are often built with little appreciation of coastal systems.

> For example: Coastal **dunes** are **eroded** and suffer **blowouts** (when grass is removed, sand gets blown away). Coastal **paths** become **eroded** and unstable. **Marinas** take more than their fair share of **sediment deposition**, which leaves **areas down the coast** vulnerable to **erosion**. **Outboard motors** damage coral. Untreated **sewage** from boats causes **marine eutrophication** and also poses a **health risk** for tourists.

Eutrophication is where excess nutrients make algae grow like crazy, taking all the oxygen out of the system so everything else dies.

Case Study — Ocean City, Maryland, USA

Background: Ocean City on the eastern US coast is a **popular beach resort** on a **barrier island**. There was a boom in development from the 1950s to the 1980s. Coastal environmental concerns were raised in the late 1970s.

The problem: To connect and maintain the quiet backwater bay behind Ocean City, engineers stabilised the Ocean City inlet by building two **stone jetties**. **Longshore drift** runs in a southerly direction, and lots of **sediment** has been **stuck** north of the jetty, south of the inlet. Assateague Island has been **starved of sediment**. In fact it's now shifted 500 m to the west.

The future: Unless **development** is **limited** and **controlled** south of Ocean City, storm waves and **storm surges** from hurricane events could **inundate** the southern Atlantic **barrier islands** — and more importantly put **mainland East Coast USA** at risk. Given the dense development of the East Coast, damages and losses would run into **billions of dollars**.

Demand for Land and Infrastructure Affects Coasts

1) Flat coastal land is really convenient for large factory development and deep-water docking facilities. Demand is outstripping supply. **Coastal wetland reclamation** and even the construction of **artificial land** are ways of artificially meeting this demand. The **Polders** in the Netherlands and areas around Felixstowe in Suffolk are reclaimed land. **Hong Kong**'s Chek Lap Kok International **Airport** is built on a **reclaimed island**. Hong Kong is very short of land.

2) Land is reclaimed by digging **drainage ditches** to let the water out. The land needs to be **rinsed** with **fresh water** to get the salt out before it can be used for cultivation.

3) A good **infrastructure** of **roads**, **railways** and **bridges** is needed to distribute imported and manufactured goods to and from ports. Building bridges over estuaries can affect **ecosystems**. There's currently a row going on over building a big bridge across **Morecambe Bay** from Morecambe to Barrow in Furness.

Practice Questions

Q1 Give two examples of coastal land uses.
Q2 Explain why dredging coastal gravel for building is bad for coastal conservation.
Q3 Give two examples of bad management of coastal tourism.
Q4 What do the Dutch Polders and Hong Kong's airport have in common?

Exam Questions

Q1 Comment on the possible environmental impact of human use of long distance footpaths which follow the UK's coastline. (4 marks)

Q2 Assess the effect of **either** urban and industrial use **or** tourist pressure on the coastal environment. (4 marks)

What a pain in the groyne...

Obviously, because so many of the world's population live so near to the sea, people need to use the coast for a variety of different activities. You need to have a good grip on a couple of examples for these human activities. In the exam, you could be asked about urban/industrial development, tourism, or land reclamation. You'll need to mention the impact on coastal processes.

Management of Coastal Systems

*Coastal management is a complex problem. Fixing up one coastal area can have the unintended effect of messing up another area nearby. Anyway, you can never quite tame Nature. There'll always be storms and waves and tides, no matter what you do. These pages are for **AQA B** (**Option Q**), **Edexcel A** and **Edexcel B**.*

There are **Several Reasons** for **Coastal Management**

Physical reasons

1) **Soft rock** such as clay, glacial tills and sedimentary rock of the lowland coastlines around the world **erodes quickly** (as fast as 2 m per year). These coasts, e.g. the **eastern UK** and the **Californian coast**, need defending, especially when exposed to maximum wave power. Hard rock coastlines don't need as much defence.

2) Remember that **human activities** speed **erosion** and **cliff collapse**. Tourists cause problems walking on and **eroding** cliff tops. Building of **harbours** limits **natural drifting** of sediment.

Social and economic reasons

1) **Vulnerable settlements**, **industry** and **populations** need to be properly and **appropriately defended**. Failure to defend industrial sites would be very costly.

2) All coastal settlements want some kind of coastal defence, but the amount of **money available** is limited. Defence strategies are based on a **cost-benefit analysis**. Small settlements and isolated properties don't have the economic clout of large settlements, so they tend not to get money spent on coastal defences.

Hard Engineering Means Built Structures

1) Coastal management used to depend on building structures to hold back the waves — this is called **hard engineering**.
2) It's now known that hard engineering causes erosion further down the coast. Artificial features catch drifting sediment, which would otherwise be deposited down the coast — in other words they **muck up** the **natural sediment budget**.

Type	Defence	Cost	Disadvantage	Example
cliff erosion defences	vertical wall	Expensive to build and maintain	Reflects waves, so strong backwash erodes under wall	Sheringham, Norfolk
	curved wall	Expensive to build and maintain	strong backwash, as above	Sheringham, Norfolk
	stepped barrier	Expensive to build and maintain	strong backwash, as above	Sheringham, Norfolk
	revetment	Expensive to maintain	strong backwash, as above	Overstrand, Norfolk
	steel sheeting	fairly cheap	can be damaged in storms and landslides	Barton, Hampshire
	gabions *wall made of cages of rocks*	cheap	ugly	West Runton, Norfolk; Studland, Dorset
	rip-rap *boulders*	fairly cheap	can shift in storms	Ventnor, Isle of Wight
coastal flood defences	earthbank	quite expensive	can be eroded	Cley-next-the-sea, Norfolk
	tidal barrier	VERY expensive	really, VERY expensive	Thames Barrier, London
beach stabilisation	groynes *longshore drift →*	quite cheap	starves down-drift beaches of sand	Walton on the Naze, Essex
offshore protection	breakwaters *waves*	expensive	can be damaged in storms	Sea Palling, Norfolk
tidal inlet management	jetties *inlet*	quite expensive	starves down-drift beaches of sand	Great Yarmouth, Norfolk

Case Study — Hard Engineering in Christchurch Bay, Hampshire

Problem: Since the 1930s, the 30 m high soft, weak cliffs at Barton on Sea have been rapidly eroded by the sea. **Groynes** protecting the settlement of Hengistbury to the west were **trapping sediment** that would normally have been deposited around Barton, protecting the cliffs. Many buildings and tourist facilities were at risk from landslides.

Response: The **hard engineering** response cost over **£6 million** (in 1975 — very expensive in today's money). It involved **groynes** (to trap sediment on Barton's beach and stop the beach eroding away) and **revetments** and **steel sheeting** (to protect the cliffs). The defences have **failed** many times since being built. Thousands of tonnes of limestone have been dumped at the cliff-foot, the cliffs have been drained and an artificial beach built to absorb wave energy.

Management of Coastal Systems

Soft Engineering Means Coaxing Natural Processes Along

Soft engineering tries to **balance** coastal **erosion** and **deposition**, so that it's **sustainable**.

1) Beach nourishment means adding **sand** and **shingle** from elsewhere.
2) Beach stabilisation can be done by **reducing slope angle** and planting **vegetation**, or by sticking **old Christmas trees** in the beach to stabilise the sand.
3) Soft engineering schemes tend to be **cheaper** than hard engineering.

Case Study — soft / sustainable approach — the Maldives (LEDC)

Background: The Maldives is a nation of **1200 tiny islands** in the middle of the Indian Ocean.

Problem: Coastal land has been taken up by **harbour development**, **land reclamation**, **tourism development** and **reef destruction**. Extreme coastal erosion because of **sea level rise** has caused loads of problems.

Response: The **importance of tourism** means that protection for the coast depends upon "coastal stewardship" rather than extreme and **unsightly** hard engineering — the islands have to **stay pretty**.

Stewardship: Coastal stewardship on the islands aims to protect the coral reefs, to set up marine parks, to educate **local people** about conservation and to teach them to protect the beaches. Beach protection is a **community** responsibility.

Or... You Can Always Do Nothing, or Retreat (Run away! Run away!)

1) Both soft and hard engineering can turn out to be **money wasted**. Big projects can be destroyed by the sea within years. Perhaps it's better to **cope** with erosion and flood as and when they happen.
2) Retreat policies encourage people to move away from the seafront. For example, in parts of **California**, new properties have to be built a **long way** from the sea, so that they won't be eroded for years to come.

Coastal Defence Policies are the Responsibility of Government Agencies

1) In the UK, DEFRA (Department for Environment, Food and Rural Affairs) is responsible for setting policies for flood and coastal defences. They don't actually do the work, or even come up with the fine details.
2) The Environment Agency handles flood defence, and local councils manage coastal erosion. Together, councils and the Environment Agency do careful research into coastal processes and resources, and they do a detailed environmental impact study before deciding what strategy to use.
3) The management strategy must be technically good, value for money and environmentally OK. It has to allow recreational use of the coast. It also has to work with natural processes, not against them.

Good luck achieving all that...

Demand for Coastal Management is Likely to Go Up in the Future

1) A large proportion of the world's population lives within 40 km of the sea. Continuing coastal development means even more people will live by the sea in the future.
2) **Rising sea levels** mean more coastal management will be needed to protect coastal settlements and developments. Storm activity also seems to be getting more frequent and more severe, even in the short term.

Practice Questions

Q1 Why is coastal management needed?
Q2 What are: a) gabions, b) groynes and c) revetments?
Q3 Give an example of a soft engineering scheme.
Q4 What other options are there for coastal management, apart from hard and soft engineering?

Exam Questions

Q1 Outline where and why different methods of coastal engineering are most likely to be used along a given stretch of coastline. (7 marks)

Do nothing? Run away? Sounds like a lousy revision strategy to me...

Coastal management sounds like a difficult and unending job. Even after spending hundreds of thousands of pounds on a nice big concrete wall to keep the waves out, and some wooden groynes to hold the beach in place — it can still all go horrendously wrong. When it goes wrong, it costs even more money. These days they try to use sustainable methods instead, but it's still hard.

Glacial Systems

I do like a nice glacier. Pity you have to go to the Alps or Norway to see the nearest ones.
*This **WHOLE SECTION** is for **AQA B (Option P)** only. If you're doing option Q or option R, skip this.*

Glaciers are Dynamic Systems

The glacial system has **inputs**, **storage** and **outputs**. It's an **open** system.

Open systems have inputs and outputs. Closed systems don't have inputs and outputs.

Inputs include:
1) **Accumulation** of snow (by **precipitation** or from **avalanches**).
2) **Condensation** of water vapour from the air (which then freezes).
3) **Sublimation** of water vapour from the air directly to ice crystals.
4) Bits of **rock** collected when the glacier carves away at the landscape.
5) **Heat** from the **Sun**, and from **friction** as the glacier grinds along the ground.

Sublimation involves a direct change of state from a gas to a solid without passing through the liquid stage.

These aren't as important as the inputs which involve water.

Stores:
1) The main store is obviously **ice**.
2) **Meltwater** is a small part of the glacier. It can be found **on the ice**, **in the ice** or **below the ice**.
3) Glaciers also carry **debris**, called moraine.

Meltwater is considered a store when it's actually in the glacier. When it's flowing down the valley well away from the glacier, it isn't a store in the system any more.

Outputs are the losses from a glacier.
1) Ice can **melt** on the surface, inside the glacier, at the base of the glacier or from the ice front.
2) Surface snow can **melt** and **evaporate**.
3) Ice and snow can **sublimate** to water vapour.
4) Snow can be **blown away** by strong winds.
5) With coastal glaciers, blocks of ice fall from the front of the ice mass into water to create **icebergs**. This is called "**calving**" — as if the glacier were a big old ice cow giving birth to a little ice calf. (It can also happen where there's a lake at the snout of the glacier.)

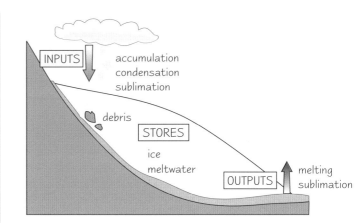

Accumulation and Ablation are the Input and Output of the Glacial Budget

1) Accumulation is the input of snow and ice into the glacial system. Most **accumulation** is snow precipitation.
2) **Ablation** is the collective loss (output) of water from an ice sheet or glacier.
3) You get **more ablation** than accumulation in the **lower** parts of a glacier, and at the end — the 'snout'.
4) You get **more ablation** during **warmer** times — which stands to reason, as ice melts more when it's warm.

A glacial budget is the balance between the inputs and outputs of the glacial system.

1) The **mass balance** is the balance between the amount of accumulation and the amount of ablation. It determines whether the front of the glacier **advances** forwards or **retreats** back.
2) If there's **more accumulation** than ablation, the glacier grows and **advances**. This is called a **positive regime**.
3) If there's **less accumulation** than ablation, the glacier retreats. This is a **negative regime**.
4) If there's the **same amount** of accumulation and ablation, the glacier is **steady**.

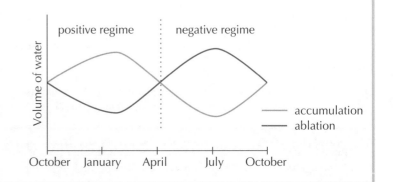

The Formation of Glaciers

Glaciers form when Snow **Accumulates** and **Turns Into Ice**

It's all very well to know that **accumulation** of snow is what makes glaciers **bigger**, but that doesn't answer the question of **how** flakes of snow turn into thick chunky glacier ice.

1) First, **snow settles**. It's in a loose, fluffy, snowflakey consistency at this point.

2) Next, the snow is converted into a **denser** and more **granular** consistency called **firn** or **névé**. Temperature changes between winter and summer and between day and night lead to the snow alternately **freezing** and **thawing** several times, which turns fluffy snow into icy granules.

3) The pressure of more snow falling on top also helps the snow become more granular. Increased pressure between individual grains causes **pressure melting**.

4) This eventually changes the loose snow into a dull, white, structureless mass. It has far less pore space so it's less **permeable** than fresh snow.

5) Air is squeezed out, and particles of ice **fuse together** as a result of further compression by the continuing accumulation of snow and ice. This is called **sintering**.

6) The resulting glacier is **ice-bluish** in colour and contains very little air. It's impermeable to water.

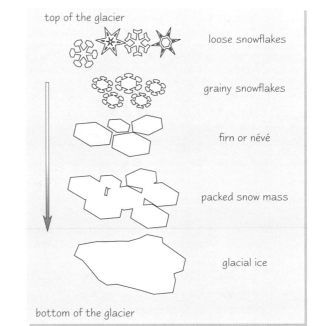

top of the glacier

loose snowflakes

grainy snowflakes

firn or névé

packed snow mass

glacial ice

bottom of the glacier

> Permeable = water <u>can</u> get through it.
>
> Impermeable = water <u>can't</u> get through it.

Glaciers can be **Cold** or **Warm**

Glaciers can be classified according to temperature.

1) In cold glaciers, the ice is very hard and frozen to the base of the valley. Cold glaciers are found in the Antarctic.

2) In **warm** or **temperate** glaciers, ice melts, and the meltwater acts as a **lubricant**, allowing the glacier to move freely. This means lots of erosion can happen. Temperate glaciers are found in the Alps.

Remember — glaciers can be warm or cold.

Practice Questions

Q1 What are the main inputs, processes and outputs in the glacial system?

Q2 What are accumulation and ablation?

Q3 If accumulation exceeds ablation what will happen to the glacier?

Q4 What is firn?

Q5 Which glaciers move more, cold glaciers or temperate glaciers?

Exam Questions

Q1 What is a glacial budget? Explain how a glacial budget shows whether the glacier is advancing or retreating. (3 marks)

Q2 Describe the sequence of events which leads to the formation of glacial ice from fresh snow. (5 marks)

<u>Brrr. Might need an extra jumper on...</u>

*Surprise surprise, glaciers are another "system". At AS level they really are mighty keen on getting you to see everything as a system. All this really means is knowing the **ins** and **outs** of the glacier. Stuff comes **in** mainly in the form of snow, and goes **out** mainly as meltwater — not so hard after all. Make sure you know how snow gets squished down into hard glacier ice, too.*

Glacial Movement and Erosion

Two important things about glaciers — one is that they're moving all the time, and the other is that they erode rocks like crazy.

Glaciers Move Downhill *under their Own* Weight

1) **Meltwater** underneath a glacier allows the glacier to **slide** over the bedrock. This is called **basal slide**, and it's the most common kind of glacial movement.

2) There's **more melting** around bits of rock protruding from the valley floor, because there's **more pressure** on the ice. Meltwater can **refreeze** downstream of the obstruction, so the flow tends to be faster around the obstruction, and slower downstream.

3) **Basal slide** can also be called **rotational flow**. The path the glacier takes is like the arc of a circle. It isn't really rotating as in "going round and round".

4) **Internal deformation** is where the whole glacier **bends** and **warps** to flow downhill. Ice crystals shift past each other, and thin layers of ice crystals slip over each other.

5) When the ice is under **strong forces** of **tension** (pulling apart) and **compression** (squeezing together), it **fractures** into thick layers, and these layers slip over each other. This is called **extending and compressing flow**.

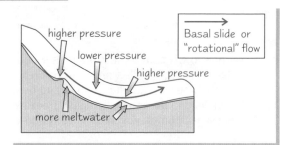

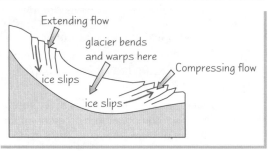

6) **Extending flow** happens at the **top** of the valley, where the ice is under **tension**. The ice layers slip **downwards**. **Compressing flow** happens at the bottom, where the ice is under **compression**. The ice layers slip **forwards**.

The main things which determine the **speed** at which a glacier flows are the **gradient** of the valley floor, the **thickness** of the ice and the **temperature** inside the glacier. The **steeper** the valley, the **faster** the glacier can flow. The **thickness** of the glacier determines how much **pressure** it exerts on the valley floor, and therefore how much **melting** goes on at the bottom of the glacier. The temperature obviously has an effect on **melting** — so warm glaciers flow more easily than cold glaciers.

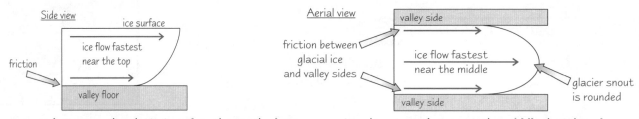

Ice moves faster near the glacier's **surface** than at the **base**.   Ice also moves faster near the **middle** than the **edges**.

Glaciers Crack *as they Move Down the Valley*

1) Stresses and strains cause **crevasses** to form at the top of the glacier. Cracks and crevasses are formed as part of **extending** and **compressing flow**.

2) Glacial flow means there's lots of **tension** between the ice attached to the back wall, and the rest of the glacier. A big **semicircular crevasse** called the **bergschrund** is formed at the back end of the glacier.

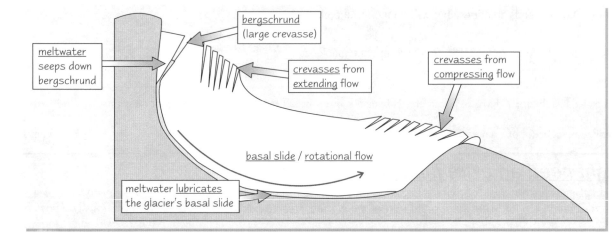

Glacial Movement and Erosion

Glaciers **Erode** the **Surrounding Rock**

Glaciers erode the valley floor and sides by plucking and abrasion

1) **Plucking** — Ice in contact with rock surfaces can thaw slightly then refreeze around rocks protruding from the bedrock. When the glacier moves forward, it **plucks** or tears the rocks away from the valley sides and floor — rather like those pore strips which pluck blackheads out of your skin.

2) **Abrasion** — Debris carried along by glacial ice can scratch and gouge at rock, leaving long scratch marks.

frost shattering breaks bits of rock off the mountain face

Ice

plucking breaks bits of rock off the mountain face and makes back wall steeper

Weathering contributes to the shaping of glacial landforms

Frost shattering helps **break up** the rocks beneath the glacier and to either side, making it easier for the glacier to pick them up and use them for **abrasion**.

abrasion grinds and gouges the valley floor

Meltwater erosion shapes the valley floor

Glaciers can produce huge quantities of **meltwater**, making streams that are powerful enough to erode the valley floor by normal **fluvial (river) processes**.

The amount and rate of erosion depends on the **local geology**, the **velocity** of the glacier, the **weight** and **thickness** of the ice, the amount of **debris** carried and what sort of debris is carried.

Glaciers **Transport** Loose and Broken **Debris**

Glaciers carry large loads ranging from **fine sediments** to **huge boulders**. There are three main methods of transporting debris:

1) **Supraglacial** material is carried **on top** of the glacier's surface.
2) **Englacial** material is carried **within** the body of the ice-sheet or glacier.
3) **Subglacial** material moves along **at the base** of the glacier. It mostly comes from the process of plucking.

This transported material is deposited as **moraine**. See p35 for more on moraines.

Glaciers **Deposit** Load as they **Move** and as they **Melt**

1) All material **deposited** by the glacier is called **till** or **moraine**. It includes massive boulders down to pebbles and clay.
2) **Lodgement till** is spread onto the valley floor beneath the ice by **moving** glaciers.
3) **Ablation till** is dropped by a **stationary** glacier as it begins to **melt**. Load is mainly deposited close to the glacier snout. This is where most ablation happens — the glacier drops debris as the ice around the debris melts.
4) **Till isn't sorted** out into big bits and small bits — glaciers drop **any old size** of till any old where.
5) Till does **point** in the **direction** where the glacier is flowing, though.

Practice Questions

Q1 What is rotational flow? What lubricates rotational flow?
Q2 What is extending flow?
Q3 What is the difference between plucking and abrasion?
Q4 What are the main methods by which a glacier transports its load?

Exam Questions

Q1 Explain how extending and compressing flow form crevasses in glaciers. (4 marks)

Q2 Name and explain the two methods of glacial erosion. (4 marks)

Glaciers move r e a l l y s l o w l y — bit like you on a Sunday morning...

Alright, I'll admit that these two pages are slightly harder than the last two. It can be tricky at first to get your head around the different ways that glaciers move. Don't worry about why it's called "rotational flow", just treat it as another name for sliding movement. Don't forget that glaciers erode rock in two different ways — by plucking and by abrasion.

The Glacial Trough and Glacial Deposition

These pages are about the landscapes that glaciers leave behind them. Mountain climbers and Geography teachers get very excited about the beauty of glacial landscape. Whether or not it moves you, you still need to learn it.

Glaciers develop in Basins called Corries (also called Cirques or Cwms)

1) Glaciers normally form on one side of a mountain peak — the side that gets **least sun** and the **coldest winds**. That's where there's **most accumulation** and **least ablation**.

2) Snow collects in hollows and turns to **ice**. **Rotational flow** with **abrasion** and **plucking** deepen the hollow into a **corrie**.

3) When the ice in the hollow is thick enough, it **flows** downhill as a glacier. Frost shattering and erosion **steepen** the back wall of the corrie.

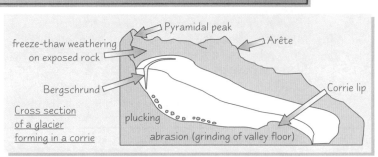

Ice Flows Down The Valley, Widening and Deepening it into a Trough

Abrasion is very forceful **under** the ice — the huge weight of ice scrapes debris against the valley floor. The valley **deepens** into a steep sided U shape called a **glacial trough**. The valley **sides** are **eroded more slowly**, so it gradually gets wider.

1) **Hanging valleys** are tributary valleys which get left at a higher level as the glacier erodes the main valley much deeper. You get waterfalls in hanging valleys, e.g. Lodore Cascades waterfall near Borrowdale in the Lake District, Cumbria.

2) **Truncated spurs** are spurs (ridges of land) between the tributary valleys which have been **chopped off** (truncated) by the powerful eroding ice. There are truncated spurs either side of Lodore Cascades.

3) **Valley steps** are formed when the glacier starts to erode more deeply. This happens when another glacier joins it or where there is less resistant rock. There are steps in the Nant-Ffrancon valley in Snowdonia, North Wales.

4) **Ribbon lakes** are long, thin lakes formed **after** the ice age. They formed in dips formed by erosion of less resistant rocks, or behind dams of terminal moraine. Windermere and Ullswater in the Lake District are examples of ribbon lakes.

5) **Fjords** are where the valley is eroded really deeply right down to the **coast** and below sea level. The valley **floods** with **sea water**, making a long deep inlet. There are lots of fjords in Norway, and the sea lochs in Scotland are mostly fjords.

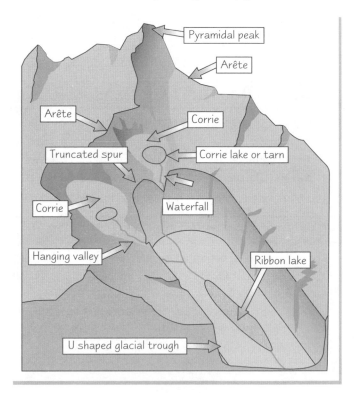

Bare Rocks are Exposed by the Ice as it Flows Down The Valley

1) A **pyramidal peak** forms where several **corries** form **back to back** so their back walls make a mountain peak, e.g. Helvellyn in the Lake District, Cumbria.

2) An **arête** is formed when two glaciers flow in parallel valleys and **sharpen** the mountain ridge in between, e.g. Striding Edge and Swirral Edge near Helvellyn.

3) A **roche moutonnée** (French for "sheepy rock") is a hard, **resistant** outcrop on the valley floor. The **upstream** (stoss) side is **smooth**, because it was smoothed by **abrasion** as the glacier went over it. The **downstream** (lee) side is steep and **rough** where the glacier **plucked** at it. There are roches moutonnées near Grasmere in the Lake District.

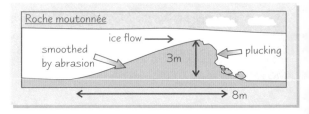

The Glacial Trough and Glacial Deposition

Deposits of **Moraine** Contribute to the **Glacial Landscape**

Moraine is a mixture of loose rocks and boulders deposited by a glacier.

1) **Lateral moraine** is deposited where the sides of the glacier were.

2) **Medial moraine** is formed where two glaciers converge, from two lateral moraines joining together.

3) **Ground moraine** is scattered all over the valley.

4) **Terminal moraine** builds up at the end of the glacier, and is deposited as little semi-circular hillocks of till.

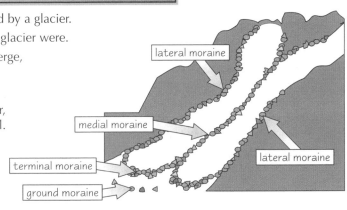

Till is all the stuff that a glacier leaves behind — unsorted boulders, stones and clay (see p33). Moraine is the name given to particular formations of till.

Till can also be Dropped in **Interesting Shapes**

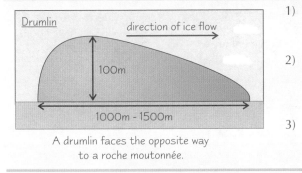

A drumlin faces the opposite way to a roche moutonnée.

1) **Drumlins** are **half-egg shaped hills** of till, up to 1500 m long and 100 m high. The **upstream** (stoss) end is **wide and tall**, and the **downstream** (lee) end is **narrow and low**.

2) It is difficult to see **why** drumlins are egg-shaped — it may be that till got stuck around a rock or a little hill sticking out into the glacier. It may be that an original mound of dropped till got streamlined by the ice sheet moving over the top of it.

3) Drumlins often form in **groups**. There are drumlins in the **Ribble Valley** in Lancashire. There are also a whole bunch of drumlins under the water level in Clew Bay, Ireland.

Erratics are **Boulders** that have been **Carried** a **Long Way** by Glaciers

1) Erratics are **completely unrelated geologically** to the rock where they're found.

2) For example, in the Yorkshire dales at Norber, loose black **Silurian** rocks sit on top of white **Carboniferous** limestone.

3) There are erratics in **Eastern England** that were originally picked up by ice sheets in **Norway** and carried all the way to England during the Ice Ages.

Practice Questions

Q1 What happens to spurs on the sides of glaciated valleys?

Q2 What is a coastal, flooded, over-deepened, glaciated valley called?

Q3 If an area of a valley is said to have the appearance of a basket of eggs, what glacial deposition features are present?

Q4 What is the name for rocks transported and dropped onto a different rock type?

Q5 Which one of these features is formed by two glaciers sharpening a ridge between them: spur, arête, fjord, cirque?

Exam Questions

Q1 Explain why, in the UK, most corries are on the north facing sides of mountains. (4 marks)

Q2 Explain the difference between a hanging valley and a fjord. (4 marks)

I wonder why they called it a sheepy rock in the first place...

There are a fair few features to learn here. The big diagram helps you see roughly what they look like, and then you also need to know how they're formed by the natural movement and processes of the glacier. The names for different bits of moraine are really quite straightforward. If you've done glaciers in GCSE Geography, this ought to be a piece of the proverbial. Cake, that is.

Fluvioglacial Landforms

Fluvioglacial landforms are things that glaciers leave behind them when they melt. Meltwater erodes the ground just like any river or stream. Meltwater also transports and deposits debris that was trapped in the ice.

Fluvioglacial Deposits Come from Glacial Meltwater

1) When glacial ice melts, water runs out and forms streams of **meltwater**. **Warm** glaciers and **retreating** glaciers produce lots of meltwater.

2) **Surface** meltwater **filters** through the glacier and flows through **tunnels** underneath the glacier, before running out of the snout of the glacier.

3) Meltwater streams are often **braided** — they split into lots of mini streams which cross over each other.

4) Glacial meltwater carries a large **load** of **sediment** of various sizes — from inside, on top of and underneath the glacier.

5) Meltwater streams **deposit** their load on the **valley floor** as they flow away from the glacier.

6) There's a difference between **glacial deposition features** formed by glaciers dropping rocks as they melt and **fluvioglacial deposition features** formed by meltwater carrying rocks and sediment away from the glacier.

7) **Fluvioglacial** deposits are **sorted**. That means that small sizes of sediment are **separated** out from larger sands, gravels and rocks.

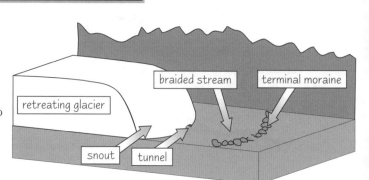

Glen Rosa on the Isle of Arran, Scotland, is a good place to compare glacial deposits and fluvioglacial deposits.

Meltwater Streams Deposit Kames and Eskers

1) **Kames** are **mounds** of meltwater deposits at the front edge of the retreating (melting) glacier roughly parallel to the front of the glacier.

2) They look a little like terminal moraine but the mounds are **smaller**.

3) **Kame terraces** are at the sides of the valley like lateral moraine but sorted into layers by varying flows of melt water.

4) **Eskers** are long, winding **ridges** of sand and gravel deposits at right angles to the snout of the glacier.

5) Eskers are fluvioglacial deposits from meltwater streams flowing in meltwater tunnels **underneath** the glacier.

Kames and eskers are illustrated on the diagram at the bottom of the page, which shows what the glacial landscape at the top of the page would look like after the glacier melts.

Melting Glaciers Leave Ribbon Lakes and Outwash Plains

1) Long thin **ribbon lakes** can be dammed by deposits from glaciers.

2) An **outwash plain** forms at the end of a glacier where the meltwater washes out onto low-lying ground.

3) Meltwater streams **drop their load** of sediment quite quickly once they leave the snout of the glacier. Sediments on outwash plains are particularly well **sorted**, and they're **stratified** into layers.

4) **Blocks of ice** carried onto the outwash plain melt to form **kettle holes**.

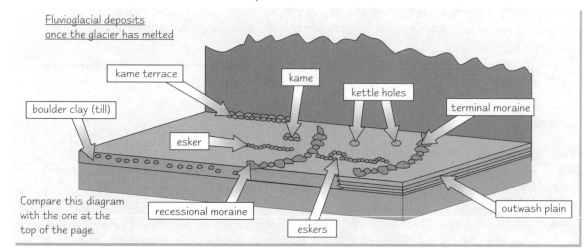

Fluvioglacial deposits once the glacier has melted

Compare this diagram with the one at the top of the page.

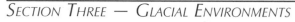

Fluvioglacial Landforms

Proglacial Lakes are Trapped Between the Glacier and High Ground

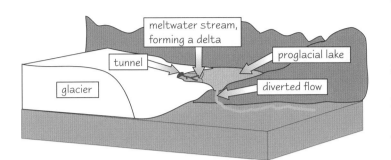

1) This is a bit weird — moving ice can **temporarily dam rivers** without freezing the river. This makes a **proglacial lake**. Melting glacier ice can also form such a lake.

2) Meltwater streams flowing into proglacial lakes deposit their sediment as a **delta**.

3) When the ice melts, these deltas are left as **delta kames**.

4) Water draining out from a proglacial lake is **diverted** by the glacier.

Example of how glaciers have diverted river drainage:

1) In the Ice Age, **proglacial lakes** were formed in the **Vale of Pickering** and **Eskdale** in Yorkshire.

2) In the **Vale of Pickering**, overflows from the proglacial lakes flowed through channels away from the glacier until the ice melted.

3) One overflow eroded the Kirkham Abbey Gorge, **diverting** the **River Derwent** through it and **away** from the sea for a considerable distance (see map).

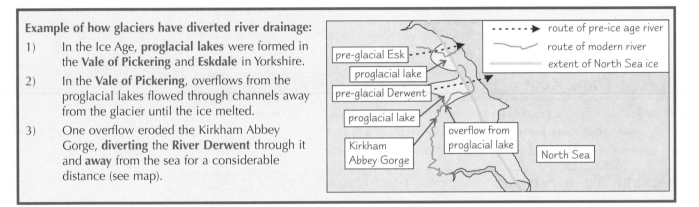

Varves are Deposits left on the Bottom of Proglacial Lakes

1) **Varves** are layers of sorted silts, sand and gravel dropped by meltwater into a proglacial lake.

2) A layer of **coarse deposits** forms when meltwater flows quickly into the lake during rapid **summer melt**.

3) A layer of **fine deposits** forms during **autumn**, when very little water flows into the lake and its surface is frozen.

4) This is because **fast** moving meltwater has the energy to carry **coarser material**, which settles to the bottom of the lake straight away. In **winter**, when there's not much water flowing into the lake, the **fine material suspended** in the lake can **settle** down to the bottom.

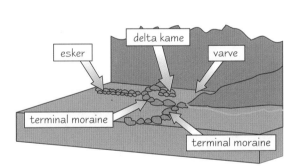

Practice Questions

Q1 What's meant by the "fluvio" part of "fluvioglacial deposits"?

Q2 What is an outwash plain?

Q3 Name the type of fluvioglacial deposits that are like lateral moraine, but sorted into layers.

Q4 Moving ice can dam a river. What does that form?

Exam Questions

Q1 How can ice cause diversion of drainage? (4 marks)

Q2 Explain why varves are made from layers of sorted material. (4 marks)

Hooray, it's another page of things that glaciers leave behind them...

Well, this is just typical of glaciers if you ask me. Not content with ripping bits of rock out of mountains and scattering them all over landscapes, glaciers then have to go and melt, and wash all kinds of bits of rock all over the place. If only they didn't have to be so, well, <u>messy</u> about it — then you wouldn't need to know what a kame or an esker or a varve was. Oh well, tough luck, eh.

Periglacial Processes and Landforms

These pages are about the land and soil on the edge of a glacial area. It's always very cold, and there's always ice in the soil. Periglacial means "on the edge of a glacial area" by the way.

Permafrost is Permanently Frozen Ground

Where glaciers and ice sheets have retreated, they leave a **periglacial** area where the **subsoil** (the layer of soil below the soil surface) is **frozen all year round**, even though the surface layer thaws for a while in summer.

1) Permafrost is **permanently frozen subsoil**.

2) Permafrost covers **20-25%** of Earth's land surface.

3) For permafrost, the temperature needs to be **very cold** — below -1.5°C for patches of permafrost and below -5°C for continuous permafrost. Above 75° latitude, it's cold enough for layers of permafrost up to **700 m deep**.

4) The layer of permafrost is **impermeable**. When the top layer melts in summer, the water can't go anywhere, so the soil gets very **waterlogged** on the surface. The waterlogged soil flows and shifts very easily. It's called the **active layer**.

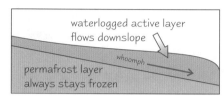

There's **continuous permafrost** in most of Greenland, Siberia and NE Canada. There's also permafrost at high altitude on mountains.

Freeze-Thaw Action and Frost Shattering Weather Rock

Water in cracks in rock **expands on freezing** and exerts **huge pressures** on the rock around it. The rock **shatters**.

1) **Frost shattering** heavily **weathers** rocks in glacial areas.

2) **Scree** is **debris** from frost shattering. There are big **scree slopes** by Wast Water in the Lake District.

Ground Water Freezes causing Frost-Heave and Contraction

1) Water in soil, sand and gravel expands on freezing.

2) When the surface layer of permafrost freezes in winter, the ice lifts or heaves up the surface layers of soil. The ice forms a kind of lens shape.

3) The process of freezing soil removes water from the dry part of the soil. The dry soil contracts, and cracks form. This is called frost contraction.

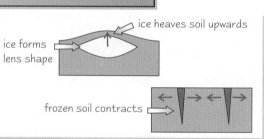

Ice Wedges Develop in Cracked Permafrost Soil

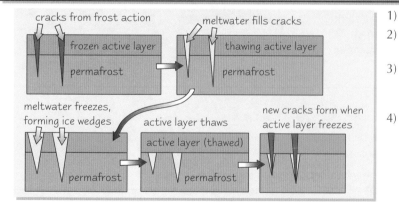

1) **Frost contraction** makes **cracks** in frozen soil.

2) In spring, ice in the active layer melts. Meltwater **seeps** into the cracks.

3) The permafrost layer is still frozen, and it **freezes** the water in the cracks. These **ice wedges** expand and **widen** the cracks.

4) In summer, the whole **active layer melts**, so you can't see the cracks any more. Each **winter**, frost contraction and frost heave **re-open** the crack. Each spring, more water seeps in, and when it freezes, the ice wedge gets thicker, **widening** the crack.

Nivation makes Hollows Deeper by Freezing and Thawing

1) A **hollow** containing a patch of **snow** gets **deeper** and **wider** by frost action. This is called **nivation**.

2) **Frost shattering** under the snow breaks bits off the underlying rock. This makes the hollow bigger.

3) In summer, the snow **melts** and meltwater carries the broken bits of rock away.

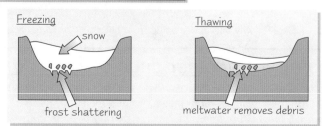

Periglacial Processes and Landforms

Solifluction is the Flow of Waterlogged Soil

1) The **waterlogged active layer** of soil **flows** easily. This flow is called **solifluction**.

2) When the flowing soil layer is cold and flowing over a **permafrost**, it's known as **gelifluction**. Because it's so **cold**, it flows in a **viscous** way, like **syrup**.

3) Solifluction and gelifluction produce **step** formations and **lobe** formations (see diagrams).

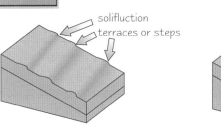

solifluction terraces or steps

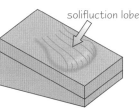

solifluction lobe

Patterned Ground has Polygon and Circle Shapes Formed by Frost Activity

1) Frost heave can result in **dome shapes** on the ground, in a pattern of **polygons** or **circles**.

2) These have **stones** marking the **edges** of each dome.

3) On **steep slopes**, the stones roll down, so you tend to get **stripe** formations instead of polygons or circles.

4) Some patterning is due to **frost contraction**. Cracks form in soil, and then get filled with ice wedges. These ice wedges are polygon shaped when viewed from above.

5) Some patterning is due to **frost heave**. Frost heave throws bigger chunks of rock up to the surface. These roll down to the edges of the polygons.

Pingoes are Ice-Filled Periglacial Hills

1) A pingo is a **conical hill** with a **core** of **ice**. Pingoes can be as large as 80 m high and about 500 m wide.

2) A pingo forms when water freezes between the permafrost and a layer of sand and gravel. The ice forms a **lens** shape, which pushes the sand and gravel up into a small hill.

3) There are two types of pingo. **Open system pingoes** are formed by water coming from **outside**, from a stream or spring. **Closed system pingoes** are formed by ice expanding in the permafrost itself, or by a frozen lake getting covered over with soil. Closed **system pingoes** tend to get **bigger** than the open system ones.

4) When the ice **thaws**, the pingo **collapses**, leaving behind a **pond** of meltwater surrounded by **ramparts** (walls of soil).

5) There are hundreds of pingoes in the **Mackenzie Delta**, way up in the North West Territories in Canada. There are collapsed pingoes near Llanberis, north Wales.

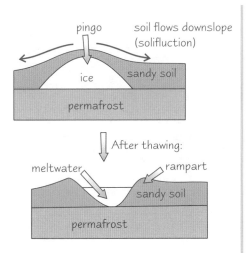

Practice Questions

Q1 What is permafrost?

Q2 Permafrost is not rare. How much of the Earth's land surface is covered in permafrost?

Q3 What's the name for a small hill pushed up by a lens shaped lump of ice?

Q4 How are polygonal shapes formed in periglacial areas?

Exam Questions

Q1 Describe solifluction terraces and the processes that lead to their formation. (4 marks)

Q2 What stages of development lead to a collapsed pingo? (4 marks)

A hill filled with ice or a cute penguin — you decide...

The trouble with this lot is that there are so many different processes going on, and all of them are to do with water freezing and then thawing. It's best to learn things bit by bit. Remember that the top layer of permafrost landscape thaws out in summer, and flows down slopes. In the exam, you could be asked about any of the landforms on these pages, and how they were formed.

Plate Tectonics

Plate tectonics is the study of the movements of the Earth's crust and their associated landforms.
*These pages are for **Edexcel A** and **OCR A**.*

There's Various **Evidence** for **Moving Tectonic Plates**

Plate tectonics theory says that the Earth's **lithosphere** (outer crust) is made up of plates, which move around.

1) One piece of evidence is that **rocks** on opposite sides of the Atlantic in Brazil and West Africa are very **similar**.

2) The South American coastline and the West African coastline also seem like they'd **fit very neatly** together.

3) Rocks in Brazil and West Africa contain **fossils** of very similar **land animals**. They couldn't have swum the Atlantic.

So, it seems that the two land masses must have been together at one point, and then they drifted apart.

Tectonic Plates Float on Semi-Molten Mantle

1) The **core** of the Earth is **very hot**, and this creates **convection currents** in the asthenosphere (see diagram).

2) The **rigid** outer plates of the **lithosphere** float on the **asthenosphere** and are moved very slowly by these currents.

3) Plates move **towards** each other, **away** from each other or **sideways** along each other.

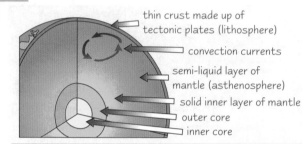

thin crust made up of tectonic plates (lithosphere)
convection currents
semi-liquid layer of mantle (asthenosphere)
solid inner layer of mantle
outer core
inner core

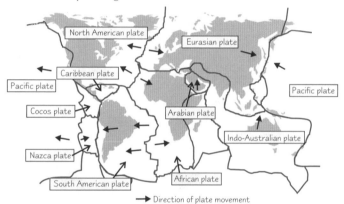

→ Direction of plate movement

The plates all move in **different directions**, and at slightly **different rates**. The North American plate and Eurasian plate move apart at 1cm per year. The Pacific plate moves at 4 cm per year.

At the **boundaries** between the plates, **tectonic processes** give rise to **volcanic activity** and **earthquakes**, and produce various **landforms**.

OCR calls plate boundaries plate margins. Edexcel uses both terms. But don't worry — they're exactly the same thing.

A **Destructive Plate Boundary** is where Plates **Converge**

e.g. between the Eurasian and Indo-Australian plates

1) When denser oceanic crust moves towards a section of continental crust, it **sinks** below the continental crust, and is destroyed. This is called **subduction**, and the area where it happens is called the **subduction zone**.

2) Subduction forms **deep ocean trenches**, e.g. the Aleutian trench between the Pacific and North America.

3) The subducted plate melts, and the **magma** produced rises up to erupt on the surface, forming **arcs** of **volcanic islands**, e.g. the Japanese island chain.

4) Where two **continental** plates meet, the collision causes complex **folding** and **faulting**, which makes **fold mountains**. The Indo-Australian and Eurasian Plates crashed together to form the Himalayas. This is called **convergence**.

5) Severe **earthquakes** can occur at destructive margins. Most of these happen around the "**Ring of Fire**" — around the edge of the Pacific plate.

oceanic plate
continental plate
volcano
subduction zone

A **Constructive Plate Boundary** is where Plates **Diverge**

e.g. between the African and South American plates

1) A constructive plate boundary is one where plates move apart creating a **rift valley**, e.g. the **East African Rift Valley** (or **Great Rift Valley**). This is called **divergence**.

2) Where plates diverge under the sea, new crust is created as magma wells up into the rift and solidifies. This creates **mid ocean ridges**, e.g. the **Mid-Atlantic Ridge**. This process is called **sea-floor spreading**.

A **Conservative Plate Margin** is where Plates **Move Past Each Other**

At a conservative plate margin, crust isn't destroyed or created, but the friction from two plates moving past each other gives frequent **earthquakes** and faulting, e.g. the San Andreas Fault in California, USA.

e.g. between the Pacific and North American plates

Plate Tectonics

Volcanoes are Common along Plate Boundaries

1) Volcanoes are formed when magma collects below the surface in a **magma chamber**.
   Pressure builds up and forces the magma up to the surface until it bursts out.

2) Volcanoes occur when a **weakness** in the Earth's crust allows material from the mantle to
   burst out onto the Earth's surface — these weaknesses tend to be on **plate boundaries**.
   Volcanoes are found at **constructive** and **destructive** plate margins.

3) You also get volcanoes at **hot spots** well out of the way of plate boundaries. Hot spots are where plumes of
   very hot magma rise up through the mantle and heat the top layer of mantle. There's a hot spot beneath **Hawaii**.

Volcanoes are Igneous Extrusions — Magma Bursts Out of Them

1) **Extrusion** means **liquid magma** bursting out of the Earth's surface. When magma reaches the surface, it's called **lava**.

2) As well as lava, volcanoes can produce gas, ash and cinder. The solid material is collectively called **tephra**.
   Pyroclastic flow is a mixture of **very hot ash**, **cinder** and **gas** which roars down the sides of a volcano at high speed.

3) The **shape** of a volcanic cone depends on the **type of lava**. Generally, **runny** non-viscous
   lava spreads out a long way, forming low **shield volcanoes** such as Mauna Kea in Hawaii.

4) **Thick viscous lava** doesn't flow far. It tends to be accompanied by gas and tephra.
   Explosive eruptions pile big bits of ash and cinder around the volcano to form a cone.
   Composite cones are a mixture of **lava** and **cinder** — they're the **steepest** cones.
   Mt. Vesuvius in Italy is a composite cone.

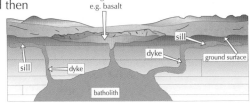

5) Very thin, **runny lava** from fissures (cracks) spreads out for miles to form a **lava plateau**.
   Iceland is an example of a lava plateau landscape, and so are the **Deccan Heights** in India.

Lava spreads out and cools to form a plateau.

Volcanic activity can have benefits — it can be great to have a volcano on your doorstep.

1) Volcanic ash makes for wonderfully fertile soil. The area around Mt. Vesuvius in Italy is rich farmland.

2) Hot springs come to the surface around dormant volcanoes, e.g. in Iceland.

3) Extinct volcanoes erode and leave behind volcanic pipes, filled with igneous rock and ash. Some of
   these pipes are rich with diamonds — the diamond mines in South Africa are in old volcanic pipes.

Igneous Intrusions are when Magma Solidifies Below The Surface

1) Magma which solidifies and crystallises when it's still below the surface is called
   an **igneous intrusion**. Magma pushes up into other rocks and slowly crystallises.

2) **Dykes** are **wall-shaped intrusions** which **cut across the strata** of the rock they're
   intruding into. They were formed when magma **oozed into a fissure** and then
   cooled. There are loads of dykes in North West Scotland.

3) **Sills** are **flat sheets** of igneous intrusion. They were formed when
   magma seeped in between two beds of sedimentary rock.

4) **Batholiths** are huge great masses of intrusive rock.
   Dartmoor is a big granite batholith.

Practice Questions

Q1 What are tectonic plates, and why do they move?

Q2 How do volcanoes form and why does their shape vary?

Q3 What is a sill, and how is it formed?

Exam Questions

Q1 Explain the relationship between volcanic and earthquake activity and plate margins. (4 marks)

Q2 Describe and explain the landforms associated with EITHER destructive OR constructive plate margins. (5 marks)

By heck, this is hot stuff...

*If you were expecting a joke about dykes as in ladies who love other ladies, you'll be sadly disappointed. You wouldn't
go to Lea DeLaria* for your Geography revision, would you. You wanna know about rift valleys, oceanic trenches,
volcanic island arcs, lava plateaux and all of that kind of fun tectonic stuff, you come here. Of course you do.*

*famous(ish) American lesbian stand-up comic

Weathering Processes

Rocks on the Earth's surface get weathered — they get worn down either by physical or chemical action.
*These pages are for **OCR A** and **Edexcel A**.*

Weathering Plays an *Important Part* in Shaping the *Land*

Weathering **degrades** rock, breaking it into fragments called **regolith**. These fragments can be **transported more easily** by running water, wind, ice or gravity. Although types of weathering are classified into groups, in real life it usually involves several processes working at once.

Weathering = breaking rock down.
Regolith = bits of broken off rock. ⟵ Regolith is an important part of soil.
Transport = regolith being carried away by water, wind, gravity, etc.

Physical or *Mechanical Weathering* is Down to *Physical Forces*

1) **Frost shattering** or **freeze-thaw action** is when water gets trapped in crevices, freezes and expands. The stresses caused by this expansion force rock fragments to **break off** the main rock face, forming **scree** e.g. **Wast Water Screes** in the Lake District.

2) **Thermal expansion** or **heating-cooling weathering** happens in areas with a big daily temperature range. Rocks expand during the day when it's hot, and contract at night when it's cold. This causes either **granular disintegration** or **exfoliation** (flaking), depending on the composition of the rocks.

3) **Pressure release** happens after overlying rocks are eroded. There's less pressure at the surface, so the rock expands, forming cracks. Layers of rock flake off. This is **exfoliation**, e.g. exfoliation domes at Sugarloaf Mountain, Rio de Janeiro and Ayers Rock, Australia.

4) **Wetting-drying weathering** happens when **clay** in rock gets wet. This makes it **swell up**, which produces cracks in the rock.

5) **Salt crystallisation weathering** is when salt crystals grow in rock crevices. They **exert pressure** on the surrounding rock and make it **crack**. This is common along **coastlines** and also in **hot deserts** where water is drawn up from below ground.

6) **Spheroidal weathering** is when lumps of rock weather more at their **corners** — so they get **rounded** off.

7) **Biological action** can cause physical damage — tree roots force rock apart, and animal burrows can let water in.

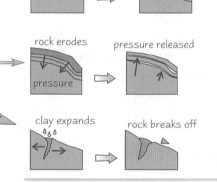

ice expands → rock breaks off

rock expands → rock contracts

rock erodes → pressure released
pressure

clay expands → rock breaks off

Chemical Weathering is Caused by *Chemical Reactions*

1) **Solution weathering** happens when **soluble minerals dissolve** and get **washed out** of the rocks.

2) **Oxidation** adds oxygen to metal ions to produce oxides. The resulting compounds can be softer and **more easily eroded** than the original metals. They can also be **bigger** in size than the original compounds. In a rock, this increase in size causes **splits** and **cracks**, weakening the rock for further weathering action.

3) **Carbonation** is when carbon dioxide mixes with rainwater to produce carbonic acid, which attacks carbonate rocks like limestone. The reaction widens natural joints in the rock, producing **limestone pavement** landscape.

4) **Hydration** is when a mineral **absorbs water**. It expands, which makes it disintegrate. Not all minerals absorb water.

5) **Hydrolysis** is a chemical reaction between water and a mineral to form clay. The breakdown of **feldspars** in granite to form **kaolinite (china clay)** is an example of hydrolysis.

6) **Biological action** can also affect rocks chemically — **bacteria** break down some minerals in the soil, and **decaying vegetation** (humus) produces **organic acids** (humic acids) which also break down minerals.

7) **Chelation** is the **removal of mineral ions** held in **organic compounds** within soil. Aluminium, iron, ⟸ There's more calcium and magnesium are removed by **humic acids** from **humus** in the upper layers of soil. about this on p67.

Oxidation: $4FeO + O_2 \rightarrow 2Fe_2O_3$
Iron (ii) oxide + oxygen → Iron (iii) oxide

Hydration: $CaSO_4 + 2H_2O \rightarrow CaSO_4 2H_2O$
anhydride + water → gypsum

Carbonation: $H_2O + CO_2 \rightarrow H_2CO_3$ $H_2CO_3 + CaCO_3 \rightarrow Ca(HCO_3)_2$
Water + carbon dioxide → Carbonic acid   Carbonic acid+ calcium carbonate → calcium bicarbonate

Weathering Processes

Various Factors Influence the Rate of Weathering

Carbon dioxide is more soluble when it's cold, though.

1) **Climate** affects weathering. Freeze-thaw and wetting-drying need water to be present. Freeze-thaw needs it to be cold. A lot of chemical weathering goes faster at higher temperatures.

2) **Rock type** affects weathering. Rocks have a variety of **chemical compositions** so they react differently. Minerals which formed at **high temperatures** tend to be most quickly affected by chemical processes, e.g. **feldspars**.

3) **Rock structure** affects weathering. **Porous** rocks have **pore spaces**, which let water through. **Permeable** rocks have routes for water to pass through them, such as along **joints**, **bedding planes** and **faults**.

4) **Relief** affects weathering. On **steep slopes** the regolith (broken off fragments) is **quickly removed**, exposing new rock for attack. On **gentle slopes** a deep **protective layer** of regolith can accumulate, due to a slow rate of removal.

5) **Vegetation** affects weathering. Vegetation can provide a protective **cover** against weathering. On the other hand, vegetation can also **contribute** to weathering, for example when tree roots prise rock apart.

6) **Human influence** affects weathering. Humans can **expose rock** to weathering by **mining** and **quarrying** or **protect** it by **building** over it. Pollution contributes to the formation of **acid rain,** which attacks rocks where it falls.

Granite Landscapes Have Distinctive Features

1) Granite is resistant to weathering. Granite landscapes have bare isolated rock outcrops called **tors**.

2) One theory of tor formation says that they're formed by physical **freeze-thaw weathering**.

3) Another theory says that they're formed by **chemical weathering**. Granite has small **joints** — splits in the rock which water can get into. Bits of granite with lots of joints get weathered away more quickly, leaving behind the less jointed granite as a tor.

4) Weathered granite landscapes like Dartmoor are very attractive, and good for **tourism**. They're also good for **quarrying**, either for granite itself, or for china clay.

Limestone Landscapes Have Distinctive Features

1) Limestone is almost completely made of **calcium carbonate**. It's weathered by **solution** and **carbonation**.

2) Limestone naturally has lots of **joints**. Weak carbonic acid seeps into joints and reacts with limestone to make calcium hydrogen carbonate ($CaHCO_3$), which is soluble in water. The $CaHCO_3$ gets washed away out of the joint. This process makes the joint wider, eventually creating **caves** and **swallow holes**.

3) **Limestone pavement** has a distinctive **slab** and **gap** pattern. The slabs are **clints**, and the gaps are **grykes**.

4) Weathered limestone landscape is called **karst**. There's a big area of karst called the Burren in County Clare, Ireland. Karst landscapes can be very attractive and popular with tourists. Limestone's also quarried and used in building.

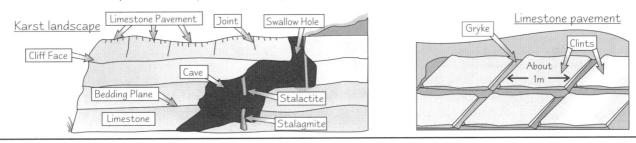

Practice Questions

Q1 Define the term 'weathering'.

Q2 How do physical and chemical weathering differ?

Q3 Describe the features of karst landscape.

Exam Questions

Q1 Describe and explain the weathering processes found in a named drainage basin which you have studied. (7 marks)

Q2 Describe the factors which affect rates of weathering. (5 marks)

Come on, don't let it wear you down, it's only a bit of geology after all...

Weathering is very important. No, really, it is. Without weathering, there wouldn't be any little rock particles to make up soil. By the way, weathering isn't the same as erosion. Weathering breaks down the rock where it is, erosion wears it away by a moving force. You do genuinely need to know the different kinds of physical and chemical weathering. It's not in the book for fun.

Mass Movement

*Mass movement is the downslope movement of regolith in response to gravity. These pages are for **OCR A** only.*

A *Slope* is a *Dynamic Open System* — it has *Inputs* and *Outputs*

1) Open systems have **inputs** and **outputs** as well as **stores** and **processes**.

2) **Slope systems** have **inputs** of **mass** from rainwater, meltwater, regolith, and vegetation (leaves, humus). They have inputs of **kinetic energy** from wind and rain, and **heat energy** from the Sun.

regolith = rock debris produced by weathering

3) **Slopes store mass** in the form of rock, soil and water. They **store energy** as **potential energy** — things at the top of a slope have more gravitational potential energy than things at the bottom.

4) **Slope processes** are **water flow** through soil and regolith, and the **mass movement** of soil and regolith.

5) Change in one input, output or process affects the others. This is **feedback** — it's what makes it a **dynamic** system.

Slope profiles are two dimensional cross sections of the slope, showing its shape from the side. Slope profiles are usually divided into elements. A standard slope has the following elements: a convex crest at the top, a free face of cliffs, a straight sloping face, and a shallow concave element at the bottom. Over time, inputs of regolith tend to pile up at the bottom and make the slope more shallow.

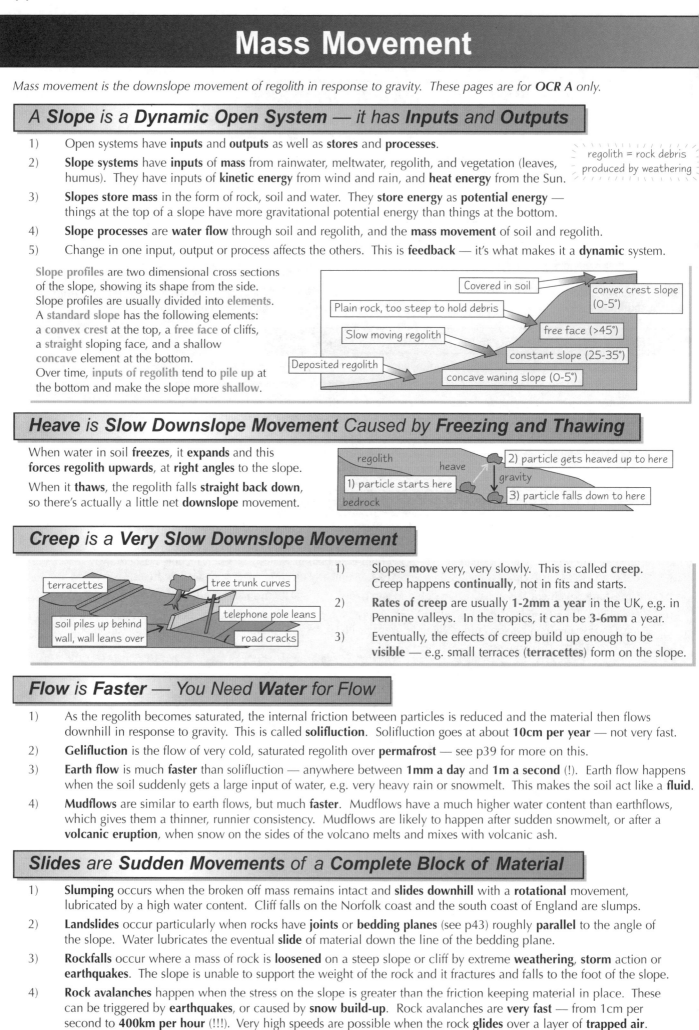

Covered in soil

convex crest slope (0-5°)

Plain rock, too steep to hold debris

free face (>45°)

Slow moving regolith

constant slope (25-35°)

Deposited regolith

concave waning slope (0-5°)

Heave is *Slow Downslope Movement* Caused by *Freezing and Thawing*

When water in soil **freezes**, it **expands** and this **forces regolith upwards**, at **right angles** to the slope.

When it **thaws**, the regolith falls **straight back down**, so there's actually a little net **downslope** movement.

regolith

heave

2) particle gets heaved up to here

gravity

1) particle starts here

3) particle falls down to here

bedrock

Creep is a *Very Slow Downslope Movement*

terracettes

tree trunk curves

telephone pole leans

soil piles up behind wall, wall leans over

road cracks

1) Slopes **move** very, very slowly. This is called **creep**. Creep happens **continually**, not in fits and starts.

2) **Rates of creep** are usually **1-2mm a year** in the UK, e.g. in Pennine valleys. In the tropics, it can be **3-6mm** a year.

3) Eventually, the effects of creep build up enough to be **visible** — e.g. small terraces (**terracettes**) form on the slope.

Flow is *Faster* — You Need *Water* for Flow

1) As the regolith becomes saturated, the internal friction between particles is reduced and the material then flows downhill in response to gravity. This is called **solifluction**. Solifluction goes at about **10cm per year** — not very fast.

2) **Gelifluction** is the flow of very cold, saturated regolith over **permafrost** — see p39 for more on this.

3) **Earth flow** is much **faster** than solifluction — anywhere between **1mm a day** and **1m a second** (!). Earth flow happens when the soil suddenly gets a large input of water, e.g. very heavy rain or snowmelt. This makes the soil act like a **fluid**.

4) **Mudflows** are similar to earth flows, but much **faster**. Mudflows have a much higher water content than earthflows, which gives them a thinner, runnier consistency. Mudflows are likely to happen after sudden snowmelt, or after a **volcanic eruption**, when snow on the sides of the volcano melts and mixes with volcanic ash.

Slides are *Sudden Movements* of a *Complete Block of Material*

1) **Slumping** occurs when the broken off mass remains intact and **slides downhill** with a **rotational** movement, lubricated by a high water content. Cliff falls on the Norfolk coast and the south coast of England are slumps.

2) **Landslides** occur particularly when rocks have **joints** or **bedding planes** (see p43) roughly **parallel** to the angle of the slope. Water lubricates the eventual **slide** of material down the line of the bedding plane.

3) **Rockfalls** occur where a mass of rock is **loosened** on a steep slope or cliff by extreme **weathering**, **storm** action or **earthquakes**. The slope is unable to support the weight of the rock and it fractures and falls to the foot of the slope.

4) **Rock avalanches** happen when the stress on the slope is greater than the friction keeping material in place. These can be triggered by **earthquakes**, or caused by **snow build-up**. Rock avalanches are **very fast** — from 1cm per second to **400km per hour** (!!!). Very high speeds are possible when the rock **glides** over a layer of **trapped air**.

Mass Movement

Various Factors Affect Slope Form and Development

Slopes are the result of **interactions** between **several factors**.

1) **Rock structure** affects slope form and processes. **Well-jointed rocks** or those with bedding planes parallel to the slope angle are more likely to suffer **landslides** or **slumping**.

2) **Lithology** (rock type) also affects slope processes and formation. Some rock types are more susceptible to weathering than others, so they **produce more regolith**. Some rocks are **impermeable** — slumps are more likely when **permeable** regolith material (e.g. sand) lies on top of impermeable rock.

3) **Vegetation** affects slope processes. A **dense cover** of plants **protects** the soil surface. When vegetation is sparse or absent, water can easily **saturate** the soil or run off the surface, increasing slope movement.

4) **Soil** affects slope processes in several ways. **Thin soils** don't support much protective **vegetation**. **Porous** soils don't stick together well, because water doesn't accumulate in them. As porous soils become saturated, the water lowers friction between particles and makes them more likely to move. **Clay** soils can become **fluidised** when they take on a lot of water, which makes for very rapid flows.

5) The **angle of slope** is another big factor, as you might expect. **Steep slopes** are less able to support the weight of the regolith and are more prone to **catastrophic slope failure** than gentle ones.

6) **Climate** has an effect. **Freeze-thaw action** in cold areas **creates regolith** and also causes downhill creep by **frost-heave action**. **Increased rainfall** adds **water** to the regolith and **lubricates movement**.

7) **Violent weather** may increase the rate of removal of regolith from the foot of slopes.

8) The **aspect** of the slope is the way it's facing. South-facing slopes tend to be warmer. More snow melts — and the meltwater lubricates movement. Slopes facing into the prevailing wind are prone to wind and rain weathering.

Human Activity may Speed Up Slope Processes

1) **Quarrying** reduces the stability of slopes, and exposes rock to weathering.

2) **Building** or **road construction** disturbs the **equilibrium** of slopes — e.g. urban development in Rio de Janeiro, and the M5 near Bristol. **Heavy buildings** can make slopes **unstable** and prone to slip.

3) **Planting forests** reduces slope movements, whereas **deforestation** increases them.

4) **Traffic vibration** can **destabilise** vulnerable slopes, e.g. around Mam Tor, Derbyshire.

5) **Industrial/mining deposition** can produce unstable artificial slopes. In 1966 a coal spoil heap in the mining village of Aberfan, Wales, suddenly fluidised and flowed downslope, killing 144 people.

6) **Grazing animals** remove vegetation cover and expose slopes to weathering.

7) **Ploughing** loosens the soil and exposes it, particularly if ploughing is across the contours (i.e. parallel to slope).

8) **Tourism** in areas of natural beauty can cause **footpath erosion**, which also destabilises slopes.

Soil erosion is a **positive feedback** process — once it starts, it gets **worse** and **worse**. Once there's a risk of erosion, **action** is needed. People can **plant trees** to anchor the soil, and use **wire mesh** to hold slope material in place.

It's important to prevent slope failure by good **slope management**. Steep slopes can be terraced before being farmed. Planning authorities can prevent the removal of trees from slopes, and prevent the construction of heavy buildings.

Practice Questions

Q1 Why is a slope described as a dynamic system?

Q2 Draw a table to show the main forms of mass movement.

Q3 Make a list of the factors affecting the development of slopes and for each write a couple of sentences to explain how they work. Cover up the top of this page first — there's no point in copying it straight out.

Exam Questions

Q1 Describe the influence of human activity on slope processes. (5 marks)

Q2. Describe the effects of mass movements. (5 marks)

Slip-sliding away, slip-sliding away...

It seems like pretty much everything in Geography is defined as a system of some kind — an open system or a closed system. All that means is that it's got various processes going on, and that it stores matter (stuff of all sorts) and energy. Slopes store soil and rock, as well as gravitational potential energy, and they've got all sorts of processes from boring old creep to mad mudslides.

The Global Energy Budget

The atmosphere is a layer of gases held close to the earth by gravity. The atmosphere is where weather happens.
*These pages are for **OCR A** and **AQA A**.*

Weather and Climate are part of the Atmosphere System

1) The atmosphere is made up of **nitrogen** (78%), **oxygen** (21%), carbon dioxide, water vapour, ozone and small amounts of other gases and dust.

2) The **earth-atmosphere system** is a **closed system**. The amount of **material** is **constant** over time. The **energy** in the system stays **constant** over time as well. We know this because the **temperature** of the Earth has been more or less **constant** for a very long time. The Earth's **winds** haven't got **faster** or **slower** either.

3) The atmosphere by itself is an **open** system. It has **inputs** of energy from the Sun.

> *Look back to p2 for more on open systems and closed systems.*

> **Weather** is the **day to day condition** of the atmosphere. **Climate** is the **long-term state** of the atmosphere. Climate is "**average weather**" for a particular place.

The Global Energy Budget Shows Energy Flow in the Earth-Atmosphere System

There are a few **conventions** in **energy budgets**. The **total amount** of **solar energy** (energy from the Sun) coming into the system is given a value of **100 units**. Don't worry about what those units are — the energy budget just says things like "for every 100 units of energy that come in from the Sun, 3 units of energy get absorbed by clouds".

The shortwave budget — shortwave energy from the Sun is absorbed and reflected

1) **3 units** of very short wave **ultraviolet** radiation are **absorbed** by **ozone** in the upper atmosphere.

2) **18 units** of radiation are **absorbed** by **dust** and **gases** in the atmosphere.

3) **25 units** of radiation go **straight through** the atmosphere to the Earth's surface.

4) **Clouds absorb 3 units** and **reflect 21 units**. Radiation reflects several times inside clouds, and eventually **10 units** of **diffuse** radiation reach the Earth's **surface**.

5) Radiation gets **scattered** by particles in the atmosphere — radiation pings about between particles, and **7 units** go back into space, with **10 units** getting scattered down to the surface.

6) **3 units** are reflected back off the Earth's surface.

7) So, that's the shortwave budget. Of **100 incoming units**, **31** are **reflected** back, **24** are **absorbed** in the **atmosphere** and **45** are **absorbed** at the **surface**.

> *Clouds look greyish white when you're underneath them — some of the Sun's energy gets through.*

> *Scattering is what makes the sky blue, by the way.*

The longwave budget — the Earth gets warm and releases longwave radiation

1) **3 units** of radiation are radiated into space by **ozone**.

2) **21 units** of radiation are radiated by the **atmosphere**.

3) **8 units** are radiated from the **surface** straight into space.

4) **14 units** are radiated via the **greenhouse effect**.

> *See pages 58 and 59 for more about the greenhouse effect.*

The non-radiation budget — the Earth transfers energy to the atmosphere in other ways

1) **4 units** are taken away by **convection**.

2) **19 units** are taken away by **evaporation** of water, which **uses up energy**.

> *Energy radiated out into space (3+21+8+14+4+19=69) equals energy absorbed by the atmosphere and the Earth (24+45=69). It all balances out. Woohoo!*

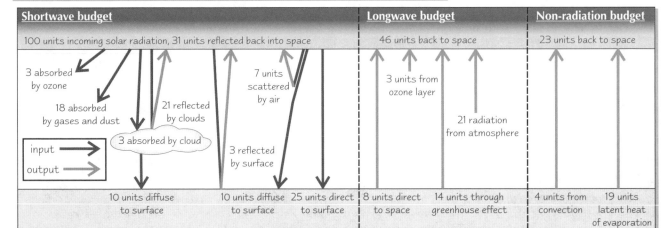

SECTION FIVE — CLIMATE

The Global Energy Budget

Energy Budgets Vary with Latitude

Imagine slicing the Earth along **lines of latitude** into **10° slices**, and doing an **energy budget** for each slice.

The slices near the **Equator** all **gain more solar energy** than they lose from longwave radiation.

The slices near the **poles** all **lose more energy** than they gain from the Sun.

This is what you'd **expect** — the Equator is hotter **because:**

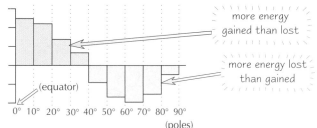

more energy gained than lost

more energy lost than gained

(equator)
0° 10° 20° 30° 40° 50° 60° 70° 80° 90°
(poles)

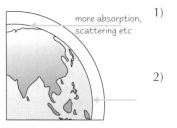

more absorption, scattering etc

1) At the Equator, solar energy comes in at right angles to the Earth's surface. Due to the **curvature** of the Earth, solar energy at the poles passes through more **atmosphere** before it reaches the ground — **more radiation** is **reflected**, **absorbed** or **scattered**. It's also spread over a bigger area.

2) At the **poles**, a lot of **insolation** (incoming solar energy) is **reflected** off the Earth's surface — polar areas are covered in snow and ice, which is all **white** and reflects light and heat. **Equatorial** areas are covered in **rain forest** — dark coloured vegetation that absorbs heat energy.

Energy Transfers Create Global Weather Patterns of Wind and Rain

1) Even though more energy reaches the Equator, the Equator doesn't get hotter and hotter. **Atmospheric circulation**, **winds** and **ocean currents** move heat energy from the Equator towards the poles.

2) The 0-40° latitude region has all the excess energy (see the diagram above). Heat is then transferred by the atmosphere, in cells e.g. the Hadley cell.

3) The transfer of energy in the atmosphere is actually quite complex. There's **horizontal air flow** from high pressure to low pressure (**advection**) and **vertical air flow** (**convection** — warm air rising).

4) "**Trade winds**" carry **cool air** towards the Equator. "**Westerly winds**" carry **warm air** towards the poles.

5) There are also very fast winds high up in the atmosphere — these are called **jet streams**.

Weather systems also transfer energy. Weather systems are big **swirling patterns of air** that move through the atmosphere, bringing **rainstorms** or fine weather. There's more about typical **British weather systems** on the next two pages.

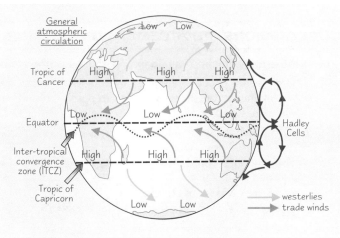

General atmospheric circulation

Tropic of Cancer

High   High   High

Equator   Low   Low   Low

Inter-tropical convergence zone (ITCZ)   High   High   High

Tropic of Capricorn   Low   Low

Hadley Cells

→ westerlies
→ trade winds

Practice Questions

Q1 What is the difference between weather and climate?

Q2 Give three examples of things that can happen to solar energy to stop it from reaching the Earth.

Q3 Why is it colder at the poles than at the Equator?

Q4 How is heat energy transferred from the Equator towards the poles?

Exam Questions

Q1 Of every 100 units of insolation, only 45 units reach the Earth's surface. Explain why this is. (4 marks)

Q2 Describe how energy budgets vary with latitude. (5 marks)

I feel like I've had the Sun on the back of my head for too long...

My oh my. A difficult pair of pages to start with, and that's for sure. The thing is, if you "get" the global energy budget and understand what happens to solar energy, you'll find the local energy budget stuff on p54-55 so much easier to get your head around. For this whole section it's also useful to know where there's excess energy and how that energy gets transferred around.

Energy Transfers and British Weather

Energy transfers in the atmosphere are responsible for all the weather we get.
*These pages are for **OCR A** and **AQA A**. They're also useful for **AQA B**.*

The British Isles are affected by *Five Air Masses*

An **air mass** has the same **temperature** and **humidity** characteristics throughout. Air masses form over **large geographical areas** that themselves have uniform characteristics. Meteorologists debate how useful the idea of an air mass is. However, they do give us some idea of expected weather.

Polar Maritime:
Source: North Atlantic near Greenland — influences British Isles for 40% of the year.
Associated weather: Cool, unstable, rain showers.

Arctic Maritime:
Source: Frozen Arctic seas.
Associated weather: Cold, unstable, rain, hail or snow showers.

Polar Continental:
Source: Scandinavia — uncommon in British Isles.
Associated weather: Dry, cold, clear skies. May pick up warmth and moisture from North Sea and bring snow showers to East Coast.

Tropical Maritime:
Source: Central Atlantic, near the Azores.
Associated weather: Warm, stable, some coastal fog, some thunderstorms.

Tropical Continental:
Source: North Africa.
Associated weather: Dry, warm, stable, heatwave conditions.

These air masses don't all affect us at the same time.

The **dividing line** between **two different air masses** is called a **front**.

Depressions are Areas of Low Pressure — Responsible for Most British Weather

1) Most of the rain received in the British Isles is **frontal rain** caused by **depressions**.

2) **Depressions** occur on the **polar front** between **warm**, **wet tropical maritime air** and **cold polar air**. A kink in the front allows **warm air** to push north into **cold air**. Where warm air pushes into cold air, there's a warm front. Where cold air pushes back into warm air, there's a **cold front**.

3) Along both the warm front and the cold front, **warm air rises** and then **cools**. Moisture in the air **condenses** and forms **clouds**.

4) As the warmer, less dense air **rises** over the colder air it creates an area of **low pressure** — a depression.

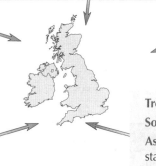

Cross section of a depression

Ci — Warm sector — Warm air rises — Ci — St — Heavy rain — Cb — Tm — Al St — Drizzle — Cold Polar air — Cold Polar air

Tm = Tropical maritime
◣◣◣ = Warm front
▲▲▲ = Cold front
Cb = Cumulonimbus
Ci = Cirrus
St = Stratus
Al St = Altostratus

Low pressure brings with it a characteristic series of **weather conditions** — this is described below:

1) As a **low** approaches, it starts to **drizzle**. The rain gets heavier as the **warm front** approaches.

2) When the warm front has passed, the **rain stops**. The weather gets **brighter** and the clouds disappear. The **temperature rises** as the warm sector passes overhead.

3) The **cold air** behind the cold front moves **faster** than the warm air, and can **overtake** and **undercut** the warm sector. This creates an **occluded front** — the warm sector is pushed upwards, giving a longer period of rainfall.

4) After several hours it gets **windier** and **colder**. Clouds build up as the **cold front** moves in. **Heavy rain** falls.

5) After the rain, conditions may settle for a short while before the next low or high. As the cold front passes, the **wind changes direction** (veers) from warm southerly to cool north-westerly.

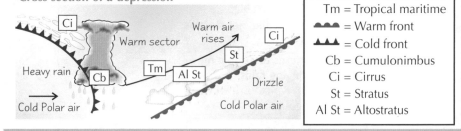

large warm sector   occluded front forms   warm sector shrinks

◣◣◣◣ cold front
◣▲◣▲ occluded front
◠◠◠ warm front
→ tropical air
→ polar air

Pressure is measured in millibars (mb).

Energy Transfers and British Weather

Anticyclones are Areas of High Pressure

Although depressions are frequent, the British Isles also often experiences conditions of **high pressure** — called **anticyclones**.

1) An anticyclone is a big ol' **mass of high pressure air** — either warm air moving north or cold air moving south.

2) In an anticyclone, **air descends**, which is what causes the **high pressure** on the ground. Descending air is calm — it doesn't have the turbulence of rising air. This means that **calm**, **settled** weather is associated with anticyclones.

3) In the **summer**, the **Azores high pressure system** (warm air) pushes northwards to influence the British Isles. **Summer anticyclones** are associated with dry, hot weather — the good old British summer **heatwave**.

4) **In winter**, polar high pressure systems (cold air) push south and influence the British Isles. They bring clear, bright skies. This causes rapid **heat loss** by radiation during the night. Night temperatures are low, and there are **heavy frosts**, even though the days are sunny.

Mr Jones reacted badly to high pressure situations.

Jet streams are very fast high altitude winds. They're caused by pressure differences across fronts.

Depressions and anticyclones are both affected by jet streams. Depressions are driven from west to east by the high altitude wind known as the polar jet stream. The polar jet stream zig zags north and south (by latitude) and up and down (by altitude). When the jet stream swings down towards the Earth it helps to create an area of high pressure — an anticyclone.

Synoptic Charts show Atmospheric Conditions

Synoptic charts show **weather data** from **several sources** — stations on the ground, aircraft, ships, cloud radar and satellite pictures. A synoptic chart is a picture of the **atmospheric conditions** — temperature, pressure, wind speed, wind direction, cloud cover and precipitation.

Chart showing anticyclone **Chart showing depression**

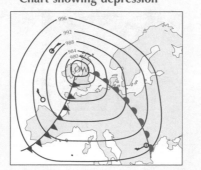

Practice Questions

Q1 Which air masses affect the British Isles?

Q2 What is a "front"?

Q3 What are the similarities and differences between anticyclones that occur in the summer and those that occur in the winter?

Exam Questions

Q1 Describe the passage of weather conditions caused by a depression. (5 marks)

Q2 Explain how low pressure systems form when tropical maritime air and polar air meet. (4 marks)

This is all too depressing...

Depressions are cloudy, wet and windy, but fairly mild. Anticyclones usually give clear skies and sunshine — hot in summer, but cold and frosty in winter. Both of these weather patterns are familiar to anyone who's spent much time in the British Isles. Make sure you know the sequence of weather events that you get when a depression passes over — it isn't as simple as "it rains".

Cool Temperate Western Maritime Climates

The Cool Western Temperate Maritime climate is the only one you need to know for the exam.
*This page is for **AQA A**.*

Cool Temperate Western Maritime Climates *occur in similar locations*

1) The **Cool Temperate Western Maritime (CTWM)** climate is found between about **40°** and **60° north** and **south** of the equator hence the '**cool**' part of the name — it's neither 'tropical' nor 'polar'.

2) CTWM climates are located on the **western edges** of continental areas, as the map shows. The whole of Great Britain has a CTWM climate.

3) The **position near the sea** is important – it affects **rainfall** and **temperatures**.

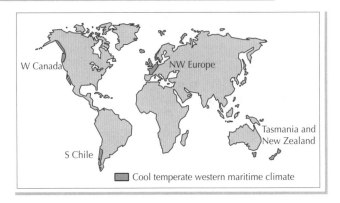
W Canada — NW Europe — Tasmania and New Zealand — S Chile
☐ Cool temperate western maritime climate

Rainfall *and* Temperature *data help you* Identify *CTWM Climates*

Rainfall — is **plentiful** in areas with CTWM climates, for example in UK it varies from about **600** mm / year in the south east to over **2000** mm / year in the north west. It comes as **frontal rain** from **depressions** (see p. 48) which is often increased by **relief**. In **summer** there is also **convectional rain** and **thunderstorms**.

Seasons — Winters are **mild** and **summers** are **cool** (averaging around 2° C in January, 17° C in July.) There are **rarely** any **extremes** of temperature. Compared to other places at similar latitudes there are **no** strong seasonal differences (but there is usually more rain in **winter**).

Atmosphere — CTWM climates tend to be **cloudy**. There is often a lot of **wind**. The rapid movement of **air masses** means that the weather can **change** very quickly.

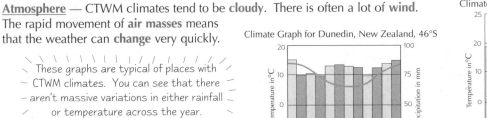

These graphs are typical of places with CTWM climates. You can see that there aren't massive variations in either rainfall or temperature across the year.

The blue lines represent temperature, and the green bars indicate rainfall.

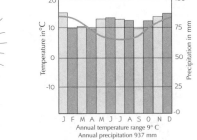

Climate Graph for Dunedin, New Zealand, 46°S
J F M A M J J A S O N D
Annual temperature range 9° C
Annual precipitation 937 mm

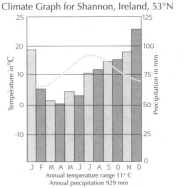

Climate Graph for Shannon, Ireland, 53°N
J F M A M J J A S O N D
Annual temperature range 11° C
Annual precipitation 929 mm

Several Factors *Affect the* Climate *in* CTWM areas

1) **Wind belts** — areas with CTWM climates always lie in the westerly wind belts. Westerlies are moist winds from oceans and they bring **cloud** and **precipitation**.

2) The '**maritime**' bit means that the climate is affected by being near to the **coast**. Coastal areas receive plentiful **rainfall**. If clouds are forced to **rise** over **mountains** then **relief rainfall** increases. This happens in north Wales when clouds uplift over the Snowdonia range.

3) As well as increasing rainfall the sea **regulates** an area's **temperature** — it keeps **summers** cooler, and winters **warmer**. That's because sea water warms up more **slowly** than land in summer, and keeps **warm** for longer during the winter so it acts like an **insulator** that regulates the land's temperature. In the British Isles the temperatures are even warmer than they should be considering the latitude because of the **North Atlantic Drift** (NAD). The NAD is a **warm** ocean current which flows north east to the British Isles from the **Gulf of Mexico**.

4) The areas which have CTWM climates are where different **air masses** meet. The constant movements of different **air masses** makes the weather very **changeable**.

Cool Temperate Western Maritime Climates

The **CTWM Climate** has many **Advantages**

1) **Temperate** conditions with **plentiful rainfall** suit many types of **farm crops**, for example wheat, barley, oats, fruit and vegetables. Some crops can even be sown in **autumn**, to start growing over the mild winter so food is available all year round e.g. **winter wheat**.

2) **Animals** can be **grazed** outside for the majority of the year — there is **no severe dry season** and pastures do not die in the winter. **Sheep** farming is more suited to the **colder**, **upland** parts of the climate zone, and **cattle** in the milder, flatter areas.

3) **Drought** is **rarely** a problem, and with careful management, the **water supply** meets **demand**. The **increasing use** of water in some areas means that water often has to be **transferred** from some drainage basins to others e.g. from Wales to the cities of the Midlands.

4) Some kind of **outdoor recreation** can take place in all seasons e.g. sports like hiking, football happen through most of the year in the UK.

5) **Buildings** do not need special construction techniques (as they do in frozen Arctic areas and places with frequent flooding).

But it has Some **Downsides** too...

1) The highly changeable weather make it **difficult** to plan **outdoor** events like fêtes and cricket matches (think about what happened when Cliff Richard was at Wimbledon when it started to rain...). Cold conditions and rain **reduce the takings** at outdoor theme parks like Alton Towers.

2) **Regular weather forecasts** are very **important**, because of the **changeability** of the weather. **Sudden, unexpected changes** in air flow affect the **accuracy** of these, e.g. the October 1987 gales, when the wind direction suddenly changed, bringing **severe damage** to the UK.

3) People in these areas **tend to expect** mild weather all the time. This makes them **unprepared** for **unexpected events** like the flash floods that hit **Boscastle** in Cornwall in 2004.

4) Relatively small amounts of **fog** and **snow** have a big impact on road and air **traffic** — it doesn't take much before **roads** and **airports** are closed.

Warm British summers are ideal for outdoor sports.

Practice Questions

Q1 Name the warm sea current that keeps Britain warmer than it should be for the latitude.

Q2 Why do CTWM climates have plentiful rain?

Q3 Why are regular weather forecasts needed in areas experiencing a CTWM climate?

Exam Questions

Q1 What is meant by the term 'temperate'? What causes CTWM climates to be temperate? (4 marks)

Q2 Describe the global distribution of the CTWM climate type. (3 marks)

Why does it always rain on me...

Basically, you need to know where CTWM climates occur, the types of weather they produce and how that weather affects people. The other thing to bear in mind is that in the southern hemisphere CTWM climates are the same but the pattern is a bit backwards cos they have summer when we have winter, you'll see what I mean if you compare the Shannon and Dunedin graphs.

Climatic Hazards: Strong Winds

*Bad weather can cause terrible damage to buildings, and it can even kill. These pages are for **AQA A**.*

Climatic Hazards — *Natural Weather Events* Putting Life and Property at **Risk**

1) A climatic hazard is a **short term variation** from the **normal climatic conditions** that would be expected for a particular place at a particular time.

2) Climatic hazards include **strong winds** or **heavy rain**.

Strong winds are caused by steep pressure gradients. Winds are air moving from regions of high pressure to regions of low pressure. The bigger the difference in pressure, the faster the air moves.

Climatic Hazards *include* **Revolving Tropical Storms** *such as* **Hurricanes**

In a hurricane, strong winds spin around a central core of calm air called the eye of the hurricane.

1) Hurricanes form as **very low pressure** systems (really low — like **920mb** low) over **tropical** oceans. **Winds** blowing into the low pressure area come together near the surface of the ocean. Warm air becomes **unstable**, rises, and starts to **spin** very fast.

2) They form over tropical oceans between **5° and 20° S** and **N** of the equator, in the **Intertropical Convergence Zone** (**ITCZ**). In this zone, the **rotation** of the Earth has a strong effect on winds, making them **spin** (this is the Coriolis effect — luckily you don't have to know it until A2).

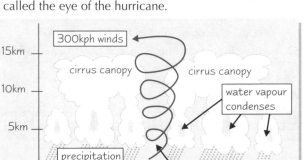

3) The sea has to be above **27-28°C** for enough water to evaporate to "**feed**" the hurricane. Water vapour from the sea condenses inside the hurricane, which provides latent heat **energy** to keep the hurricane going. Hurricanes always **die out** quickly once they move over **land**.

4) The **eye** is 5-50 km in diameter and is an area of calm, clear air. The area around the eye consists of **cumulonimbus clouds** towering as high as **15km**, due to intense convection. The heaviest rain falls from this part of the hurricane. There are smaller weather subsystems all around the hurricane. Wind speeds inside the hurricane can be up to 300kph.

Spinning tropical storms have different names around the world — in the Indian Ocean they're called <u>cyclones</u>, in the Pacific they're called <u>typhoons</u>, the ones that affect Australia are called <u>Willy-Willies</u> (top name), and in the Gulf of Mexico and west Atlantic they're hurricanes.

The **Impact of Hurricanes** *and* **Human Responses** *to them Vary Greatly*

Hurricanes vary in magnitude, which affects their impact. There are also differences between **MEDCs** and **LEDCs**.

1) **MEDCs** can afford **early warning systems** to warn people of the approach of a hurricane. Early warning systems are **expensive**, so **LEDCs** often don't have this option.

2) In **MEDCs** people have the **ability** to **act** on advice and warnings — they can **afford** to **protect their homes** and **stockpile food**. In **LEDCs** people are often unable to take advantage of any warning.

3) **MEDCs** are able to **organise relief efforts** quickly. They can offer financial, medical, and social support to people who have been affected by the hurricane. **LEDCs** don't have the **infrastructure** or **money** for big relief efforts.

Cyclone in the Indian state of Orissa, 2nd November 1999 (LEDC)

Event:	Wind speeds up to 300 kilometres per hour, tidal waves of 10 metres. Heavy rain.
Short term:	9887 people died. $1.3 billion of public and private property was damaged. The annual rice crop was destroyed. 500 000 draught animals died. 90 million crop-producing trees uprooted, e.g. coconut and cashew nut trees.
Long term:	5 million people depended on food aid for at least 7 months afterwards. Many fell into a cycle of poverty and bad health, as farming jobs and livelihoods were destroyed. Repairing the damage to infrastructure took months.

Hurricane Andrew, Florida, USA 24th August 1992 (MEDC)

Event:	Gusts of up to 270 kilometres per hour battered the Florida coast for 8 hours. Heavy rain.
Short term:	Millions evacuated. 43 died. 50 000 homes destroyed, 2 million without electricity. Boats and marinas destroyed. Jumbo jets blown off runways at Miami International airport. There was some looting of property.
Long term:	Rebuilding was expensive. Building regulations were tightened to make houses safer — so the equally strong Hurricane Charley in 2004 ended up destroying fewer houses than Hurricane Andrew. Insurance companies made it easier for people to claim house insurance money.

Climatic Hazards: Strong Winds

Tornadoes are Very Violent Funnel Shaped Winds

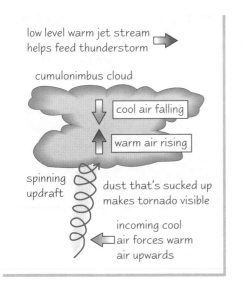

low level warm jet stream helps feed thunderstorm

cumulonimbus cloud

cool air falling

warm air rising

spinning updraft

dust that's sucked up makes tornado visible

incoming cool air forces warm air upwards

1) **Tornadoes** are incredibly **rapidly spinning winds** in a **funnel** shape (vortex) that form over flat areas of land.

2) They form over land in **mid latitudes**, about **20-60° N or S** of the Equator, where tropical and polar air masses meet, e.g. **Great Plains of USA**.

3) In the USA, **warm air** flowing north from the **Gulf of Mexico** meets cold air flowing south from the **Rockies** or **Canadian Arctic**. Daytime **heating** causes the air to **rise**, forming **cumulonimbus clouds** and creating a **low pressure** area. The rising air begins to **spiral**, and the **jet stream** makes it **rise faster**. A massive "**supercell**" thunderstorm forms — the **tornado** develops **inside the supercell**. The tornado develops close to the **cold front** of the two air masses.

4) The **diameter** of the tornado funnel is **300-400 metres** — not very wide. The wind inside the tornado funnel can be greater than **500kph**. At this speed, **buildings** are simply **picked up** off the ground and turned into **matchstick splinters**. There's usually heavy rain or hail.

5) The extreme **low pressure** inside a tornado **sucks** dust and debris up into the tornado. Sucked up dust makes the tornado **visible**.

6) Tornadoes move **SW to NE** at speeds of **100 kph**. You can't outrun a tornado.

Tornadoes frequently bring Devastation in the USA

"**Tornado Alley**" is the part of the USA where **most big tornadoes** touch down. It averages about 1000 tornadoes a year. **Nebraska**, **Kansas**, **Oklahoma** and **Texas** are the states most commonly considered as Tornado Alley.

Case Study — Super Tornado Outbreak, USA, 2nd April 1974

Location:	Georgia, Illinois, Indiana, Kentucky, Michigan, Mississippi, North Carolina, Ohio, South Carolina, Tennessee, Virginia, West Virginia.
Event:	147 tornadoes "touched ground" in just 16 hours.
Damage:	335 deaths and 1200 people injured, 13 500 homes destroyed or severely damaged, 4000 farm buildings destroyed, 1500 small businesses destroyed or severely damaged.

Severe Gales cause Problems in the UK

1) Britain suffers **severe gales** fairly often in autumn and winter. There's often minor damage to trees and houses.

2) In **1987**, a massive storm hit the British Isles. Winds of over **100mph** (**160kph**) caused widespread serious damage to **buildings**, and knocked down millions of **trees** across southern England.

Practice Questions

Q1   What is a climatic hazard?

Q2   Name a part of the world where tornadoes are common.

Q3   What are the characteristics of a hurricane?

Q4   How do hurricanes form?

Exam Questions

Q1   Compare the human impact of a tropical revolving storm in an LEDC and in an MEDC.   (7 marks)

Q2   Hurricanes eventually decay and disappear. Why does this happen?   (3 marks)

Kinda blows you away, really...

If I lived in Kansas or Oklahoma I'd be scared witless of tornadoes, let me tell you. Tornado winds can pick up a paperclip (seriously, a freaking paperclip) and run it right through you, killing you stone dead. Count me out of that. Anyway, you have to know what causes tornadoes and hurricanes — the air masses, the pressure conditions, how they're formed. All that malarkey.

Local Energy Budgets

As well as investigating the global energy budget (see p46-47), geographers look at energy budgets on smaller scales.
*These pages are for **OCR A**, but they're also rather helpful for **AQA B (option R)**.*

Local Energy Budgets show Energy Inputs and Outputs at the Earth's Surface

The diagram on the right is a **daytime energy budget** for a **flat portion** of the Earth's surface. It's for a **standard surface** with a layer of **grass** over a layer of **soil**.

This energy budget shows the **energy transfers** which give energy to the Earth's surface and take energy away from the Earth's surface.

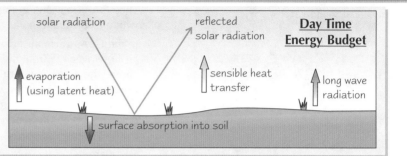

1) Energy comes in as **incoming solar radiation**. The amount of solar radiation coming in depends on the amount of cloud in the sky — the more clouds there are, the less radiation reaches Earth.

2) The amount of energy reflected by a surface depends on what the **surface** is **like**. The **albedo** of a surface is a measure of **how reflective** it is — how much of the energy it gets is reflected back.

Grass has an albedo of **0.25** or **25%** — it reflects a quarter of the solar energy it receives.
Fresh snow has an albedo of up to **95%**.
Thick clouds have an albedo of **60%** to **90%** — clouds reflect the Sun's energy before it can get to the Earth's surface.

3) **Evaporation** of **water** into **water vapour** uses up a lot of **energy** (this is called the **latent heat** of evaporation). Some of the Sun's energy is **used up** in **evaporating surface puddles**, so it doesn't get used to heat up the grass and soil.

4) Heat energy from the Sun **heats up the soil**. Some kinds of soil are better at **conducting heat** down to the lower layers of soil than others. When heat is conducted away, the surface isn't as hot.

5) **Sensible heat transfer** means the transfer of energy via **cold air flowing in** to **replace warm air**. It's not "sensible" as in the opposite of daft — it's "sensible" as in "you can sense it". When **cold air** blows onto the **warm surface**, heat is transferred by conduction from the Earth's surface to the air, and the surface gets **colder**. Also, air rises (convection) when it's heated up by the Sun's energy, or by contact with the warm surface. **Cool air** comes in to **replace** the **warm air**, which again makes the Earth's surface get colder.

6) **Longwave radiation** is another form of energy transfer from the Earth's surface. All warm objects emit longwave radiation — as the Earth's surface warms up during the day, it starts to **radiate** heat. There's **more longwave radiation emitted** from the surface than received by the surface (but the Earth's surface receives lots of **shortwave** radiation from the **Sun** during the day, don't forget — that's what makes it warm up).

The Night Time Energy Budget is Simpler

The night time budget is **simpler**, because the **Sun isn't shining**.

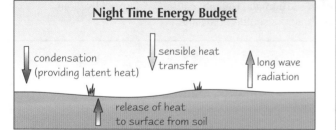

1) At night, water vapour near the Earth's surface cools and **condenses** into liquid water — **dew**. **Condensation gives energy out** to the surroundings (this is called **latent heat** of condensation).

2) The surface gets **colder** at night. However, **heat energy** stored in the **soil** during the day transfers to the surface, which **reduces** the **total temperature drop**.

3) **Sensible heat transfer** still applies during the night. **Warm air** can blow onto the surface to **raise surface temperatures**. **Cold air** can blow onto the surface to **lower surface temperatures**.

4) At night, there's **more radiation emitted** from the surface than **received** by the surface, which means there's a net loss of energy and the surface temperature goes down.

Cloud Cover Affects Local Energy Budgets During Day and Night

1) During the **day**, **cloud cover** affects the amount of **solar radiation** coming in. Thick **stratus**, **stratocumulus** and **nimbostratus** clouds transmit the **least** solar radiation to Earth.

2) Cloud cover **reflects** some **longwave radiation** back down to the surface, so the surface doesn't get as **cold at night** when it's **overcast**.

Local Energy Budgets

Local Energy Budgets show how Ground and Air Frosts Happen

1) Ground frost happens when the **temperature** of the **Earth's surface** falls **below freezing**. If it's above freezing, **dew** forms.

2) The **night time energy budget** helps to work out when there'll be a ground frost. A **ground frost** is most likely to happen when there's **most cooling** of the surface — when **loss of energy** due to **longwave radiation** is highest, and when there's the **lowest amount** of sensible heat transfer. In other words, **clear still nights** are most likely to be frosty.

3) **Air frost** happens when the temperature of the **air** is **below 0°C**. The **ground surface** must be cooled **below 0°C**, and the **air** touching the ground is chilled by **conduction** to below freezing.

4) For there to be an **air frost**, there has to be plenty of heat loss from **longwave radiation** and **very little sensible heat** transfer. It's particularly important to have **very calm conditions**.

5) **Frost damages crops**. Crops can be protected against frost by spraying them with water. When the water freezes, the latent heat of freezing actually keeps the crops warmer. Sounds crazy, I know, but it's true.

Mist and Fog are Tiny Droplets of Water in the Air

Fog's thicker than mist — visibility between 5000 and 1000m is mist, visibility lower than 1000m is fog.

1) Air can hold water as **water vapour** — but only a limited amount. When the air is saturated with water, it can't hold any more water vapour. The vapour starts to **condense** into little **droplets** of liquid water — a **mist** or **fog**. A **light wind** is needed to **suspend** the droplets in the air.

2) The **warmer** the temperature, the **more water vapour** the air can hold. So, **cooling** the air makes water vapour **condense** into **mist**. The temperature at which mist starts to form is called the **dewpoint**.

3) Fog is more likely in **low lying dips** and **hollows**. The temperature is likely to be **low anyway** because there's not much **sensible heat transfer**.

This is a pain on roads, where good visibility's important. It can be dangerous to drive into a dip and suddenly plunge into thick fog.

Temperature Inversions can Trap Air Close to the Surface

1) Air usually gets **cooler** as **altitude** increases. The rate of change of temperature with height is called the **environmental lapse rate**. Rising warm air **cools** as it **rises** — and keeps rising as long as it's warmer than the air around it.

2) Sometimes, there's a layer where **temperature increases with height** for a while. This is a **temperature inversion**.

3) When rising **warm**, dirty air from factories rises up to this **inversion layer** and reaches air that's at the same temperature, it **stops** and can't rise any more. Polluted air gets **trapped** under the inversion layer.

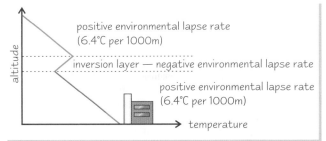

positive environmental lapse rate (6.4°C per 1000m)

inversion layer — negative environmental lapse rate

positive environmental lapse rate (6.4°C per 1000m)

altitude

temperature

4) Temperature inversions occur during **anticyclonic conditions** with **clear skies** and **little or no wind** (autumn nights in particular). These conditions lead the Earth to **radiate heat** out into space. The surface gets **cold** and **cools** the **air** by **conduction**. There's **little** wind to mix the **colder lower layers** with **warmer air** above, so you get an **inversion**.

Practice Questions

Q1 What are: a) "sensible heat transfer", b) "latent heat", and c) "albedo"?

Q2 Under what atmospheric conditions does air frost form?

Q3 What is a temperature inversion?

Exam Questions

Q1 Explain why ground frost does not tend to form on overcast, cloudy nights. (3 marks)

Q2 Explain why urban air pollution is worse during autumn anticyclones. (4 marks)

Dew wanna learn about weather, or not...

Local energy budgets have a touch of "possibly pointless faff" about them at first glance. They're actually a useful way of figuring out if it's likely to be frosty, or if there'll be fog. Yeah, yeah, "big deal", I know. You don't have to be fired up about it in everyday life, but you do need to learn it for the exam. If you know the basic energy transfers it should be nice and straightforward.

Urban Climates

*Large urban areas have their own microclimate. These pages are for **AQA A** and **AQA B (Option R)**.*

Urban Areas are Often Warmer than the Surrounding Land

This is called the **urban heat island** effect (UHI for short).

There are four main causes of the UHI:

1) The **dark coloured roofs** and **concrete**, **brick** and **tarmac** surfaces are non-reflective (they have a low albedo), so they **absorb** and store heat during the **day**. They **release** the heat slowly at **night**.

2) **Pollution and smog** trap outgoing heat radiation.

3) **Car fumes**, **factories**, **power stations**, **central heating** and **people themselves** all release heat.

4) **Less heat energy** is used up by **evapotranspiration** in urban areas. Most rain **runs off** through the city's **drainage** system, so it doesn't lie around and then **evaporate**. There isn't much **vegetation**, so there's little **transpiration**.

1) **London** has a **clearly defined heat island**. It experiences less snow and fewer frosts than surrounding rural areas.

2) Large urban parks can show up as an **anomaly** of **cooler temperature** within the heat island.

3) The **highest temperature** is found in the most **densely built up** area – usually the **CBD** (Central Business District).

4) The **UHI effect varies** between **day** and **night**. Urban daytime temperatures can be **1-2°C warmer** than surrounding countryside areas. **Urban night time** temperatures can be about **5-6°C warmer**. This is because the city doesn't lose much **heat** during the night — both urban and rural areas warm up during the day, but rural areas cool down a lot more at night.

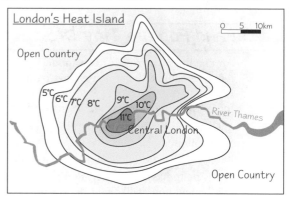

5) It also varies between **summer** and **winter**. Average **winter** temperatures can be **2°C warmer**. Average summer temperatures can be up to **5°C warmer**. In winter, the UHI is more noticeable when there's an anticyclone (see p49).

Urban Areas Affect the Normal Wind Patterns

1) Higher temperatures in urban areas cause **convection** — air rises. This creates an area of **low pressure**. Air is **drawn in** to the low pressure area from surrounding areas.

2) Tall buildings create friction and act as windbreaks, so **average wind velocities tend to be lower** in cities than in rural areas. In cities there are completely sheltered areas where the wind drops to zero.

3) **There's small-scale turbulence** around buildings. Wind gets channelled down streets leading to **powerful gusts** in some streets — this is known as the **canyon effect**. The canyon effect can have implications for **architectural design** and **town planning** — e.g. layout of **paths** and **positioning** of buildings, and the location of **doorways** on larger buildings.

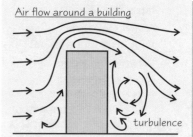

Urban Areas Experience More Fog and Precipitation

There's more fog, cloud and rain in urban areas than in the surrounding countryside.

1) Urban areas generate huge amounts of dust and pollution. Particles of dust and pollution floating about in the air act as condensation nuclei (water condenses around them) and encourage clouds and fog to form.

2) Because there are higher temperatures and thicker, more frequent cloud cover in urban areas, there's less frost. There's less snow in towns than in the countryside.

3) Urban areas experience more intense storms especially on hot summer evenings compared with surrounding countryside areas. There also tend to be more thunderstorms. St. Louis in the USA experiences an average of 29 summer thunder days compared with less than 15 in the surrounding countryside. This is a direct result of the higher temperatures which force warm air to rise (convection).

Urban Areas Have Temperature Inversions

1) Usually, the atmosphere gets **cooler** with **increasing height**. Warm air rising will **cool**, but carry on rising as long as it's warmer than the **surrounding air**. A temperature inversion is a layer where temperatures **increase with height**, which **stops** rising air currents.

2) **Warm, polluted urban air** rises up to this **inversion layer**, reaches air that's at the same temperature, and **stops**. Polluted air gets **trapped** under the inversion layer, causing **smog**. There's more about this on p57.

Urban Climates

Urban Areas Have Poorer Air Quality than Rural Areas

Ozone (O_3), carbon monoxide (CO), nitrogen oxides (NO_x) and sulphur dioxide (SO_2) are the main pollutants of urban air. Vehicle exhausts and industrial emissions are the main sources of this pollution, which causes fog and smog.

1) In bright sunshine **nitrous oxides** become **nitrogen dioxide**.
2) Car exhaust fumes react with sunlight to create **ozone**.
3) **Carbon monoxide** is produced when there is incomplete burning of fuel.
4) **Sulphur dioxide** is produced by car exhausts.

This "chemical soup" created from car exhaust fumes and bright sunlight is known as **photochemical smog**. This can irritate the eyes and cause headaches, and it's a particular **health hazard** for people with **respiratory diseases** such as asthma. Particles such as dust and cement can also irritate the respiratory system.

Air Pollution can be Fought by Technology, Politics, or Changes in Behaviour

1) **Technological solutions** include things like the use of **catalytic converters** in cars. These remove nitrous oxides, carbon monoxide and unburned hydrocarbons. In 1993 they were made compulsory on all new cars in the UK.
2) **Economic and political solutions** include decisions such as **road tolls**, **congestion charges** and **taxes on fuel**. These can be risky decisions to make — the public don't like it when "ordinary" things suddenly get more expensive.
3) **Social and behavioural solutions** include things like **staying indoors** when there's a poor air quality forecast (especially if you suffer from asthma or bronchitis), **car sharing**, **using more public transport** or **walking.**

Planners and Decision Makers have tried to Reduce Air Pollution

Case study: Mexico City

LPG = Liquid Petroleum Gas, which produces a lot less pollution than petrol.

Strategies: Building a new **underground system**.

Introducing '**hoy no circular**' (**no driving today**) days for cars with certain number plates.

Converting vehicles in intensive use such as buses, taxis and delivery trucks from **petrol to LPG.**

Evaluation: Rich people buy **second or third cars** to get round the 'hoy no circular' restrictions. Air quality continues to deteriorate. Enforcing pollution control is **difficult** and **expensive**. **Industrial** development continues.

Case study: Los Angeles

Strategies: LA Air Quality Management Plan (1989) aims to reduce sulphur dioxide pollution by 62% and nitrogen dioxide by 80% in the next 20 years. The authorities encourage **car sharing** (there are lanes on the highway specifically for cars with more than one occupant), park and ride, **telecommuting** (working from home) and **staggered work hours**. **Electric cars** have been introduced.

Evaluation: Number of **vehicles** on the road **continues to rise** — 2.3 million in 1950 to 10.6 million in 1990. LA is **still** a heavily polluted city — 63 days in 1993 posed a significant danger to health because of poor air quality.

Practice Questions

Q1 What is an "urban heat island"?
Q2 Describe the effect that urban areas have on wind speeds.
Q3 Why do you think cloud cover is higher in urban areas compared with rural areas?
Q4 What is "photochemical smog"?

Exam Questions

Q1 Describe and explain the urban heat island effect. (4 marks)

Q2 What are the main obstacles to improving air quality in towns and cities? (4 marks)

There you are. That's why London is so... sweaty...

Make sure you can scribble down a rough account of what causes the urban heat island effect. Remember to include the effects of albedo, impermeable surfaces, lack of vegetation and pollution. As well as the urban microclimate, you also need to know about urban air quality. They want you to mention how the "attitudes and values of decision makers" affect clean air schemes.

Global Warming

*The media loves global warming. There's hype, some unscientific argument and sensational writing about global warming and its causes and consequences. It's important to take a balanced and questioning approach into this topic area. For **AQA A**.*

The **Greenhouse Effect** and **Global Warming** are Not Exactly the Same Thing

The **greenhouse effect** is a **natural phenomenon** that makes life on earth possible — if the Earth's atmosphere wasn't able to trap heat, the temperature on Earth would be **-33ºC**, which would make life on Earth impossible.

Global warming refers to the **noticeable rise** in global **temperatures** as a result of **human activity**. More greenhouse gases in the atmosphere makes for a **stronger greenhouse effect** than **normal**, which makes for higher temperatures (see p144).

Evidence for global warming includes:

1) **Average global temperatures** have risen by **0.5ºC** in the last 100 years and the years since **1980** have been the **hottest** on record — even when you allow for natural temperature fluctuations.

2) The amount of **carbon dioxide**, a major greenhouse gas, has increased since the Industrial Revolution. Before the Industrial Revolution there were **270 parts per million** by volume (ppmv) of carbon dioxide in the atmosphere. By 2000 this had risen to **360 ppmv**.

3) The **Arctic ice cap** is **thinning** and there's evidence that some **mountain glaciers** are **retreating**.

There are **Six Greenhouse Gases**

"Run away!"

1) **Water vapour** comes from surface water, and from plant and animal respiration. **Clouds** account for **97%** of the **natural greenhouse effect**.

2) **Carbon dioxide** comes from plant and animal respiration, and from burning fossil fuels and fresh wood. CO_2 can stay in the atmosphere for **200 years**.

3) **Methane** is released when **bacteria** break down **organic matter**. Animal digestion processes produce methane. The bacteria in **cows' stomachs** are a particular culprit and the number of cows in the world has gone up a lot in the last 200 years. Methane is also released by **marshes**, **swamps** and **rice paddy fields**. Methane can stay in the atmosphere for **12 years**.

4) **Nitrous oxides** come from the burning of fossil fuels — in power stations and in cars, trains, planes etc. Nitrous oxides can stay in the atmosphere for **120 years**.

5) **CFCs** are used in refrigeration. They used to be used in aerosol sprays. They can remain in the atmosphere for **1000 years**.

6) **Ozone** is a greenhouse gas as well.

Global Warming has **Physical, Economic** and **Social** Consequences

Potential Physical Consequences World Wide

1) The polar ice and glaciers could melt and sea levels rise. Some coastal locations could experience accelerated coastal erosion. Some low-lying island nations are already under some threat of flooding, e.g. the Maldives.

2) Some areas could become wetter or more humid, e.g. North Africa. Some areas will become drier, e.g. Great Plains of North America. The British Isles could experience a more Mediterranean climate.

3) Hurricanes could become stronger. There'd be more avalanches, more landslides, and more flooding.

4) Distributions of plants and animals could change and some species could become extinct. The incidence of tropical diseases like malaria and cholera could change.

Potential Social Consequences in the UK

1) There could be more pressure on medical services as patterns of disease change — e.g. people getting malaria.

2) There could be population displacement from densely populated coastal areas.

3) Coastal conservation areas like Chesil Beach could be lost, and coastal and cold climate species could be lost.

Potential Economic Consequences in the UK

1) Industrial development could be displaced from estuary locations, e.g. the Humber Estuary.

2) Loss of coastal farmland in East Anglia would cause food prices to rise. There'd be new capacity to grow warm weather crops like olives and sunflowers. Dairy farming would be forced northwards.

3) Summer water shortages may have financial implications for water companies.

4) More money would need to be spent on flood defences like the Thames Barrier.

5) There would be further loss of jobs in the Scottish skiing industry.

There'd be political consequences from all these changes as well.

Global Warming

Governments can Try To Reduce the Amount of Greenhouse Gases

However, all the possible measures governments can take bring some kind of **problem** with them.

Change	Potential Problem
Change use of fossil fuels from **coal** to **oil** and **gas**.	New **power stations** may have to be built.
Use more **alternative sources of energy** (e.g. Wind-turbines, solar power, nuclear energy, hydroelectric energy).	**Renewable** energy can be **expensive** to set up. Not all areas are suitable for all types of renewable energy. **Nuclear** energy is **controversial** — there's risk of **accidents**, **waste disposal** is a problem, and nuclear plants are a **target** for **terrorism**.
Increase **fuel efficiency** of **buildings** (e.g. double or triple glazing, cavity wall insulation, new boilers).	You can introduce new standards in **building regulations**, but all the **old building stock** won't comply with new rules.
Encourage **green transport** and use **pricing strategy** that reflects **environmental costs**.	**Transport** and **fuel pricing policies** may be a tadge **unpopular**.
Control **deforestation**, especially in rainforests.	It's hard to **persuade** countries to change **forestry strategies**.
Programmes to **replant trees**.	This would **cost** a lot of money. It's hard to decide whose **responsibility** it is to plant trees, and **where** trees should go.

It's likely that a **mixed policy** that incorporates several of these ideas will be the way forward for most countries.

Political Responses to Global Warming Require International Co-operation

For a strategy to reduce greenhouse gases to **work**, people all over the world have to take a little bit of action — "think globally, act locally" is the idea. For example, individuals need to be prepared to use more public transport, and **businesses** need to accept the **higher production costs** that come with using **alternative energy sources**.

The **government** needs to **encourage** individuals and businesses to make the "right" choices. This means governments need to be prepared to take **political risks** — people might **prefer to vote** for a political party which isn't going to **raise petrol taxes**, or a party which isn't going to **force businesses** to do lots of "green compliance" **paperwork**.

There's also a **financial risk** — if one country pushes businesses to reduce greenhouse gases, and all its **international competitors** don't, then that country's businesses will be at a **financial disadvantage** and the country will **lose money**.

That's why **international co-operation** is **important**. It's best if countries can arrange to **take action** at the **same time**.

Global Warming has been on the Agenda of Three International Conferences

1) **Earth Summit in 1992**. 150 nations signed non-binding treaties aimed at reducing emissions of greenhouse gases. Short term **economic costs** and worries about **political consequences** meant there wasn't a huge amount of action.
2) **Kyoto Conference in 1997**. 84 countries signed the Kyoto Protocol, which laid down compulsory reductions in carbon dioxide emissions. Environmentalists didn't think these reductions were big enough.
3) **World Environmental Summit in South Africa in 2002**. Countries reaffirmed their commitment to the **Kyoto Protocol**. As of 2004, the USA still wasn't signed up to the Kyoto Protocol, though.

Practice Questions

Q1 What's the difference between global warming and the greenhouse effect?
Q2 What evidence exists for global warming?
Q3 Name six greenhouse gases.
Q4 What consequences could there be for the UK as a result of global warming?

Exam Questions

Q1 Why is an international approach necessary in order to reduce the impacts of global warming? (5 marks)

Q2 Describe how a house could be built with energy conservation and fuel efficiency in mind. (4 marks)

It's getting hot in here...

Examiners like you to be able to juggle different points of view about controversial issues like "Who is responsible for global warming?" Practise the debate by picking an argument with someone about global warming today. The examiners also like you to be aware of the political side of the debate and the reasons why a government might not go all out to reduce greenhouse gases.

Systems, Flows and Cycles

Ecosystems have stores and flows just like all the other systems you have to study. These pages are for AQA A and OCR A.

Ecosystems and Biomes are Different

1) An **ecosystem** is a **community** of plants, animals and micro organisms and their **environment** — taken as a unit.

2) An ecosystem can be as **small** as a potted plant, a pond or a hedge or as large as planet Earth.

3) A biome is a **large area** of **similar climate** and **habitats**. Examples include **rainforest**, **grassland**, **tundra**, **desert**.

4) A biome includes the same type of **community** wherever in the world it occurs.

Biome	Climate	Flora (Vegetation)	Fauna (Animals)
desert	very hot, dry climate	drought resistant plants with long roots	insects, reptiles, small mammals
grassland	rainy season and dry season	grasses, scattered shrubs	large mammals
rainforest	hot, very rainy	fast, lush plant growth, trees	diverse animal species
tundra	cold, snow in winter	mosses and lichens on permafrost	birds and mammals

Ecosystems are Made up of Biotic and Abiotic Components

1) **Biotic components** are all the **organic (living) things** in the ecosystem — **flora** (plants) and **fauna** (animals).

2) **Biomass** is the mass of **dry organic matter** per **unit area**. In the diagram below, it's shown as metric tonnes of dry matter per hectare (1 hectare = 10 000m²).

3) **Abiotic components** are all the **non-living items** including rock, soil particles, minerals, air and water.

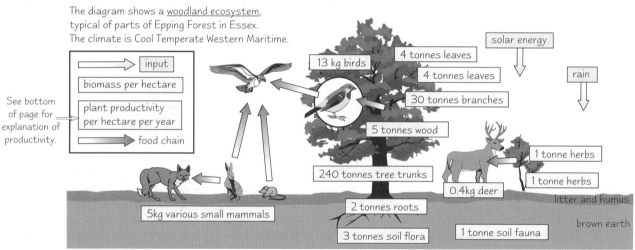

The diagram shows a woodland ecosystem, typical of parts of Epping Forest in Essex. The climate is Cool Temperate Western Maritime.

See bottom of page for explanation of productivity.

input
biomass per hectare
plant productivity per hectare per year
food chain

solar energy
rain
13 kg birds
4 tonnes leaves
4 tonnes leaves
30 tonnes branches
5 tonnes wood
240 tonnes tree trunks
1 tonne herbs
1 tonne herbs
0.4kg deer
litter and humus
brown earth
2 tonnes roots
5kg various small mammals
3 tonnes soil flora
1 tonne soil fauna

Energy Flows through the Trophic Levels of a Food Chain

1) All the energy in an ecosystem comes from the **Sun**.   Photosynthesis: Carbon dioxide + water + energy = glucose + oxygen

2) Plants use the Sun's energy to produce glucose, in the process of photosynthesis. Plants are **primary producers**, and they are the first trophic level in the food chain.

   Remember, food webs are just lots of linked food chains showing all the feeding relationships in an ecosystem.

3) Plants are eaten by **herbivores (primary consumers)**, e.g. rabbits, mice, beetles — this is trophic level 2.

4) Herbivores are eaten by **carnivores (secondary consumers)**, e.g. rabbits are eaten by foxes and some birds of prey, and beetles are eaten by shrews and weasels. This is the third trophic level. Some food chains have a **tertiary consumer** or **top carnivore**, which eats other carnivores, e.g. a cat eating a shrew.

5) Not all the **energy** in each level is **passed on** to the **next level**. At each level a large amount of energy is used up by **respiration** and other life processes, and lost in the form of **waste matter**.

Productivity Varies in Different types of Biomes and Ecosystems

1) **Productivity** is how much **biomass** is fixed into an ecosystem by **plants** over a certain **time**. There are two ways to measure it: **gross primary productivity** is the rate at which an ecosystem builds up biomass, including the mass lost via **respiration** (e.g. as heat). **Net primary productivity** doesn't count biomass lost due to respiration — just the **new biomass**.

2) Gross productivity is shown in the **diagram** above of temperate woodland, in the blue boxes. For a temperate woodland it's about 1200g/m². For a **tropical rainforest** it's **higher** — 2200g/m². **Tundra** and desert have very **low productivity**.

Systems, Flows and Cycles

Nutrients Cycle Through the Ecosystem

1) Plants need **nitrogen, potassium, phosphorus, carbon, oxygen, hydrogen, sulphur, magnesium** and **trace elements**.

2) These nutrients are **stored** in the **soil**, in **biomass** and in **litter**.

3) Nutrients **flow** or **cycle** from one **store** to another. The **diagram** on the right shows the nutrient cycle for a rainforest.

4) The **stores** are always shown as **circles**. The **bigger** the circle, the **more** of that store there is.

5) The **flows** are shown as **arrows**. The **thicker** the arrow, the **more** of that process is going on.

Nutrient cycle diagrams can look quite different for different biomes. But the only thing that really changes are the size of the circles and the width of the arrows.

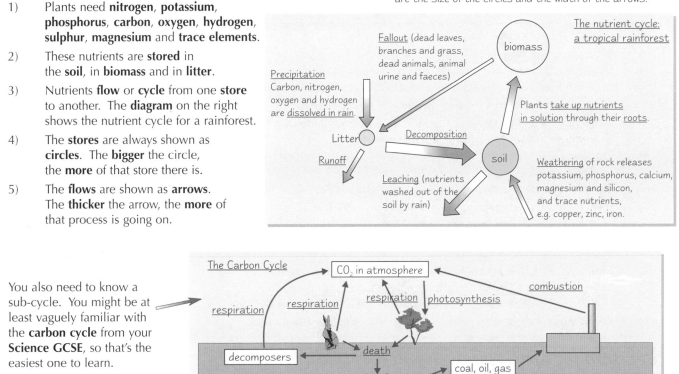

You also need to know a sub-cycle. You might be at least vaguely familiar with the **carbon cycle** from your **Science GCSE**, so that's the easiest one to learn.

People Affect Natural Processes e.g. in Broadleaved Deciduous Woodland

1) Removing **trees** and **undergrowth** reduces the **biomass store** and the **litter store** in the woodland. Less litter means **less decomposition** and fewer **soil nutrients**, so the **fertility** declines.

2) If the cleared woodland is used for **farming**, **fertiliser** and **manure** are added which alter the nutrient cycles.

3) **Deforestation** reduces **interception** and increases **runoff**. This increases the risk of **flooding** and **soil erosion**. Tree **roots** hold soil together, so removing them **increases** soil erosion.

4) Clearing woodlands changes **atmospheric processes**. It increases **wind speed** and **evaporation** and reduces **shade** and **transpiration**, so overall the area becomes **warmer** and **drier**. Fewer trees means that less **CO_2** is absorbed so the level of CO_2 in the atmosphere **increases**.

5) Food chains and webs are **disturbed** and can be **destroyed** altogether, so the **diversity** of species falls.

Practice Questions

Q1 What is a biome?

Q2 Define the term biomass.

Q3 Draw a circles and arrows nutrient cycling diagram for a rainforest (lots of rain, lush plant growth, fast decomposition).

Q4 What are the effects of deforestation on a) stores and b) processes in the nutrient cycle?

Exam Questions

Q1 Define food chain and food web. Explain why there is a loss of energy at each stage in a food chain/web. (5 marks)

Q2 Explain how nutrients flow into and out of the soil as part of the nutrient cycle. (4 marks)

Don't just sit there and stare at the page like a great lump of biomass...

Ecosystems are in GCSE Science, so they shouldn't be too new — there are a few more details for AS Geography, though. In your exam, you might get one of those circle and arrow diagrams of the nutrient cycle, so you need to know those. Oh, and if you're doing AQA A, you need to know the characteristics of the Tropical Rain Forest biome.

Plant Succession

Ecosystems develop over time. They can start off with a lichen spore landing on bare rock.
*These pages are for **AQA A** and **OCR A**.*

Ecosystems Change And Develop — There'll be Another one Along in a Minute

OK, not quite a "minute", more like several thousand years.

1) Ecosystems start with **pioneer organisms** colonising **bare rock** or **sand**. These contribute to the formation of **soil**, which lets more plants grow and compete.

2) Successful plants become **dominant**, and make up a **community**. The first community to form after the pioneer plants is the **herb** layer.

3) Eventually the soil develops enough to support **shrubs** and **trees**, which **outcompete** grasses and herbs and replace them.

4) This sequence of events is called a **plant succession**. Each different kind of succession is called a **sere**. Think of it as a <u>series</u> of stages. Each stage in the succession is called a **seral community**.

5) If left alone, ecosystems develop to the **maximum** that the **climate** will support — the **climatic climax**. This depends on the **climate type**, particularly the amount of **water** and the **temperature**. Dense **tropical rainforest** is the most developed climatic climax but elsewhere, other biomes are the climax.

6) **Climax vegetation** is generally **stable** and made up of **long lived species**. Unless the climate changes, or there's an event like a fire or volcanic eruption, or human activity changes, climax vegetation keeps on reproducing itself.

7) Events which stop or slow plant succession are called **arresting factors**.

> "Herbs" means small plants without woody bits — it includes plants like grass, not just kitchen herbs like mint and basil.

> <u>Lithosere</u> is a succession starting on bare rock. <u>Hydrosere</u> develops in fresh water. <u>Halosere</u> is salt marsh vegetation developing on the coast. <u>Xerosere</u> develops in arid conditions with drought resistant plants.

> In the UK, deciduous woodland is the climatic climax.

Sand Dunes are a Harsh Dry Xerosere Environment

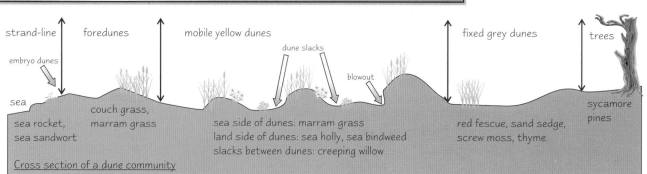

strand-line foredunes mobile yellow dunes dune slacks blowout fixed grey dunes trees

embryo dunes

sea
sea rocket, sea sandwort
couch grass, marram grass
sea side of dunes: marram grass
land side of dunes: sea holly, sea bindweed
slacks between dunes: creeping willow
red fescue, sand sedge, screw moss, thyme.
sycamore pines

<u>Cross section of a dune community</u>

1) The sand dune succession **progresses** as you get further **inland**. Nearest the sea, new dunes are forming in front of the old dunes as more sand is blown in.

2) The pioneer **primary community** species are salt-tolerant succulent plants like **sea rocket** and **sea sandwort**. They grow on the strand line and get nutrients from rotting seaweed. They have to cope with being covered by sea water.

3) **Embryo dunes** form as wind blown sand is trapped by these plants. Drought resistant couch grass grows on these embryo dunes. Its long roots anchor the dune. Couch grass **outcompetes** the pioneer succulents, and the rotting material of the dead succulents helps the couch grass to grow.

4) **Foredunes** develop as couch and marram grass trap more sand. Yellow or white **main ridge dunes** are anchored by vigorous **marram grass**. Where patches of vegetation cover are lost, the **wind** quickly removes the sand. This forms hollows called **blow-outs**.

5) When primary community plants and foredune grasses **die**, they add organic material to the **soil**. This **traps moisture** and provides **nutrients** for the **next community** of plants. More plants colonise the land side of the dunes. As each community replaces the last, the plant communities on the sand dunes get more **diverse**.

6) Depressions between the dunes are called **dune slacks**. These are more damp than the dunes themselves. **Creeping willow** and **small shrubs** grow in the slacks.

7) **New embryo dunes** form in front of the older dunes, keeping the sequence going. Eventually the dunes nearest the sea are big enough to stop sand getting to the oldest yellow dunes. The yellow dunes stop getting any bigger.

8) **Grey dunes** form where **humus** accumulates. The humus supports a community of plants replacing marram grass — first **mosses** and **lichens**, then **red fescue**, **sand sedge**, **herbs** and **heather**. The **soil** is more **acidic** here because decomposing plant material produces organic acids called **humic acids** which leach through the soil.

9) Eventually, the soil on the **grey dunes** is rich enough to support **trees**. Trees **outcompete** dune plants and replace them.

Plant Succession

Human Activity may Interfere with Plant Succession

A **plagioclimax** community is a community that's **stopped** from reaching its natural climatic climax by human activity.
Secondary succession is the succession that takes place after a destructive event — e.g. a fire, flood or forest clearance.

Human activity can have an effect on sand dune succession

- Dunes become **weakened** by people **walking** all over them, and **blow-outs** (where wind erodes the sand) can form. Riding **quad bikes** over the dunes is horrendously bad for them.
- Humans **plant more marram grass** to stabilise dunes. **Fencing** is also used to stabilise dunes. This is especially necessary in popular **recreational** areas like Bantham in South Devon.
- **Conifers** and other **new plants** can be planted on dunes. These new plants can **outcompete** native dune plants.
- The most mature dunes can be cleared of shrubs and used for **pasture**. Grazing sheep reduce the amount of vegetation, which can result in increasing the risk of blow-outs.

Not particularly good or bad, just a change from the natural succession.

Human activity can have an effect on succession in a forest

- **Coppicing** is when young trees are cut low down near to the base of the trunk so that lots of thin straight branches will grow upwards from the stump. Coppiced trees don't form a thick **canopy**. This means that **light** can still get through to the forest floor, so **herbs** and small shrubs don't get **deprived of light**, and therefore aren't outcompeted. The community is **stopped** from reaching its **climatic climax**.
- People also manage woodland by **clearing undergrowth** and **planting** exotic and native plant species. This alters the natural course of plant succession.

British Forests have been Affected by Clearance and Chemical Pollution

1) Thousands of years ago, most of the UK was covered in **dense deciduous forest**.
2) As the human population increased, people **felled** and **coppiced** trees for firewood and for building.
3) People also cut down trees to make room for **farmland**.

1) Most of the UK and north west Europe is now covered in **plagioclimax** — even in mountain and moorland areas.
2) This is because the land is used for **farming**. E.g. sheep don't cut down trees themselves, but they're responsible for the change from forest to grassland.
3) Grazing **stops** forests **re-growing**. Grazing herbivores eat seedlings, so new trees don't grow to replace old trees when they die.
4) Grasses **survive grazing**, but tree seedlings don't. So, when trees die and new trees don't replace them, grass takes advantage of the lack of shade to grow.

Acid rain is caused by sulphur oxides and nitrogen oxides in air pollution. It damages trees and soils in UK woodlands.

Practice Questions

Q1 What is the first species to colonise a bare surface called?
Q2 What is a succession on sand dunes called?
Q3 What's "coppicing"?
Q4 What type of pollution has been particularly damaging to forests in NW Europe?

Exam Questions

Q1 Arresting factors can halt or delay the plant succession. Give four examples of natural arresting factors. (4 marks)

Q2 How has human population increase resulted in plagioclimax in many areas? (6 marks)

Ooooh... reaching climatic climax now...

Ecosystems have a knack of looking like they've been there since the dawn of time. But they haven't. That's the thing, you see — you start off with bare naked rock (hurr hurr hurr, I said "bare" and indeed "naked") and stuff grows on it, then rots down to make soil which other stuff can grow in. It's deeply cunning, is what it is. Of course, human activity can alter things.

Rainforest Destruction

*Cutting down rainforests has been a hot topic for quite a few years now. These pages are just for **AQA A**.*

Humans *Cut Down Rainforest* for their Own Purposes

Rainforests are **rapidly disappearing**, because we humans are chopping down trees for our own social and economic purposes. The best known example is the **Brazilian** rainforest in the **River Amazon Basin**. Forests in **Malaysia** and **Indonesia** in S.E. Asia are also being cut down at quite a rate.

Indigenous People *Use the Forest on a Small Scale*

Indigenous people just means the people who originally lived there.

Indigenous tribes use plants for **food**, **clothing**, **shelter** and **medicines**.

They live mainly as **hunter gatherers**, with just a bit of farming on the side. Traditional farming techniques rely on **slash and burn**. This is where you **cut down** an small area of forest, **burn** it, then **farm** the soil. When the soil runs out of nutrients, you **move on** to another little patch of forest.

Indigenous people also plant **brazil nuts** and **rattan palms** for their own use.

Timber *Attracts* Logging Companies *and Earns* Foreign Currency

1) Commercial timber organisations want **tropical hardwood** like **mahogany**, **teak** and **iroko** because there's an **economic demand** for it. People want to use it for doors and furniture because it's **strong** and looks nice when it's varnished.

2) To get at valuable hardwood trees in tropical forests, large numbers of **other trees** and plants are **torn down** and burnt — this includes productive **brazil nut trees**, **rubber trees** and **fruit trees**. It seems like a big **waste**, but the logging companies can make a bigger **profit** on selling a mahogany tree than a farmer can by selling a few brazil nuts.

3) Some **governments** encourage this. Exports of hardwood earn foreign currency, which they need to pay interest on debts and import goods made in other countries.

4) In the last 50 years, logging has moved on from picking out individual mahogany trees, to **large scale clearance** of trees for wood pulp, plywood, woodchip, etc.

5) Lots of **roads** and **bulldozer tracks** have been created in order to shift vast quantities of logs around.

Settlers *Were Moved to the* Amazon *by the* Brazilian Government

In Brazil, huge numbers of people from the over populated, impoverished, drought-hit North East were **encouraged** to go to the tropical rainforest to do **slash and burn** farming. This may not have been such a great plan.

1) Most of the **nutrients** were **stored in the trees**, and were **burned** with the trees.

2) Nutrients in exposed soils were **leached away** by the heavy rainfall.

3) Removing vegetation caused **soil erosion** on slopes.

4) The **first crop** often **succeeded**, but took so many nutrients out of the soil that the **later crops** would **fail**.

5) Settlers had to **move on** to clear more forest. They often sold the land to **cattle ranchers**.

6) **Cattle ranches** suffered from **poor soil** because of **overgrazing**. This poor soil was colonised by more vigorous tropical plants that cattle don't eat. Often, the cattle ranchers had to **move on**, too.

7) **Mining** is a big industry in many LEDCs — Brazil is no exception. Waste from mining causes **pollution**. Also, **roads** built for mining operations open up **new areas** of forest to settlers, who start **slashing** and **burning** a new patch of forest.

Slash and burn on this scale isn't sustainable.

Natural Disasters *Threaten Rainforest*

Hot weather can sometimes spark off **natural fires**, which spread rapidly through the trees in tropical rainforests, ruining the ecosystem — e.g. the recent fires in **Malaysia** and **Singapore**. These fires are becoming more common — they're linked to the El Niño weather phenomenon. This can itself be linked to **global warming**, so in fact these natural events might not be quite as natural as they first sound.

Rainforest Destruction

Ecosystems Collapse when the Trees are Removed

1) Once the trees are gone, the normal **plant succession** and animal community can't re-establish itself.

2) Trees help **anchor soil**. When they're cut down, soil is washed away.

3) Trees **store** large amounts of **nutrients**. Normally, those nutrients are released to the soil when **leaves fall**, and when the tree **dies** and **rots down**. When the tree is cut down, these things can't happen, and the soil loses out on nutrients.

4) With fewer trees, there's **less evapotranspiration** and less moisture in the air, so **less rainfall**.

5) The result of all this is a fairly useless **plagioclimax** (see p63) that isn't much good for growing anything.

Clearing Rainforest Makes a Difference

1) Rainforest uses up carbon dioxide and produces oxygen. Everyone needs oxygen. Without the rainforest, excess carbon dioxide in the air could contribute to global warming and worldwide climate change.

2) It's important to preserve biodiversity — i.e. to prevent species from becoming extinct. Once gone, extinct species can't be replaced.

3) A lot of medicines are based on chemicals from plants, trees and animals, many of them from tropical rainforest. A cure for a currently fatal disease could potentially be found in the rainforest — no one'll find it if the rainforest is destroyed.

4) Clearing and burning trees can affect urban areas. In 1998, burning of forests got out of control in Malaysia, which polluted the air for millions of people in densely populated Kuala Lumpur and Singapore.

5) Clearing rainforest for farming doesn't make economic sense. One brazil nut tree can produce more protein than cattle on the same area of land — yeah, OK, cattle are big and brazil nuts are tiny, but cattle need a lot of land to graze. Farming tree products is part of the sustainable way forward for the rainforest.

Banks, Corporations, Pressure Groups and Governments Have Influence

1) In the past, some multinational companies have been actively **encouraged** by LEDCS such as Brazil to diversify into **forest clearance** and **ranching** in exchange for **tax concessions** and other **incentives** to locate new factories in the country.

2) **Indigenous people** protest about indiscriminate logging, but they need help from larger, **international pressure groups** in order to get **governments** and **corporations** to pay attention.

3) Recently, **governments** have responded to environmental pressure group campaigns and tried to **restrict** deforestation — but laws are often **ignored** or not properly enforced.

4) **Banks** in MEDCs have lent huge amounts of money to LEDCs which then have to resort to **desperate measures** to pay back the **interest** — including damage to rainforests in attempts to make money from them. Some debts have been **written off** but a lot more can be done by MEDCs to reduce the **debt burden**.

5) Governments can encourage **sustainable development** of species used in **medicines**.

6) **Ecotourism** offers potential **profits** to local communities and helps **conserve** the rainforest. See p77 for more on ecotourism.

Practice Questions

Q1 What is slash and burn agriculture?

Q2 Give an economic reason for allowing logging companies to cut down trees.

Q3 Where did forest burning get out of control in recent years and cause massive air pollution?

Q4 Give an example of financial pressure on LEDCs to exploit rainforests.

Exam Questions

Q1 In a hot and humid environment tree growth is rapid and nutrients are recycled as soon as they are available in the soil. How is this significant to the management of tropical rainforest? (4 marks)

Q2 Why is it important to preserve biodiversity in tropical rainforests? (4 marks)

Tree conservation — not just for hippies any more...

Back in the 1980s and 1990s, it was singer and eco-preacher Sting who brought the problems of the Amazonian Indians to public attention, schlepping his new best buddy the Yanomami chief around from chat-show to chat-show. Since then it's been a hot topic. For the exam, they actually want you to consider your own attitudes about deforestation, as well as the facts.

Soil Characteristics

*Soil. Dirt. Honest muck. These pages are for **AQA A** and **OCR A**.*

Soil contains Water, Air, Organic and Inorganic Matter

1) **Organic matter** is stuff from **living** or **once-living** organisms. **Inorganic** matter is everything else, like **air** and **rocks**.

2) Organic matter in soil includes things like **animal faeces** and bits of **decomposed plants** and **animals**.

3) All these components are needed for **healthy soil** that plants can grow in. Plant roots need **oxygen** from the air and **water**. Both **regolith** and **humus** are sources of **nutrients**.

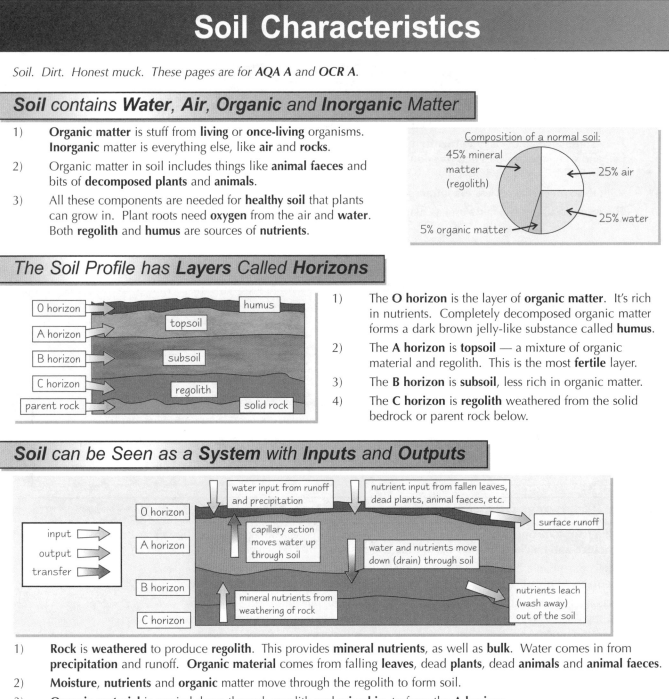

Composition of a normal soil:
45% mineral matter (regolith)
25% air
25% water
5% organic matter

The Soil Profile has Layers Called Horizons

O horizon — humus
A horizon — topsoil
B horizon — subsoil
C horizon — regolith
parent rock — solid rock

1) The **O horizon** is the layer of **organic matter**. It's rich in nutrients. Completely decomposed organic matter forms a dark brown jelly-like substance called **humus**.

2) The **A horizon** is **topsoil** — a mixture of organic material and regolith. This is the most **fertile** layer.

3) The **B horizon** is **subsoil**, less rich in organic matter.

4) The **C horizon** is **regolith** weathered from the solid bedrock or parent rock below.

Soil can be Seen as a System with Inputs and Outputs

input
output
transfer

O horizon
A horizon
B horizon
C horizon

water input from runoff and precipitation
nutrient input from fallen leaves, dead plants, animal faeces, etc.
surface runoff
capillary action moves water up through soil
water and nutrients move down (drain) through soil
mineral nutrients from weathering of rock
nutrients leach (wash away) out of the soil

1) **Rock** is **weathered** to produce **regolith**. This provides **mineral nutrients**, as well as **bulk**. Water comes in from **precipitation** and runoff. **Organic material** comes from falling **leaves**, dead **plants**, dead **animals** and **animal faeces**.

2) **Moisture**, **nutrients** and **organic** matter move through the regolith to form soil.

3) **Organic material** is carried down through regolith and **mixed in**, to form the **A horizon**.

4) Water flows through the soil and carries **dissolved nutrients** down to the **B horizon**.

5) Water can **rise** through the soil by **capillary action** and bring mineral nutrients with it to re-enrich the A horizon.

6) **Living organisms** work together to form and enrich soil. Bacteria, flora (that's plants and fungi) and fauna (that's animals), e.g. moles and worms, are all at work in the soil. Fungi and bacteria work to **decompose** leaf and twig litter and turn it into **humus**. **Worms** heave up soil, letting **air get in** and **water drain out**, and they help **mix** the different soil components together. Good old worms, eh.

The Process of Soil Formation is Affected by Several Factors

1) The **rock type** of the parent material affects rate of weathering.

2) **Climate** affects soil formation. **Precipitation** affects the amount of **water** and sunshine can bake the soil hard.

3) **Relief** (amount of slope) and **topography** (shape of the land) affect how soil develops. Higher ground gets more rain and lower temperatures. Some slopes get more **sunshine** than others. The **steeper** the slope, the more **drainage** and soil **creep**. Low flat areas can get **waterlogged**.

4) **The amount of living organisms** in the soil affects how well the components of soil are mixed together.

5) **Time** is a big factor — half a metre depth of fertile soil can take 8 000 or more years to form, depending on the influences of the other factors above.

6) **Human activity** (e.g. farming) is, as usual, a big factor.

Soil Characteristics

Soil has **Texture** — It has Small or Large **Particles** and Small or Large **Pores**

Texture	Clay	Silt	Fine sand	Coarse sand
Diameter in mm	Less than 0.002	0.002 to 0.02	0.02 to 0.2	0.2 to 2
Feels like	Sticky when wet	Like wet soap	Gritty	Very gritty and crumbly
Drainage properties	Holds water tightly	Holds water	Drains well	Drains rapidly, dries

1) Texture affects **drainage**. Sand drains very quickly, and clay drains very slowly.

2) Texture affects **aeration**. For example, sandy soils have **big airy pore spaces** between particles, but clay soils have very small air spaces.

3) **Nutrient availability** is also down to texture. Smaller particles hold nutrients well in **small pores** — nutrients stick to **clay particles**.

4) The ideal soil for farming is **loam**, which is 15% clay, 45% sand and 40% silt. Loams have a **combination** of the characteristics of the different soils in the table above.

Soils are made of a mixture of particle sizes. Some soils are mostly sand, some mostly clay, some a mixture of sand, clay and silt, etc.

Soil also has **Structure** — Particles **Clump Together** in Different Ways

1) Soil particles **clump together** to form chunks called **peds**.

2) The best soil for farming is called **crumb**. Crumb soil is made of small, round-ish peds with plenty of pore spaces. It **drains** well.

3) Soil made up of **plate-like peds** isn't so good for growing plants. Plates **lock together** and hinder drainage, aeration and root penetration.

4) **Columns** and **prisms** drain well and are fairly good for farming.

Which is chocolate, which is soil — you decide.

Soil Moisture is Important for Soil

1) The **pore spaces** in soil hold water. When it rains, water infiltrates the ground and fills the pore spaces. Excess water then drains away. The amount of water left in the soil is called its **field capacity**.

2) Water can flow **upwards** through the soil by **capillary action** to replace water evaporating from the surface of the soil.

3) When water flows through the soil, it can take **minerals** and **nutrients** with it, washing them out of the soil. This is called **leaching**. **Lessivage** is a particular type of leaching which washes out clay particles.

4) Soil becomes **waterlogged** when not enough water flows downhill through and away from the soil.

Soils can be **Acidic** or **Alkaline**

Some **humus**, e.g. under pine trees, is **acidic**. Rainwater passing through it becomes acidic (it's ever so slightly acidic anyway). Acidic water **reacts** with basic (alkaline) minerals in soil like **calcium** and **potassium**. It dissolves them, and leaches them down through the soil profile. This leaves behind an **acidic A horizon**, and makes the **B horizon** more **alkaline**.

Practice Questions

Q1 What is a typical percentage for organic matter in a mature soil?

Q2 What is regolith?

Q3 What is the best soil structure for farming?

Q4 What term is used for water draining down through the soil, taking nutrients with it?

Exam Questions

Q1 Describe the role of the following in soil formation: a) water b) organic matter, c) inorganic matter. (6 marks)

Q2 Explain how the texture and structure of soil affect its suitability for farming. (7 marks)

It's not "hummus" ,OK...

Cos that's the chickpea dip thing. I have to say, though, humus does sound really weird. I always thought it was just like potting compost that you get from the garden centre, but no, it's some kind of blackish brown "jelly-like" substance. Hmmm. Anyway, the things you need to know about soil are texture, structure, acidity and profile. Get those straight and you won't go far wrong.

Types of Soil

Excited by soil? Read on. Not in the least bit excited by soil? Read on anyway.
*These pages are for **AQA A**, but they're kind of useful for **OCR A** as well.*

Remember the Differences Between Zonal, Azonal and Intrazonal Soils

1) **Zonal** soils have clear horizons. They occur in particular **climate** areas, and they're often linked with particular **biomes** — for example, **podsol** is linked with cold **coniferous forest**.

2) **Intrazonal** soils are more influenced by **other factors** than by **climate**. The influencing factor can be **rock type** (e.g. rendzina on chalk) or **relief** (amount of slope), e.g. gley.

3) **Azonal** soils have only one **layer** or **horizon**. They aren't fully formed, e.g. they're often just regolith, so they're also called **immature** soils. **Alluvium** deposited by a river is azonal.

Podsol is a Type of Zonal Soil Found in Coniferous Forests

A true podsol has a very clear series of **horizons** (layers).

Conditions for the formation of podsol

1) **Annual precipitation** is **high**, and precipitation is **spread throughout** the **year**.
2) **Long, cold winters** slow the **decomposition** of organic material.
3) **Snow-melt** in spring suddenly provides lots of water which **infiltrates** soil to **leach out nutrients** and **minerals**.
4) **Conifer trees** drop **needles** which make the soil humus **acidic**.

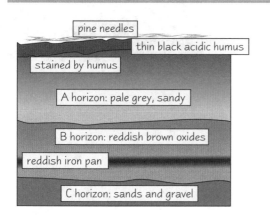

pine needles
thin black acidic humus
stained by humus
A horizon: pale grey, sandy
B horizon: reddish brown oxides
reddish iron pan
C horizon: sands and gravel

Characteristics of podsol

1) **Organic acids** remove alkaline **iron** and **aluminium oxides** through leaching from the A horizon, leaving lots of grey silica.
2) There's a **sandy upper zone** near the surface in the A horizon.
3) The **B horizon** is more like clay and is **brown** or **yellow**. The iron and aluminium **oxides** are deposited here.
4) Oxides may **cement together** to make a solid **pan** in the B horizon, which restricts drainage and causes waterlogging.
5) Acidity means **few earthworms** are present to mix the soil.
6) The acidity has to be **neutralised** with **lime** before podsols can be used for **agriculture**.

Brown Earth is a Type of Zonal Soil Found in Broadleaved Forests

Conditions for the formation of brown earth

1) **Moderate rainfall** is spread throughout the year, so leaching is slow and steady all year long.
2) Temperatures **above freezing** for most of the winter and **mild** in summer, allowing growth of **deciduous forest**.
3) Lots of **leaves** fall from the trees, and they're **quickly decomposed** by bacteria.
4) There's plenty of **soil fauna**, such as worms, mixing humus in with topsoil.

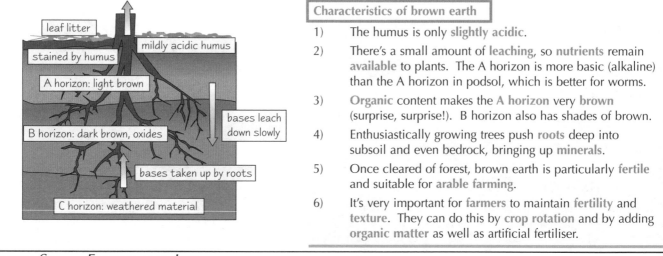

leaf litter
stained by humus
mildly acidic humus
A horizon: light brown
B horizon: dark brown, oxides
bases leach down slowly
bases taken up by roots
C horizon: weathered material

Characteristics of brown earth

1) The humus is only **slightly acidic**.
2) There's a small amount of **leaching**, so **nutrients** remain **available** to plants. The A horizon is more basic (alkaline) than the A horizon in podsol, which is better for worms.
3) **Organic** content makes the **A horizon** very **brown** (surprise, surprise!). B horizon also has shades of brown.
4) Enthusiastically growing trees push **roots** deep into subsoil and even bedrock, bringing up **minerals**.
5) Once cleared of forest, brown earth is particularly **fertile** and suitable for **arable farming**.
6) It's very important for **farmers** to maintain **fertility** and **texture**. They can do this by **crop rotation** and by adding **organic matter** as well as artificial fertiliser.

Types of Soil

Gley Forms in Waterlogged Soil

1) Waterlogged soil doesn't have any room for **air**. That means the biological and chemical processes that need **oxygen** can't happen.

2) In **waterlogged** soil, iron oxides get **reduced** (it's a chemistry thing, don't bother about the details). This changes their colour from **reddish-brown rust colour** to **grey**. So, gley is **grey**.

3) Where there are **air pockets**, the iron compounds don't change colour. This gives gleyed soils a **patchy**, **mottled** appearance. There are air pockets along the lines of **plant roots** and animal **burrows**.

4) Gley has a **clayey** texture. Gley soils are **intrazonal** soils.

Soils Can Change Significantly Down a Slope

1) On **steep slopes**, **mass movement** removes soil as soon as it's formed. You don't get much soil on **cliffs**.

2) On **less steep slopes**, there's still enough mass movement to carry soil away before it gets the chance to form clear horizons. Soils on shallow slopes tend to be **thin** and **azonal**.

3) **Nutrients leach down** from the top of a slope to the bottom.

4) On a slope, you get a **sequence** of different soils, which is called a **catena**. The differences between the soils in the catena are usually caused by the **slope** rather than differences in **climate** or **rock type** — because the climate and often the rock type are the same at the top and at the bottom of the slope.

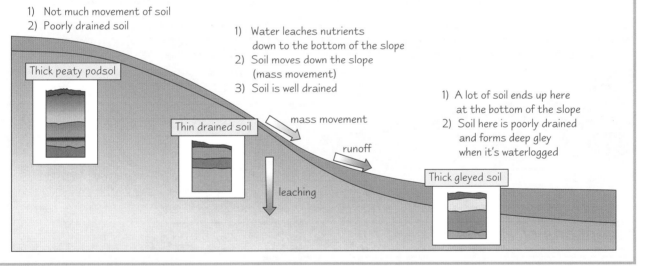

1) Not much movement of soil
2) Poorly drained soil

Thick peaty podsol

1) Water leaches nutrients down to the bottom of the slope
2) Soil moves down the slope (mass movement)
3) Soil is well drained

Thin drained soil

mass movement

leaching

runoff

1) A lot of soil ends up here at the bottom of the slope
2) Soil here is poorly drained and forms deep gley when it's waterlogged

Thick gleyed soil

There are **really obvious catenas** on many of the slopes of the **Isle of Arran** in Scotland — another thing to check out if you happen to go to Arran for a Geography field trip.

Practice Questions

Q1 What soil is most likely to form under coniferous forest?

Q2 What soil is most likely to form under deciduous forest?

Q3 What soil is most likely to be influenced mainly by rock type, out of: zonal, intrazonal and azonal?

Q4 What soil is most likely to form in waterlogged conditions at the base of a slope?

Exam Questions

Q1 Podsol has clear horizons. Explain how these horizons form. (4 marks)

Q2 How can slopes influence soils? (4 marks)

"Gleying" actually is "greying". Whodathunkit, eh...

You're supposed to know the characteristics of brown earth and podsol — so all that stuff on the other page needs actually learning, I'm afraid. Soil catenas might seem a bit weird and confusing at first glance. The way to make it easy is to remember that stuff flows downhill — soil ends up at the bottom of the hill, and water seeps downhill to make the soil waterlogged. See, not hard.

Introducing Rural Areas

Ask several geographers to define the term "rural area" and they'll probably all give you a different answer.
*These pages are for **Edexcel B** and **OCR A**.*

There **Isn't** a **Simple Definition** of "Rural Area"

Geographers use various factors to determine what is a rural area, and what isn't:

1) **Population** — the minimum number of people needed for a settlement to be classed as a town varies.
In the UK it's about 10 000 per settlement. In France, it's 2 000. In Ireland it's only 500. The UN definition gives 20 000 as the minimum for an urban settlement, leaving anything smaller as rural.

2) **Employment** — traditionally rural employment is in primary activities (e.g. farming), whereas in urban areas economic activity is mostly in secondary and tertiary industry. However, service employment in rural areas is increasing.

3) **Land use** — rural settlements are usually widely spaced, with open farmland between villages.
Urban settlements are more closely packed together with a mixture of land use.

4) **Social character** — rural settlements tend to have a sense of community, but fewer services than urban settlements.

Cloke's "**Index of Rurality**" is a measure of the extent to which an area can be considered as rural or urban.

It's based on information from the **Census** — things like **population density**, **population change** (if it's going up or down), **commuting pattern** (how far people travel to work), **distance** from an **urban centre**, population **over 65**, and **amenities**.

The index has a **five-point scale** of extreme rural, intermediate rural, intermediate non-rural, extreme non-rural, and urban.

Cloke's Index shows rural and urban as extreme ends of a **rural-urban continuum**. It's appropriate to see "urban" and "rural" in this way, because many former agricultural rural dwellers now work in towns and many former urban dwellers now live in rural areas and **commute to work**. The **vague boundary** between the two is the **rural-urban fringe**.

A good way to look at the **rural-urban continuum** is to take a **transect** from a city centre out to a remote rural area. The more **accessible** a place is, the less rural it is. Settlements can be a **long way** from the city as the crow flies, but still be quite accessible as long as there's a **good main road** linking them to the city.

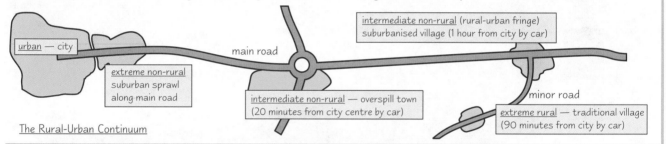

The Rural-Urban Continuum

Perceptions of Rural Areas and Rural "Quality of Life" **Vary**

Good perceptions of rural life	**Negative perceptions** of rural life
It's safe for kids to play out.	It's boring, there's nothing to do.
It's peaceful and beautiful.	It's difficult to get to the shops and the bank.
The air quality is good.	There are hardly any jobs.

These are example perceptions — you can probably think of more ideas that people have about the countryside.

A mental picture of an English rural area is usually one of countryside with fields, hedgerows, trees and farmsteads. However, much of the countryside isn't like that any more, because agricultural methods have changed. Some urban dwellers have a **romantic fantasy** of the countryside, at odds with the reality of everyday life in rural areas.

Global Patterns Show **Differences** Between **MEDCs** and **LEDCs**

Generally, the higher a country's gross domestic product (**GDP**), the lower its **rural population**, as the table shows.

GDP is a measure of economic output. It's the amount of money made in a country each year by trading goods and services.

For example:

1) **Malawi's** population almost **all** live in **rural areas**. **78%** of the people make their living from **agriculture**. 90% of exports are agricultural.

2) **Mexico** has started moving from agriculture to **industry**. Its GDP has **increased**.

3) There isn't always a **direct** relationship between GDP and rurality. **Japan** is **highly developed**, but **agriculture** is still very **important**.

	% living in rural areas	GDP per head (in US $)
Malawi	85	170
Bangladesh	74	350
Kenya	66	370
Kazakhstan	55	1500
Malaysia	42	3700
Hungary	35	5100
Mexico	25	6120
Japan	21	32600
UK	11	24220

Introducing Rural Areas

Rural Settlements Vary in their Site and Situation

1) The **site** of a settlement is where it is in the **physical landscape**. A village usually needs to be fairly **flat** and **well drained**. Back in prehistoric times, when humans first settled the land, they often chose sites on high ground which were **dry** and **easy to defend**.

2) The **situation** of a settlement is where it is **in relation to resources**. Early villages needed **water**, **wood** and **stone** for building, and **good farmland**. They also needed to be **close** to other settlements. Villages often grew up in places where it was easy to **bridge a river**, or where there was already a **road**.

3) Settlements **evolve** over time. Some villages in favourable sites and situations have developed into **towns** and **cities** — even London was once a small prehistoric hunter-gatherer village. Some villages have **moved**, **shrunk** or **disappeared**.

Villages can be **classified** according to their **shape**.

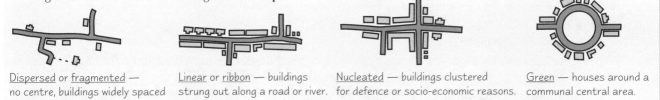

Dispersed or fragmented — no centre, buildings widely spaced

Linear or ribbon — buildings strung out along a road or river.

Nucleated — buildings clustered for defence or socio-economic reasons.

Green — houses around a communal central area.

Rural settlement patterns can vary widely throughout the world — people may be fairly **evenly spread** in rural areas in **India** or **Kenya** but settlement is far more **patchy** in places like the **Australian outback** or **Iceland**.

There are Differences Between Rural Areas in LEDCs and MEDCs

1) The differences between rural areas across the world are based on **physical**, **socio-economic** and **cultural factors**.

2) In **LEDCs**, **traditional** rural activities such as **farming** still dominate the economy and the society although **new activities** such as **manufacturing** or **service** industry have been introduced to rural areas. **Rural amenities** are **poor**, and **urban amenities** aren't accessible from rural areas. Settlements are quite **evenly spread**. Culture is **traditional**.

3) In **MEDCs**, new activities are often well **established** in the rural economy — especially tourism and the service industry. The population density is higher as more people stay in rural areas either to work, or to commute out to nearby **towns**. **Urban amenities** are accessible. **Larger settlements** are close to urban areas, and are often **suburbanised**.

Rural Areas are Served by Nearby Towns

There's more about central places on p82-83.

1) People in MEDC rural settlements depend on nearby **towns** for **goods** and **services** such as supermarkets, banks, secondary schools, health centres, etc. Usually their **place of work** is in town too. The town is called a **central place**, and it serves all the rural settlements in the **market area** surrounding it.

2) A central place with a **lot of important services** will have a lot of people travelling in to use those services. This means it has a **large market area**. Settlements are ranked in a hierarchy according to the size of their market area.

3) The **range** of goods or a service is the distance that people are prepared to go to get it. Low order goods like milk have a short range. High order goods like top range audio equipment have a long range.

4) The **threshold** of a product or service is the smallest population needed to make it worth selling the product or service. **Hospitals** need a **large** threshold population. A **corner shop** only needs a **small** threshold population.

Practice Questions

Q1 Give four factors which geographers use to classify an area as rural or urban.

Q2 What is the boundary between the city and the countryside called?

Q3 Name three different shapes of village settlement.

Exam Questions

Q1 What is the rural-urban continuum? (2 marks)

Q2 Describe the similarities and differences between a named rural area in the UK and a rural area in a named LEDC. (7 marks)

Look out the window. Do you see any sheep? Well, there you are then...

If only my simple "sheep/no sheep" definition of the rural/urban divide would catch on. Unfortunately, for AS level it gets slightly more complicated than that. It's not too bad, though — things like population density, land use and whether there's a sense of community are fairly easy to get your head round.

Changes in Rural Areas

Changes in the structure of society and in the global economy have effects on rural environments.
*These pages are for **Edexcel B**, and for **AQA B**, option T (first 2 sections on p72 only).*

The **Rural Landscape** Evolved from the **Ancient Open Field System**

The **open field system** of agriculture (open field because they had neither fences nor hedges as boundaries) grew up around villages in **Anglo-Saxon times** and continued until the early 19th century.

1) The land around all rural settlements was split into **three fields** that contained all the arable land. Two of the fields were normally devoted to cereal crops like **rye** and **wheat**, and the third was **fallow** (uncultivated).

2) Each field was divided into separate strips, **shared out** among the villagers according to the amount of land rented. The strips making up a total holding were **scattered about the fields** so the good soil could be evenly distributed between the villagers. The **pattern** of ridges and furrows is still visible in some places.

3) Most of the work was done on a **community** basis. Few families owned either a plough or enough oxen to make up a ploughing team, so families usually **shared**. There was **common grazing land** for everyone's livestock.

> **Problems with the open field system:**
>
> 1) The system **wasted land** — the **fallow** field produced **nothing**, and in the other fields land was wasted on the **paths** required for access between each strip.
>
> 2) The system **wasted labour** — even though the fallow field wasn't sown, it still had to be **ploughed**.
>
> 3) The system **wasted time** — families had to **travel** between their strips in different fields.

Enclosure Created **Small Fields** Divided by **Hedges**

The open field landscape couldn't produce enough food for the 18th century's rapidly expanding **urban** settlements, so in the 19th century, landlords converted open fields into **separate enclosed units**. Common land was also enclosed and cultivated.

Fences, **hedges**, and **ditches** separated one field from another. This **changed the look** of the rural landscape from open expanses of farmland to smaller hedged and fenced fields.

Many farmers **benefited** from these changes. They could spend more time on cultivation, which **increased productivity**. Other farmers were **worse off**. The **common grazing land** was **gone**, and they couldn't afford to buy land to graze their cattle and sheep. Many people were **displaced** from the land and drifted towards the **towns** in search of work.

Changes in **Agriculture** in MEDCs Affected **Rural Communities**

1) Farming in MEDCs has become more and more **intensive** and **high-tech.** since the middle of the 20th century. Farmers have been keen to use intensive farming methods to make their farms more **productive** and more profitable.

2) Increased **mechanisation** means that there are far **fewer manual jobs** in farming. Approximately 29% of farm workers now work **part time**, while 13% work **seasonally** — e.g. only at harvest or lambing time. In the year 2000 just **4.4% of the rural population** were involved in agriculture. Former farm workers have left their villages in search of work — see p74 for the effects of **rural depopulation**.

3) Farms have become a lot **bigger** on average. Most farms in the UK are still fairly small (less than 20 hectares), but a few **agribusiness** farmers who cultivate huge areas of land (over 300 hectares) own almost half of the farmland.

4) The **average field size** has increased, especially in arable farming areas like East Anglia. This is due to the increasing use of **mechanisation** — it's more **efficient** to run a **combine harvester** over one massive field than over two medium sized fields. For one thing, you spend longer going in a straight line, and **less time turning around**.

5) The EU's **Common Agricultural Policy** has had huge effects on farming in the UK. The basic aim was to make farming more efficient and it offered subsidies to farmers to produce certain products. One result was **over-production** — farmers made more than they could sell, and there were vast stores of unused products.

> **Solutions to the problems of European agricultural over-production**
>
> 1) The EU introduced **quotas** (limits) for milk production. As a result, many UK farmers have had to give up their dairy herds and turn to other activities.
>
> 2) **Diversification** has been encouraged. This is where farmers carry on farming, but also develop other business activities, e.g. running a **bed and breakfast**.
>
> 3) The **set-aside** scheme pays farmers to leave land **uncultivated**, which makes overall production fall. Under the scheme, any farm over 20 hectares in size must leave 15% uncultivated for at least 5 years. The land can be woodland, fallow or a wildlife area.
>
> 4) **Environmentally Sensitive Areas** (ESAs) have been designated. In these areas, farmers are given **incentives** to farm in an **environmentally friendly** way, e.g. become organic farms.

You could say that the decline in farming has left farmers with no choice but to diversify.

Farmers receive **less profit** from the food they sell than they did 50 years ago — nowadays most food is sold through **supermarkets**, and the supermarkets keep most of the price that consumers pay.

Changes in Rural Areas

The Development of *Tourism* has *Changed* the *Function* of some Settlements

The massive growth in **tourism** over the last 50 years has brought many changes to some rural areas, particularly those in **coastal** areas and **National Parks**, with social, economic and environmental impacts.

1) Instead of being farming communities some villages now function mainly as **tourist centres**, and the services offered there reflect the **needs of visitors** rather than the needs of the **inhabitants**.

2) For example, **tea shops** and restaurants open and shops selling **gifts** and equipment for **outdoor activities** appear. The need for visitors' **car parks** can cause big changes to land use patterns.

3) In the UK, most tourism is **seasonal**. This can have serious effects on seasonal unemployment in the area.

Case Study: Malham, Yorkshire Dales National Park (UK)

Background: Malham has **150 permanent residents**, and **100 000 visitors** per year.

Advantages: The tourist facilities (e.g. 6 cafes, 2 pubs, 5 shops, and 2 campsites) **generate jobs**. The **money** spent by tourists keeps local businesses afloat, transforming a struggling rural community into a community with a **sustainable income**.

Problems: **Erosion** of local footpaths, damaging local flora and fauna.
Holiday traffic restricts local mobility.
Parking spaces are limited, resulting in many tourists parking inappropriately.
More **holiday homes**, so house prices are going up beyond the reach of locals.
The area has become **noisier**.

1) Tourist areas need to be **managed**. The **Lake District National Park** has a management plan some 244 pages long. It covers **recreation**, **quiet enjoyment** of the pretty landscape, local **economic** and **social wellbeing**, **traffic management**, **recreation** and **environmental** issues like wildlife and pollution.

2) There are separate chapters on managing the **fells**, the **valleys**, the **lakes**, the **forests** and the **settlements**. As well as protecting the landscape, the National Park Authority have to use and exploit the landscape in order to get plenty of tourists to visit the area and spend their money there. It's a balancing act.

Tourism can *Raise Rural House Prices*

1) Visitors who like an area try to **buy houses** there. This pushes up house prices beyond the reach of **locals**. This in turn forces **young first time buyers** to **leave** the village to find housing, which makes the **average age** of residents **older**, changing the character of the village.

2) If newcomers use the house as a **second home** it'll be left **empty** for parts of the year. An empty house can't contribute to the **local economy** unless it's rented out as a **holiday** cottage. This isn't **practical** out of the holiday season. Villages can end up almost empty in winter — **not good news** for non-tourism related businesses such as local shops and services.

3) But **second homes** have their **good side**, too. Buying up derelict cottages and modernising them provides **employment** for local **builders/plumbers** etc. and makes the village look nicer.

You could have bought a 3-storey mansion for that in my day, and still had enough change for a sack of offal.

Practice Questions

Q1 Why have fields in MEDCs become larger over the last 50 years?

Q2 What was the open field system?

Q3 Why can second homes pose a threat to rural communities?

Exam Questions

Q1 Describe the effects of mechanisation in farming on the economy and landscape of rural England. (8 marks)

Q2 Why did the open field system come to an end in the 1700s? (8 marks)

Q3 With reference to a named case study, explain how tourists change the nature of a rural area. (14 marks)

So why are farmyards always full of blue plastic and old cars, then...?

Farming was always the number one activity in rural areas, so it's not surprising that changes in farming have had such a big effect on the rural landscape and economy. For AQA B, you need to know about changes to field structure in the 1700s. For Edexcel you need to know about changes that happened in the last 50 years. The rise of tourism is a particularly important change.

Changes in Rural Areas

*People move from rural areas to cities for various reasons, often socio-economic. In MEDCs, people also move the other way, from the city into the countryside. These pages are for **Edexcel B**, **AQA A** and **OCR A**. Page 74 is also useful for **AQA B option S**.*

Rural Depopulation is the Movement of People Out of Rural Areas into Towns

1) **Rural depopulation** is a serious decline in the population of rural areas.

2) **Reasons for moving** can be divided into **push** factors and **pull** factors.

3) Rural-urban migration in the UK started in the **19th century**, as the **Industrial Revolution** created more jobs in towns and cities. The rate of rural depopulation has slowed down in recent years in most MEDCs but not yet in LEDCs.

4) The people who move away tend to be **young people looking for work**, so the average age in villages increases.

Push factors (away from village)	Pull factors (towards town)
lack of job opportunities	potential job opportunities
low paid jobs	well paid jobs
poor housing and services	better housing and services
natural disasters (famine, drought)	

5) In **MEDCs**, **services** such as transport, libraries and banks start to be **withdrawn** because there aren't enough people to keep them profitable. This hits hard in remote areas. The very young and very old are particularly affected.

Case Study — Rural Depopulation in Remote Central Wales in the 1980s

- Local people migrated out to look for work, and English people migrated in. The number of Welsh speakers went down.
- There was conflict between locals and newcomers over housing. Councils built less housing.
- Many jobs in rural Wales were "low status" low paid jobs. Most jobs were limited to the more accessible areas.
- Decline in population resulted in transport services to villages being cut.
- Many small villages had no shop (except a mobile shop visiting once a week), and some had no post office, school or bus service.

Counter-Urbanisation is the Movement of People Into Rural Areas

1) **Counter-urbanisation** (also called urban-rural migration) is where people seem to react against city life and move away to live in **rural areas**. In the UK many people dislike the traffic congestion, air and noise pollution, higher crime rates and rising house prices of the urban environment.

2) **Better transport** has allowed people to live in rural villages and **commute** to their urban place of work. At the same time, **changes** in **employment styles** and the increased availability of **broadband internet** access in rural areas have led to more people being able to **work from home**.

3) There are more **jobs** in rural areas now. The Government gives **grants** to **businesses** setting up in some rural areas.

Effects of counter-urbanisation

1) **Professional families** and **wealthier retired people** migrate into villages and replace labouring families. The socio-economic profile of the settlement changes from mostly agricultural to a diverse mix of social groups.

2) The closure of shops and services has been avoided because of the inward migration of commuters. For example, in the Craven District in North Yorkshire, village schools have been saved by the young families moving into the area.

3) The type of services in a village also tends to change. Commuters have very limited leisure and shopping time available during the week. Village convenience stores usually shut as people opt to shop in supermarkets at the weekend. This creates space for businesses like trendy restaurants which are popular with young professionals.

4) To cater for inward migration, villages often have to expand. New housing estates are built, which changes the appearance of the village, and often changes its character. Building new estates, and infill building between existing houses, increases the amount of impermeable surface. This increases flood risk (see Section 1).

5) House prices rise because the incomers can afford higher prices. This means locals can't afford houses in their own villages. Second homes also mean that fewer houses are available to locals.

6) There's an increase in congestion on country roads which weren't built to cope with lots of traffic. Traffic pollution affects the air quality of the area.

Effects of Migration Depend on How Close the Village is to an Urban Centre

Villages **a long way from cities** are **particularly affected** by rural-urban migration, and by the **loss of services**.

Villages **close** to cities aren't particularly hurt by the loss of services, because people can **easily travel** to the city. Villages near cities are also the most likely to be **repopulated** by **counter-urbanisation** — people like to be able to commute quickly to work. **Accessibility of services** varies depending on how remote the village is.

Changes in Rural Areas

Rural Areas are Also Changing in LEDCs

1) **Rural-urban migration** is **more marked** in LEDCs than in MEDCs — the push and pull factors are greater. The **rural** areas are perceived as an **economic dead end**, and the urban areas are believed to offer great potential.

2) The introduction of **mechanisation** in farming has caused **job losses**. Farm workers have to move away to seek jobs. The lack of other sorts of job opportunities is another factor.

3) As the migrants tend to be the **economically active population**, the situation in the rural area becomes even **worse** once they start leaving. The very young and the elderly who remain there are unable to farm the land efficiently and the problem of **under-production of food** becomes **more serious**.

4) Diseases such as **HIV/AIDS** have an effect on rural areas. The **economically active age group** die of AIDS related illnesses (because they're the **adults** — the **sexually active** age group, and the most likely to contract HIV through sexual contact), and this has a brutal effect on the **economy** of rural settlements.

Case Study: HIV/AIDS, poverty and migration in Uganda

Background:	Very high rates of HIV infection in the 1990s (21% of pregnant women aged 15-24 infected in 1991).
Effects of HIV:	Sick people **sold possessions** to pay for healthcare, and bereaved people sold possessions to pay for funerals. AIDS tends to affect both parents in a family, so children left **orphaned** and cared for by **grandparents** or by **each other**.
Effects of poverty:	Poor people less likely to have good **health education**. Poverty makes people more likely to **migrate** from rural to urban environments. Men went to the city to get temporary work — and some used **prostitutes** while in the city, increasing the rate of HIV infection. **Poor women** more likely to **become prostitutes** out of desperation.
Labour:	The **economically productive age group** is most likely to become infected with HIV, and therefore the most likely to die of AIDS related illnesses. The **local economy** loses their **labour**, and the labour of anyone **looking after** them.

Stemming the tide of rural-urban migration — Land Reform

Land reform is where land is taken away from landlords and given to local people. The idea of land reform is to make **rural life** more **appealing** and more **profitable** for local people, so that they won't feel the need to migrate to the city.

Farmers who **own** their own land don't have to pay **rent** to a landlord, so they can keep more of their profits.

As well as helping people to own their own land, land reform schemes can help people to **manage** and **irrigate** their land.

Rural Change Creates Conflict

1) There's conflict between **private landowners** and **recreational walkers** over access to land.
2) **Recreational walkers** conflict with **mountain bikers** over the use of paths, e.g. in the Lake District and North Wales.
3) There's conflict between **recreational** land use and **conservation**.
4) There's conflict between **tourist traffic** and **local people** driving to work.
5) Counter-urbanisation causes conflict, especially where newcomers have a romanticised view of what a village "ought" to be like, or where locals perceive newcomers as "yuppies" who are ruining the village.
6) Counter-urbanisation creates need for new housing development which puts **pressure** on the area.

Practice Questions

Q1 Give two examples of push factors and two examples of pull factors contributing to rural-urban migration.
Q2 Describe and explain three effects that counter-urbanisation can have on rural areas.
Q3 Give three causes of conflict in rural areas.

In the exam, you'll get better marks if your pull factors aren't straight opposites of your push factors, i.e. lack of jobs vs job opportunities.

Exam Questions

Q1 Define rural depopulation and suggest reasons for rural depopulation in a named area of England or Wales. (7 marks)

Q2 Explain how high levels of HIV infection in Sub-Saharan Africa can cause a spiral of rural poverty and outmigration. (8 marks)

This is a local page for local people — nothing here for you...

Rural-urban migration is similar in LEDCs to MEDCs, except the push/pull factors are more extreme. Rural conflict takes a whole load of different forms. It's always caused by something changing, and someone getting bothered by it. Watch out for the environmental impacts of counter-urbanisation as well as the socio-economic impacts.

Challenges Facing Rural Areas

*Managing the countryside is a bit of a balancing act. For this topic, they want you to be able to say who decides how rural areas develop, and how they manage conflict between different groups who want different things. These pages are for **Edexcel B**.*

Managing Rural Deprivation is Important

Rural deprivation means the extent to which an area **lacks services** or **amenities**. Often, deprivation results in **depopulation**, which results in **more deprivation** and **decline** — this is the **cycle of deprivation**.

Managing rural deprivation needs strategies to boost rural incomes. This is something that government departments can do by giving development grants to businesses, so that they can create more jobs.

It's necessary to stop rural services from closing down, so that people can enjoy a reasonable quality of life. Local and national government can **subsidise bus routes**, for example.

Case study: Managing rural deprivation in an MEDC — Llangurig, Wales

Agency:	Local Housing Association
Problem:	The local rural school has only 18 pupils. It'll be closed down unless it can attract more students.
Solution:	The local housing agency has advertised in the local and national press for a large Welsh speaking family to become tenants of one of their properties, at a reduced rent. The idea is that the family's children will attend the local school.
Result:	A family with 4 children moved into the property. 3 of the children attended the local primary school.

Case study: Managing rural deprivation in an LEDC — Malawi

Agency:	The United Nations Development Programme
Problem:	80% of rural households have no access to financial services, such as banks.
Solution:	The agency provides credit to help the poor. A simple loan can help small rural communities to set up their own small scale, sustainable businesses.

Managing and Developing Resources in the Countryside is Important

1) Rural areas provide lots of important resources.

- **Reservoirs** in the countryside provide **water** for both rural and urban areas, e.g. Thirlmere in Cumbria provides water for Greater Manchester.
- **Quarries** provide **stone** for building and for the chemical industry.
- **Forestry** provides **wood** for building and for the paper industry.

2) All these resources need to be **managed** so that they provide **profit** for the people owning and running them.

3) It's important to avoid **ruining** the **look** of the countryside, or ruining too many wildlife habitats.

4) Resource development needs to provide **jobs** for local people. It can also provide **recreation** where appropriate — reservoirs are often used for boating and windsurfing, and forestry plantations can include paths and cycle tracks.

5) It's important to be **sustainable**. Sustainable development "meets the needs of the **present** without **compromising** the ability of **future** generations to meet their needs". In other words, sustainability means that the resource will **still be there** to use and make money out of — using a resource unsustainably isn't in anyone's **long-term interests**.

Case Study: Coastal Superquarries in Scotland

Advantages: It makes **economic sense** to dig huge "superquarries". The quarries would bring new **jobs** to the area. Stone from the quarry would be taken away by **ship**, which would mean developing a **port** — a positive impact on the local area. The environmental impact of one superquarry might actually be **less** than the impact of **several small quarries**.

Disadvantages: **Environmentalists** say superquarries ruin the **natural beauty** of rural areas. When quarrying is finished, a huge hole will be left, which would cost a lot of money to **landscape**. Superquarries would ruin some **wildlife** and plant habitats. Where a superquarry is to be dug in a **tourist** area, people worry that a big, **ugly**, **noisy** quarry would drive tourists away. **Ships** carrying stone from the quarry could **disrupt** the **fishing industry**.

Who Decides: **Local councils** decide whether quarry owners should have planning permission to dig quarries. **National government** gave firm **guidelines** after consulting with quarrying companies, environmentalists and local councils.

The Decision: Only **4 superquarries** could be dug in Scotland up until 2009. They'd have to be in remote areas where they'd benefit the local job market, and where they wouldn't affect tourism and fishing. The government would have a say in planning permission — it wouldn't all be up to local councils. *Sticky problems like this are often managed by a final decision from central government.*

Challenges Facing Rural Areas

Rural Environment Problems Need to be Tackled

Farmers work hard to **intensify production** and maximise their **profits.**
Unfortunately this has caused environmental problems.

They've been so successful that the EU produced vast surpluses for a while, and had to actually persuade farmers to limit production.

Problem	Managing the Problem
Groundwater contamination: Slurry and fertilisers contaminate groundwater reserves.	1) **EU authorities** offer **incentives** to farmers to restrict use of nitrates. 2) **Consumer concern** about the **environment** and "chemicals in food" has also forced farmers to review their practices.
Hedgerow Removal: Hedges are removed to make fields bigger. This destroys habitats.	DEFRA's **Countryside Stewardship** scheme gives **grants** to farmers for **improving hedges**, and requires that they **don't trim hedges** too often.
Land Exhaustion: Farmers apply lots of fertiliser and pesticides to get higher yields. This can decrease the soil's fertility.	Farmers can use **alternative pest control** measures, e.g. insect predators instead of pesticides.
Soil Erosion: The misuse or overuse of land results in the topsoil being removed.	**Mixed farming** and **crop rotation** are coming back into "fashion". These have less impact on the soil than traditional **monoculture**.

It's **tricky** to manage these problems. Most of the solutions result in farmers **losing income**, which encourages rural communities to **diversify** into less traditional activities. Agencies generally want farmers to **keep farming** — people like the **traditional look of farmland**. Without farmers, the job of keeping the countryside looking nice would be a lot **harder**.

The **Green Revolution** was a programme of plant breeding which produced new **high yielding varieties of crops** — increasing **food production** and economic viability of farms. It was adopted widely by **LEDCs** between 1960-1970.

Unfortunately, the new seeds were **too expensive** for poorer farmers. High yields meant **demand** for grain **decreased**, so the **price** of grain went down. Poorer farmers couldn't compete, and had to move to the city. The Green Revolution encouraged **mechanisation**, so agricultural **jobs** were lost. Farmers had to use a lot of **fertilisers**, which damaged the **environment**.

Tourism can be an *Effective Development Strategy* in *LEDCs*

1) Getting people from MEDCs to spend money in your village sounds like a real **winner**.
2) However, **tourism impacts** on **local communities**. People who work with tourism companies are paid well — this causes **conflict** between local people. **Begging** increases when there are lots of **wealthy visitors** from MEDCs. Communities may have to **change** to offer visitors the amenities they want — discos, restaurants, etc.
3) **Mass tourism** impacts on the environment — lots of tourists create lots of **rubbish**. Erosion can also be a problem.
4) Deciding on a **tourism strategy** means taking all these things into account. Communities need to manage **new land use** (e.g. building a hotel) alongside **traditional land use** (farming). They need to **manage conflict** between people who want to make money from tourism and people who fear losing their farming income.

1) **Ecotourism** aims to **conserve** fragile and rare environments, and **make money** for locals at the same time.
2) For example, ecotourism trekking expeditions in **Nepal** use local guides and **respect local culture**. They carefully dispose of non-biological **waste**, and use relatively **environmentally friendly** paraffin stoves.
3) **Ecotourism** is now the **fastest growing sector** in global tourism.
4) Nice though ecotourism is, it doesn't do away with **begging** or **conflicts** between local people.

Practice Questions

Q1 Describe and explain the cycle of rural deprivation.
Q2 List four environmental problems generated by the intensification of farming practices.
Q3 Define "ecotourism".

Exam Questions

Q1 Describe the management of rural deprivation in a) an MEDC and b) an LEDC. (11 marks)

Q2 Describe how rural communities in LEDCs manage conflict when setting a strategy for tourism. (8 marks)

Learning all this Geography — it's a challenge all right...

For this, they want you to describe what the challenge is and say how successful the big decision makers are at resolving conflict and making plans for future development. In class, you might have done tourism, rural deprivation, resource management or environmental problems from farming. Pick the ones you've done in class to revise — no point learning more than you have to.

Rural Futures

*Rural areas need sustainable development strategies for the future, so that solutions to today's problems don't create further problems for future generations. This requires planning — an awful lot of planning. These pages are for **Edexcel B**.*

Non Governmental Organisations *Have a Role in* Rural Development

Non Governmental Organisations (**NGOs**) like **Oxfam** and **CAFOD** do a lot of **rural development work** in LEDCs. Smaller charities and individual churches are also active in rural development projects. They're all keen on **sustainable development** —

"Economic and social development that meets the needs of the current generation without undermining the ability of future generations to meet their own needs."

CAFOD = Catholic Agency for Overseas Development

CIDSE = International Cooperation for Development and Solidarity

Case Study — Rice and Pig Banks in Cambodia

Background: Poor families in rural Cambodia **couldn't afford** to buy rice to plant in their fields, or pigs to keep.

Project: CAFOD partner, CIDSE, set up a rice and pig bank. The idea is that a farmer can "borrow" some **rice**, plant it, and **pay back** the loan in **rice that they grow**. They can "borrow" a **sow** from the bank and then pay back the loan in **piglets**. The farmer can **keep** or **sell** the **spare rice** and **piglets** left over.

Result: Farmers can **afford to farm**, and they can **make a profit** by selling spare rice and piglets. Bonus!

Fair trade is a big movement in sustainable development. Traditionally, people selling goods or crops have had to sell at the **market price**. If the market price goes **down**, they suddenly **earn a lot less**. Fair trade gives a minimum "**fair**" price that allows farmers and craftspeople to make a **decent living**. Fair trade goods in MEDC shops **cost** a little more, but a lot of people are willing to pay a touch more in order to help out people in LEDCs.

Case Study: Rikchary Warmy Craft Cooperative, Peru

Background: Knitting, weaving and metalwork skills are part of traditional culture in Peru. Women usually find it difficult to make a living from these skills, though.

Project: A **women's artisan cooperative** produces sweaters for the Western **fair trade market**. The cooperative was initially founded and funded with the help of a **church** in the USA.

Result: The women earn a good **income** from **fair trade**. The cooperative buys raw materials from **local producers** to boost the local economy.

The Swiss cheese makers were happy with their new fair trade deal and celebrated with a new set of costumes for the boys.

Rural Planning *in MEDCs Needs to be Integrated*

1) **Land use planning** determines what kind of developments can go where. E.g. in the UK **National government** gives broad guidance to local authorities. **Councils** then draw up **Structure Plans** to say where new housing, industrial developments, shops and recreational land should go. **District councils** fill in the **fine detail**.

2) **Structure Plans** state the county council's policy on future development. They state what **changes** and **problems** are going on in the area, and set out what kind of **development** will be done to **solve** them.

3) The decline of **traditional economic activities** means rural areas in the UK have to find solutions to a **range** of challenges. Rural areas usually have several problems at once — e.g. lack of **services**, poor **transport** and lack of **jobs**.

4) The trick is in planning carefully to solve **all of the problems** with the **least amount of effort**. Rural planning needs to be able to kill two or more birds with one stone — it needs to take an **integrated** approach.

1) The Countryside Agency is England's rural development agency (Wales and Scotland have development agencies of their own). Their aim is to "make the quality of life better for people in the countryside and the quality of the countryside better for everyone". I guess everyone has to have a good slogan these days.

2) The Countryside Agency is an integrated development agency — they bring together economic, environmental, community and recreational issues under one roof. They don't actually set policy or provide services. Their role is to research, analyse and advise national and local government — the agencies who actually do make decisions affecting rural areas. They also give grants to local authorities to help them pay for development projects.

Case Study: Welsh Development Agency

Problem: Long-term **unemployment** and poor **housing** conditions in former slate mining communities in North Wales.

Scheme: The **Slate Valleys Initiative** — designed to empower communities to start their own sustainable development projects. Money from the initiative was used to set up a centre for teaching **traditional building skills**, and to create "slate trails" to encourage **tourists** to explore the area.

Cost: £28 million, funded by **EU** and **Welsh Development Agency** in partnership with Gwynedd Council, CELTEC.

Rural Futures

Development can be *Top-Down* or *Bottom-Up*

1) **Top-down development** is forced onto local communities by national government.
   Top-down development is usually planned and carried out on a **national scale.**

2) This type of development lumps all rural settlements together in one category — it's a **one size fits all** approach.

3) Because it's usually enforced by government organisations, top-down development is open to **corruption**.
   Sometimes, government agencies can be **tempted** by bribes to act in the interest of **commercial organisations**, rather than in the interests of local people. The welfare of the local community isn't always at the top of the agenda.

1) **Bottom-up development** tackles development from the "grass roots" up.
   Bottom-up development is usually planned and done on a small, **local scale**.

2) Bottom-up management strategies are **tailor made** in consultation with the **local community**.

In the past decade, geographers have gradually begun to realise that **small scale**, **bottom-up** projects are the way forward. Help tends to be successful when it's given at the **community level**, because community projects are more **sustainable**. Local people are more likely to make a project work if they feel that their **interests are represented**. Hugely **expensive** top-down projects often **don't work out**.

Case Study — Large scale top-down development in Egypt

Aim: To provide a **constant and reliable water supply** to the agricultural land surrounding the Nile catchment.

Scheme: Building the **Aswan Dam**. The dam took **8 years** to construct at a cost of **$1 billion**.
Its 12 turbines have a generating capacity of 2100 megawatts of electricity (that's a LOT of electricity).

Advantages: **Reliable water source**. Egyptian government got **international recognition** for the project.

Disadvantages: **Some** land was flooded during the construction, and villages had to be **resettled**.
The dam trapped silt, decreasing the fertility of the land — **crop yield went down**.
The delta is under threat from **flooding** due to reduced sediment levels in the river.

Case Study — Small scale bottom-up development in Nepal

Background: Nepal is a country with steep **mountains** and high year-round **rainfall** — ideal for **hydro-electric power**.

Scheme: Micro hydro-electric power scheme. **Community** involved in **planning**, **installation** and **management** of the scheme. Machinery locally made from materials available in the area. **Water** power also used to grind grain.

Advantages: Much **faster** at grinding grain than traditional water wheel. Supplies **electricity** to houses — no need to travel to buy kerosene. Powers electric stoves, so less need for **firewood** — this slows **deforestation** and **soil erosion**. Success has spread to other parts of Nepal.

Development agencies can "help people to help themselves" by giving **training courses** in **accounting** and **financial management**, so that local people can **run their own businesses** more effectively.

They can also help provide **credit** facilities so that people can take out a **small loan** to **start their own business**. The **Grameen Bank** in Bangladesh was one of the first of these **microcredit schemes**. The Grameen Bank gives small loans to people who are **too poor** to prove that they can pay back a loan from a traditional bank.

Practice Questions

Q1 What is fair trade?

Q2 What is a Structure Plan?

Q3 What is the role of the Countryside Agency?

Q4 Describe the difference between top-down and bottom-up development.

Exam Questions

Q1 Define integrated development and explain why it is needed in the English countryside. (7 marks)

Q2 Use named examples to explain why bottom-up development tends to succeed more than top-down development. (7 marks)

Give a man a fish, feed him for a day. Teach him to fish, feed him for the rest of his life...

The rice and pig bank is a really brilliant idea, I reckon. Borrow a pig and pay the bank back in piglets — cash doesn't come into it at all. There are lots of imaginative ideas like that in development these days. Helping people to help themselves out and use the skills they've already got is the modern way of doing things. Bottom-up development is the way forward. Chin chin.

Urban Areas and Urbanisation

Defining urban areas isn't any easier than defining rural areas.
*These pages are for **Edexcel A**, **Edexcel B**, **OCR A**, **AQA A** and **AQA B (Option S)**.*

Urban Areas are Built Up Areas — But there are Several Definitions

1) **Urban areas** are described by the United Nations as **settlements with a population of over 20 000** but the number needed to make a town varies between countries. In Japan it's 30 000, in the USA it's 2,500, in Denmark it's 250, in Peru it's only 100.

2) **Urban areas have high population density** — in India 368 people per km² defines a town, but this varies between different countries.

3) **Urban areas have plenty of services** — as a general rule, the larger the town the more services it has.

4) **Urban areas have specialised functions** — the **more functions** a settlement has, and the **more specialised** they are, the **more urban** it is. For example, a village may have a doctor's surgery, a larger town may have a hospital, and a big city will have a large hospital and specialised clinics.

Cities can be carefully planned, or they can be developed in a haphazard, unplanned way.
Extreme examples of planned urban areas are Brasilia (the capital of Brazil) and Milton Keynes.
Extreme examples of unplanned cities are Mexico City (especially the suburbs) and Kolkata, India.

Urbanisation is the Trend for More People to Live in Towns

Urbanisation is the process by which an **increasing proportion** of people **live in towns** and **cities**.

1) **Urbanisation** occurs when **rural-urban migration** is greater than **urban-rural migration**.

2) **Urbanisation** also happens when the **natural increase** in **population** is greater in urban areas than in rural areas — when there are more births than deaths, population goes up. Simple as that.

There are **big contrasts** in the **size** of cities across the world, and in their **population density**.

Urban growth causes **urban inequality** — differences in standards of living, the range of services available and quality of life for the inhabitants.

> The patterns and causes of this social segregation will be covered on later pages.

Millionaire Cities have over 1 Million People, Mega Cities have Over 10 Million

1) A **millionaire city** has **over one million inhabitants**. There are now more than **400** millionaire cities in the world and their number is continuing to grow. The distribution of these millionaire cities is shown on the map on the right. Until the **1970s**, most of them were in **MEDCs** but by **2000**, most of the millionaire cities were in **LEDCs**.

2) **Mega cities** are those with more than **10 million** inhabitants. There were **19** of them in 2000, most in **LEDCs**.

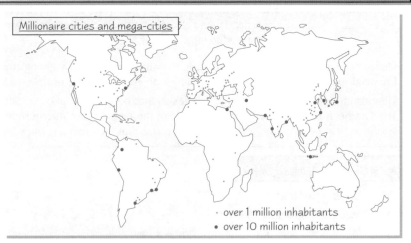

Millionaire cities and mega-cities

· over 1 million inhabitants
• over 10 million inhabitants

There are a Few World Cities of Global Importance

1) As **cities** have **grown very large** their **influence** has become wider and wider. Changes in transport and information technology have meant that this influence can now be **international**.

2) There's now a **global hierarchy** of cities. New York, Tokyo and London are at the top. They **control** the **global economy** — the **headquarters** of many **corporations**, **financial institutions**, and **international** services are sited there.

3) Below these global cities there are 3 lower tiers:
   i) Cities linked to **large international areas**, e.g. **Los Angeles** (Pacific coast and Mexico), **Singapore** (south east Asia).
   ii) Cities linking **large national economies** with the global system, e.g. **São Paulo** (Brazil), **Paris** (France).
   iii) Cities which link **sub-regional economies** with **global** systems, e.g. **Seattle** (USA, Pacific North West) and **Vancouver** (Canada, Pacific North West), **Osaka-Kobe** (Southern Honshu, Japan).

Urban Areas and Urbanisation

Urbanisation in LEDCs Happens Mainly Because of Rural-Urban Migration

1) People migrate to urban areas because of problems in the **rural areas** where they live — e.g. no jobs, decline in agriculture, poverty, poor service provision etc. These are called **push factors**.

2) There are also **pull factors** attracting people to urban areas. Services like **education** and **healthcare** are better in cities. There's more chance of a **job** in the city, and also more opportunity for work in the **informal sector**, e.g. selling cigarettes on the street, shining shoes, collecting recyclables and selling them. There's also more opportunity to make money from **crime** or **begging**.

(See p74 and p121 for more about push and pull factors.)

3) The **actual advantages** of rural-urban migration often turn out to be not quite as good as people **expect**. People may **imagine** that they'll be **well-off** in the city, only to find themselves having to **beg** on the streets.

Rapid growth of LEDC cities causes **housing**, **employment** and **pollution** problems.

1) Houses can't be built fast enough for incoming people to move into. Inward migrants build their own settlements, called **shanty towns**.

2) People migrate to towns in search of jobs — but often there **aren't enough jobs** to go around.

3) A rapidly increasing population produces rapidly increasing amounts of **pollution**.

There's more on all this later in the section.

Case Study: Urbanisation of Mexico City

Background: 1900 population 344 000. Population **doubled** every 15 years or so up to the 1970s. Migrants mainly from nearby areas.

Effects: High growth rate led to lack of space for **housing**. New areas (e.g. Chalco) developed for housing without very good services. **Pollution** increased. Central district began to decline in the 1980s, as people moved out to seek more space in the outer districts. **Squatter settlements** built with barely any services at all, and bad poverty.

Economy: Growth in **manufacturing** and **service** industries. Manufacturing based in huge **complexes**. Services in centre.

Present day: 10 million live in the central area, **18-20 million** in the whole metropolitan area. **1000-2000** people still arrive every single day. Mexico City is **financial** and **industrial** centre of Mexico.

Urbanisation in MEDCs is Currently Slower than in LEDCs

In 1990 the UN estimated that over **70%** of the population in **MEDCs** was **urbanised**, in contrast to **less than 40% in LEDCs**. They predict that by 2020 the percentages will be 77% and 53% respectively.

Urbanisation in MEDCs happened in the **19th century**, when there was a **rapid increase** in urban populations as a result of **job opportunities** offered by the **Industrial Revolution**.

Case study: Urbanisation of Manchester

Background: Original **Roman** settlement. Grew during **Industrial Revolution** in 18th century. **Population doubled** in 19th century.

Effects: Unplanned developments led to high levels of pollution and high death rates from water-borne diseases.

Management: Housing regulations post 1868 brought improvements in council and private houses. Many new estates were built. High density housing built after wartime bomb damage rebuilding and slum clearance.

Present day: Decline in industry and start of **counter-urbanisation** — people moved from the city into rural areas.

Practice Questions

Q1 What is an urban area?

Q2 What two processes contribute to urbanisation?

Q3 What's the difference between a "millionaire city" and a "mega city"?

Exam Questions

Q1 (a) What are the main causes of urbanisation in MEDCs? (2 marks)
(b) What are the main causes of urbanisation in LEDCs? (2 marks)

Q2 Most mega cities are in Asia. What does this tell you about urbanisation in the LEDC? (2 marks)

Who wants to be a millionaire city...?

It used to be that not many cities had a population of over a million. Now there are millionaire cities almost everywhere you look. Everywhere on the world map, that is, not everywhere in the house — there are no major world cities down the back of the sofa. Urbanisation, especially in LEDCs, has been happening at an incredibly fast rate. Check out that Mexico City case study. Wow.

Settlement Hierarchies

*There are quite a few different ways of looking at settlements of different sizes — that's what all this hierarchy lark is all about. These pages are for **AQA A**, **Edexcel A** and **OCR A**.*

For Each **Large Settlement**, *there's Loads of* **Smaller** *Ones*

1) The **hierarchy pyramid** shows the relationship between the **size** and **number** of settlements. Basically, there are **more small** settlements than larger ones.

2) Lots of people have tried to explain **why** there are different **sizes**, **numbers** and **spacings** of settlements. These **ideas** are covered over the next few pages, so read on...

The **Rank Size Rule** *Says* **Settlement Size** *Relates to* **Rank**

1) The **Rank Size Rule** says the **size of settlements is inversely proportional to their rank** — i.e. the **second biggest** settlement should be **half** the size of the biggest settlement, the **third biggest** settlement one **third** the size of the biggest one, and so on. A graph plotted on **logarithmic** graph paper will give a straight line if the relationship is perfect.

2) It's **rare** to find a perfect relationship because one city often **dominates** a country and becomes **much larger** than the second city — it becomes a **primate city**. These cities are usually the capital of a country, and they become the centre for **political**, **economic** and **cultural** activities. Economic growth tends to attract **investment** so the cities carry on getting bigger. **Mexico City** and **London** are examples of primate cities. Countries with primate cities are said to have a **primary distribution**.

3) Some countries have two cities of **almost equal size**, e.g. Sydney and Melbourne in Australia, or Madrid and Barcelona in Spain. This is called a **binary distribution**.

The **Size** *and* **Spacing** *of* **Settlements** *are related to their* **Services**

1) Any **settlement** that provides **services** (e.g. shops and schools) that are used by people from the surrounding settlements is known as a '**central place**'.

2) The surrounding area is called the **sphere of influence**, **urban field**, **market area** or **hinterland**.

Scattergraph of population and number of services in a part of Shropshire

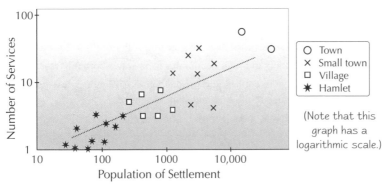

(Note that this graph has a logarithmic scale.)

Small places (e.g. villages) have small spheres of influence because the services they have only attract local people (e.g. post offices and small shops). **Large places** have a **wider range of services**, which people are prepared to **travel** to to use (e.g. universities, hospitals, or shopping centres). Because of this large places have larger spheres of influence.

All Goods and Services have a **Range** and a **Threshold**

1) A **good** or **service** has a **range** — the maximum **distance** people are prepared to travel for it. Goods or services that people are prepared to travel a long way for (e.g. a big museum) are called **high order** goods and services. Goods and services that people don't travel far to use (e.g. a newsagent) are called **low order** goods or services.

2) The **minimum number of people** needed to support a good or service is called the **threshold**. A large department store needs more customers than a village store to make a profit.

3) **London** has an enormous **variety** of services such as shops, theatres, restaurants and museums, many with **huge** ranges (even worldwide) and thresholds. This means its **sphere of influence** is very large. Lots of settlements of this size could **not** exist very close together, because there would be too much **competition**.

Settlement Hierarchies

Reilly's Law Lets You Work Out Theoretical Sphere of Influence

Before you read this check that you **really** understand the term '**sphere of influence**' because things are about to get silly.

Reilly's law of retail gravitation says "two centres interact by **attracting trade** from other places in **direct proportion** to the **size** of each centre and in **inverse proportion** to the square of the **distance** between them". This basically means...

1) **Larger** centres **attract more business** than smaller ones. ← *More people go to large towns to shop than to small towns.*

2) The **amount of trade** one town gets from another town **increases** the **closer together** the two towns are. There's **less and less trade** the **further** the two towns are **apart**. This is called **distance decay**. *People go to nearby large towns, not large towns hundreds of miles away.*

3) Reilly's Law lets you calculate the edge of the **sphere of influence** between two settlements by using the **break point** formula:

$$\text{Break point between 2 towns} = \frac{\text{distance from town A to town B}}{1+\sqrt{\text{population of town A} \div \text{population of town B}}}$$

... where A is the larger town and B is the smaller town.

If two towns are the **same size** and **importance** the dividing line or **break point** between two spheres of influence should be exactly **halfway** between the two towns.

Working out the Actual Sphere of Influence is Trickier

Reilly's Law gives you the **theoretical** sphere of influence. This probably won't be the same as the **actual** sphere of influence.

Reilly's Law uses some **basic assumptions** that might not be correct. It assumes that the **larger** the town the **greater the attraction**, and that people **always** go to the **nearest** town. But in reality, other factors might affect where people go too e.g.:

1) There may be **traffic problems** in getting to the larger town, and parking may be more **expensive** once you're there.

2) Shops in the smaller centre may be **fewer** but of **higher quality**.

3) The smaller centre may be **less congested**, **cleaner** and **safer**.

4) The smaller town may **advertise** its services better.

5) People's positive or negative **perceptions** of a place may **override other factors**.

Spheres of influence are also influenced by infrastructure and physical geography.

1) The sphere of influence may be **stretched out** in the direction of a **good road**, e.g. a **motorway**. Customers can reach the central place faster on the motorway, so people from **further away** will go into the town from that direction.

2) **Natural features** like **hills** and **rivers** can act as **barriers** making it harder for people to get to central places. This can change the **shape** of the sphere of influence, for example it might get **squashed in** on the hilly side of a town.

3) Settlements on the **coast** would have a semi-circular sphere of influence — rather obvious, you might think, as people don't come into town from the bottom of the sea. It'll still get you marks in the exam, though.

Practice Questions

Q1 What is the "range" of a good?

Q2 What is a primate city? Name one example from an MEDC, and one from an LEDC.

Q3 Using Reilly's formula calculate the breakpoint between towns A and B if:
the population of town A is 36 000, the population of town B is 4 000 and the distance between A and B is 32km.

Exam Questions

Q1 Explain why a centre's actual sphere of influence might be different from its theoretical sphere of influence (6 marks)

That's quite a lot of fuss to make about where people go shopping...

You know, I really wish I knew why geographers felt the need for all these theories. The idea that people go to the most convenient place to shop is fairly sensible, though, especially when you take traffic, attitudes and physical factors into account. Think about where the biggest shops near where you live are and where you go to get small items like sweets and magazines.

SECTION EIGHT — THE URBAN ENVIRONMENT

Cycle of Urbanisation

Cities grow and develop in a cycle. First there's urbanisation, then suburbanisation and counter-urbanisation. Finally, there's reurbanisation — people move back into the city. These pages are for **OCR A**, **AQA A**, **AQA B** *and* **Edexcel B**.

Suburbanisation is Migration from City Centre to Suburbs

All your urbanisation gubbins is on pages 80-81.

1) In MEDCs, suburbanisation started in the **19th and early 20th** centuries.

2) Suburbanisation is made possible by the growth in public and private transport — people living in suburbs need to be able to travel easily to work in the city centre. **Early suburban growth** tended to be **along railway lines** but as **public transport** systems **spread** throughout the town, the areas between these routes were developed as well. Recent suburbanisation has been made possible by the huge increase in car ownership (see p104).

3) The following table shows the **push factors** and **pull factors** which cause **suburbanisation**.

	Push factors (away from the city)	Pull factors (towards the suburbs)
public	Crowded housing, with no gardens. Traffic congestion, pollution. Fear of crime.	Low density housing with gardens. Pleasant open spaces. Suburbs are seen as safer.
employers	Office space is expensive. Land is expensive. Transport systems overstretched.	Cheaper land for development, with room for spacious office developments. New roads, railways etc.

4) Cities **grow outwards** into the surrounding area, **engulfing** the surrounding **villages** and **towns**, until they eventually form an almost **continuous urban area** called a **conurbation**. This "**exurban growth**" (growth out of the urban area) causes problems.

5) There are **environmental problems** — air pollution, water pollution and damage to natural habitats (see p106-107).

6) **Urban sprawl** is huge, spreading suburbs, characterised by low density housing and business developments. People travel by car, because their homes are out of reach of public transport systems. This increases **congestion** on the roads. Urban sprawl doesn't mean a city is increasing in population — it means it's spreading out over a large area.

Suburbanisation in Manchester:

Inner city:	In the 1960s, high rise flats and high density housing were built in central districts, e.g. Hulme and Moss Side. Many of these areas became ghettos of social deprivation and high unemployment with inner city riots and continuing high levels of crime.
Outward growth:	Housing estates were added to the city edge.
Suburbanisation:	Commuter villages on outskirts became suburbanised. These are still growing, e.g. Cheadle Hulme, Wilmslow, Alderley Edge, Shaw, Middleton.

Urban Sprawl

Urban growth in LEDCs generally occurred later than in MEDCs. It's been fastest since 1950.

Growth in LEDCs tends to be more haphazard. When migrants come into the town faster than the town can provide houses, they build their own makeshift houses — these are called squatter settlements (shanty towns).

As well as housing, there are often industrial developments in the suburbs of LEDC cities, e.g. Mexico City.

Rapid urban growth has had an impact on LEDC cities. Shortages of jobs and housing and increased pollution have caused problems in Mexico City (squatter settlements, pollution), Kolkata (slums, begging) and São Paulo (squatter settlements).

Counter-Urbanisation is Migration Away from the City to Rural Areas

1) In the **late 20th century** in MEDCs, people have begun to **move out** from **cities** and **suburbs** into **surrounding villages**. People move to rural areas because they dislike the traffic, pollution, crime rates and high house prices in towns, and fancy a quieter, rural life.

2) Counter-urbanisation has been made easier first by **commuter transport** and more recently by the **growth in working from home** and using **email** to communicate with the office.

3) This **movement out** from cities causes many **changes, problems and conflicts** in the **rural-urban fringe** area. The impacts on rural areas are covered in Section 7. The impacts on the rural-urban fringe are covered in detail on p96-p97.

4) Don't get **suburbanisation** and **counter-urbanisation** mixed up. Suburbanisation is when people move to the **suburbs**, not out into **rural areas**.

Cycle of Urbanisation

Suburbanisation and Counter-Urbanisation Can Cause Inner City Decline

After **urban-suburban migration**, and **urban-rural migration**, inner city residential areas are **depopulated**. They don't have enough people living there to support local businesses, so **shops and businesses close down**. Empty, boarded-up shops look horrible, and attract **crime** and **vandalism**.

The people who still live in run-down inner cities usually **don't have high-paid job**s — they may be **unemployed** or in **low-paid work**. This means that there isn't **local wealth** to **invest** in maintaining the local environment, and things **just get worse**. This is called a "**multiplier effect**".

Reurbanisation is Migration Back to the City Centre

1) Most **MEDC cities** have made major improvements to their **town centre** areas in recent years and the latest **trend** is for people to **move back into the city centre**. Former **office blocks**, **factory units** and **warehouses** have been **converted** into **up-market apartment blocks** which are very attractive to young affluent people.

2) Residents are **close** to the **leisure** and **cultural activities** on offer in the town centre. They don't have to commute any more — commuting to work can be a huge hassle. The **money** and **time** they save on transport to work can be spent on **luxury housing** and **leisure**.

3) These developments often go hand in hand with **urban rejuvenation projects.**

Urban rejuvenation is covered on p95.

4) Reurbanisation is not seen in cities in LEDCs.

Reurbanisation in Manchester:

New Housing:	**High** rise flats in Hulme were demolished, and new housing has been built on the site. Warehouses have been redeveloped into flats, e.g. in Castlefields. There are penthouses above the Arndale Shopping Centre. Council flats and terraced council houses have been replaced by low-rise, low-density houses.
Occupants:	Mainly single professionals and young couples with no children.
City Centre:	City centre locations are safer with CCTV.

There's also been serious reurbanisation in Birmingham and Glasgow.

All This Lot is Often Called the Cycle Of Urbanisation

First comes **urbanisation** — cities grow as people move in from rural areas, and as more kids are born in urban areas.

Population growth in urban areas and the development of transport mean **suburbanisation** happens.

Next comes **counter-urbanisation** — people fancy a nice new life out in the country.

Finally there's **reurbanisation** — a tired old city centre gets a **make-over**, and young trendies come flooding back.

It's <u>called</u> a cycle, but that doesn't mean that once reurbanisation happens, all the other stages happen again, and again, and again.

Practice Questions

Q1   Define each of the following terms relating to the growth and development of towns and cities. Make sure that your definitions show the differences between the terms:
a) urbanisation   b) suburbanisation   c) counter-urbanisation   d) reurbanisation

Q2   Explain why suburbanisation can cause inner city decline.

Exam Questions

Q1   Describe how cities grow and develop. Discuss both LEDCs and MEDCs in your answer.   (8 marks)

Q2   With reference to a named city in an MEDC, describe and explain what has been done to reurbanise and regenerate the inner city area.   (7 marks)

This is all a bit too much like the Hokey Cokey...

Move in to the city, move out of the city, move back in to the city again... in, out, shake it all about... Anyway, there are altogether far too many words ending in -urbanisation on this page. Make sure you've got the definitions learned, and get the cycle of urbanisation sorted in your head while you're at it. Learn what causes the main movements, and what the effects are.

British Cities Through History

*You can see evidence of the past in British cities — Roman walls, medieval churches, Georgian town houses, minging 1960s office blocks — it's all there. These pages are for **AQA B Option T** — the historical option.*

Towns Developed over Hundreds of Years

1) **Roman towns** were usually small, **rectangular**, based round the **forum** (a complex of buildings where the administrative buildings and temples were), and within **protective walls**.

2) **Medieval towns** typically have a **grid-iron street pattern** and land divided into regular plots called **chequers**. There was usually a **market place**, a **Guildhall** and a **parish church**. Some new towns were established in the Middle Ages, e.g. Liverpool, but most failed to survive the **Black Death**. The "**Bastide**" **towns** of North Wales e.g. Caernarfon are medieval, built quickly to a set plan to defend territory in newly occupied areas.

3) **Tudor** architecture is characterised by **timber framed houses** with whitewashing between the timbers.

You can see evidence of the **historical development** of towns in their **present day structure**. Most evidence of the past is removed as newer building phases build over earlier stages though.

1) There's evidence of Roman towns in **street patterns**, e.g. in York. Evidence of Roman buildings such as **baths** and **town halls** is seen in Roman settlements of the south and east of Britain, and in **York**, **Chester** and **Leicester**.

2) Evidence of medieval towns is seen in the street pattern — a **network** of **small narrow streets** is typical of a medieval town. Some castles and city walls still remain, e.g. **Conwy**, **Caernarfon**, **Ludlow**.

3) Some **half-timbered Tudor houses** remain, especially in central England, e.g. in **Worcester**, **Leominster** and **Ludlow**.

Case Study — York

Roman:	York was a main town in northern Britain. There was a legionary fortress. The town walls had corner towers, e.g. the Multangular Tower. There were gates through the walls, e.g. Bootham Bar.
Medieval:	Present city walls are medieval. Micklegate Bar was built as the gate to the road to London. York Minster was built over the Roman fortress. The narrow winding streets followed the Roman street pattern. The Shambles was built as a butchery area with meat hooks — it's still there today.
Renaissance:	Half-timbered buildings remain from the Renaissance period, e.g. Merchant Adventurers Hall, and houses on Lady Row, Goodramgate.
Georgian:	Castle Green prison opened (it's now a museum). Mansion House, Fairfax House and the Assembly Rooms were built.
19th century:	New Earswick garden village was built by Rowntree.
20th century:	New estates on the outskirts, e.g. Acomb.

Georgian and Regency Towns Were Inspired by Greek and Roman Buildings

Georgian (1714-1830) and **Regency** (1811-1820) architecture was inspired by **classical Greek** and **Roman** architecture. It's often called **neo-classical** architecture. It used a lot of columns, and generally tried to give buildings the look of an Ancient Greek temple (like the Parthenon in Athens).

Georgian and Regency buildings are likely to have these features:

1) They're built on a **rectangular** plan, and they have a **symmetrical** front.

2) The windows are **sash windows**, divided into **several panes of glass**. Top floor windows are much smaller than bottom floor windows — the top floors were the servants' quarters.

3) There's an ornate **portico** (porch) above the front door, with **columns** at the side of the door.

4) There are **wrought iron railings** outside, and **wrought iron decoration** outside the windows.

Case Study — Bath

Bath is the best example of **neo-classical architecture** and town planning in the UK.

Architects:	John Wood and Robert Adam rebuilt a lot of Bath in the neo-classical style. John Wood researched the Roman origins of Bath, and decided to design houses and public buildings in a Roman style.
Buildings:	The Pump Rooms (built 1796) used the natural spa to attract wealthy visitors (Bath became very fashionable in Georgian and Regency times). The Assembly Rooms were built in 1769 as public meeting rooms. Lawns, trees, and avenues were part of the plan to create a beautiful town. Identical, elegant three-storey houses were built in semicircular crescents, e.g. Royal Crescent and Lansdowne Crescent. There's even a completely circular street of houses — Bath Circus.

British Cities Through History

The **Industrial Town** of the **19th Century** Developed Around **Factories**

As industries developed in the 19th century, people flocked to work in the factories. In **1801**, **17%** of the population lived in towns with over 20 000 people. In **1891**, **53%** lived in towns with over 20 000 inhabitants.

1) People had **little choice** but to live near to their workplace, so lots of high-density, **poorly-built houses** were built **around the mills and factories**. There were **no planning regulations** so **speculative builders** packed as many houses as possible into the smallest space possible — houses were **tiny back-to-back terraces** around **unpaved courts** with **no sewers**, **refuse disposal** or fresh **clean water**.

2) Because there were **no sewers**, and **no clean water**, **diseases** such as **tuberculosis**, **cholera** and **typhoid** were **very common**. **Life expectancy** was **low** and **infant mortality rates** were very **high** — more than 200 children per 1000 died before they were 5 years old. Few realised the **connection** between **housing conditions** and **health**, so public health improvements were very slow. The **1844 Public Health Act** to provide clean water wasn't compulsory, so it didn't achieve much.

3) The **1875 Public Health Act** finally **forced** local authorities to provide and maintain **sewage** and **rubbish disposal**, provide a clean drinking water supply, pave and light streets and monitor public health — including the control of infectious diseases.

4) **Prosperity** brought by manufacturing and foreign trade links encouraged wealthy people to be proud of their towns. They **built civic buildings**, e.g. town halls, libraries and museums. This caused even more overcrowding, because town centre houses were knocked down to accommodate them.

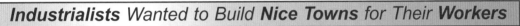

Fresh, clean drinking water, 1874.

1) By-Law Housing was built to provide homes for the large number of rural-urban migrants in the 19th century. The building of this housing was controlled by Local Authorities.

2) Back-to-back housing was made illegal in 1864, because of the health risks. After 1864, long terraces of houses were built, with back alleys between the rows — there are still terraces of streets just like this in towns all over Britain. Streets were laid out in a linear (straight line) pattern.

Industrialists Wanted to Build Nice Towns for Their Workers

1) Some **employers** reacted against the **appalling conditions** of the industrial towns. They realised that a **happy, healthy workforce** was **better for the company**, and set about building decent housing for their workers.

2) Enlightened industrialists like Titus Salt and George Cadbury built **garden villages** with **lower density housing** and a **garden** for each house to encourage workers to grow produce to improve their diet and health.

3) **Trees** and **green recreational space** were provided. Community facilities such as a **church**, a **school** and a **library** encouraged community pride and encouraged workers to "better themselves".

4) Examples include **Saltaire** (built 1850-1876 by Titus Salt for his mill workers), **Port Sunlight** (built in 1888 by Lord Lever for his soap factory workers), **Bournville** (built by the Cadbury family for workers in the Cadbury chocolate factory) and **New Earswick** (founded by Joseph Rowntree in 1904).

Practice Questions

Q1 How do we know that towns have undergone periods of growth in the past?
Q2 What sort of buildings and street patterns were characteristic of the following periods of urban growth?
 a) Roman b) Medieval c) Georgian/Regency d) The 19th century industrial town
Q3 Why was urban reform needed in the 19th century?

Exam Questions

Q1 Describe the evidence of the past growth of a town you have studied. (5 marks)

Q2 Describe and explain the problems of urban slums in the industrial towns of the 19th century. (7 marks)

Features of Bath — 1) rubber ducky, 2) taps...

If you're doing AQA B Option T, then you need to be prepared to give some detail. That means knowing a few facts about Roman, medieval and Tudor features, and knowing several facts about Georgian and Regency features — including the names of places where you'd see them. You'll also need a few facts about back-to-back housing, by-law terraces and garden villages.

New Towns

*New Towns were planned and built in the 20th century to solve overcrowding problems. This page is for **AQA B (Option T)**, **Edexcel A** and **Edexcel B**. It's useful for **AQA A** and **OCR A** too. But the next page is just for **AQA B (Option T)**.*

In the **20th Century**, "New Towns" were built in the UK

Urban planning began after World War 2, with two main purposes:
1) To **stop**, **limit** or **guide** the **outward spread** of large urban areas.
2) To improve the **economic** and **social** conditions within the towns.

1) The **Town and Country Planning Act** of **1947** introduced a **green belt** around London to try to curb urban sprawl. Green belts are broad bands of countryside around a town, where **planning regulations** prevent house building.

2) Excess population was accommodated beyond the green belt in either **New Towns** or pre-existing towns.

3) The **New Towns Act** of **1946** was an attempt to **relieve overcrowding** within the major UK cities, and to **regulate** the amount of **migration** to **existing cities**.

4) **Eight New Towns** were built around London between 1946 and 1949. People were **moved out of inner city** slum areas into the New Towns. New Towns also met the need for housing after bomb damage from World War 2.

5) New Towns were designed to be **self-sufficient and balanced** with a range of manufacturing, shopping, services and entertainment facilities. They were designed to provide employment for all the inhabitants. They were also intended to have a good mix of ethnic groups.

6) Two further phases of New Town developments followed. Some were built as "**growth poles**" in areas of high unemployment, e.g. Washington in the North East. No New Towns have been built since 1970.

Location of New Towns in the United Kingdom

Growth poles are places which stimulate growth around them — the idea is that growth tends to happen in a few specific areas, not everywhere at once.

Note — Welwyn Garden City was actually founded back in 1920 as a "garden city". Garden cities were early forerunners of New Towns — planned towns with lots of nice green open space. Welwyn was reclassified as a New Town under the New Towns Act.

New Towns have had Mixed Success

Successes of New Towns:
1) They provide **spacious homes** with **modern conveniences**.
2) They're in **semi-rural surroundings** with low levels of pollution.
3) There are **job opportunities** in **modern industrial premises**.
4) Some have attracted **foreign** companies to open up factories there.
5) Some have become "**growth poles**" in their own right, e.g. Milton Keynes.

Another advantage of New Towns is that the land uses are separated — industry is in a separate zone to housing.

Failures of New Towns:
1) New Towns were **rarely self-sufficient**, particularly in the early days — the provision of services tends to **follow demand**, so services weren't there ready and waiting for new residents.
2) There aren't always **new jobs** in New Towns. Increased mobility allows commuters to occupy the New Towns and travel to their **original** place of work.
3) The provision of **services** (e.g. leisure amenities and shops) is often **inadequate** for the size of the population.
4) Modern architectural styles (especially 1960s concrete) are seen as **ugly**.
5) The desired **social mixing** wasn't achieved. Residents who didn't fit in with their neighbours asked the council to be transferred to another neighbourhood.

Building Materials and Techniques

Building Materials and Techniques have Changed in Recent Years

Post-war building of **high rise flats** and **office blocks** in pre-cast concrete
were influenced by the idea that a house should be "a machine for living in".

Prefabrication

1) Prefabricated houses ("prefabs" for short) were built after World War 2,
   to replace bombed out city centre housing, and inner city slums.
   They were made from **steel panels**, **concrete** and **asbestos**.

2) **Asbestos** is light, easy to cut to shape, and fireproof.
   Unfortunately, it's also very **dangerous** — it causes a nasty lung disease.
   The designers of prefabricated buildings didn't know this though.

3) Prefabricated houses had **"all mod cons"** — hot and cold running
   water, a flush toilet, etc. This was a step up from London slums.
   Inhabitants **loved** them, and there was **huge demand** for prefabs.

4) The post-war prefabricated houses were meant to be **temporary**.
   Prefabricated houses and public buildings (e.g. schools) are now **worn
   out**, and most have been demolished. There are still some of the old
   prefabs in Newport, Bristol and Birmingham.

_Concrete and shiny reinforced glass
skyscrapers in London's Docklands_

New Materials

1) New materials have allowed architects to push the boat out.

2) Reinforced **concrete** and **plate glass** are commonly used.
   Reinforced concrete is reinforced with **steel rods**.

3) **Flat roofed** buildings have waterproof **felt** roofs.

4) **Cladding** has been used to give fancy finishes to the external
   walls of buildings.

High rise buildings

1) Modern cities include **high rise buildings**. It wouldn't be possible to
   build **high buildings** without using **steel girders** to make a frame.

2) The invention of the **lift** also made it possible to build high rise blocks.

3) **Elevated walkways** were used in 1960s housing blocks. The idea was that they'd be
   "cities in the sky" — unfortunately, a lot of them turned out to attract crime.

Practice Questions

Q1 Name three New Towns in the South East, one in the North East and one in Wales.

Q2 Give three good points and three bad points of New Towns.

Q3 Name three technologies that were necessary to allow the building of skyscrapers with glass walls.

Exam Questions

Q1 With reference to a specific New Town(s), describe the reasons for its construction and explain its layout. (7 marks)

Q2 Many people consider New Towns in the UK to have been a great success.
Other people disagree. Discuss the reasons for these two contrasting views. (7 marks)

Q3 Describe the ways in which named new building technologies changed the look of cities in England. (6 marks)

One thing about these New Towns — they have too many roundabouts...

_It's true — part of the plan for New Towns included lots of roundabouts on the road. Hemel Hempstead even has a big
roundabout with six small roundabouts on the way around it. It's a shame that New Towns turned out to be not as good as the
"urban utopia" of the post war plan. Some turned out alright, though. Don't forget the new building styles if you're doing AQA B._

Urban Land Use

Geographers have come up with various different models of land use in cities and towns. These pages are for **OCR A**, **AQA A**, **Edexcel A** and **Edexcel B**.

Note that AQA people don't need to know the names or details of the models — just the general gist of how urban land is used in different places.

Here's a Quick Run-Down of **Urban Land Functions**

Land in cities has to be used for **residential**, **industrial**, **office**, **retail** and **recreational** uses.
Office, **retail** and **entertainment** are all based in the **Central Business District** (**CBD** for short).

The **Burgess** Land Use Model is Based on **Concentric Rings**

Burgess (1925) based his urban land use model on Chicago. He suggested that **towns grow outwards evenly from a central core** and each zone gradually colonises the next outward zone. His model suggests **five concentric zones**:

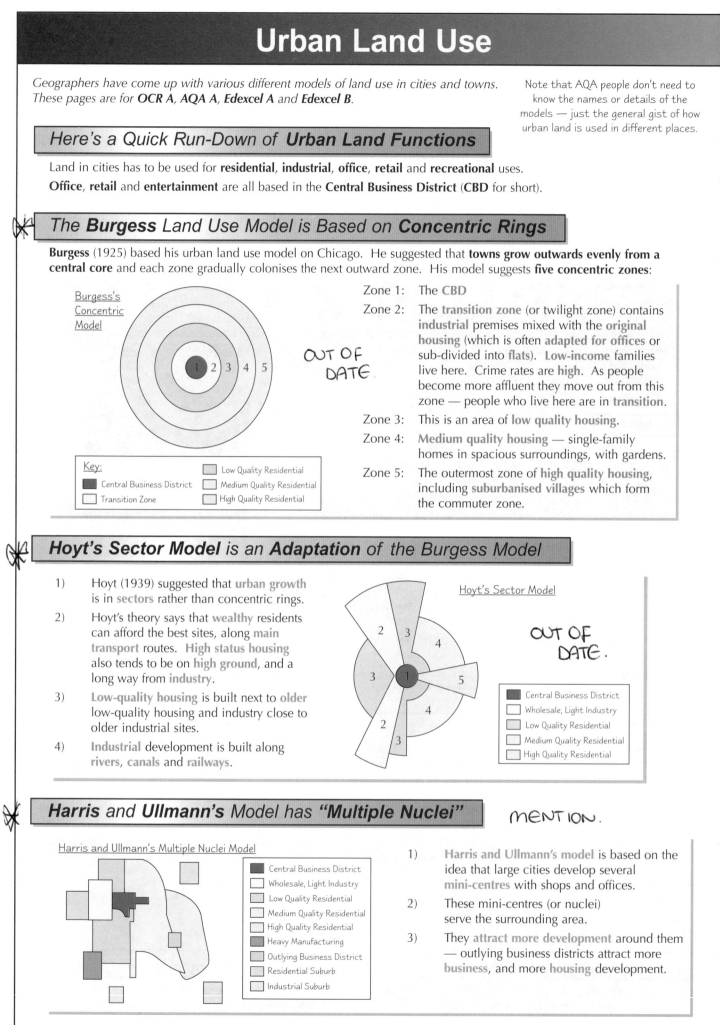

Burgess's Concentric Model

OUT OF DATE.

Key:
- Central Business District
- Transition Zone
- Low Quality Residential
- Medium Quality Residential
- High Quality Residential

Zone 1: The **CBD**

Zone 2: The **transition zone** (or twilight zone) contains **industrial** premises mixed with the **original housing** (which is often **adapted for offices** or sub-divided into **flats**). **Low-income** families live here. Crime rates are **high**. As people become more affluent they move out from this zone — people who live here are in **transition**.

Zone 3: This is an area of **low quality housing**.

Zone 4: **Medium quality housing** — single-family homes in spacious surroundings, with gardens.

Zone 5: The outermost zone of **high quality housing**, including **suburbanised villages** which form the commuter zone.

Hoyt's Sector Model is an Adaptation of the Burgess Model

1) Hoyt (1939) suggested that **urban growth** is in **sectors** rather than concentric rings.

2) Hoyt's theory says that **wealthy** residents can afford the best sites, along **main transport** routes. **High status housing** also tends to be on **high ground**, and a long way from **industry**.

3) **Low-quality housing** is built next to **older** low-quality housing and industry close to older industrial sites.

4) **Industrial** development is built along **rivers**, **canals** and **railways**.

Hoyt's Sector Model

OUT OF DATE.

- Central Business District
- Wholesale, Light Industry
- Low Quality Residential
- Medium Quality Residential
- High Quality Residential

Harris and Ullmann's Model has "Multiple Nuclei"

MENTION.

Harris and Ullmann's Multiple Nuclei Model

- Central Business District
- Wholesale, Light Industry
- Low Quality Residential
- Medium Quality Residential
- High Quality Residential
- Heavy Manufacturing
- Outlying Business District
- Residential Suburb
- Industrial Suburb

1) **Harris and Ullmann's model** is based on the idea that large cities develop several **mini-centres** with shops and offices.

2) These mini-centres (or nuclei) serve the surrounding area.

3) They **attract more development** around them — outlying business districts attract more **business**, and more **housing** development.

Urban Land Use

Mann Developed a Model for British Cities

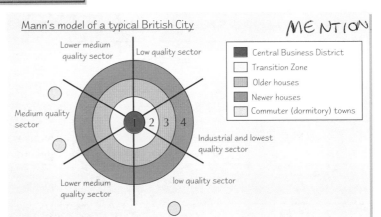

1) **Mann** (1965) combined the Burgess and Hoyt models to produce a model for the **typical British city**.

2) He thought that **cities develop outwards** in **concentric circles**, but **income groups** cluster in **sectors**. So, you'd have a **low quality sector** with old houses in the middle, and newer council houses towards the outside, and a **medium quality sector** with old houses in the middle and newer executive homes towards the outside.

3) Prevailing wind direction means that **higher quality housing** would be to the west, upwind of industrial air pollution.

4) Since **car ownership** is now more common, there are **commuter villages** outside the urban area.

5) In this model, zone 3 (older houses) is made up of **terraced houses** in the lower quality sectors, **medium to large houses** in the lower medium quality sector and **large older villas** in the medium quality sector.

Robson Developed a Model Specifically for Sunderland

Come on, you Mackems...

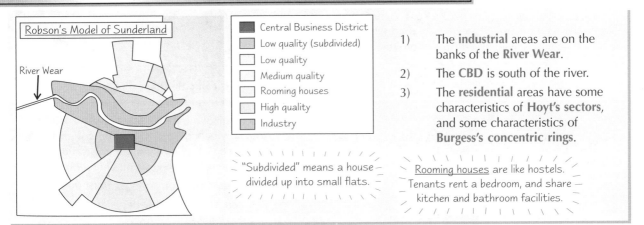

1) The **industrial** areas are on the banks of the **River Wear**.

2) The **CBD** is south of the river.

3) The **residential** areas have some characteristics of **Hoyt's sectors**, and some characteristics of **Burgess's concentric rings**.

"Subdivided" means a house divided up into small flats.

Rooming houses are like hostels. Tenants rent a bedroom, and share kitchen and bathroom facilities.

Be Careful if You're Using These Models in the Exam...

If you only mention the **Burgess** or **Hoyt** models, you won't get the **best marks available** — they're very simplified models, and they're out of date. You'll be fine if you can compare them to one of the better models (e.g. **Mann** or **Robson**).

If you want to **compare** MEDC land use with LEDC land use, or if you want to give **reasons** behind these models, you'll need the next page.

Practice Questions

Q1   What are the main types of land use found in towns?

Q2   What city was Burgess's model based on, and when did Burgess come up with his ideas?

Q3   In Mann's urban land use model, why is the medium quality housing to the west of the city?

Q4   Give a reason why the high quality residential districts of Sunderland are situated a long way from the city centre.

Exam Questions

Q1   Draw and describe a land use model for a standard MEDC city.   (5 marks)

Oooh, pretty pictures...

The annoying thing here is that all the pretty pictures look so similar. Make sure you don't get them mixed up — a good way to do this is to talk your way through the diagram as you look through it. Make sure you can explain what's where, and why it might be there. Definitely learn one of the UK specific models, either Mann or Robson.

Urban Land Use

Land Use models tend to be different for LEDCs.
*These pages are for **Edexcel A**, **Edexcel B**, **AQA A**, **AQA B** and **OCR A**.*

Sjoberg's Model Shows Land Use in *Pre-Industrial Cities* in *LEDCs*

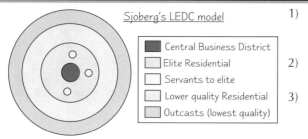

Sjoberg's LEDC model

- █ Central Business District
- ☐ Elite Residential
- ☐ Servants to elite
- ☐ Lower quality Residential
- ☐ Outcasts (lowest quality)

1) **Sjoberg** saw that some **LEDC urban areas** had got quite large without going through industrialisation. He called these **pre-industrial cities**.

2) In these cities, most transport is still on foot, so the wealthiest choose to live close to the CBD. The poorest live furthest away.

3) Sjoberg's model applies to many **LEDC cities** where the **governing elite** lives **centrally** and the lower the status of the social group, the further out they live. Foreign and minority groups are often segregated into distinct areas of the town.

Different Models Were Developed for *Different LEDCs*

1) **Griffin and Ford** based their model on **Latin America**.

2) The **main difference** is the **location of housing types**. **Higher quality** houses are **close to the CBD**, and the **poorest** housing is on the **outskirts**, often in the form of squatter settlements.

3) Many Latin American cities have a **commercial spine**, including **high quality residential areas** and the main cultural activities, leading outwards from the CBD.

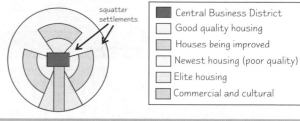

Griffin and Ford's model of a typical Latin American City

squatter settlements

- █ Central Business District
- ☐ Good quality housing
- ▨ Houses being improved
- ☐ Newest housing (poor quality)
- ☐ Elite housing
- ▨ Commercial and cultural

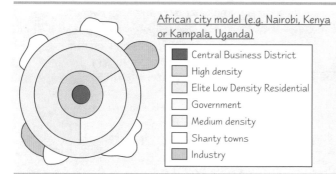

African city model (e.g. Nairobi, Kenya or Kampala, Uganda)

- ● Central Business District
- ☐ High density
- ☐ Elite Low Density Residential
- ☐ Government
- ☐ Medium density
- ☐ Shanty towns
- ▨ Industry

1) Many **African cities** have a **high-density core** occupied by **indigenous groups**.

2) **This is surrounded by** a **low-density** zone **originally** occupied by the **white colonial elite**. This zone is now used for **administration**, and **housing for the governmental elite**.

3) Medium density housing surrounds this zone.

4) There are **squatter settlements** and **industry** on the outskirts of the town.

1) Many **South Asian** (Indian) cities were originally **colonial ports** with a central **walled fort**.

2) The **CBD** is **separate** and surrounded by **low-density housing**, originally occupied by European colonists.

3) The **indigenous people** originally lived in **segregated areas** of **unplanned** housing.

Model of an Indian City
(such as Mumbai, Chennai, Cochin etc)

sea

- ☐ Fort
- ☐ Port
- ▨ Port extension
- ☐ Open space
- ▨ Administration
- █ CBD

- ☐ Anglo-Indian residential
- ☐ Indian residential
- ☐ European residential
- ▨ Bazaar — commercial/residential
- ☐ Stages of new wealthy middle-income residential extensions

Various Factors Explain *Land Use Patterns* in both *LEDCs* and *MEDCs*

1) **Accessibility** is the most important factor. Businesses which need lots of customers or lots of workers need to locate somewhere very accessible. **City centres** are very **accessible**. Roads, bus routes and railways converge on the city centre. Areas on **main transport routes** are also **accessible**. Industries need to be close to road, rail, rivers, canals or ports so they can easily bring in supplies and parts, and distribute finished products.

2) **Mobility** is a factor — the more people have **cars**, the further away from their place of work they can live. **Low income** families in MEDCs without a private car tend to live near **city centres** and on main **bus routes**.

3) Some land uses **attract similar users**. **Families** tend to live in neighbourhoods with **similar people** — birds of a feather flock together and all that. **Shops cluster together** so that they can benefit from the same customers.

4) Some land uses **repel other land uses**. Factories which produce lots of **pollution** put people off living near them. People who can **afford** it choose to live or work away from sources of air pollution.

Urban Land Use

Bid-Rent Theory is All About Desirability and Money

1) An explanation for urban land use patterns is that some parts of the town are **more desirable** than others. This **creates competition** — in a free market whoever can make most **profit** from the site bids highest and buys the land.

2) The amount that land users are prepared to pay for a site is called the **bid rent**.

3) Competition is **fiercest** in the **town centre** because it's most **accessible** and **land is scarce**. Land is **most expensive** here. **Away** from the city centre, **demand** for land **falls**, so people are prepared to pay less for it.

4) **Bid rent theory** produces a **concentric** pattern of land use — banks will pay most in the CBD, and don't much bother with land outside the CBD, so they're concentrated in the CBD. (Factories aren't willing to pay as much as banks in the CBD, but they'll pay more than banks and shops in outer zones.)

5) Nowadays other sites in a town have become sought after — along main roads, or close to out of town **business parks**, **shopping centres** and **industrial estates**. This has caused the shapes of traditional land use models to change.

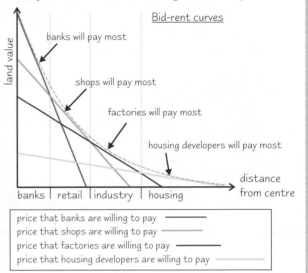

Bid-rent curves

banks will pay most

shops will pay most

factories will pay most

housing developers will pay most

land value / distance from centre

banks | retail | industry | housing

price that banks are willing to pay ————
price that shops are willing to pay ————
price that factories are willing to pay ————
price that housing developers are willing to pay ————

Urban Morphology Means the Way Streets are Laid Out

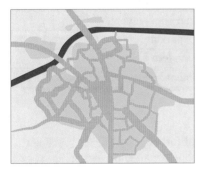

Traditional **medieval** town centre, with **narrow, irregular** streets. The older parts of LEDC cities are often like this, as are some MEDC cities.

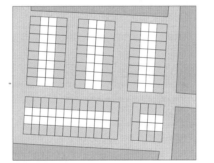

19th century low quality **housing**, in long terraces with a small back yard.

Late 20th century **medium quality suburban housing. Detached houses** and **gardens** are important to people in MEDC countries, especially the **UK**.

Practice Questions

Q1 Sketch out Sjoberg's simple LEDC land use model, and label it.

Q2 Where are the commercial functions found in Griffin & Ford's model of a Latin American city?

Q3 Draw and explain a bid-rent graph for a typical town.

Q4 How is the morphology of 19th century workers' terraced cottages different from that of suburban housing?

Exam Questions

Q1 Urban land use structure in MEDCs is often very different to that in LEDCs.
Describe some of the main differences and suggest reasons for them.

(7 marks)

That's all very well, but where's the Burger King and the KFC...?

On these pages, you don't have to learn all the LEDC models. You should know at least one or two, though. You need to be able to contrast them with MEDC land use models. One thing that you definitely need to be clear on is the list of reasons why land use arranges itself in sectors, concentric rings and the like. Bid rents are part of this, so take your time to get them stuck in your head.

Changing Urban Structure

Social and economic conditions change, and this forces changes on the structure of cities.
These pages are for **Edexcel A**, **Edexcel B**, **AQA A** *and* **AQA B**. *Also useful for* **OCR A**.

The **Central Business District** (CBD) is **Changing**

1) The CBD is traditionally the centre for **business**, **commercial** and **government** activities. It's the focus of **transport routes** and it has the highest **land values**, the **tallest buildings** and the **most pedestrians**.

2) However there's often **segregation** of different activities within the CBD — **retailing** tends to form an **inner core**, surrounded by an outer core of **professional** and **commercial services** and entertainment. Beyond this is the "**frame**" — the outer part of the CBD which contains light industries, wholesaling, railway stations and car parks.

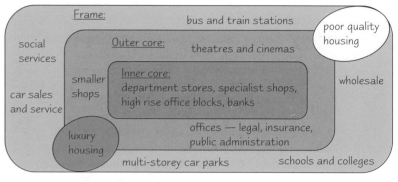

Structure of the Central Business District

3) The CBD is an area of constant change. Many CBDs seem to be **moving outwards** in some areas — creating "**assimilation zones**". In others, the CBD is shrinking — forming "**discard zones**".

Decentralisation is the **Movement Away** from the **CBD**

Decentralisation includes both residential and business movement away from the CBD. The table shows the **push factors** (away from the CBD) and the **pull factors** (towards the outskirts and suburbs).

Push factors away from the CBD	Pull factors towards the periphery (outskirts)
High **land cost** and high **rent**.	Pleasant, **attractive** environment.
High **crime rate**.	**Safe**, **quiet** environment.
Traffic congestion and **noise**.	Plenty of **parking**.
Air pollution.	Newer, **modern** buildings.
Very **limited space** to expand.	**Government grants** and **incentives**.

There are **Pushes** and **Pulls** in City Centres

1) Factors which push people and businesses away from the city are called **centrifugal forces**. **Retail stores** move to **out of town** sites because these are more **convenient** for shoppers with cars (and for one-stop shopping), and have much more **space** for **large stores**. Pubs and bars have taken over from shops and banks in some CBDs, e.g. Nottingham.

2) Factors which pull people towards the city centre are called **centripetal forces**. Major **redevelopments** have taken place in most major cities to attract affluent residents back into the city centre. **Rejuvenated** city centres are **attractive** because they offer convenient access to workplaces and leisure facilities.

Case Study of Manchester CBD

Background:	The commercial heart of **Manchester** can be delimited within an area bounded by rail and road routes. Building **densities** are very **high**, reflecting the **competition** for space there.
Road:	Road networks give the area good **accessibility** — the M602 brings traffic from the West to just outside the CBD and the A57(M) runs along its southern edge. The M60 forms an outer ring road well away from the CBD, to help cut down on congestion caused by through traffic.
Rail:	There are two mainline **stations** (Victoria and Piccadilly) at the edges of the CBD, plus Deansgate and Oxford Road stations, which serve commuter passengers.
Trams:	The **Metrolink** tram system opened in 1992 to improve **access** for commuters and cut down on traffic congestion and pollution. It's now being extended and expanded.
Land Use:	Main land use is for **shops**, **finance**, **education**, **administration**, **leisure** and **offices**. Similar functions tend to **cluster** together.
Revitalising:	**Gentrification** of old run down buildings (see next page) has revitalised parts of the CBD, e.g. flats developed in old warehouses in **Castlefield** which are occupied by young professionals. There's also a huge amount of new building of offices and trendy apartment blocks. Manchester is marketed as a "**hip**" city, and posh department stores **Selfridges** and **Harvey Nichols** opened branches there in the late 1990s and early 2000s.

Changing Urban Structure

Rejuvenation or Urban Regeneration Projects Help Fight Urban Decline

1) **Rejuvenation** or **regeneration** of run-down inner city areas has been going on since the 1980s.

2) The **physical environment is redeveloped** by clearing old buildings and developing new buildings. The idea is to improve quality of life, create job opportunities and try to get enough businesses and investment into the area so that it can stand on its own two feet. A lot of this **property-led regeneration** was done by **Urban Development Corporations** (UDCs) — temporary companies set up to manage the development of run-down inner cities.

3) There are various other schemes to plan and fund urban rejuvenation including: the URBAN Programme (EU funded), Derelict Land grants, Enterprise Zones and City Challenge projects. These urban regeneration projects are often done by **partnerships** between **central government**, **local authorities** and the **private sector**.

4) **Housing Associations** have a role in improving inner cities.

Case Study: Rejuvenation in Ancoats, Manchester

Background: Inner city **Ancoats** or "Little Italy" was a busy area during the Industrial Revolution. It's an area of mixed housing types. Since 1950, it's declined — crime and unemployment increased and environmental quality was poor.

New projects: These include "Safe as Houses" (improving **home security**), the Oldham Road Business Watch (a **neighbourhood watch** project), a **car crime** education initiative, and a **drug education** programme.

Redevelopment: The Ancoats Building Preservation Trust, the Urban Village project and the Italian community are trying to recreate Little Italy around a central square with flats above the shops, restaurants and bars. **English Heritage money** is being used to restore Victorian buildings. Once complete the Ancoats area, the Rochdale canal and the Castlefields area will become a **World Heritage Site**.

Other regeneration schemes in Manchester include: the Hulme estate, the Trafford Park industrial area and the Salford Quays redevelopment.

Gentrification is when Run Down Houses are Done Up

1) When an area's gentrified, **well-off people** (e.g. professionals or managers) move in, displacing low income families.

2) Individuals and families do up individual houses — it's not an **official** or **government** thing. Local authorities tend to be all for gentrification though.

3) The **purchasing power** in the area **increases**, so local businesses can do well. There's an increase in the number of **bars** and **restaurants**.

4) Gentrification creates **employment** for **builders**, **plumbers**, **decorators**, etc.

5) Gentrification has **disadvantages** though. House prices shoot up, and local people can't afford to buy. As more properties are bought and done up, there are fewer houses to rent too. There's often friction between newcomers and the original residents.

6) Examples of gentrified areas include **Notting Hill** in London, the **Brindley Place** area in Birmingham, and the **Castlefield** area of Manchester.

Some people say that these areas are "yuppified" and lose their original character.

Practice Questions

Q1 What are the main functions of the CBD?

Q2 What is meant by the terms "core" and "frame" when applied to studies of the CBD?

Q3 What are the aims of property-led regeneration?

Q4 Give an advantage and a disadvantage of gentrification.

Exam Questions

Q1 Describe and explain land use changes in the CBD of a named city you have studied. (7 marks)

Q2 With reference to a named city in an MEDC, describe and explain what has been done to reurbanise and regenerate the inner city area. (7 marks)

From slums to posh flats in two easy steps...

Inner cities are near the CBD, and are changing a lot these days. It seems to me that inner city residential areas can go one of two ways — either "run down, crime ridden and generally depressing", or "trendy and yuppified and full of tapas bars and really expensive flats". There actually, genuinely, doesn't seem to be much middle ground there.

Conflict on the Rural-Urban Fringe

*The rural-urban fringe is an area of change and conflict. It's developing, but not everyone wants to see development.
These pages are for **Edexcel A**, **Edexcel B**, **OCR A**, **AQA A** and **AQA B**.*

New Developments on the Rural-Urban Fringe Cause Conflict

1) As the population of urban areas grows, there's an **increased demand** for **services**, e.g. retail, business and office, light industry, hospitals, leisure. Obviously, there's also an increased demand for housing.

2) As towns develop, there's also **less and less land** left to develop **within** the town. Land in towns can get very expensive because of increased competition. Services have to go somewhere — the rural-urban fringe is very inviting. There's room to expand, land is cheaper, and urban traffic is avoided.

3) There is a **conflict** between the **need for housing developments**, business and science parks and out-of-town shopping centres and the **ecological arguments** in favour of retaining areas of relatively undisturbed countryside.

Retail Parks have been Developed in the Suburbs and Rural-Urban Fringe

This move to the rural-urban fringe has been caused by **several factors** — room to develop, cheap land etc.
The **increase** in **car ownership** means that consumers can drive to a retail development wherever it's situated.
Retail has **followed** the **wealthier customers** out to the rural-urban fringe — e.g. the John Lewis store in Cheadle, Cheshire draws its customers from the wealthy commuter towns and villages of Cheshire to the south.

Negative effects of retail parks	Positive effects of retail parks
Retail parks **take customers away** from local **town centres**.	Retail parks **create jobs** in the rural-urban fringe.
Retail parks massively increase **consumer** and **HGV traffic** on roads leading to them — causing **congestion**, which is a hassle for local residents.	**Inner city traffic congestion** is **reduced**.
	Local roads are sometimes **improved** when the retail park is developed. This **benefits local people**.
Building retail parks on **green open land** destroys natural wildlife habitats. Locals may find the new development **ugly**.	Some retail parks such as **Bluewater**, Kent and **Lakeside**, Thurrock have nice **landscaped gardens**, managed woodland areas, boating lakes, etc.

Not all retail parks were built on green open land, though — Bluewater in Kent was built on the site of an old chalk quarry.

Case Study — Impact of Bluewater on Gravesend Town Centre

Background: Bluewater retail park opened in **March, 1999** — 350 shops, about 75 000 visitors per day.

Impact: Local people went to Bluewater a lot in the first months that it was open, but this eased off. There's been a **reduction in sales** in Gravesend — about 6% in the first 2 years. Some shops in Gravesend have begun to **recover**. Impact on Gravesend town centre has been **far less** than had been predicted. **Car park use** in Gravesend has stayed the **same**. The **Lakeside** retail park in Thurrock was already open, and there were already out of town and suburban supermarkets, so Gravesend town centre had **already been affected** by those developments.

Schemes: Gravesend town centre has been done up to look more **attractive**.
Town centre shopping centres and **individual stores** have been **renovated**.

Leisure Facilities are Also Built in the Rural-Urban Fringe

1) In MEDCs, people have **leisure time**, and **money to spend**. There's lots of **demand** for **leisure facilities** for people in urban and suburban areas.

2) Some new **football stadiums** are located in industrial or retail parks — e.g. the **Bolton Wanderers Reebok Stadium** is in the Middlebrook retail and leisure development on Bolton's rural-urban fringe.

3) **Golf courses** take up a lot of **land**, and often incorporate **hotels** and other leisure facilities. Lots of golf courses were built in the 1980s and early 1990s. This caused conflict — people saw golf courses as **artificial** and **suburban**, and felt they didn't belong in rural areas.

4) There was also concern about the **impact** of golf course development on **wildlife**. Some land on golf courses is tightly managed — greens and fairways are kept as neat, tidy, trimmed grass. Other than that, though, "rough" and trees provide great habitats for wildlife.

Transport Developments Also Affect the Rural-Urban Fringe

Bypasses, ring roads and motorways are built in the rural-urban fringe, to improve transport into urban areas.

Air travel is increasing in popularity, so there's increasing demand for new airports and new airport runways to be built.
Manchester Airport's second runway was eventually built after a public inquiry.

Conflict on the Rural-Urban Fringe

Suburbanised Villages are Villages with Suburban Characteristics

Many **villages** on the rural-urban fringe have had their character completely **changed** as **urban commuters** have moved in.

1) Land use changes from **agricultural** to **residential**. The number of working farms decreases.

2) The village **grows**, as new houses are built. **New housing estates** can almost **dwarf** the original village.

3) New housing estates on the outskirts of villages change the **shape** and **physical look** of the village. The new houses are usually in **standard modern styles**, with perhaps a vague nod towards the traditional local architecture — they usually look **identical** to **similar housing estates** in suburbs. They're usually **detached** or **semi-detached** "executive homes" with a garden and a garage, to appeal to affluent commuters.

4) The **social profile** of the village changes — there are more affluent middle income professionals.

5) Newcomers travel to work outside the village. This causes **traffic problems**.

6) Services **not used by commuters** don't benefit, e.g. **public transport**, because urban newcomers all have cars so the demand for bus services goes down. This often results in bus services being **cut**.

7) Wealthy newcomers can have a **positive** effect on the local economy, e.g. **pubs** and **restaurants** often do well.

Green Belts Protect the Rural-Urban Fringe

1) The first **green belt** in England was created around London after the Town and Country Planning Act of 1947. Rapid and uncontrolled growth of cities (London in particular) threatened to engulf the countryside. The creation of the green belt was an attempt to **restrict housing** developments and other **building** and to **conserve** areas of **countryside** for farming and recreation.

2) Many of the original green belts still exist in more or less their **original state**, which is a tribute to their **success**. However, they **failed** to halt urban sprawl — further development simply "**leapfrogged**" the green belt and was built **further out** from the city.

3) **Shortage of building land** in and close to cities, particularly in the south-east around London, has led to increased **pressure on green belt** land. It is an area with great **potential** for housing, commercial and leisure developments. This is because the rural-urban fringe has a typically **affluent, mobile population**.

4) There are green belts around many of the UK's cities, e.g. Newcastle, York, Manchester, Liverpool, Birmingham, Bristol, Bournemouth, Oxford and Cambridge.

Case Study: The Green Belt around London and the M25

The Green Belt Act of 1938 created a 25km wide zone around London in which building is controlled.

Aims:	To stop London sprawling out into the countryside, to prevent neighbouring towns from merging, to protect farmland, to restrict "harmful activities" within the green belt.
Rules:	There are strict planning regulations on building. Existing towns can only be expanded by infilling between existing buildings. Planning regulations were relaxed for strategic purposes, e.g. building the M25.
Results:	New Towns were built outside the green belt so commuting across it has increased.
The M25:	The M25 (London's orbital motorway) is 117km long, and cuts through the green belt. It was built in the 1980s with 3 lanes — many sections have been widened to 5 lanes. Further development of the M25 would destroy SSSIs (Sites of Special Scientific interest), woodlands and many wildlife sites. It would also add to noise and air pollution.

Practice Questions

Q1 What's the "rural-urban fringe"?

Q2 Name four different types of land use that can occur on the rural-urban fringe.

Q3 What is a "green belt"?

Exam Questions

Q1 With reference to a named example you have studied, describe and explain some of the changes that have occurred as the village has become suburbanised. (5 marks)

Q2 Describe, with reference to specific examples, some of the conflicts which occur in the rural-urban fringe. (7 marks)

Not what you get if you pass your third Judo test...

What have airports, golf courses, humungous retail parks and Bolton Wanderers Football Club got in common — why, they're all nicer places to be than a Geography lesson, of course. The "sensible" answer is that they've all developed on the rural-urban fringe, on exactly the sort of land that green belts were designed to protect. By the way, learn the two case studies, they're useful.

Urban Quality of Life

*Every city is different and everyone in a city has a different view of life there. However there are broad generalisations and similarities found in all cities. These pages are for **Edexcel B**, **AQA B Option S** and **OCR A**, and are useful for **Edexcel A** and **AQA A**.*

Economic and Social Indicators Measure Quality of Life at National Level

1) **Economic indicators** include things such as GDP (Gross Domestic Product), GDP per capita (per person), the number of cars per 100 people etc. Common **social indicators** include things like the percentage of children receiving education, life expectancy, number of patients per doctor etc.

2) The UN produces the **Human Development Index** (HDI) which combines GDP per capita, life expectancy, percentage of children in school and adult literacy into a single number. The **Physical Quality of Life Index** (PQLI) combines infant mortality, life expectancy and literacy rate into a single number.

3) All these are **average figures for a country** which **mask** the **inequalities** between people and regions **within** a country. They're great for comparing countries, but not good for comparing or investigating cities.

You Can Measure Quality of Life in Individual Urban Areas

1) Measurement at local level involves local **fieldwork** — looking at access to services and amenities, investigating pollution levels, and asking people questions about their daily lives.

2) The annual **Local Environmental Quality Survey** reports on how clean and tidy a local area is. It covers issues like dog fouling and litter.

3) The **House Condition Survey** reports on the state of housing. It covers the physical condition of homes and their energy efficiency.

4) Fieldwork is backed up by **secondary data** from the **census**, which is carried out every 10 years. The census collects **demographic** data (people's ages, how many children they have), **economic** facts (how much people earn) and **social status** information (what kind of job they do, how many rooms are in their house) — **enough detail** to let you spot variation within a town. **Census** data is now collected worldwide, but it's more reliable for **MEDC** countries.

> Perception is a major factor in considering the quality of life in urban areas. It's important that surveys and questionnaires ask people what they think of the environment they live in.

There's Deprivation in Urban Areas in MEDCs — the Inner City Problem

1) **Inner city areas** are generally areas of **decline**, often close to the CBD, where **population** numbers are **decreasing**, and **job** opportunities are **limited**.

2) **Public perception** of these areas is generally **negative** — with images of crime, poverty, poor housing conditions, dirt, unemployment, overcrowding and racial tension.

3) Areas of deprivation are classified by the Department for the Environment, Food and Rural Affairs (**DEFRA**) as areas where "an individual's well-being falls below a level generally regarded as a reasonable minimum for Britain today". There are over **5 million people** living in some **3 000** such neighbourhoods in British cities.

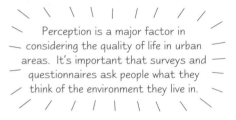

DEFRA uses several indicators of deprivation, including:
- levels of **unemployment**,
- proportions of **long-term unemployed** and adults on **income support**,
- proportion of housing which is **overcrowded**,
- households **lacking basic amenities**, e.g. bathroom,
- number of children in "**unsuitable accommodation**",
- **low educational achievement** at GCSE,
- amount of **crime**,
- amount of **derelict land**.

1) As well as being deprived, people in inner city areas often suffer from **social exclusion**. Social exclusion means people having **problems getting on** in society because of **unemployment**, **discrimination**, **poor skills**, **low incomes**, poor **housing**, high **crime**, **poor health** or **family breakdown**.

2) Without outside intervention these areas suffer a **downward spiral** — few jobs means very little wealth and not enough investment in the area. This causes an even greater concentration of deprivation and social exclusion.

3) **Homeless people** tend to **cluster together** in **certain areas** within a town, so they can give each other mutual support. However this often gets that area a bad reputation.

There's more on these issues later in the section.

Urban Quality of Life

There's Deprivation in Urban Areas in LEDCs — Shanty Towns and Squatters

1) **Urbanisation** has occurred at such a **rapid** rate in many LEDCs that it is **impossible to keep up with housing demand**. For example, 500 000 migrants arrive in Delhi each year, creating a demand for a further 200 000 houses per year, but less than 20 000 are actually built.

2) People have to live somewhere — they build illegal, unplanned high density **squatter settlements**, building makeshift houses out of anything that they can get hold of. More than **50%** of the population of many LEDC cities **live in squatter settlements**. Squatter settlements are also often called **shanty towns**.

3) Most cities have **low-cost housing developments** for the poor, but people often prefer to live in self-built squatter settlements where they don't have to pay rent.

4) The **location of shanty towns** is usually as **close to the CBD, or to industrial areas** as possible. However, land is often only available on the **edge** of the city or on **unsuitable sites** such as **steep land** (susceptible to landslides), close to polluting industries, close to landfill sites or on swampy **flood plains**.

5) At first **urban authorities resisted the growth** of these squatter settlements, regularly evicting people and destroying their homes because they thought they were the sites for political dissent, disease and crime.

6) The attitude of the authorities has now changed and shanty towns are seen as a way to get round the housing problems in LEDCs. Once squatters are given **legal ownership** of the land they quickly work to **upgrade** the area.

7) **Site and services** schemes are a growing, **low-cost** solution to the problem. The authority **provides plots** with **basic services** — mains water, sewerage, electricity and roads and the immigrants then **build their own houses** on the land. They can then sell the house later to move to a "better" area of town.

Case study: Slums in Mumbai

Slums:	**13 million people** live on the streets of Mumbai — that's over 50% of the population. Over 2 million do not have a toilet and 6 million do not have clean drinking water.
Dharavi:	Dharavi (probably the largest slum in Asia) is 11 km north of Mumbai's CBD. It's difficult to estimate the population density because so many of the people live on the streets, but the census of 1991 calculated a population density of about **17 000 people per km²**. There are many local industries within the slum, including metalwork, leather, ceramics, furniture and recycling, plus many **self-help groups**. Plans to build tenements instead have been resisted by the inhabitants — they preferred a **railway** station to allow them to access the **suburban rail network**.

Urban Overcrowding isn't the Same as High Population Density

All urban areas have **high population density**. Population density is measured as people per km². Population density varies within a town. In MEDCs it's usually low in the CBD, high in the inner city, and low in the suburbs. In LEDCs with squatter settlements, population density is high in the suburbs.

Overcrowding is where there are **too many people** living in each individual house or flat — e.g. a family of seven in a two bedroomed flat.

Practice Questions

Q1   Make a list of the indicators that can be used to measure quality of life.

Q2   Give an example of a survey that collects data on urban quality of life.

Q3   Give a definition of the term "deprivation" as applied to urban geography, and as used by the UK government.

Q4   What's meant by "site and services", in relation to squatter settlements?

Exam Questions

Q1   Describe the social issues that result from inner city depopulation and decline in MEDCs.   (4 marks)

Q2   Describe some of the causes of squatter settlements in LEDCs and, with reference to (a) named example(s), describe the conditions there.   (7 marks)

As the Pogues pointed out, it's a dirty old town...

Well, it sure can be grim in cities and no mistake. There are patches of "social exclusion" and general horribleness in MEDC cities, even in the capital cities of rich countries. Just to clarify — in MEDCs like the UK, a squatter is someone who breaks into an empty house and lives there. In LEDCs, a squatter is someone who builds a house or a shack on disused land.

Urban Ecosystems

*Urban environments aren't all buildings. All cities and towns have areas which aren't built up — e.g. parks, gardens, playing fields and derelict land. These all have their own communities of plants and animals. These pages are only for **AQA B (Option R)**.*

New Species are Introduced and Other Species are Removed

In **urban gardens** and **parks**, people plant "**exotic**" species which aren't native to the UK. In fact, **almost all plant species** in urban areas have been **introduced** by humans.

People also **get rid of weeds**. Weeds such as dandelions and daisies are **native** plants which you'd find in a natural, undisturbed rural ecosystem.

Planting species	Removing species
Trees (e.g. sycamore, plane, cherry, poplar) are planted beside **roads** to give **shade**, to look **pretty** and to reduce noise. In **Victorian** times, lots of trees were planted in urban **parks**.	Trees are **cut down** if their **roots** are too close to buildings.
Grass is planted in **lawns**, **parks** and **playing fields**.	**Undergrowth** is cleared in **parks** and **urban woodland**.
Border plants and **bedding plants** are planted in parks and gardens to look colourful and pretty.	**Weeds** are **removed** from gardens, parks and pavements.

Grassed Areas Don't Have Much Biodiversity

1) Lawns are carefully managed to be **grass**, and **nothing but grass** — daisies, dandelions, moss and other **weeds** are considered **undesirable**.

2) Lawns **don't support many animals**. A few insects are about the lot. Lawns are sometimes called "**wildlife deserts**". Areas with **shrubs** and **trees** support much more wildlife.

Urban Areas have Distinctive Ecologies

Individual urban areas provide **ecological niches** for plants and animals. An ecological niche is a plant or animal's position in an ecosystem.

Some areas are **highly managed** — e.g. gardens, parks.

1) **Gardens** and allotments are **cultivated** with fancy garden plants, vegetables, etc. Most garden plants aren't native to the UK, and definitely wouldn't be expected in the normal succession of the area.

2) **Parks** are **carefully managed** by the local authorities. Formal gardens and large expanses of grassland are typical, often with a **pond** (with a hydrosere ecosystem). They also contain exotic non-native plant species.

3) There aren't **proper forests** in urban areas, but there are small areas of **woodland** in most large urban environments. Urban woodland is managed.

Some residential areas have communal patches of land which are usually kept as grass by the local authority.

Areas along **traffic corridors** are relatively **unmanaged**.

1) **Roads** themselves aren't colonised by plants, but the **verges beside them** frequently are. The high levels of **carbon monoxide** from traffic exhausts mean that plants don't grow as well as on open ground.

2) **Land alongside railways** isn't influenced by humans very much, so plant successions can develop **without interference**. However the succession is affected by **pollution** emitted by the trains, and it **doesn't reach maturity** because it's systematically **cleared** by the railway authorities to stop it interfering with the lines. Leaves on the line, anyone...

Former industrial sites are **unmanaged**.

1) When industries close down and buildings are **demolished**, a plant succession will begin on the open ground that's left. The succession may not be the same as on open ground nearby — this is because of **localised pollution** and **chemical differences** in the soil. Species which are **tolerant** of the conditions grow there.

2) **Waste disposal sites** — municipal landfill sites are now **landscaped** as they're filled, but this usually just means **covering them in grass** prior to future development. Other waste sites (fly-tipping sites in particular) can give rise to **odd** successions of plants because of **local pollution** in the soil.

Urban Ecosystems

Plant Succession is the Change in Vegetation Over Time

1) The series of **changes in vegetation** over **time** is called a **succession**. Each stage of the succession has its own group of species which changes the micro-environment and creates conditions which allow new species to dominate.

2) Eventually the **community** of plants reaches a **dynamic equilibrium** for the particular environmental conditions. This equilibrium is called the **climax** community. In the **UK** this would naturally be **oak woodland** over most of the country.

3) Over most of the UK the **plant community** is permanently **prevented from** reaching its **climatic climax** type because of the **influence of humans**. A plant community like this is called a **plagioclimax**. This particularly applies to urban areas.

> See pages 62-63 in Section 6 for more on succession.

Gilbert Described Succession on Waste Ground

1) **Mosses and lichens** develop on **bare concrete** or **rubble**. Mosses and lichens can cope with very little water. They extract nutrients from the bare material below, and weather the material slightly. When they die they leave **organic matter** and some **weathered material**, which makes a soil for other plants to grow in.

2) The next stage is **flowering plants** such as **Oxford Ragwort**. Seeds blow in on the wind, and germinate in cracks in the concrete — cracks retain water and soil.

3) As the ragwort plants die, they rot down and produce humus, which slowly makes the soil more nutrient rich. Bigger, taller plants can grow, e.g. **Rosebay Willowherb**. These shade out the smaller plants. **Grass** also starts to grow at this stage.

4) After **5 years** or so, herbs and grass can be replaced by **shrubs** and **trees**. **Sycamore** and **Rowan** are fast growing trees, so they'll get going first, followed later by **Ash** and **Oak**. Derelict sites are often **redeveloped** way before this stage, though.

> In fact, Sycamore saplings can germinate in small amounts of soil — they can send down roots through cracks in concrete, or in walls or gutters. They don't grow very big unless there's plenty of soil, water, sunlight and nutrients, though.

Plant succession on bare land **varies** depending on the following factors — the **original state** of the derelict site (whether soil or rubble is **acid** or **alkali**, how much **water** there is, if it's **waterlogged**), **regional variations** and **human intervention**.

1) Succession on land which has already had plants on it and then been cleared is called **secondary succession**. It's faster than succession starting from bare rock, concrete or rubble.

2) Succession on land that's **deliberately been set aside** for **conservation** is allowed to continue to its **natural climax**.

Many Cities have Urban Conservation Areas

1) **Boston** in the USA has an "**Urban Wilds**" initiative. Areas of the original ecosystems that were there before the city was built are left undisturbed. They're protected from development, and used for recreation.

2) **London** has relatively undisturbed habitats for rare birds such as the **black redstart** and rare mammals such as the **water vole**. The **London Wildlife Trust** collects information on wildlife in London and manages some reserves in the Greater London area. Urban wildlife conservation is relatively **new** in the UK, compared to the USA.

Practice Questions

Q1 Define a) exotic species b) native species c) ecological niche.

Q2 Why isn't a grassy lawn a great place for wildlife conservation?

Q3 What is "plant succession"?

Exam Questions

Q1 Urban environments are varied. With reference to an urban area you have studied, describe some of the environments to be found there. (5 marks)

Q2 Outline a typical plant succession on an urban wasteland. (5 marks)

No, the "urban jungle" does NOT count...

Luckily, all this is only for AQA B students, and only for those AQA B students doing Option R. Oh, what's that — you're doing AQA B Option R? Well, in truth it's not horrendously difficult. You do need to learn the plant succession on wasteland, because they can ask you about it in the exam. It's worth being able to mention an urban conservation area, too.

Managing Urban Housing

*Housing is one of the most expensive things on which most people spend their money. The size, cost and location of housing is therefore important in determining where people live in a city. For **AQA A**, **AQA B**, **Edexcel B** and **OCR A**, and useful for **Edexcel A**.*

It's Important to Have the Right Mix of Housing Stock in MEDCs

It's important to have the right mix of **house types** and **house prices** to suit the population.

1) The **size** of housing has to suit the **size of household**. A country where people have **big families** needs **large family homes**. A country where lots of people **live on their own** needs small houses or flats.

2) The **price** of housing has to suit people's **incomes**. You need big luxury houses for the wealthy, and no-frills affordable housing for low income households. Housing developers in the UK have to include some "affordable housing" in new housing estates.

3) The **style** of housing also has to be right. In the UK, people tend to like **detached houses** with a garden. In the rest of Europe, more people are happy to live in **flats**. Also, people who want to buy a property tend to want a house. Flats are more often rented.

4) The **kind of housing** a person lives in depends on their **age**. After leaving home, **young people** often live in **shared houses** where they only have a room to themselves. Their **first house** or flat is likely to be **small**. When they **have kids**, they need a **bigger house**. When they retire they might move to a small **retirement bungalow**.

New Housing in MEDCs can be either on Greenfield Sites or Brownfield Sites

Greenfield sites are places that **haven't been used** for building before.
Brownfield sites are places that are **already in urban use**, or with **derelict buildings**.

1) When the Labour Government came to power in 1997 they aimed to build 60% of new homes on **brownfield sites**. There are **plenty of brownfield sites** to use — more sites become available each year than are redeveloped, but builders are reluctant to use them.

2) **Greenfield sites** are attractive to builders — housing on greenfield sites has nice views of countryside, so it'll easily sell. Building on greenfield sites is **controversial** — many people are against the loss of countryside. Building houses on greenfield sites can make for **more journeys to work**, because they're further away from the CBD and industrial districts than brownfield sites.

3) **Competitors** for greenfield sites include house building, road construction, industrial expansion, retail parks, and golf courses. The highest bidders are often house builders.

Demographic and Social Trends in the Last 30 Years have Affected UK Housing

1) Even though the UK birth rate is falling, the demand for housing is increasing. There are more and more **single person households**. The increase in **divorce** means that many households are splitting into two.

2) **In the UK, demand** for housing is **greatest in the South East** — highly-paid jobs in and around London have attracted large-scale migration to the region. There aren't really enough houses in the South East to **cope** with the demand, and there isn't enough space to build houses on, either. This causes **conflicts** in the rural-urban fringe.

3) The **price of housing** has **increased** to reflect the increased competition for houses. **Lower income groups** can't **afford high prices**.

4) The number of **older people** is increasing, so more homes which are **suitable for the elderly** are needed.

5) The number of **single occupancy households** is **increasing**, and the number of large families is decreasing. Large townhouses have been **subdivided into flats** to meet the changing demand for housing.

6) More people **own their own home**. The government sold off council houses in the 1980s — they thought that people who owned their houses had a reason to look after their neighbourhood.

7) As people have become more **well-off** and more **ambitious**, they've wanted **bigger**, **fancier** houses. There's been a trend towards large **detached** and **semi-detached** "executive homes" in the suburbs and on the rural-urban fringe.

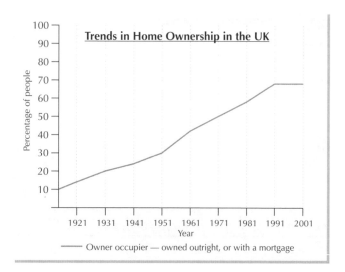

Managing Urban Housing

Urban Renewal *Provides* **Better Housing**, *but not always* **Affordable Housing**

1) **Regeneration schemes** in **inner cities** have included housing development. Planning permission isn't usually a problem — local authorities encourage development on **brownfield sites**. There's more about inner city regeneration on p95.

2) Inner city development **can** provide pleasant and **affordable housing** for low income and middle income households. However, it tends to provide **luxury flats** for **well-off single people** and well-off **couples without kids**.

3) **Gentrification** of an area (doing up houses, see p95) makes the houses a lot **better**, makes the area **look** a lot nicer, increases the area's **wealth**, and **reduces crime**. However, nicely done-up houses are expensive to buy — gentrification makes areas inaccessible to lower income families.

There's **Low Quality Housing** for Many **Poor People** in **MEDCs**

1) Inner city housing in MEDCs tends to be **poor** — unless the area's been regenerated.

2) Low quality housing in MEDCs often suffers from the following problems:
   - **Inadequate heating**
   - **Damp**
   - **Vermin infestation**, e.g. rats and cockroaches
   - **Overcrowding**

3) The poorest areas suffer **social exclusion** (see p98).

4) **Homelessness** is a problem in MEDCs. In MEDCs, homelessness isn't generally caused by **overpopulation**, although there may be a shortage of housing available to rehouse homeless people. **Substance abuse**, **mental illness** and **relationship breakdown** are sometimes contributing factors to homelessness in MEDCs.

5) In the UK, local authorities move homeless people into **temporary accommodation** in hostels and B&Bs. This is better than sleeping rough on the streets, but it isn't a great way to live, especially for a family with young children.

There's a **Shortage** of **Good Housing** in Many **LEDCs**

1) **Lack of finance** and very **high rates of in-migration** are the **main problems** in maintaining an adequate housing stock **in LEDCs**.

2) The growth of **squatter settlements** is typical in LEDC cities. See p99 for more on squatter settlements.

3) Local authorities in some LEDCS have set up self-help housing schemes, often called "site and services" schemes. The authority provides plots of land, and offers low-cost basic building materials for people to build their own house. The plots of land have a **clean water supply** and **sewers**.

4) LEDC authorities also try to spread the population into the surrounding area by building **satellite towns** around the main city e.g. towns built around Cairo and building **new towns**, e.g. New Bombay.

Practice Questions

Q1 Other than population increase, give two reasons why the demand for housing in the UK is increasing.

Q2 What is the difference between a greenfield and brownfield site?

Q3 What effect does the increase in single people have on the demand for housing?

Q4 What is a subdivided house?

Q5 Give two examples of housing problems in MEDCs.

Exam Questions

Q1 With reference to specific examples in MEDCs, describe the types and locations of some new housing developments. (7 marks)

Q2 What sort of solutions are used to try to manage the housing stock in LEDCs? Illustrate your answer by referring to examples you have studied. (7 marks)

Gentrification — nothing to do with blokes...

It's almost fascinating, how many more people own their own homes now than 40 years ago. It's become much more expected for people to own their own house. Anyway, for this topic you need to know the social and demographic reasons behind trends in house building, development and ownership. You also need to know how the authorities try to manage the housing stock.

Managing Urban Transport

Most towns developed before cars were invented — they weren't designed for traffic at all. So, traffic in towns is yet another thing that needs to be carefully managed. These pages are for Edexcel B and OCR A. Also useful for Edexcel A, AQA A and AQA B.

Car Ownership has Gone Up in MEDCs

1) Cars were a **luxury** item in the **1950s** — they're now seen as a **necessity.** **Disposable incomes** have **increased. Improved production** methods have made **cars more affordable.** Both of these factors have **increased** car **ownership.** Most UK households have a car, and the number of households with more than one car has increased dramatically.

Year	1950	1960	1970	1980	1990	2000
% of households with cars	13	28	52	56	62	68
% with 2 or more cars	1	2	6	12	22	30

2) Although the urban population in MEDCs is either increasing very slowly, or actually decreasing, the number of **car journeys isn't going down** — many people who move out of cities continue to work there and **commute daily.** People with cars make **more journeys per day** than those without a car. People don't just use their cars to travel to **work** but **also** for **social and leisure** purposes — because they can.

3) Recent **growth** in the **retail and service industries** has led to **more delivery traffic** in urban areas. The growth of **out-of-town retail parks** also causes additional **car journeys** to the suburbs.

> Because most people in MEDCs own cars, retail can locate out of town without losing customers.

Cars cause pollution (see p.107). Car exhausts contain **nitrogen oxides** and **sulphur oxides**, **carbon monoxide** and **particulates.** Exhaust from **leaded petrol** contains poisonous **lead.**

Car use **isn't sustainable.** The **more cars** there are on the road, the **worse traffic** will get — the worst case scenario is that it would take **too long to drive anywhere**, because of the other cars on the road. Increasing car use would also **increase pollution** beyond acceptable

There's Also Huge Demand for Public Transport in MEDCs

1) As cities grow, the **demand for public transport grows.** Public transport is a **convenient** way to get to work. Sure, trains and buses and the Tube can be cramped and delayed, but commuters on public transport don't have the hassle of driving in heavy traffic or of finding somewhere to park in town.

2) **New mass transit systems** have been developed, e.g. the **Metro** underground rail system in **Tyneside**, and the **Metrolink** tram system in **Manchester.** Both of these schemes have been very successful in attracting commuters to use them. The **BART** (Bay Area Rapid Transport) system in **San Francisco** has been **less successful** — Californians aren't as easily persuaded to leave their cars behind.

3) **Existing public transport systems** like the **London Underground** and London's bus service have been improved. The new **Jubilee Line extension** and the **Docklands Light Railway** were built to serve new financial centres in East London.

Sustainable Transport Strategies in MEDCs

Cities need to think up transport strategies to get cars off the streets, or to reduce the amount of pollution that each car causes.

1) It's **hard** to **persuade** people to leave their cars at home and take public transport. Some transport schemes try to **attract people to use public transport** and others try to **discourage people from using their cars**.

2) London's **Congestion Charge** is £5 per journey into Central London. It's reduced the traffic flow in central London by 20%. At the same time, the number of buses was increased so people could still travel in central London. Some **roads** leading to town centres have **charges levied** on them, e.g. in Leicester, UK.

3) **Park and ride** schemes are common in most large UK cities (where cheap or free car parks are provided on the city outskirts with a regular bus service into the city centre).

4) Many main roads have **bus and cycle lanes** where cars aren't allowed. They're meant to encourage travel by bus or bike, because they're supposed to be faster than travelling by car.

5) **High parking charges** in town centres are designed to deter motorists.

6) "**Tidal flows**" for traffic provide more lanes of traffic in the direction of greatest demand. These can be reversed, depending on the time of day — so there'd be more lanes going into the city in the morning and more lanes going out of the city at night. There are examples in London and Manchester.

7) **Leaded petrol** has been **phased out** in Europe. There's **lower car tax** for cars with **smaller**, more fuel efficient engines.

8) The UK has strict **emission controls** — cars with excessively polluting exhausts fail their MOT.

9) **Building new roads** is **no longer** seen as **a solution** to transport problems — it increases car usage.

Managing Urban Transport

Transport Poses Challenges in LEDCs As Well

1) Car ownership figures are lower in **LEDCs**, but they're going up very quickly. The rate of increase of car ownership in LEDCs is overtaking the rate in MEDCs. This **particularly** applies to the **NICs** (Newly Industrialised Countries) of Asia — such as South Korea, Malaysia and Indonesia.

2) Rapid, **unplanned urban growth** hasn't included **traffic** requirements — traffic planning has **lower priority** than housing and basic service needs. Traffic **congestion** and the **air pollution** it causes are **major problems** in LEDCs.

3) Only the **newest vehicles** have catalytic converters fitted. **Lead** and **particulate** emissions pose a serious health hazard to urban dwellers.

There are a billion people in China, and the market for cars in China is growing and growing and growing. This could cause big pollution problems in the future. It's all very well for some of the world's people to have a polluting car — we can kind of, sort of cope with that level of pollution (although it's still not nice). If everyone in the world has a polluting car — that's a problem.

LEDCs Need Traffic Management

1) Without some form of **traffic management** many LEDC cities will suffer more and more traffic congestion and health problems. Any measures which can reduce traffic-related illness will bring big economic benefits to the community.

2) It's hard for local authorities in LEDCs to implement a good sustainable transport policy, because they usually just don't have the money. **Basic services** and **housing** are a bigger priority. This means that in LEDCS, there tends to be more **private mass transit** — e.g. private minibuses, water taxis, private ferry services.

Case study: Traffic problems and solutions in Bangkok, Thailand.

Cars:	In 1995 45% of new cars in Thailand were registered in Bangkok. 1000+ new vehicles are on the streets every day.
Pollution:	Over 50% of air pollution in Bangkok comes from road traffic. Most traffic policemen suffer from respiratory diseases. Levels of lead in the blood of inhabitants are amongst the highest in the world — over 2× level regarded as dangerous. Thousands of premature deaths and millions of work days are lost due to exposure to air pollution.
Traffic jams:	Estimated average journey speeds in 1998 were only 5km per hour. A 200km-long tailback was recorded in 1995 which took 18 hours to clear. Traffic jams make the pollution problem worse.
Solutions:	Lead-based petrol has been phased out. City centre car parking charges are very high to discourage people from driving into the city . BMTA (Bangkok Mass Transit Authority) set up to oversee traffic management. Elevated expressways built with toll charges to help finance them. Skytrain elevated rail system opened late 1999. An elevated tramway system is being built and also a subway system.
Mass Transit:	Public transport now accounts for over 80% of journeys to work.

Evaluate Transport Strategies — See What's Happened

The **Congestion Charge** in London has been a victim of its own success, in a way. The £5 charge has **put more people off** travelling by car than **expected**. They're all taking the bus or the Tube instead, and public transport services have had trouble **keeping up with demand**. Manchester's **Metrolink** has been successful, and there's demand to expand the service.

The town's public transport system was really in need of modernisation.

Practice Questions

Q1 Make a list of the reasons for the increase in car ownership.

Q2 Name four pollutants emitted by vehicles.

Exam Questions

Q1 Explain the relationship between car ownership and the provision of public transport. (3 marks)

Q2 With reference to a named city in an MEDC, describe and explain transport strategies to reduce traffic problems. (7 marks)

Q3 Describe and explain the causes, effects and attempted solutions to the transport problems in a named LEDC. (9 marks)

I say I say — why is London like a bunged-up nose...?

Some gags are too bad to finish. Anyway, ever played the computer game Sim City? — you need to build a lot of roads and railways in your city to cope with congestion, and funnily enough no matter how many railways you build, the people still use their cars. At least, they do when I'm playing. You on the other hand may be a Sim City whiz, in which case, I salute you.

Urban Environmental Problems

*One of the important factors affecting urban quality of life is the environment. This includes the amount of open space, the pollution levels (air, noise, visual and water) and waste disposal. These pages are for **Edexcel B** and **OCR A**.*

Urban Pollution affects Health

1) Statistics show that the **general health of urban dwellers** in both MEDCs and LEDCs is **worse than their rural** counterparts, particularly with respect to respiratory diseases.

2) Cities are usually the site of major industries, which cause air pollution. Levels of **sulphur dioxide**, **hydrocarbons, carbon dioxide** and **nitrogen oxide** are many times **higher** in urban areas than in surrounding rural areas. When atmospheric conditions cause **photochemical smog** to form, it brings serious **health problems** — particularly to people with **respiratory diseases** such as asthma and bronchitis.

In Delhi, over 70% of the city's air pollution comes from motor vehicles. Over 50% of the children have asthma. The incidence of lung disease is 12 times above average.

3) **Motor traffic** is a major source of carbon, nitrogen oxides and particulate matter in MEDC and LEDC cities.

4) **Links between respiratory disease and industry and traffic** have long been suggested and researched, but it's likely that **other factors of deprivation** are also important, e.g. poverty and the quality of housing.

In Mexico City, ozone levels are well above the World Health Organisation safe limits. The main causes are motor vehicles and industry.

Clean Water Supply is a Big Issue in LEDCs

1) **MEDC** cities all have **clean water**. Lack of **clean drinking water** is still a big **cause of illness** in many LEDC cities.

2) Too many people in LEDCs only have access to clean **drinking water from standpipes**. These are usually **shared** between large numbers of people and often aren't safe. Dirty water causes outbreaks of **water-borne diseases** like typhoid and cholera. There's often **cross-contamination** from inadequate **sewage disposal** systems.

3) Domestic and industrial **waste** is still **discharged** directly into **rivers** and the **sea** in many LEDCs, which threatens the **marine environment** and food chains. River water is often used for washing, putting **people** at risk of infection, too.

4) Accidental or deliberate leaks of **toxic chemicals** into rivers can kill aquatic wildlife and enter food chains, causing longer-term damage. Although these discharges are strictly controlled in MEDCs, accidents still happen.

5) **Hindu funerals** in India can be a problem. The dead are **cremated** on a funeral pyre, and their ashes scattered into the sacred **River Ganges**. A combination of **population increase** and **deforestation** means there's **not enough wood** for all the funeral pyres. Partly burned coffins and **corpses** end up going straight into the river.

There's Always Noise Pollution In Urban Areas

1) Cities are **noisy places**. For a start, there's a lot of traffic noise.

2) Factories create noise, and delivery lorries travelling to and from factories create even more noise.

3) The **leisure industry** creates a lot of noise. Town and city centres contain lots of **pubs** and **nightclubs**, which are particularly noisy at **closing time** as **loud, drunk punters** spill out onto the street. Noise pollution isn't the only problem — violence and other **antisocial behaviour** also annoy nearby residents, and **stretch police resources**.

4) **High population density** forces people to practically live on top of each other. **Noisy neighbours** are a problem.

5) In the UK, **Environmental Health officers** try to enforce noise restrictions, but there's often not much they can do.

Waste Management isn't just a Load of Rubbish

1) All urban areas generate large amounts of **household rubbish** and **industrial waste**. There are more and more people on the planet, and we're all producing more and more rubbish. This is a problem.

2) **Modern materials** are less easily biodegradable and some are hazardous — so they're **more difficult to get rid of**.

3) Traditionally, **domestic rubbish** and **chemical waste** have been put into **landfill sites** but these are quickly **filling up**.

4) **Low-level chemical waste** and **treated sewage effluent** are still discharged **into rivers and the sea**, despite increasing protests from environmentally aware groups such as **Greenpeace**. More **stringent limits** have cut down the levels of pollution from these sources in MEDCs but regulations are often ignored in many LEDC cities.

5) **Domestic waste** accounts for about half of the waste in MEDC cities. **Campaigns** to persuade us to **use less** and therefore produce less waste are very slow to take effect. **Recycling** is beginning to make inroads in MEDCs. Most **governments** now have **targets** for the amount of waste that should be recycled. This includes paper, textiles, glass, cans, cartons, batteries, garden refuse for compost, etc. Some countries have better records at this than others.

6) **Recycling** is also an **important industry** in many shanty town developments in LEDCs. People (well, often little kids, actually) collect recyclable things from landfill sites and sell them on to other people. It's a **source of income**.

Urban Environmental Problems

Most MEDC Cities Have Pollution Problems

Case Study — Los Angeles

Background: Smog has been a problem in Los Angeles since the 1950s. In the 1970s, Los Angeles had more than 300 days per year where air quality was below acceptable levels. (Physical factors also affect the development of smog. Pollution is trapped in the Los Angeles valley — onshore breezes are hemmed in by mountains to the east, south and north of the city.)

Vehicles: 75% of Los Angeles' smog comes from motor vehicles. Los Angeles has **over 9 million vehicles**.

Public Transport: Los Angeles has a **metrorail** (underground and light rail) system, but there are **only four lines**. There's also a **bus** system. Only about **5%** of people use **public transport** to travel to work.

Urban Sprawl: Los Angeles is an enormous, sprawling city. It covers a huge area, and journeys to work are long.

Solutions: Cars in LA have to pass a "**smog test**" — a strict test of emissions. Cars which fail have to get repaired and retested, by law. The use of **clean vehicles** running on **natural gas** or **electricity** is being encouraged — these vehicles are allowed to use the **carpool** lane usually reserved for vehicles carrying passengers. Urban planners are encouraged to **limit urban sprawl**.

The Brown Agenda is an International Urban Environment Scheme

The **Brown Agenda** is a major initiative to improve **urban environmental quality** in LEDCs and resolve some of the environmental health problems faced by LEDC cities. It began after the **1992 Earth Summit** in **Rio de Janeiro**.

A quarter of the world's preventable diseases, such as respiratory infections and diarrhoea, can be directly attributed to poor environmental quality, but **lack of money** for effective preventative schemes is a major issue for LEDC countries.

Case Study: The Brown Agenda in Mumbai

Problems: Air pollution, too many slum developments, inadequate clean water supplies and ineffective sewage and waste disposal.

Solutions:
• Unleaded petrol introduced. All new cars now have catalytic converters fitted. Motorised rickshaws banned from the city.
• Two new sewage treatment plants built. Outflow pipes now extend 3km into the sea to allow better dispersal of waste.
• Tree planting schemes to increase oxygen in the environment.
• Satellite towns to spread the population away from the city centre.

It's called the "Brown Agenda" to distinguish it from the "Green Agenda". The "Green Agenda" is about solving the world's environmental problems. The "Brown Agenda" is about sorting out the environment in cities, and making cities nicer, healthier places to live.

Urban Conservation Areas Make the City Greener

1) **Green areas** such as parks and gardens often provide an **oasis of peace** in busy urban areas.
2) They also provide areas with a **local microclimate** and where **pollution levels** are **slightly lower**. These areas are rarely very large as pressure on any available building land is always high.
3) See the bottom of p101 for more on urban conservation.

Practice Questions

Q1 Make a list of the main causes of environmental health problems.
Q2 What sort of solutions are tried to help solve environmental health problems?

Exam Questions

Q1 With reference to examples, describe how the health of city dwellers can be affected by the urban environment. (7 marks)

Q2 With reference to a named city in an MEDC, describe what is being done to try to improve air quality and comment on the level of success of the schemes. (7 marks)
N.B. This question could equally be tied to a named LEDC example. You should be prepared to answer a question this like by learning a case study from both an MEDC and an LEDC.

"The Brown Agenda" — planning to make sure toast gets well done...

For these pages, it's not enough to know what the problems are — you also have to show that you know what's being done to sort them out. This means you need to learn about recycling campaigns, laws to control pollution in the sea, smog tests, unleaded petrol and sewage treatment.

Managing Urban Social Problems

*The issue of social inequality within cities applies to both MEDCs and LEDCs, although the actual problems may be slightly different. These pages are for **Edexcel B**. P109 is also for **AQA B** and **OCR A**.*

Crime is a Problem for Urban Areas

1) **Statistics** of crime are often **unreliable** because a lot of crime goes **unreported**. People may think the police won't do much. They may be worried about reprisals and revenge from the offender, or scared of going to court.

2) Statistics are fairly reliable for **burglary** — most buildings are insured, so people have to report the incident to get the insurance money. Serious robberies are reported, but less serious muggings often aren't.

3) **Vehicle theft** is well reported because of **insurance claims**. Theft **from** vehicles is not often reported.

4) **Sexual crime** often **isn't reported** because victims feel ashamed, or because they're worried that the police or the court won't believe them — especially when the attacker is someone they know.

> The **British Crime Survey** is a survey of people's **individual experience** of crime.
> It aims to **fill in the gaps** in official crime figures, and find out how much crime there really is.

Different types of crime tend to happen in different areas of a city.

1) **Burglary** and **robbery** (theft with violence or the threat of violence) are most frequent in **inner cities**.

2) **Vehicle theft** is common in **large car parks,** e.g. park and ride, hospitals, work place car parks.

3) **Sexual attacks** are clustered in areas where there's **opportunity** for attackers, e.g. parks, river/canal banks, poorly lit areas, low density housing, areas of low police presence.

Urban Residents and Authorities have Different Responses to Crime

Crime has **direct** effects — the **financial** effect of losing property, the **trauma** of the actual event and fear of future attacks, and **physical** injuries from violent crime. These can result in **days lost from work**, which has a knock-on **economic** effect.

Crime also has **indirect** effects. **Property values go down** in areas with a high incidence of crime. **Insurance premiums go up** because its a high-risk area. The area becomes less attractive to further **investment**, which can make it fall into decline.

1) The most obvious response to crime is to put **more police** on the streets. This is very **expensive**.

2) **Zero tolerance policing** means arresting and prosecuting for all offences, even the not very serious ones (police and authorities are often tempted to **ignore** the "little" crimes such as graffiti and concentrate on the "big" crimes such as murder and large scale drug dealing). The big idea of zero tolerance policing is that people will **raise their standards** when they see that **no crimes are tolerated** at all. Zero tolerance policing has been used in **New York**, **Middlesbrough** and **Liverpool**.

3) **Private individuals** and **businesses** respond to crime by installing **burglar alarms** and **security cameras**, and employing **security guards**. People **insure** their homes and businesses against theft. People set up **neighbourhood watch schemes**, in partnership with the police.

4) People often **move away** from high crime areas if they can. Poorer people and people suffering **social exclusion** usually can't move away, though.

Strategy	Pros	Cons
More police on the streets	More crime is **detected**, and there's a big **deterrent** effect.	This is very **expensive**.
Zero tolerance policing	Zero tolerance sends a **clear message** that crime isn't tolerated. Criminals are **put off crime** at an early stage.	Zero tolerance doesn't always deter **drug addicts** from committing theft.
	In **principle**, there's **no room** for police officers to target people based on their **race**.	In **reality**, police officers may **still target people** based on their **race** (or the public might think this is what the police are doing).

Urban regeneration programmes help to fight crime. People are less likely to commit crime in nice, pleasant neighbourhoods than in run-down, slum neighbourhoods.

Race relations between police and public in some parts of New York suffered when Zero Tolerance was implemented.

Authorities Tackle Inequality in Access to Services

The **Social Exclusion unit** is part of the UK government. It reports on things like inequality in access to **health** services, **transport** services and **education**. The Social Exclusion unit recommends strategies to government departments.

Managing Urban Social Problems

There's **Segregation** of Different Groups in **Residential Areas**

1) Different ethnic and religious groups often live in segregated areas.

2) Reasons for segregation can be **positive**, e.g. sharing a common language or religious and cultural traditions.

3) Negative reasons include **discrimination** in the **housing market**, safety and defence against **racial prejudice** or high **unemployment** which gives rise to **poverty**, concentrating people in cheap, low-quality housing.

Ghettos are disadvantaged areas where a minority group lives

1) The minority group lives apart from others because they are forced to by **economic** or **social reasons**.

2) Ghettos are generally associated with **poverty**, **low incomes**, **high unemployment**, **poor quality housing** and **high crime levels**. Public **perception** of ghettos is partly due to their portrayal in the media.

3) **Inhabitants** of ghettos often feel that their services are the first to be cut back. They **feel unjustly treated** in comparison to wealthier neighbours. This **leads to social friction,** which often spills into violence.

The first ghettos were set up in European cities in the 16th century. The Christian majority forced Jews to live in segregated, walled-off areas of the city. The word "ghetto" is now used for any area where minorities are segregated.

Divisions Caused by **Religion** and **Ethnicity** are a **Challenge** for Cities

1) In **Northern Ireland**, **religious** and **political tension** exists between **Protestant Unionists** (in favour of belonging to the UK) and **Catholic Nationalists** (in favour of being part of Ireland instead).

2) In **Belfast** and **Derry/Londonderry**, the groups are segregated. They don't live on separate sides of the city, but in **small patches** of the city which are **intermingled** — one street can be Catholic and another street 50 metres away Protestant. In the late 20th century, there were frequent **confrontations** and **outbreaks** of **violence** between the two communities, known as the Troubles.

3) **Political action** (e.g. the Stormont talks) has done a lot to reduce the violence.

4) **Community groups** have been set up to bring young Protestants and Catholics together.

1) **Political division of land** in Palestine after the Second World War created the country of **Israel** as a **Jewish homeland**. This caused a lot of unrest between **Jews** and **Palestinian Arabs**, to put it mildly.

2) The city of Jerusalem is divided between **Jews** and **Arabs**. Both have claims to some of the city's **holiest sites**. Both would like to have the city as the **capital** of their **own country**.

3) **Peace talks** in the 1990s went some way to bringing peace to Jerusalem. The United Nations have made a plan to try and solve the problems in Palestine called the '**Road Map to Peace**'.

1) In Bradford, there's been **religious** and **ethnic** segregation, and **tension** between **whites** and **young Muslims of Pakistani origin**. Extreme right wing political organisations such as the BNP (British National Party) played on pre-existing fear and resentment. Tensions spilled over into **race riots** in 2001.

2) **Ethnic tensions** were made worse by **deprivation**. Only 31% of young ethnic minority people aged 16-24 had a job.

3) **Official reports** recommend projects which would develop a sense of **community spirit**, and get different ethnic groups **mixing together**. The recommended strategies all try to **avoid segregation** of different ethnic groups.

Practice Questions

Q1 Make a list of the various types of crime that affect people in urban areas.

Q2 Give two pros and two cons of zero tolerance policing.

Exam Questions

Q1 Describe, with reference to examples, strategies which can be tried to combat the problem of urban crime. (6 marks)

Q2 Describe what is meant by the term ghetto and describe reasons for the formation of ghettos in urban areas. (7 marks)

Unfortunately, these pages are emphatically NOT ghettofabulous...

Again, for this topic they want you to know what the problem is, and more importantly what's being done about it. The examiners like you to be able to weigh up a strategy and point out its successes and failures. They also like you to know about both public (paid for by the government out of taxes) and private (what Joe Public and the company he works for can do) strategies.

Urban Futures

*So, I wonder what's in store for cities in the future... These pages are for **Edexcel B**.*

Cities are **Regenerated** and **Redeveloped** for the **Future**

1) **Local and central governments want cities to be attractive places** where businesses would like to **invest**. Huge amounts of **central government finance** have been spent on **grants** to **regenerate** inner cities. There's lots more about urban regeneration on p94-95.

2) A recent trend in urban development is towards the "**24-hour city**".   Leisure and retail facilities stay open later at night.

3) A European city is selected each year to be "**City of Culture**". Gaining City of Culture status brings finance and investment, **prestige developments** and the potential for huge amounts of income from visitors during the year. It also helps bring about a big **improvement in public perception** of the city.

4) An important **international event** (such as the Commonwealth Games in Manchester in 2002 or the Olympic Games in Sydney 2000 and Athens 2004) brings large amounts of public finance and leaves the city with a wide **variety of facilities** which can be used by the population after the event. The **public image** of the city is improved.

Flagship projects are major initiatives to bring in lots of investment and show what the city can do

1) Many **flagship projects** have involved the **investment of large amounts of money** to improve the environment and quality of life in waterfront areas and to attract further investment, e.g. the Albert Dock in Liverpool, the Quayside in Newcastle, Salford Quays in Salford/Manchester, Canary Wharf in East London.

2) Former dockland areas were **renovated**, **converted** and **redeveloped** into modern, vibrant areas of **high quality housing**, **business premises** and **leisure facilities**. This was paid for by **government grants** and money from **private investors** — private investors hoped to make money by charging high rents to businesses.

3) These have **mostly** been very **successful** in attracting people back into inner city areas and in **creating** much-needed **employment** in the new high-tech industries which are attracted to these sites.

Case Study — London Docklands

Background: In the early 1980s, Docklands and the Isle of Dogs was an area of decaying 19th century **docks**, **poor quality housing** and **derelict** land. Male **unemployment** was at 24%. Local population was in **decline**, despite high rates of **immigration** from abroad. Housing in the area was 80% council housing, 30% of which was "**unfit for human habitation**".

Development: **London Docklands Development Corporation** (LDDC) was set up in 1981 to **renew** the area. Canary Wharf flagship office development on the Isle of Dogs provided 30,000 **jobs**. London Docklands Light Railway was built to connect the area to central London.

Successes: A derelict area of London has been **transformed**. The DLR and the Jubilee Line Extension put Central London just 10 minutes away. There are also links to London City Airport. By 2000 over 16 000 worked in Docklands. 20 000 new homes have been built and 8 000 council homes refurbished.

Limitations: There aren't many **opportunities** for the largely **unskilled** traditional population — 13 000 to 14 000 manual jobs have been lost since Docklands opened. Original residents can't afford to live in the new housing. There's still not enough **investment** in transport. Many so-called new jobs have been transferred from elsewhere in the City of London. A new young affluent population has **displaced** the traditional population.

Heritage tourism is a way forward for historic cities

1) Cities with a **historic background** have taken advantage of their cultural heritage to **attract tourists** and their money.

2) Chester and York have Roman walls, which can be developed as tourist attractions to generate income.

3) The Roman Fort at Castlefields, Manchester has been developed as part of the Rochdale Canal regeneration scheme which will become part of a World Heritage Site — a very important boost for the city.

4) Most heritage sites are not within cities but in **smaller towns**, e.g. Coalbrookdale (Ironbridge), Shropshire.

Urban Planners **Plan for the Future** and **Learn From Past Ideas**

There's more detail on New Towns and building materials on p88-89.

1) **Garden cities** were built to give people a better quality of life in spacious environments where pollution levels were low. They were the precursors of post war New Towns.

2) **New Towns** used modern materials, like concrete. People thought this was ultra-modern and super-cool at the time. Later, the architecture of the New Towns was harshly criticised. Pre-cast concrete doesn't look so nice any more.

3) Building on the lessons learned from the early New Towns, later towns like Milton Keynes had more **varied designs** and made more use of steel and glass. Of course, now some people think Milton Keynes has too much glass...

4) Urban planners still try to create an **ideal environment** in cities.

Urban Futures

Sustainable Cities are Set Up to Last

> "A sustainable city is one where achievements in social, economic and physical development are made to last" (UNCHS Sustainable Cities Programme)

1) A sustainable city should **encourage economic growth** and development, provide opportunities for individuals to **advance socially** and **reduce poverty**.

2) Sustainable cities must be able to **manage growth and change** on their own. **Local businesses** should be **adaptable** to **global competition**. **Local government** should have enough **power** to make changes.

3) Sustainable cities need a good infrastructure, and reliable provision of utilities like electricity, water and sewerage.

4) It's very important to manage the **consumption of resources** to avoid **stretching ecosystems** too far. **Waste management** and **recycling** are the way to go.

There are Obstacles in the way of Making a City Sustainable

Sustainable urbanisation needs action at **all levels** — local, national and international — and by a wide range of agencies, including governments and society in general. This is difficult to pull off.

1) There's **conflict** between **economic growth** in the here and now and **environmental sustainability**. Also, **changing urban economies** to make them sustainable **threatens** urban economic growth.

2) Social and political changes can **undermine traditional social structures**, which means people are likely to **resist** them.

3) Essential **infrastructure changes** (plumbing houses into mains water, putting electricity cables in) affect the natural and built environments. They need to be made in financially and environmentally sustainable ways.

4) It's **plain hard** to **manage the changes** to sustainability, and often **easier** to **not bother** with it.

There's Sustainable Urban Development in some LEDCs

Curitiba, capital of Parana State in **Brazil** is a good example of what can be done when planners and decision makers really **push for sustainability** and push to meet the "**Brown Agenda**" for improving the urban environment.

Case Study: Sustainable Development in Curitiba, Brazil

Background: Urban planning has been a focus for 30 years.

Management: Administrators set tasks and goals according to a master plan. There are 24 core projects, each project with its own co-ordinator who directs activities and liaises with other leaders, so all projects evolve simultaneously.

Transport: The transport system combines **low operating costs** with **quality service**, and carries 1.9 million passengers daily. It's an **integrated** system — people can travel through the city for a **single flat rate fare**, using either **bus** or **rail**, whichever's most convenient. **Longer distance travellers** (usually poorer commuters) are therefore subsidised by **short-distance travellers**. The transport system has won several **international awards**.

Green Areas: There's **52m² green area per inhabitant**. Green areas are a priority for municipal environmental and sanitation policy. Over 150 000 people visit the 21 million m² of maintained parkland every weekend. Most parks are along riverbanks or in valleys. Lakes are used as **flood control reservoirs**.

Recycling: Curitiba has pioneered **recyclable waste exchange schemes** — recyclables are exchanged for sacks of foodstuffs, teaching materials and toys. The city has won **international awards** for the amounts of rubbish recycled.

Other: School children help in monitoring water quality in some parts of the city.

Practice Questions

Q1 What is a "flagship development"?
Q2 What is "heritage tourism"?
Q3 Give two characteristics of sustainable urban development.

Exam Questions

Q1 With reference to specific examples, describe some of the ways in which cities regenerate and gain a new image. (4 marks)

Q2 With reference to a named example, describe the measures which have been taken to try to make the city sustainable. How successful have they been? (7 marks)

If Milton Keynes is anything to go by, urban futures are looking dodgy...

"Flagship development" is one of those phrases that officials use a lot, without ever really saying what it means. All it means is an important development that shows the world what the city's all about. For this urban futures topic, they want you to be able to make a few points about regeneration (it's worth looking back through the section), planning and sustainability.

Population Distribution and Density

This section is about where people live, why they live there, where they're moving to and why they're going there.
These two pages are just for OCR A.

Population Distribution and Density Aren't the Same

1) **Population distribution** is about **where** people live.

2) **Dot maps** are used to show population distribution. The world's population is **unevenly spread**, with many people in certain areas, e.g. Bangladesh, and very few people in others, e.g. Alaska.

3) **Population density** describes the **number** of people per **square kilometre**. It's the **total population** of an area divided by the **area**.

4) **Choropleth maps** show population density, using darker colours for **greater densities**. These maps show the **average density** for an area.

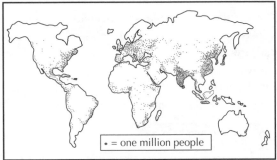

Dot map showing population distribution

• = one million people

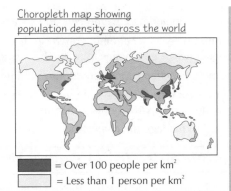

Choropleth map showing population density across the world

■ = Over 100 people per km²
□ = Less than 1 person per km²

There are Physical Factors Affecting Population Distribution and Density

Factor	Sparse population	Dense population
Climate	Areas of **extremes** — very **cold**, e.g. North Canada or very **hot**, e.g. Australian Outback. **Arid** and **semi-arid** land, e.g. Sahara desert, and very **humid** areas, e.g. Amazonia.	**Moderate climates**, e.g. NW Europe. **Monsoon lands**, e.g. India.
Relief	**High altitudes** and **steep slopes**, e.g. Rocky Mountains, Himalayas.	**Lowlands** and **coastal plains**, e.g. East USA.
Vegetation and soil	**Coniferous forest**, e.g. North Canada. **Rainforest**, e.g. Amazonia. **Tundra** e.g. Siberia.	**Fertile grassland** and cleared deciduous woodland, e.g. UK. **Alluvial soils**, e.g. Nile delta and Hwang-he floodplain.

There are Human Factors Affecting Population Distribution and Density

Factor	Sparse population	Dense population
Resources	**Few minerals** (e.g. Ethiopia), few **energy sources**, **poor soils**, poor **water** supplies.	**Rich resources** for **farming** or **industry**, e.g. Ruhr coalfield, Germany.
Accessibility	Mountains, deserts and forests make **transport** difficult.	Communications are easier in **lowlands**, **valleys** and **coasts**, e.g. SE England, Rhine Valley.
Farming potential	**Shifting cultivation**, e.g. Amazonia. **Nomadic herding**, e.g. Lapland or Siberia.	**Intensive farming**, e.g. India or the Netherlands.
Political factors	Low government **investment**, e.g rural Mexico.	**High investment**, e.g Tokyo, or Brasilia.

There are Global Patterns of Population Distribution and Density

1) World patterns are the result of combinations of the above physical and human factors.

2) Harsh environments such as **mountains**, **cold lands**, **deserts** and **rainforests** have a **small percentage** of the world's population. **Far more** of the world's people live in **lowlands** with **good soils**, **moderate** or **monsoon climates**, and **rich resources**. Which makes sense, when you think about it for longer than a nanosecond.

Population Distribution and Density

Population Distribution and Density in Brazil (LEDC)

- < 1 per km²
- 1 - 4.9 per km²
- 5 - 50 per km²
- > 50 per km²

1) Over **90%** of the population live near the **coast**.

2) Most people live in the **south east**. The south east has good **resources**, **natural harbours**, **industry** and plenty of **government investment**.

3) Very few people live in the **north** and **west**. The **Amazon basin** is hot, humid and difficult to farm. **Transport** is **difficult**.

4) **Brasilia** is a **New Town**, built as the new capital of Brazil.

5) **Manaus** and **Belem** are **river ports**.

Population Distribution and Density in the UK

Fewer people live in the **north** and **west**.

- There are inhospitable **mountains**.
- The **climate** is **wetter** and **colder**.
- **Soils** are poorer.
- There are **fewer jobs**, and more **accessibility** problems.

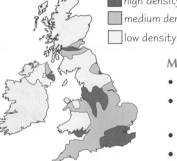

- high density
- medium density
- low density

More people live in the **south** and **east**.

- These were originally **industrial** areas.
- There are now many **conurbations** (big cities) with **tertiary** and **high tech** jobs.
- **Lowlands** are easier to build roads on.
- Soils are **more fertile**.

Population Distribution and Density in Northern England

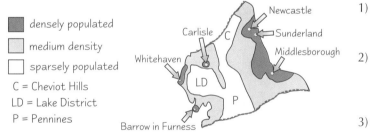

- densely populated
- medium density
- sparsely populated

C = Cheviot Hills
LD = Lake District
P = Pennines

1) There's high population density in the lowland areas around the mouths of the **Tyne**, **Wear** and **Tees** rivers. **Shipbuilding** was a major industry here.

2) There's high population density where **natural resources** were found — e.g. coal around Middlesborough and Whitehaven and **iron ore** around Barrow in Furness.

3) There's **medium** population density in **lowlands** and **valleys**, and **sparse** population in **mountain** areas.

Distribution and **density** often vary a lot over small distances. At the local scale, UK cities have denser concentrations of people living in inner city areas, with lower concentrations in suburbs, and very few people in the CBD.

Practice Questions

Q1 Define population distribution.

Q2 How is population density measured? (Give the formula.)

Q3 Name the type of map used to show population distribution.

Q4 Name and locate 3 world regions that have sparse populations.

Exam Questions

Q1 Explain, with an example, why river valleys are often densely populated. (4 marks)

Q2 Describe the population distribution of a named LEDC. (4 marks)

The people round here don't look all that dense to me...

It's useful to learn the lists of physical and human factors — they explain lots of other things in Geography too. It'd also be well worth swotting up on a bit of "world knowledge" — dig out a world map and see if you can pick out the densely populated areas and the sparsely populated areas. You can compare desert and mountain areas to areas of low population. It's almost fun.

Population Terms and Definitions

*Populations are **dynamic** — always changing. These pages will help you understand how and why — it's all to do with birth and death rates and population migrations. These two pages are for **AQA A**, **AQA B**, **OCR A** and **Edexcel A**.*

Population in **LEDCs** is **Growing Faster** than in **MEDCs**

Note: AQA A people don't need to learn carrying capacity, Malthus or Boserup.

Continent	Asia	Africa	Europe	S America	N America	Oceania
Years taken for population to double	46	28	n/a	38	119	63

Some areas have a higher birth rate or death rate than others.
Some have a lot of people migrating into the area.

The population of Europe is actually going down.

There are **Loads** of **Terms and Definitions** to Learn

(Crude) birth rate — **live births per thousand people per year**.

(Crude) death rate — **deaths per thousand people per year**.

Malawi has a very high birth rate — 51 per 1000. UK has 13 per 1000, Spain 9 per 1000. Sierra Leone has a high death rate — 30 per 1000. UK's is 11 per 1000. Kuwait's is only 2 per 1000.

Natural change — when **birth rate > death rate**, the population grows naturally unless people migrate away.
when **death rate > birth rate**, population falls unless people migrate in.

< means less than
> means more than

Replacement rate — a **birth rate** that's enough to **replace** the population, so the population doesn't go down. It's often given as the **number of babies** each woman needs to have, e.g. 2.1.

Zero growth rate — the population is **neither growing** nor **falling**.

Fertility rate — number of **live births per thousand women in the age range 15 – 44**.
It can also be given as the average number of children per female.

Infant mortality rate — number of **deaths of babies under 1 year old per thousand live births**.

Life expectancy — number of **years** a person can **expect to live** (also called **longevity**).

Dependency ratio — $\dfrac{\text{the number of } \textbf{children} \text{ (0-15 years)} + \text{number of } \textbf{elderly} \text{ (65+)}}{\text{number of people of } \textbf{working age} \text{ (16-64)}} \times 100$

MEDCs usually have a dependency ratio of 50-70. LEDCs often have a dependency ratio of over 100.

e.g. a figure of 54 means that for every 100 working people, there are 54 dependants.

Carrying Capacity Limits Population Size

1) The **rate** of growth of the world's population **increased massively** in the 20th century, in the **population explosion**.

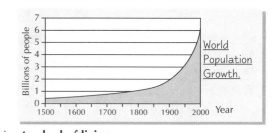

World Population Growth.

2) People are concerned that many areas have **reached** or **exceeded** the **carrying capacity** — the **largest population** an area's **resources** can support at a certain **standard of living**.

3) In the 1970s, 10 countries (the **Club of Rome**) forecasted that Earth's carrying capacity would be exceeded, resources would start to run out and **famine**, **pollution** and general doom would result.

4) Many countries have **too many people** in relation to their **resources** and level of **technology**. They are **overpopulated**. Ethiopia can be considered to be overpopulated.

5) Other areas are **underpopulated** — they have **more resources** than their populations can use, and with **high levels** of technology. Australia is underpopulated.

6) If resources and technology exactly suit the population, it has **optimum population** — a theoretical perfect situation.

Case studies:

	NE Brazil (overpopulation)	**Canada (underpopulation)**
Population density:	3 per km²	3 per km²
Climate:	semi-arid, droughts	mild to cold — good for farming or winter sports
Soil:	infertile, soil erosion	good, well managed soils
Standard of living:	poverty, poor housing, job shortages	wealthy, good housing, many jobs
Literacy levels:	low literacy	high level of literacy
Health:	poor, lots of disease, low life expectancy	good, high life expectancy
Technology:	poor	high
Resources:	some exploitation of minerals	rich in minerals, well exploited

density is too much for Brazil, but Canada could handle more people

Population Terms and Definitions

Malthusians have a Pessimistic View of Population and Resources

1) **Malthus** warned of **doom and gloom** way back in the 18th century. He wrote in 1798 that **population growth** would increase faster than **food supplies** could grow. Eventually, a "**population ceiling**" (carrying capacity) would be reached — people would run out of food and starve, reducing the population again.

2) He said **population checks** (e.g. people having kids **later in life** and having **smaller families**, or **disasters** like famine, war and disease), would end up happening to keep the lid on population growth. Malthus called the decision to have a **smaller family** a **preventive check** — it'd **prevent** the population growing so much in the first place. He called famine and disease **positive checks** — people would be born, but then they'd be killed off by starvation or poor health.

Boserup had an Optimistic View of Population and Resources

1) In 1965, she wrote that as populations grew, people's **skill** and **ingenuity** would **invent new technologies**.

2) The **18th century population explosion** in the UK coincided with the **Agricultural Revolution** and the **Industrial Revolution** — there were improvements in crops, and new inventions, e.g. steam engines.

3) The **Green Revolution** of the 1960s helped **India** deal with population increase, and improvements in **farming** and **industry** helped **Mauritius** in their overpopulation crisis.

Some Countries are Trying to Reduce their Rate of Population Growth

Case Study — China

Background: In 1949, China was **overpopulated**. There was famine, poverty, very low life expectancy (32 years), poor farming and industry. High birth rate of 45 per 1000.

Policy: In 1979, the **one-child policy** started. Each family could only have one child. The government used "carrots", e.g. free education, and "sticks", e.g. forced abortion, if a mother got pregnant again. The state provided contraception and abortion facilities.

Effects: By 1994, the birth rate had halved. However **boy babies** are more valued than girl babies. The sexes are now **imbalanced** — it's said this is because girls are sometimes killed at birth.

Future: With fewer new babies being born, the Chinese population will become elderly.

Other Countries are Worried about Low Growth Rates

Case Study — Singapore

Background: The government **reduced** rapid population growth with **birth control** (1960s).

Effects: This caused **zero growth** and concerns about **shortages of skilled workers**.

Policy: From 1987 the government encouraged middle income people to have several kids, and discouraged poor people from having kids at all. They paid **middle income parents** to have 2-3 children, and paid unskilled women to get sterilised.

Practice Questions

Q1 Which have lowest rates of population growth — LEDCs or MEDCs?

Q2 Define "zero growth rate" and "life expectancy".

Q3 How is the Dependency Ratio worked out?

Q4 What did Malthus say would happen when populations grew too large?

Q5 What does "carrying capacity" mean?

Exam Questions

Q1 For an area of your choice, outline some of its symptoms of overpopulation. (4 marks)

Q2 Outline the potential problems resulting from government policies to reduce population growth. (5 marks)

Ah, Social Darwinism...

It's entirely possible that you might, erm, "have views" about the Chinese policy of forced abortions, and the Singaporean policy of engineering a society full of Nice Well Educated Middle Class People. So if you want to have a quick rant now, feel free. In the exam, you'll be expected to cover the facts and evaluate/analyse calmly — looking at the pros and cons of the situation.

Population Change

You might well have met the Demographic Transition Model before if you did GCSE Geography.
*There's more detail at AS level though. These pages are for **AQA A**, **OCR A** and **Edexcel A**.*

The **Demographic Transition Model** (DTM) Describes **Population Growth**

This shows how the **populations** of countries **change** through time as they pass through **4 stages** (in some cases **5 stages**). The model shows changes in birth rates, death rates and total population.

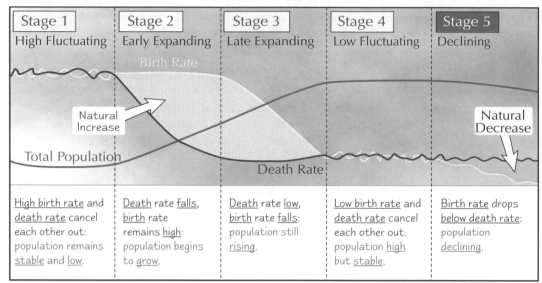

Stage 1	Stage 2	Stage 3	Stage 4	Stage 5
High Fluctuating	Early Expanding	Late Expanding	Low Fluctuating	Declining
High birth rate and death rate cancel each other out: population remains stable and low.	Death rate falls, birth rate remains high: population begins to grow.	Death rate low, birth rate falls: population still rising.	Low birth rate and death rate cancel each other out: population high but stable.	Birth rate drops below death rate: population declining.

At the moment, **tribes** in the **tropical rainforests** of Brazil and Papua New Guinea are in **Stage 1**.
Sri Lanka is in **Stage 2**, with a rapidly increasing population. **China** is in **Stage 3** — the birth rate has gone down, but the population is still rising. **South Korea** is in **stage 4**, and **Japan**, **Germany,** and **Italy** are in **Stage 5**.

There are **Reasons** why **Birth Rates Change** Through **Time**

Stages 1 and 2 — High Birth Rates around 35/1000

Social factors
1) There is no **birth control/family planning**, and **poor education**.
2) **Lots** of children are born **to replace** those who die.
3) Some **religions** favour large families, e.g. Islam, Catholicism.
4) Children are seen as a sign of **success** or **virility**.

Economic factors
1) Children are needed as **workers**.
2) Children help look after **elderly parents**. The more kids you have, the more money for your needs in old age.

In Gwyneth and Norman's case, having babies just seemed too cruel.

Stages 3 & 4 — Birth rates fall to between 20/1000 and 16/1000

Social factors
1) **Birth control/family planning** is increasingly used. **Education** is improved.
2) Infant mortality falls so there's **less need** to have lots of children.
3) **More women work**, rather than stay at home bearing children.

Stage 5 — births < deaths

Economic factors
1) Growth of **industry** and **mechanisation** means fewer workers are needed.
2) People want **possessions** and **wealth** rather than large families.

Political factors
Government **population policies** start in some countries.

Population Change

There are Reasons why Death Rates Change Through Time

Stage 1 — High Death Rates around 35/1000

Social factors

1) **Poor health**, **poor diet** and **disease** cause many deaths, especially of children.
2) **Health care** is **poor**, and **medical knowledge** in the past was limited.
3) **Poor hygiene**, **contaminated water**, no or poor **sanitation**.

Economic Factors

1) **Inadequate food production** and **transport** cause **famines**.
2) **Poverty**.

Political factors

Wars cause high death rates.

Just imagine life with no running water, no bathrooms, no loos...

Stages 2 (death rates falling to around 20/1000), 3 (16/1000) and 4 (12/1000)

Social factors

1) **Health improves** due to medical advances, e.g. vaccinations, new drugs, and **better diet**.
2) **Improved sewage disposal** and **clean water supplies** also increase life expectancy.

Economic factors

1) **Food production** and **transport of food** improve.
2) **Industrialisation** (in some countries) brings **wealth** for improved education and medical services.

Stage 5 — Death rates fall, but they're higher than birth rates

An increasingly **elderly population** means that more people die (of old age) than are born.

Governments Collect Data on Population Size, Births and Deaths

1) Governments like to be kept informed of population trends. This helps them to plan their policies. They need to know how much they'll have to spend on education, health care, pensions and looking after the elderly and ill.
2) Governments do a **census** every few years. A census basically counts the number of people in the country. In the UK, the census is done every **10** years (the last one was in 2001). The UK census form asks for information about people's age, job, state of health, and the type of house they live in.
3) **Births** and **deaths** in the UK also have to be **officially registered**, by law.

Practice Questions

Q1 What does the demographic transition model show?
Q2 In which stage of the demographic transition model is population growth the fastest?
Q3 In which stage do death rates start to fall?
Q4 In which stage do birth rates start to fall?

Exam Questions

Q1 Explain one social and one economic factor which contribute to a fall in the death rate. (4 marks)

Q2 Explain two factors that lead to a decline in birth rates. (4 marks)

Rabbits never seem to get much past Stage 2...

You're expected to know your way around the DTM. First off, it's worth making sure that you understand the diagram, and what happens to birth rate, death rate and the total population at each stage. Then, look at the reasons why the birth and death rates change. If you don't understand the model, there's no way you'll be able to say how well it applies to some random country.

Applying the DTM

These pages are about how well LEDCs and MEDCs compare to the DTM, and how useful the DTM really is as a tool.
*For **AQA A**, **OCR A** and **Edexcel A**.*

The UK's **Demographic History** Conforms Well to the **DTM**

1) **Stage 1 (prehistoric times to about 1760).** Population totals were **small**. Wars, the Black Death and other diseases such as cholera, typhoid and diphtheria meant **death rates** were **high**. Poor diet and hygiene helped kill people off. The high death rates cancelled out **high birth rates**. By 1700, the UK's population reached about 6 million.

2) **Stage 2 (1760-1880).** This had the **fastest** rate of population growth. Improved farming, industry and medical science made **death rates fall**, while **birth rates** remained **high**. By 1811 the population was about 12 million. There was high economic growth, and urban populations grew particularly fast.

3) **Stage 3 (1880-1940).** The 1881 population was 30 million. As birth control methods were improved, **birth rates fell**, and **death rates continued to fall** (except during World War 1). The population still grew, but at a **slower** rate.

4) **Stage 4 (1940 onwards).** This had **low birth and death rates** (although death rates were high during World War 2, with a "baby boom" afterwards). By 1941 the population was 47 million. Growth rates **slowed down**.

5) Today, we're reaching **Stage 5**, with **death rates exceeding birth rates** as the population grows older. The UK's total population is approximately 58 million, with pensioners outnumbering children and teenagers, and almost **zero growth**, and possible **decline**. By 2050, **a quarter** of UK's population will be **over 65**.

Most MEDCs Compare Fairly Well to the DTM

1) **Looking at history, MEDCs** have passed through Stages 1, 2 and 3 to reach **Stage 4 and beyond**, with low birth and death rates, long life expectancies and slow population growth.

2) During Stages 2 and 3 their **rapid growth** was accompanied by **great industrial growth**, **farming improvements** and **increasing wealth**. This is where they changed from being LEDCs to MEDCs.

3) Some MEDCs are in stage 5. Their birth rates are now **lower** than death rates, because the population is **ageing**. The population **declines**.

Examples of Stage 5: Germany, Italy, Russia, Japan, France, UK.

4) Governments' worries about Stage 5 are:

   - **Too few children** to **replace workforce** — e.g. Japanese women only have on average 1.4 children.
   - **Schools** will **close down** because there won't be enough children in their catchment area.
   - **Smaller workforce** and **less spending** will cause **economic decline**.
   - There'll be **fewer taxpayers** to support the growing numbers of elderly people.
   - It'll cost the state to provide care, residential homes, transport and hospital care for the elderly.

LEDCs are Mostly in the **Early Stages** — Pretty Much by Definition

1) The LEDCs are mostly in **Stages 2** (e.g. Sri Lanka) or **3** (e.g. China).

2) Many LEDCs entered **Stage 2** in the **1950s** (mostly due to medical improvements), but many of these population explosions **haven't** been accompanied by increases in **food supplies** or **economic wealth**. They've become **overpopulated** (e.g. Kenya, Bangladesh).

3) Some **former LEDCs** have had **rapid economic growth** and **population explosions** in the last few decades — they are the **NICs**, e.g. Malaysia and Taiwan, and are in **Stage 3** with strong policies to control population growth.

NICs stands for Newly Industrialised Countries. There's lots more about them on p132-133.

Case Study — India

Stage 1:	India was in Stage 1 until **1921** with high birth and death rates.
Stage 2:	Between **1921-81**, there were **falling death rates**. The birth rate varied, and a 1960s birth control policy wasn't successful (so India's stage 2 isn't exactly the same as the model).
Stage 3:	Began in 1981, with **birth rates clearly falling**.

Case Study — Kerala state, S. India
(successfully moving towards Stage 4)

One tenth of **government spending** is on health care and medical services.

Women are **better educated** and more **literate** than in other parts of India.

Women have traditionally had high social status in Kerala. Don't make the mistake of thinking "LEDC = Oppressed Wimmin".

They understand the benefits of **family planning**.

Birth rates are lower and life expectancy higher than the Indian averages.

Applying the DTM

The DTM can help to Inform Population Policies

1) The model shows governments what may happen to populations in the **future**.
2) This helps their **planning**, e.g. for housing or health care.

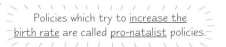
Policies which try to <u>increase the birth rate</u> are called <u>pro-natalist</u> policies.

France's Policy Aims to Increase the Birth Rate:

1) **Fertility rates** are below **2 children** per woman.
2) Population growth is **very low**.
3) **Life expectancy** is now 74 (men) and 82 (women) and the population is **ageing**.
4) Without immigration, the population (and workforce) will **fall**.
5) The government encourages **larger families** with poster campaigns, generous social security payments and pre-school care.

China's Policy is to Reduce the Birth Rate:

1) In **1950** China's population was 550 million and **rapidly growing**.
2) **Strong government policy** on family planning brought in the **one-child policy** in **1979**.
3) The population **will continue to grow** until the people who were born between 1950 and 1979 have all had their one child. Only **then** will they move into **Stage 4**.
4) By around **2040**, population **decline** will start and China will be into **Stage 5**.

There's more detail about the one-child policy on p115.

The DTM is Useful, but it Also Has Limitations

1) The DTM gives a **generalised** picture of **population changes**.
2) It **forecasts** what may happen in the **future**, helping government **policies**.
3) It's **easy to compare countries** with the DTM — you can say "this country is in Stage 2 and this one is in Stage 4", and then scratch your chin and attempt to look intellectual...

BUT...

4) The original research was done in Europe. It might not be valid to apply the model world-wide. What happens in Europe might not be the same as what happens in Asia or Africa.
5) The original model **doesn't** have Stage 5 — that was added later.
6) It doesn't consider **migration**, and there's a whole lot of international migration going on.
7) The original model didn't consider things like **education** and the role of **women** which affect the number of people who have babies (e.g. increased higher education means many people **delay** having a family).
8) Countries with **different customs** may change in different ways (e.g. Catholic countries still favour large families and frown on birth control, but some countries welcome birth control within marriage). In India, population growth has slowed more quickly than the model predicts.
9) **Poverty** and low levels of development may **prevent** many LEDCs from passing through all the stages.
10) The DTM **can't predict exactly when** countries will reach each stage, or how long each stage will last.

Practice Questions

Q1 Which stage of the DTM are most LEDCs in?
Q2 Name 4 countries in Stage 5.
Q3 Describe what happens to: a) birth rates, b) death rates, and c) average age of the people in Stage 5.
Q4 What problems do countries in Stage 2 face? Name a country in Stage 2.

Exam Questions

Q1 For a named MEDC, explain why the government has a policy in favour of more births. (3 marks)

Q2 What challenges face countries in Stage 5 of the DTM? (4 marks)

Yes, that really was ANOTHER two pages about the DTM...

But you know, beggars can't be choosers. And in this game, "beggars" = "you". The only choosing you get to do is to choose which case studies you're going to learn for the exam. You can learn the ones in here, or if your teacher taught you different ones in class, you can learn those if you prefer. But learn you must — the Demographic Transition Model, the examples, the whole lot.

Types and Theories of Migration

Migration is the **movement** of people. People can move into an area (**immigration**) or out of an area (**emigration**).
Migration is an important part of **population change**. These pages are for **AQA A** and **OCR A**. They're useful for **Edexcel A**, too.

There are Many Different Categories of Migration

(1) **You can classify by the causes.**
1) There are **voluntary** moves, when people decide freely to migrate.
2) **Forced** moves are compulsory, e.g. foreigners expelled from a country.

(2) **You can classify by distance.**
1) **Internal migration is within the same country** (e.g. a move from Blackburn to a new job in Newcastle).
2) **International migrants** go abroad (e.g. Britons retiring to Spain).

(3) **You can classify by duration.**
Moves can be **daily** (e.g. commuting), **periodic** (e.g. a holiday),
seasonal (e.g. tourism workers, nomadic herders) and **permanent** (people move to a new address).

(4) **You can classify by type of area.**
1) There are **rural to urban** moves (e.g. from Mexican villages to Mexico City),
and **urban to rural** moves (e.g. UK city family moving to the countryside).
2) There are **MEDC to MEDC** moves (e.g. Britons going to work in USA).
3) There are **MEDC to LEDC** moves (e.g. an aid worker or volunteer moving from the UK to Eritrea).
4) There are **LEDC to LEDC** moves (e.g. people escaping from harsh governments or civil war).
5) And finally, there are **LEDC to MEDC** moves (e.g. Bangladeshis moving to the UK to seek work).

Ravenstein (1880s) Came Up with some Common Patterns of Migration

1) Most migrants move **short distances**.
2) Moves go in **stages** or **waves** — as people move on,
so other migrants move in to take their place.

> Movement in stages is called <u>step migration</u>.

3) Migration is a two-way process — **immigration** and **emigration**.
Net migration is the difference between the two.
4) **Long-distance migrants** usually go to **major cities**.
5) **Rural** people **migrate more** than **urban** people. Remember, Ravenstein was writing in
the **19th century**, when farm workers in UK and USA were flocking to the cities for jobs.
6) **Women** move more in **internal migrations**, while **men** are more likely to move **abroad**.

The Gravity Model is Based on the Law of Gravity

The **Gravity Model** says that cities pull people towards them, just like a large object pulls things towards it by gravity.
The Gravity Model suggests that the **larger** the town, the **greater** its pull on migrants.
This is true today in LEDCs, where rural migrants have heard more about the big cities.

> If you want to put names to this theory, Zipf and Reilly are the ones.

Zelinsky Described Migration in the Mobility Transition Model

Zelinsky Described Five Stages of Migration

Stage 1: There **isn't much migration** in **pre-industrial** times.
Stage 2: There's **rural to urban migration**, and **emigration** to colonise new lands.
Stage 3: There are **rural to urban**, and **inter-urban** movements.
Stage 4: Now, there's **less rural to urban** movement. **Inter-urban moves continue**,
though. There's **immigration** of labourers, and international **exchanges** of
professionals in TNCs (Trans-National Companies).
Stage 5: There are advanced societies with **intra-urban** and **inter-urban** moves.
There's **less need for movement** because advances in IT mean people can work
together over the internet and email. **Governments** may **restrict** migration.

> Inter-urban migration means movement <u>between</u> towns. Intra-urban moves are <u>within</u> towns.

Types and Theories of Migration

The Causes of *Voluntary Migration* Involve *Push Factors* and *Pull Factors*

Push factors are what's **bad** about the **current situation** that people want to **get away** from.

Type	Examples of Push factors
Physical	Harsh environment, poor soils, hazards, e.g. flood or drought, extreme climate, noise, pollution.
Economic	Poverty, unemployment, low wages, low status jobs.
Social	Isolation, inadequate services, poor housing, health and education.
Political	Fear caused by ethnic persecution or war.

Pull factors are what's **good** about the area that people are **moving to**. They're all the **opposites** of the push factors above. Pull factors can be **real** or **perceived** — if someone genuinely **believes** that the streets of London are **paved with gold**, they'll want to move there, even though no London Borough **really** has enough money for gold-based pavements. Not even Kensington and Chelsea.

If you're asked to give two factors influencing migration, don't give a push factor and its immediate opposite, e.g. "there are jobs in the destination area and no jobs in the area of origin". This doesn't count as two different factors, so you won't get all the marks.

Lee's Model Describes *How* People *Decide* to Move

1) People **weigh up** the push and pull factors. Both the **home area** and the **destination area** will have push and pull factors. People's **attitude** to their home area and their **perception** of the destination are important.

2) There may be **intervening obstacles** making it **difficult** to move, e.g. the cost, or the hassle of finding a new job, or a new school for the kids.

3) There are also **intervening opportunities**. For example, people may not get to their planned eventual destination because they **find work on the way**.

4) **Distance** affects migration. **Long distance moves are costly**, and places will be **less familiar**, and far from relatives, so most people move **short** distances. The **longer** the **distance**, the **more hassle** it is to move. This is called the principle of **distance decay**.

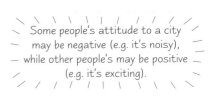
Some people's attitude to a city may be negative (e.g. it's noisy), while other people's may be positive (e.g. it's exciting).

Place of origin
Advantages — pull factors.
Disadvantages — push factors.

Intervening obstacles
- It's a long way.
- It's expensive to move.
- The destination may have different language or culture.
- Government policy may not support the move.

Intervening opportunities
Nice places on the way, with good jobs.

Destination
Advantages — pull factors.
Disadvantages — push factors.

Practice Questions

Q1 Define "internal migration" and "voluntary migration".
Q2 Write down two of Ravenstein's ideas about migration.
Q3 Explain how something like Newton's Law of Gravity can be applied to migration.
Q4 What does Lee's model say stands in between the place of origin and the destination place?

Exam Questions

Q1 State and explain two possible reasons for internal migration. (4 marks)

Q2 Describe the principle of distance decay, and explain its effects on migration. (3 marks)

It's not like the days when you were born, lived and died in the same village...

There are standard push and pull factors — job prospects, physical factors, services and political factors. I wouldn't be tempted to apply them all to every single situation — if the question is about a specific country, you have to be careful to give an answer that actually fits that country. Take care when learning the Ravenstein, Zelinsky and Lee Models — don't get them mixed up.

Causes of Migration

P122 is about international migration, and p123 is about migration within the same country.
*These pages are for **AQA A** and **OCR A**. They're also useful for **Edexcel A**.*

There are **Various Causes** of Migration

1) Many people emigrate for **economic reasons** — to find work or higher pay. In the 1970s, Indian and Chinese workers went to the growing industries of east and south east Asia.

2) Skilled and professional people move for **higher salaries**, e.g. **Indian** and **South African** doctors to the **UK**, **British scientists** to the **USA** — these moves are called "the **Brain Drain**" because countries **lose** their brightest and best trained people.

3) Some people move to **retire**, e.g. from the UK to Tenerife in the Canary Islands.

4) Some people are **forced** abroad, e.g. Kosovan refugees forced by ethnic conflict and civil war in Kosovo to move first to Albania, and then to western European countries.

Learn the **Causes** of **West Indians** Moving to the **UK**

After World War 2, the UK Government **welcomed** immigrants from the Caribbean as workers in many lower paid jobs. West Indian immigrants went to **conurbations** such as London or Birmingham. The migrants' **negative attitudes** to conditions in the West Indies were the push factors. Their **positive perceptions** of the UK were the pull factors.

Push factors — disadvantages of the West Indies

Physical — There was a **shortage** of **farmland**. There had been a high birth rate, and each family had to share its land around among several children.

Economic — There were shortages of **jobs**, poor **wages** and **poverty**.

Social/cultural — **High birth rates** added to the overpopulation problem.

Pull factors — advantages of moving to the UK

Economic — There were good **job opportunities** and higher wages in the UK.

Social/cultural — Migrants were attracted by better services, housing, schools and health care, and by the **encouraging news** sent home by **previous migrants** to their families.

Political — The **UK Government** helped migrants to move. The West Indies were **colonies** of the United Kingdom. Everyone there had been encouraged to see **England** as the "**mother country**", and felt that they would be **welcomed** with open arms and feel at home in England.

To start with, everyone from Commonwealth countries (former British Empire colonies) had the right to live in the UK. Immigration restrictions for people from Commonwealth countries have only applied since 1962.

Learn the **Causes** of **Mexicans** Moving to **California**

Many migrants cross from Mexico (LEDC) into California (USA — MEDC) every year. Some are **legal immigrants** (who obtain a Green Card and can legally work), but many try to cross the heavily-patrolled border at night **illegally**.

Push factors

Physical — The climate is **semi-arid**, with droughts. The **soil** is **poor**.

Economic — There were shortages of **jobs**, poor **wages** and a low standard of living. In 1987, the Peso (Mexico's currency) crashed, and the economy looked dire.

Social/cultural — There's **overpopulation** in some parts of Mexico.

Pull factors

Physical — Better **soil** for farming, **well irrigated**.

Economic — Lots of **job opportunities** in casual farm labour, e.g. **fruit picking**.

Social/cultural — There's a high **quality of life** in the USA. Also, there are Mexican immigrants already in California — there's already a **Mexican community**.

Fruit farms in California depend on Mexican immigrants coming in each year for the fruit picking season.

People with friends and relatives already in the USA are more likely to emigrate than people who don't know anyone in the USA.

Causes of Migration

In the **UK**, There was a **Drift to the South** in the 20th Century

From **1930s to 1980s**, people were leaving **Northern** and **Western** areas (e.g. Tyneside, Merseyside, Scotland) and moving to the **South** and **East** (London suburbs and southern counties).

Factor	The push of the north and west	The pull of the south and east
Physical	Colder, wetter climate. High land, difficult transport.	Warmer, drier climate. Low lying, easy to build roads.
Economic	Decline in farm jobs and heavy industry / shipbuilding. Lower wages and standard of living.	Growth of jobs in offices, and high tech industry. Higher wages and standard of living.
Social/ cultural	Poorer quality of life and services. Less entertainment.	Better quality of life and services. More theatres, sport facilities, etc.

There are Lots of **Rural to Urban** Moves in **LEDCs**

The movement of **rural people** to **cities** in LEDCs is an **enormous** and **accelerating** one. Hundreds of people arrive every week in Mexico City.

Rural to urban migration, plus the high birth rates among the younger migrants, is the cause of the rapid urbanisation (the increase in the urban population) in LEDCs today.

Case Study — Causes of Migration to Mexico City

Factor	Push factors of villages	Pull factors of Mexico City
Physical	Poor soils, soil erosion, drought. Shortage of land. Inhospitable semi-arid climate.	Freedom from physical hazards. Low lying, easy to build roads.
Economic	Poverty, job shortage, low pay, very hard labour on farms.	Hope of better jobs and higher wages in factories.
Social and Cultural	Poor access to services, e.g. schools and doctors.	Cities look attractive, with services, entertainment, etc.
Political	Not much investment.	More government investment.

In the **UK**, People **Move House** a Lot Within their **Local Area**

Some people move house many times, e.g. from **inner city** to the **suburbs**, from **urban** to **rural** areas (in the **counter-urbanisation** process), from **cities** to **New Towns**, and today some are moving back into **new housing areas** or expensive **apartments** near the city centre. The **causes** of the moves are people's **different attitudes** and **changing circumstances**.

Counter-urbanisation is the reverse of urbanisation — people moving from urban to rural areas. There's lots more about it in both Sections 7 (Rural) and 8 (Urban).

Practice Questions

Q1 Name an example of an international migration from an LEDC to an MEDC.

Q2 What are the economic pull factors that caused this migration?

Q3 Define urbanisation and counter-urbanisation.

Q4 Name two regions of the UK that had a net loss of migrants because of the Drift to the South.

Exam Questions

Q1 Explain how people's negative attitudes to their rural home have pushed them to a named city in an LEDC. (5 marks)

Q2 Explain the economic factors which led to the Drift to the South in the UK. (4 marks)

That's it, I'm emigrating to South Georgia to live with the penguins...

You're supposed to know the causes of migration — economic, physical, social and political. The easiest way is to divide them up into push factors and pull factors. It's worth having a really good grasp of one MEDC example and one LEDC example — the examiners can ask you to refer to an example in your answer. No example, bad student, no (biscuit) marks.

Effects of Migration

*Migration has **positive** and **negative** impacts on the **migrants**, the area of **emigration** and the area of **immigration**. People sometimes have particularly strong attitudes to **international** migration. These pages are for **AQA A**, **Edexcel A** and **OCR A**.*

There are Positive and Negative Effects of International Migration

	Positive effects of international migration	Negative effects of international migration
Social	Many **immigrants** are teachers and health care workers. This helps the health and education system.	**Tension** between races can lead to **violence**, (e.g. UK inner city riots in 1980s).
Cultural	Different **cultures** are introduced (e.g. West Indian food, music, carnivals).	**Immigrants** may face **language** problems.
Economic	**Caribbean** workers **helped UK recover after WW2**, filling vacancies in the NHS, construction, transport, etc. **Mexicans** in **California** work hard for low pay. **Immigrants** earn **higher wages** than they can at home.	Immigrants put a strain on **schools**, **health services** and **housing**. Immigrants are **resented** when **unemployment** rises.
Environmental	Damage to the **environment** (e.g. by over-farming) is **lessened** in the **emigration** area.	Many immigrants **remain poor**, and live in **slums** and **ghettos**, which suffer ongoing poverty.
Demographic	Immigration can **help** countries with an **ageing population** and **population decline** (e.g. Germany), because immigrants are usually of working age.	Immigrants are **young** — the **birth rate rises**. The population of the **emigration** area becomes **elderly** as young people leave.

Southall in **West London** is an area with a large population of **South Asian immigrants**, in particular Sikhs from the **Punjab** region of India. Southall grew very quickly in the 1950s and 1960s, when immigrants from Commonwealth countries were invited to the UK. There are lots of **Punjabi** food shops, clothes shops, music shops and restaurants — the area is known by some people as "**Little India**".

Brixton in **South London** has a large population of **black** people of **Caribbean** and **African** origin — from the original West Indian immigration of the 1950s. Brixton has a thriving multi-ethnic **cultural scene**. There was bad deprivation and **racially motivated rioting** in Brixton in the early 1980s, and small amounts of deprivation still remain.

The Effects of Internal Migration – Rural to Urban Migration in LEDCs

	Positive effects of LEDC rural-urban migration	Negative effects of LEDC rural-urban migration
Social	Migrants have access to **better services**, e.g. schools and shops.	Crowded **shanty towns** have **disease**, e.g. cholera, and lack **clean water** and **sanitation**.
Economic	There are **more jobs** to go round in the **villages**.	City authorities don't have enough **money** for **houses**, **medical services** and **schools** for immigrants.
Environmental	**Pressure** on the environment in **rural** areas is eased.	LEDC cities are **growing too rapidly** (urban sprawl). Shanty towns are built in **hazardous** environments like steep landslide-prone slopes (e.g. São Paulo).
Demographic	**Village birth rates fall**, easing problems of famine and overpopulation.	**Village** populations become **elderly**, while **city birth rates rise rapidly**.

There's more about rural to urban migration on pages 80-81 and shanty towns on page 99.

Learn These Effects of Internal Moves in the UK

1) The **"Drift to the South"** reduced demand for housing in the North and increased demand for housing in the South. **House prices** in the **North fell**, and house prices in the **South rose**.

2) Some areas lost many people (**rural depopulation**). There are **abandoned farms** in some rural areas, especially the North Pennines.

3) **Urban to rural** moves lead to **rises** in **village house prices**, increases in **commuting traffic**, and **environmental damage** as more houses are built. There's more about this in Section 7.

4) **Recent trends in internal moves** have been back from the suburbs into city centres. This is **re-urbanisation**, which has **improved** the inner city **environment**, e.g. London's Docklands and Birmingham's Brindley Place. Counter-urbanisation of the wealthy to rural homes is another recent trend.

Government Migration Policy

Resettlement Policies *Force People to Move*

Governments sometimes have a policy of **forced** migration.

Most government migration policies aren't as extreme as this — they usually encourage or discourage voluntary moves.

1) China's **resettlement policy** forced over 2 million people to move to the western province of Xinjiang (1990s). The government wanted to **develop** the area, **relieve overpopulation** elsewhere and make the area more culturally Chinese (ethnic Chinese were previously a minority in Xinjiang). Also, the Three Gorges dam project (completion 2009) will **displace** over 1 million people in order to build a huge reservoir.

2) **Transmigration** is a forced movement of people from a **densely populated area** to **less crowded areas**, e.g. in Indonesia from Java to Sumatra.

Development of less crowded Indonesian islands has caused deforestation, and conflicts with locals.

3) South Africa's **white** government's **apartheid** policy forced **black** people (the majority) to move to "Bantu homelands" often on the poorest land or to "black townships" in cities (e.g. Soweto on the outskirts of Johannesburg).

Apartheid, a policy of separating the races, was abolished in 1994, and segregation ended.

Guest Workers *are* Actively Encouraged *to Migrate, e.g. Turks to Germany*

1) The German government **welcomed** Turks into Germany to help **re-build** the country after World War 2 and solve their **labour shortage**. The Turkish workers were called guest workers (*Gastarbeitern* in German), and classified as **temporary migrants**, even when they'd been in Germany for years.

2) Germany now wants guest workers to **return to Turkey**, because of **unemployment** caused by the **reintegration of Germany**. Unemployed workers from **former East Germany** compete with Turks for limited jobs.

3) But this is problematic, because the **children** of the original Turkish guest workers consider **Germany** to be their home.

Italian and Spanish workers went to Germany as guest workers too. Italy and Spain are part of the EU along with Germany, but Turkey isn't. EU workers can work anywhere in the EU, and can't be chucked out of Germany.

The Number of *Refugees and* Asylum Seekers *is* Increasing World Wide

1) In **international law**, a refugee is a person who has **migrated to another country** because they **fear persecution**. People who have to move because of **natural disasters** are often called refugees, too.

2) In the early **1990s**, there were large numbers of refugees from civil wars in Somalia, Eritrea, Ethiopia and Liberia.

3) In **1994** in **Rwanda**, horrendous violence based on ethnic divisions killed 500 000 people and caused 5 million people to be displaced both within Rwanda and in neighbouring countries. There were **2 million Rwandan refugees** in the Democratic Republic of Congo (formerly Zaire), Tanzania and Burundi.

4) In **1999** over 2 million **Kosovans** fled from civil war in the **former Yugoslavia**.

5) Most refugees go from one LEDC to another — over 80% of refugees are in LEDCs.

Asylum seekers are people who enter a country and want to be **officially classified as refugees**. Once they've been **granted asylum**, they can **stay** in the country. Many are fleeing from **poverty** rather than persecution, though.

MEDCs now tend to take a **tough line** on asylum seekers. In the late 1990s and early 2000s, the **Sangatte Red Cross camp** near Calais provided a temporary home for asylum seekers. Large numbers of people were leaving Sangatte and crossing the Channel to **enter the UK illegally**, so the camp was disbanded and demolished in 2002.

Practice Questions

Q1 Describe one social and one economic advantage of international migration.

Q2 Name an area of the UK with a net gain of internal migrants.

Q3 Name an area of the UK with a net loss of migrants.

Q4 Define "transmigration" and "resettlement".

Exam Questions

Q1 What are "guest workers"? Using an example, explain why they have become a problem to some countries. (5 marks)

Q2 What are some of the negative impacts on cities in LEDCs as a result of rural to urban migration? (4 marks)

Sometimes it works out, sometimes it doesn't...

You might have to answer a question about the physical impact of migration in an LEDC, or it might be about the cultural impact in an MEDC. There's no way of knowing which it'll be until you're sat there in the exam room — so the best bet is to learn a decent example for each subheading section on the page. Make sure you know about government policies on migration, too.

Population Structure

*It's not just population size, growth and movement that are important. Population **structure** is important, too. Some countries have a lot of children, some have a lot of old people. For **AQA A**, **Edexcel A** and **OCR A**.*

Population Structure is How the Population is Made Up

Population structure is the **number** or **%** of **males** and **females** in the different **age groups**.
Population **pyramids** (age-sex pyramids) show population structure, and reveal **lots** of information.

Population pyramid for France (MEDC), 1997

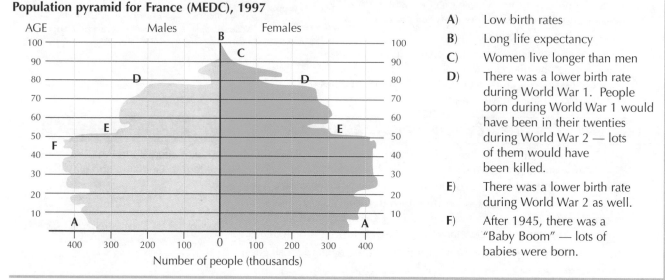

A) Low birth rates

B) Long life expectancy

C) Women live longer than men

D) There was a lower birth rate during World War 1. People born during World War 1 would have been in their twenties during World War 2 — lots of them would have been killed.

E) There was a lower birth rate during World War 2 as well.

F) After 1945, there was a "Baby Boom" — lots of babies were born.

Population pyramids show how many dependants there are. You can work out the dependency ratio from the number or percentage of **young dependants** (aged 0–14), **economically active people** (aged 15-64) and **elderly** people (see page 114).

Population Structure Varies from Place to Place, and Over Time

1) Pyramids for different countries vary because of **demographic factors** (different birth, death and fertility rates), **wars** and **migration**.

2) Pyramid shapes show which **stage** of the Demographic Transition Model a country is in (p116-119). A country's structure **changes** through **time** as it moves into the next stage.

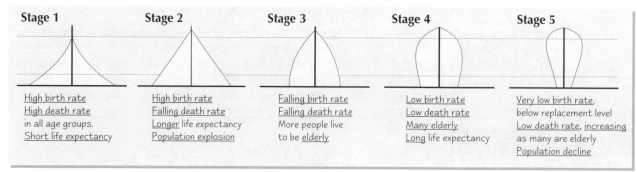

Stage 1
High birth rate
High death rate
in all age groups.
Short life expectancy

Stage 2
High birth rate
Falling death rate
Longer life expectancy
Population explosion

Stage 3
Falling birth rate
Falling death rate
More people live
to be elderly

Stage 4
Low birth rate
Low death rate
Many elderly
Long life expectancy

Stage 5
Very low birth rate,
below replacement level
Low death rate, increasing
as many are elderly
Population decline

3) Some pyramids show the effects of **immigration** and **emigration**.

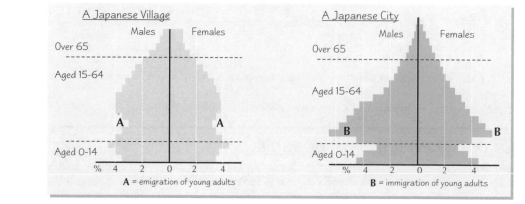

Population Structure

A *Youthful Population* has *Socio-Economic* and *Political* Impacts

Malawi is an LEDC with a particularly large number of young dependants.

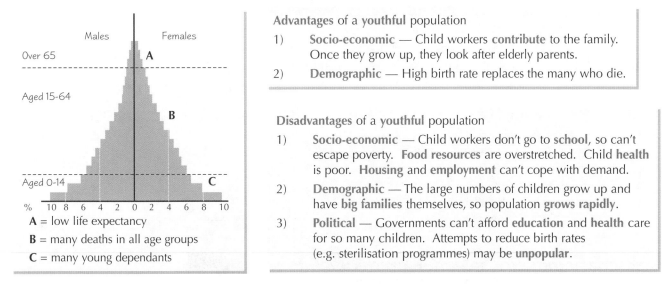

A = low life expectancy
B = many deaths in all age groups
C = many young dependants

Advantages of a **youthful** population

1) **Socio-economic** — Child workers **contribute** to the family. Once they grow up, they look after elderly parents.

2) **Demographic** — High birth rate replaces the many who die.

Disadvantages of a **youthful** population

1) **Socio-economic** — Child workers don't go to **school**, so can't escape poverty. **Food resources** are overstretched. Child **health** is poor. **Housing** and **employment** can't cope with demand.

2) **Demographic** — The large numbers of children grow up and have **big families** themselves, so population **grows rapidly**.

3) **Political** — Governments can't afford **education** and **health** care for so many children. Attempts to reduce birth rates (e.g. sterilisation programmes) may be **unpopular**.

An *Ageing Population* has *Socio-economic* and *Political* Impacts

Holiday resorts on the south coast of the UK have a large percentage of over 65s.

Advantages of an **elderly** population

1) **Socio-economic** — Children have grandparents for longer. Some elderly people have wealth to spend, e.g. on travel.

2) **Demographic** — Slow rate of population growth.

Disadvantages of an **elderly** population

1) **Socio-economic** — Greater **demand** for public services, e.g. hospitals, but **fewer working people** paying **taxes** to fund these services. Many elderly live in poverty.

2) **Demographic** — Birth rates **fall** and the population may **decline**.

3) **Political** — Governments may have to close schools. They may recruit **workers from abroad** (e.g. nurses), but locals often object. They may try to **increase the birth rate** — this costs money.

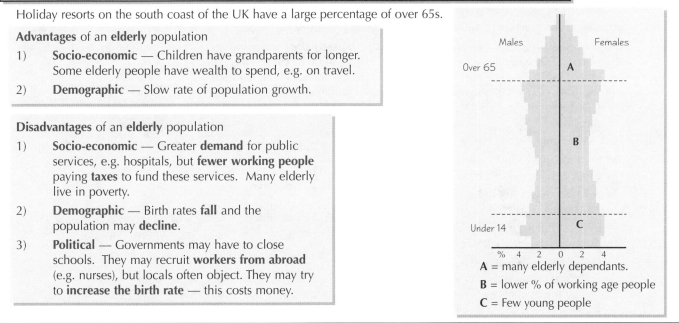

A = many elderly dependants.
B = lower % of working age people
C = Few young people

Practice Questions

Q1 Define population structure.
Q2 What is the other name for a population pyramid?
Q3 If a pyramid has a narrow base, what does this tell you?
Q4 Name two countries with a pyramid like the one described in Q3.

Exam Questions

Q1 Describe and explain the shape of the Malawi population pyramid. (6 marks)

Q2 Explain how wars affect the shape of population pyramids. (3 marks)

The idea of population pyramids reminds me of those Russian acrobats...

There are as many disadvantages to having too many little kids in the population as there are to having too many old people. Either way, lots of dependants means that there's a big strain on services like schools and hospitals, and not enough working people around to foot the bill. Countries like the UK who are in Stage 5 of the DTM face a future with a very large elderly population.

Sectors of Economic Activity

There are different ways of classifying industries — these are the classifications that the AQA exam board uses.
*These pages are for **AQA A** and **AQA B**.*

Primary Industry *is **Extraction** and **Collection***

1) **Primary industry** is the **extraction** or **collection** of resources.

2) Primary industries include **quarrying**, **mining**, **forestry** and **farming**.

3) Primary activities **provide** the resources for **secondary industry**.

4) Primary employment is more associated with **LEDCs** — as countries **develop**, primary industry and employment **decreases**.

Primary employment in the UK

1) In 1790, most employment was in **farming**.

2) In 1890, after the Industrial Revolution, most people were working in **manufacturing** (secondary industry).

3) By 1990, primary industry was affected by **competition** from abroad. Most people in the UK were employed in **other sectors**.

% primary employment

75% (1790)   15% (1890)   3% (1990)

Secondary Industry *is **Manufacturing** and **Processing***

1) Secondary industries involve **processing raw materials** and **manufacturing products** out of them — e.g. turning iron ore into steel, turning wheat into bread, making paper out of wood pulp, making cars, televisions, microwave ovens, etc. **Construction** (building) is also a secondary industry.

2) Over the last 30 years, the percentage employed in the secondary sector has increased in LEDCs and decreased in MEDCs. In **Bangladesh in 1996, 10%** were employed in the secondary sector — the economy still has an **agricultural** (primary) base. In the **UK**, the percentage employed in the secondary sector is **falling** — it went down from **28%** in 1990 to **25%** in 2000.

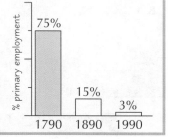

Bangladesh   Brazil
63% 10%   23% 20%
     25%   57%

UK   2%
     25%
  73%

primary ☐
secondary ☐
tertiary ☐

Secondary employment in the UK

1) In 1790, people had just started to **migrate** to urban areas to work in **manufacturing**.

2) In 1890, there was **full industrialisation** in the UK following the Industrial Revolution — secondary employment was pretty much at a **peak**.

3) By 1990, much of the UK had **de-industrialised**.

4) In the UK, there's a marked **regional variation** in secondary activity. In the **north** of the UK, **35%** of the workforce is employed in **secondary** activity. In the **south** of the UK, only **23%** of the workforce is employed in **secondary** activity.

% secondary employment

15% (1790)   55% (1890)   28% (1990)

Tertiary Industry *is **Services***

1) "**Services**" is one heck of a broad classification. It includes:

- Transport
- Communication
- Retail
- Entertainment, leisure and tourism
- Finance

Some geographers divide the tertiary sector into services for producers (i.e. businesses), services for consumers and services for the public. Producer services are lumped together as the quaternary sector, and public services are lumped together as the quinary sector. Consumer services stay as the tertiary sector.

2) **Tertiary industry** is strong in **MEDCs** — these countries have a great **demand** for **services**. In the **UK**, **tertiary activity** accounts for **two thirds** of total **economic output**. There's been a **huge increase** in **service** employment in the **UK** over the last 30 years.

3) **Cities** attract most service employment. High rents, high salaries, traffic congestion and shortage of space to expand are forcing offices to the **edges of cities**, e.g. from Central London to Croydon.

Sectors of Economic Activity

Quaternary Industry is Finance and Insurance for Producers

1) **Quaternary** industry provides services to **producers**, to help them sell their products.
2) These services include **advertising** and **wholesaling**, which both help distribute products.
3) Quaternary industry provides **financial services** to businesses, e.g. **banking**, **insurance** and real estate (**property**) services.
4) Quaternary industry also includes **legal** services, **IT** and **consultancy** (management consultancy, IT consultancy etc).
5) Quaternary industry is mainly concerned with generating, collecting, storing and retrieving **specialised information** — **financial information**, **market research information**, specialist **IT information**, etc.
6) These "**producer services**" tend to **clump together**. They all need a **skilled workforce**, which tends to be found around **universities**. They often need to be **close** to their **clients** (the businesses) and their clients tend to be clustered together.

Case Study: The financial service industry in Leeds

Background:	In the 1980s and 1990s, there was fast growth in financial services jobs in and around several European cities — e.g. Turin, Stuttgart, Lyon, Birmingham, Norwich and Leeds.
Why Leeds?:	There's good **transport access**. Several government policies have helped launch Leeds as a financial "growth pole" — to encourage further office growth and related developments.
Examples:	Leeds has six of the largest legal groups outside London. Banks such as Yorkshire Bank and Barclays have a major presence in the city. There are major corporate and finance groups, outsourced services (telephone call centres for customer services and credit control), architects, marketing services and advertising agencies.

Case Study: High-tech industries along motorways in the UK

Background:	Major concentrations of high-tech industries are found along two major routeways — the M4 (Reading and Newbury) and the M11 (Cambridge).
Reasons:	1) The availability of a highly skilled, university educated labour force (e.g. from Oxford and Cambridge Universities). 2) There are good motorway and rail networks nearby.

Quinary Industry includes Education, Health, and Government

1) Quinary industry provides services to the **public**.
2) These services include **education**, **government** and **health**. Some geographers also class **recreation** and **tourism** as quinary services.
3) In the UK, many **quinary services** are in the **public sector**. This means they're organised by the **government** and paid for by the taxpayer.
4) There was a huge **increase** in the number of **public service employees** between **1970** and **1990**.
5) Quinary industry has to grow in line with **population increase**.

Quinary industry also includes the sort of specialised research that government departments do.

The **quaternary sector** and the **quinary sector** are both **subdivisions** of the **tertiary sector**.

Well, as far as the AQA board are concerned, anyway.

It's **important** that you **understand** that — or everything will be oh-so-very-very-very **confusing**.

Practice Questions

Q1   Which sector of industry develops first?
Q2   What is the difference between the quaternary and quinary sectors?
Q3   What is the basic difference between the employment sector structures of LEDCs and MEDCs?
Q4   Name one factor that has caused the percentages within the different sectors to change over the last 25 years in the UK.
Q5   In which sector is each of the following organisations — a fish farm, HSBC, Marks and Spencer, the NHS?

Exam Questions

Q1   Contrast the location needs of primary sector, secondary sector and quaternary sector industries.   (5 marks)

Good job secondary school doesn't lead to quinary school...

Get these economic sectors completely sorted in your mind, otherwise the rest of this section will be a big blurry mess. In the exam, you'll be expected to know what's meant by each sector. The tertiary/quaternary/quinary divide is a little confusing at first, but work on it and you'll get it. Quaternary = services for business, quinary = services for the public (like hospitals and schools).

Secondary Activity in MEDCs

*MEDCs have gone from manufacturing economies to service economies. 40 years ago, manufacturing employed most of the workforce and contributed the most to national wealth, but now this has all changed. These pages are for **AQA A** and **AQA B**.*

Deindustrialisation *Means the* Decline *of* Manufacturing

1) **Deindustrialisation** can be **relative** or **absolute**. **Relative** decline is where less of a country's economic output comes from manufacture. Manufacturing productivity could actually be rising, but its **share** of the **economy** would be **going down**, e.g. because of growth in **services**. **Absolute** decline is where manufacturing is **falling in output**.

2) In the EU and the UK massive deindustrialisation happened from the mid **1970s** to mid **1980s**.

3) Deindustrialisation in the UK was **relative overall**, looking at the **whole** of the UK economy. But some **regions** suffered **absolute deindustrialisation** — their industries **packed up completely**:

   These are often called "smokestack industries".

   - The **coal** industry suffered in **South Wales** and the **North East of England**.
   - The **shipbuilding** industry declined in **Newcastle**, **Glasgow**, **Belfast** and **Barrow in Furness**.
   - The **iron and steel** industry of **Sheffield** has declined.
   - The **textile** industry declined in **Manchester**, **Yorkshire** and the **Midlands**.

4) Deindustrialisation has affected the **rest of Europe**, too. The "**heavy industry triangle**" of the German **Rhine-Ruhr**, the **Franco-Belgian coalfield** and **Alsace-Lorraine** was hit **hard** by decline in the **coal** and **steel** industries.

Reasons *for* Deindustrialisation *are Linked to* Coal *and* Competition

1) Traditionally, industries relied on **coal** as a source of electricity and needed to be **near coalfields** — it was **cheaper** to bring the **factory** to the **coal** than to bring the coal to the factory. Nowadays, there are other ways of generating electricity. Heavy industry doesn't **need** to be near the coalfields any more.

2) **Competition from abroad** is also responsible for the decline of European manufacturing industry. Countries like Japan, Taiwan and Malaysia could **undercut** European manufacture partly because their **labour costs** were **lower** and they didn't have to follow strict **health and safety** laws. They could make and sell stuff cheaper than EU countries.

3) Many industries in the UK didn't keep up with changes in **technology**, and didn't **modernise** their working practices. During the 1970s, **trade unions** actively **resisted modernisation**.

Deindustrialisation is also linked to increased demand for services. As economies grow, incomes rise, and there's demand for consumer durables and services. However, someone has to make all those lovely consumer durables — the EU doesn't make half as many of them as the newly industrialised Asian countries do. This is where competition comes in — other countries can make consumer goods cheaper than the EU, and EU consumers buy the cheaper foreign-made goods.

Deindustrialisation *has Impacted on* Communities *and* Areas

1) **Deindustrialisation** can create a **vicious circle** of **unemployment**, loss of **demand** for **local goods** and **services**, and **further decline** in local industry.

2) To break this cycle, **investment** from **outside** is needed.

3) The **EU** has been keen to set up **investment** programmes to help **reindustrialisation**.

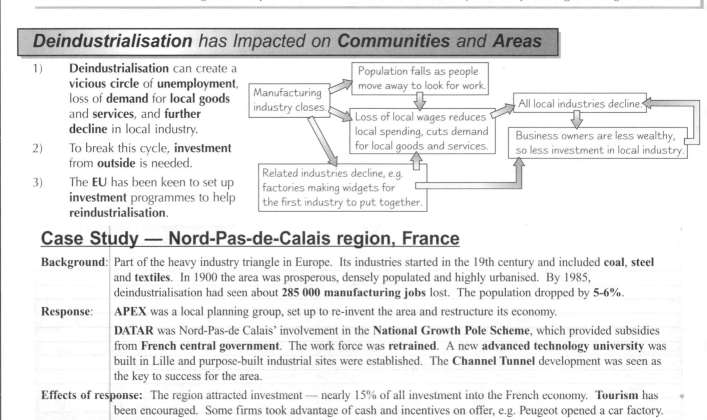

Case Study — Nord-Pas-de-Calais region, France

Background:	Part of the heavy industry triangle in Europe. Its industries started in the 19th century and included **coal**, **steel** and **textiles**. In 1900 the area was prosperous, densely populated and highly urbanised. By 1985, deindustrialisation had seen about **285 000 manufacturing jobs** lost. The population dropped by **5-6%**.
Response:	**APEX** was a local planning group, set up to re-invent the area and restructure its economy.
	DATAR was Nord-Pas-de Calais' involvement in the **National Growth Pole Scheme**, which provided subsidies from **French central government**. The work force was **retrained**. A new **advanced technology university** was built in Lille and purpose-built industrial sites were established. The **Channel Tunnel** development was seen as the key to success for the area.
Effects of response:	The region attracted investment — nearly 15% of all investment into the French economy. **Tourism** has been encouraged. Some firms took advantage of cash and incentives on offer, e.g. Peugeot opened a car factory.

Secondary Activity in MEDCs

There's Been New Industrial Growth in the UK since the 1960s

New industries include computer equipment, pharmaceuticals and of course, the entire tertiary services sector. New industries are sometimes called "sunrise" industries. The heavy industries they replace are "sunset" industries. Areas which suit new industries (e.g. the M4 corridor around Reading) aren't usually the areas where heavy industry jobs have been lost.

1) Since World War 2, the UK government has helped businesses to move to areas of high unemployment or declining industry, under the Assisted Areas Scheme. Encouragement includes: grants, loans, planning permission to build industrial estates, retraining of the work force and tax allowances. The government has also made it harder to build industrial developments in areas where there aren't many employment problems.

2) This policy has created 800 000 new jobs. However, areas which were poorest 65 years ago are still relatively poor.

Investment from Abroad has Helped UK Manufacturing Industry

Foreign manufacturers have opened factories in the UK. They've invested lots of money in facilities and training.

Case Study — Toyota car plant in Burnaston, near Derby

The EU puts trade barriers in place to stop people importing things that can be made in the EU.

Background: Japanese car manufacturer Toyota wanted a foothold in Europe. In 1989, they decided to locate in the UK, in Derbyshire. Production started in 1992.

Locating in the UK: Locating in the EU gets around trade barriers. Burnaston in Derbyshire was ideal. There's space to expand. There are lots of skilled workers in the area. There are good road (M1 and M42) and rail links for bringing in parts and distributing finished cars.

Advantages to the UK: Since 1989, Toyota has invested over a billion pounds in the factory. Toyota trained the workforce. Money has been injected into the local economy.

Problems for Toyota: Weak Euro and strong pound have caused problems — exported cars cost a lot in Euros when the pound is strong, and sales in Euro-zone countries suffer.

Problems for the UK: Profits leave the country for Japan. Decisions about the plant are taken abroad.

Here's a UK Case Study that Gives the Whole Story

Case Study — Industrial Heritage and change in Lancashire

Heritage: In the 19th century Lancashire's economy was based on cotton manufacturing. Mills were powered by fast flowing Pennine streams and later by coal from local coalfields. Access to the port of Liverpool meant raw cotton could be imported from the USA and India. The building of the Manchester Ship Canal helped the region contribute up to 25% of the UK's GDP.

Change: There was a decline in cotton production in the 1950s to 1970s. Industrialisation abroad meant that cheaper products from abroad outcompeted UK textiles. There was also a change in demand from cotton to synthetic fabrics, e.g. nylon. There was little investment. By the 1980s, the textile industry was almost all gone.

New industries: In the 1990s, the area was identified by the UK government as an area that needed help. Local and national government invested in the area. Many services and high-tech operations have moved to the area, e.g. financial, retail and chemical manufacture in Manchester. Blackburn diversified into electronics manufacturing.

Practice Questions

Q1 Name two UK areas and two EU areas which have suffered in the process of deindustrialistion.

Q2 A shipyard closes down. Explain why this would badly affect non-related businesses in the area.

Q3 What are "sunrise" and "sunset" industries?

Exam Questions

Q1 Describe how the distribution of industrial activity in the UK has changed in the last 40 years. (8 marks)

Q2 Identify and explain the causes of deindustrialisation in the EU. Refer to two named areas. (18 marks)

No need for you to deindustrialise yourself — keep revising...

There's a lot to learn here. The questions you need to answer are "What's deindustrialisation?", "Why did it happen?", "Where did it happen?", "What effect did it have?", "How did governments try to help?" and "What new industries are there?" — the answers are all somewhere on these 2 pages. In the exam you can get a short question about some of it, or a monster question about all of it.

Newly Industrialised Countries

*Some countries in the LEDW (less economically developed world) have industrialised very quickly. These pages are for **AQA A**.*

There are **Newly Industrialised Countries** in **Asia** and **Latin America**

1) In the **1970s-1990s** some countries of Asia and South America **industrialised very quickly**. They're collectively called **Newly Industrialised Countries** (**NICs** for short). NICs include South Korea, Thailand, Malaysia, Singapore, Mexico and Brazil.

NICs export their products to MEDCs.

2) NICs have experienced **massive growth** in their **manufacturing output** and **exports**. They now have more manufacturing industry than the **traditional** manufacturing areas of Europe and North America.

3) **South Korea** is a **first generation** NIC. **Malaysia** is a **second generation** NIC. **India** is part of the **third generation**, and **Vietnam** and the **Philippines** are part of the **latest generation** of industrialising countries.

4) The **Asian NICs** have on the whole been far **more successful** than the **South American NICs**. They are sometimes given the nickname of "**Asian Tigers**" or "**Tiger Economies**".

5) Several of the Asian NICs suffered a **severe economic downturn** during the global recession of **1997-1998**.

Reasons for fast economic growth in NICs:

1) A **large, flexible, educated work force** makes up for a shortage of natural resources.

2) **Political stability** helps economic development.

3) The NICs are willing to **trade abroad** — their domestic markets are too small to make **bulk manufacturing** worthwhile, so they really need export markets.

4) The NICs chose appropriate **low skill manufacturing** activities to begin with and then diversified into more skilled industries as the workforce became **more skilled**.

5) **Governments** in NICs offer **subsidies** and **support** to export industries.

6) Foreign capital from **large multinational corporations** is used to support industry.

Case Study — South Korea, a first generation NIC

Background: After the Korean War in the 1950s, South Korea was a poor agricultural country. The **division** of Korea into **North** and **South Korea** left North Korea with **most of the industrial institutions** and **resources**.

Growth: Carefully **planned**, using **overseas investment** (mostly from USA and Japan). The South Korean government put **trade barriers** in place to **stop Korea importing goods** it could make itself. Huge **conglomerate firms** (called **chaebols**) dominate the economy — e.g. **Hyundai**, Lucky Goldstar (**LG**), **Daewoo** and **Samsung**. Korean technology **copied** and improved upon the systems used in MEDCs.

Reasons for Success: South Korea has a **large, loyal, hardworking** and **educated labour force**, willing to work for **low wages**. There's been **government encouragement** and **subsidies** as well as help from **abroad**.

Consequences: Rapid **urbanisation** and the building of squatter settlements has caused **water** and air pollution.

Future: There's now **competition** from **third generation NICs**, e.g. **India**.

Korean development has been in stages:

Stage 1 — **subsistence**: Post-war South Korea's economy was based on subsistence farming.

Stage 2 — **getting ready for take-off**: Support from the USA and Japan in the form of money and technology.

Stage 3 — **take off**: By 1980, South Korea was producing the same as the UK's manufacturing output.

Stage 4 — **drive to maturity**: The Korean economy has diversified. It's gone from textiles to shipbuilding and heavy industry to electronics. There's a future in high-tech industry based on Korean research and development.

Rapid Economic Growth has Costs and Benefits

Advantages of fast growth	Disadvantages of fast growth
Lots of **employment for local people**.	**Water and air pollution** can be a **big** problem.
Investment of **capital** (money to help business develop).	**Deforestation** to clear land for factories etc (see p64-65). Burning forest adds to **air pollution**.
Improvements in **infrastructure** (roads, railways, ports etc).	**Unsafe working practices** may cause human or environmental disasters, e.g. Bhopal disaster 1985.
Average incomes rise, and there's more **spending** power in the **home market**.	
	Resource exploitation (e.g. mining) can **damage ecosystems**.
Reduces dependency on **selling primary goods** (ores, crops, coal, etc). There's more money in manufacture.	**Rural-urban migration** creates **overcrowding** and slums.

Newly Industrialised Countries

Multinationals, e.g. Philips, Sony and Nike, Have a Large Role in NICs

1) **Multinationals** are **large corporations** with high turnovers (the top five multinationals' turnover exceeds the GNP of large groups of African countries). They're also called **transnational corporations** or **TNCs**.

2) Multinationals have several **branches** or **affiliate companies** in foreign countries. Their **headquarters** are usually in a big **MEDC** city such as **New York** or **Tokyo**. **Routine manufacturing** can go anywhere in the world where **labour is cheap**.

A branch is part of the multinational company. An affiliate is a separate company, partly controlled by the multinational parent company.

3) Multinationals have **invested** in NICs, and have a big impact on the economy of NICs.

4) Investment from a multinational is great — as long as it lasts. Multinationals are happy to pack up and go to another NIC with **cheaper labour**. For example, Nike had shoe factories in **South Korea** in the late 1980s. They moved a lot of these to **China** and **Indonesia** in the mid 1990s, and they're now getting their shoes assembled in **Vietnam**.

5) Multinational involvement in the LEDW has been **controversial**. Some people think that workers in LEDCs are **exploited** by multinational corporations.

LEDC Case Study — US "Branch Plants" in Mexico.

Background: Many **US companies** do their **manufacturing** in Mexico, in **branch factories** called **Maquiladoras**.

Why Mexico?: There are **low labour costs** and **minimal health and safety** constraints. **Components** are easily and quickly **transported** from the USA, and finished items can be **quickly delivered** back to the USA, so Mexico is preferred over south east Asia. The local workforce will work for lower pay than in the USA.

Advantages to Mexico: **Jobs**. **Cash** to support Mexico's economy. Mexico benefits from **technology** developed in the USA.

Disadvantages to Mexico: Most **profits go to the USA**. Generally, only **manual** work is available, not R&D (research and development) or higher management jobs. There's **environmental damage**. The Mexican economy could **rely on US businesses** too much.

Multinational Involvement Has Advantages and Disadvantages

Advantages of multinational involvement	Disadvantages of multinational involvement
Lots of **employment**.	**Low wages**. **Working conditions** can be **poor**. **Child labour**.
Investment of **capital**.	Multinational may pack up and leave for another LEDC if locals **demand higher wages** or better working conditions.
Increased **productivity**.	
Labour force learns **new skills**, especially when the multinational introduces **new technology**.	Most profit goes **overseas**.
	Goods often **don't meet local needs**.
	Multinationals **outcompete** local businesses.

Practice Questions

Q1   What is a "second generation" NIC?

Q2   Outline some of the costs (disadvantages) created by rapid economic growth.

Q3   Why do multinationals locate in NICs?

Q4   What benefits can a large company like Nike bring to an area?

Exam Questions

Q1   Examine and explain the present day location of manufacturing industry in Newly Industrialised Countries.   (8 marks)

Q2   Analyse the economic, environmental and social issues arising from economic change in NICs.   (6 marks)

Make the trainers for £2, sell the trainers for £60 — makes sense, eh...

Now that MEDCs have deindustrialised, someone's got to manufacture the clothes and consumer durables that people in MEDCs love to buy. Enter stage right, the newly industrialised country. Big multinational manufacturers build factories in NICs to make their products — which is why a lot of stuff you buy has "made in China" or "made in Vietnam" on the label.

Changes in the Retail Industry

As the retail sector has grown, the UK's urban and suburban areas have changed in form and function.
These pages are for AQA A, and AQA B option S, and useful for Edexcel A and Edexcel B.

There's Traditionally been a Hierarchy of Retail

1) The **CBD** (**Central Business District**) was at the **top** of this hierarchy, and the **corner shop** was at the **bottom**.

2) In this hierarchy, the **lower levels** provide **convenience** goods or **low order** goods — stuff like **milk** that you go to the corner shop to buy. Shops in the CBD sell **high order** goods or **comparison** goods. These are goods like **shoes** that you'd probably travel a fair distance to buy, and that you need to **compare** to make sure you're getting the nicest ones.

3) The concept of **threshold** is important. Threshold is the **number of people needed** to shop at a retail store. **Low order** centres like **corner shops** only require a **small threshold** population living within **walking distance**. **Large threshold** populations are required by the **highest order goods** and shops that are found in the **CBD**.

4) The traditional hierarchy has now changed. The table below shows the **retail hierarchy today** for a large town or small city (e.g. Norwich or Preston).

Level	Shopping type	Purchase type	Transport	Trade radius	Number of shops	Trend
5	**Regional** shopping centres	Bulk buying, chain stores	car, bus, train	up to 50km	1-20	growing
4	**CBD** (city centre)	High order, specialist goods, services	car, bus, train	10km	200+	declining
3	**Transition zone** (near centre)	Bulk and DIY	car, bus, train	5km	less than 20	growing
2	**Suburban** and **district** shopping centres	Low order, convenience	foot, car	2km	less than 20	growing
1	**Ribbon Development** (along main roads)	Low order, convenience	foot, local bus	less than 1km	about 20, scattered	declining

There Are Now Fewer Independent Shops and More Big Out-of-Town Stores

1) There has been a **decline** in the number of **small independent shops** in city centres and in villages.

2) Shopping has been **decentralised**. More and more new shops are in **out-of-town** locations.

3) There's been an increase in **one-stop shopping**. Time to shop is limited — there's isn't time to make several trips.

4) Now that most households have a **car**, people can choose where to shop based on **price** and on **convenience**. They don't have to go to the **nearest** shop, and they don't have to go to the **CBD**.

5) More shops are open at **non-traditional times** — especially supermarkets. This is **convenient** for working people.

6) Moving shops to **suburban** and **out-of-town** locations cuts down on **city centre congestion**.

7) However, there are downsides to the retail revolution. Many people have to **travel further** for **basic shopping** — tough if you are old or poor.

8) Town centre shops can't **compete** with brand new shopping centres and big spacious out-of-town supermarkets.

9) The spread of **convenience stores** in **garages** has made the chore of **late opening** even more of a hassle for **corner shops**. Many garages now sell a wide range of **convenience goods** and are **open 24/7**.

Example 1 — Food

1) Food shopping is now mainly done **weekly** or **fortnightly**. Because almost everyone has a **freezer**, people don't **need** to shop for fresh food every day. Because most people **go out to work**, they don't have **time** to shop every day.

2) Most households have a **car**, so they can drive to **wherever the supermarket is** and put the week's shopping in the boot.

3) Supermarkets have moved to **out-of-town** locations — these are cheap to build on.

4) **Out-of-town supermarkets** sell more and more **non-food items** — e.g. clothing, books, homewares and household electrical goods. This takes more custom away from the CBD.

Example 2 — DIY

1) DIY has become a **popular leisure activity** — people like to buy DIY equipment and do some light home and garden development at the weekend. (Whatever floats your boat, I suppose.)

2) As with supermarket food shopping, now that most people have **access to a car**, they can drive to wherever the DIY store happens to be — people no longer have to go into busy city traffic to shop.

3) Big DIY superstores such as B&Q, Homebase, Wickes etc have built on **out-of-town** sites.

Changes in the Retail Industry

First Come *Malls*, Then *Retail Parks*

1) Purpose built **shopping centres** and **malls** have revolutionised shopping in central city areas — e.g. Newcastle's Eldon Square, Norwich's Castle Mall, Manchester's Arndale Centre.

2) As these shopping centres get **old** and **tatty**, they can suffer the same fate as the original town centre shops — people prefer to go to the big, **new**, shiny **out-of-town** retail park instead.

3) **Retail parks** are in **out-of-town** locations. They're like shopping centres on growth hormone.

4) As well as being big, retail parks try to be **attractive** to consumers. They often have **entertainment** and **food** functions as well as shops — this makes consumers want to spend the **whole day** there (and give the credit card a good workout while they're there, obviously). The **Trafford Centre** is a good example of a superglitzy retail park — it's got a **cinema** and a massive **food court** with lots of restaurants.

5) You don't really get independent stores in retail parks. It's **chain stores** all the way.

Case Study — Taunton's Riverside Retail Park

Background: Taunton Riverside is a £40 million office, amenities and shops complex. It's situated on the banks of the River Tone and Junction 25 on the M5.

Advantages: Taunton is a growing regional centre for Somerset. The site's easily accessible and perfect for one-stop customers.

Positives: New jobs created bringing new money into the economy. People now travel from far away to shop in Taunton. The retail park puts Taunton on the same level as Exeter and Bridgewater.

Negatives: Trade is being taken from the CBD. Profits go to **large chains** instead of small independent shops.

The *Retail Revolution* has Caused *Conflict*

1) There's **conflict** between the established centres and new out-of-town developments. Town centre shops are **threatened** by competition with out-of-town developments.

2) If town centre shops **close down**, they'll leave behind **empty**, **boarded-up** buildings. This increases the risk of crime, and **lowers property rents** in the area — there's a **downward spiral** effect where **no retailers** want to rent a shop unit in a street of manky old **boarded-up shops**.

Local Authorities have tried to make life **easier** for town centre businesses.

1) Most towns and cities have a **pedestrianised** town centre area, to make it more pleasant for people to shop there.

2) **Park and ride schemes** link **suburban** and **rural** areas with **city centres**, encouraging people to shop in town.

3) Some cities have re-invented themselves as **trendy** and **hip**, and spent money on making the CBD attractive. As a result, retailing returns to the CBD. For example, the exceptionally posh retail stores **Selfridges** and **Harvey Nichols** have opened branches in Manchester.

The first place to pedestrianise was Stevenage, which is a New Town.

See p95 for more on urban regeneration.

Practice Questions

Q1 What's a "low order good"?

Q2 Give one reason why people do more "one-stop shopping" these days.

Q3 Give two reasons why supermarkets have moved from town centres to suburbs and beyond.

Q4 How has pedestrianisation helped retailing in the city centre?

Exam Questions

Q1 Give advantages and disadvantages of the development of out-of-town retail parks. (7 marks)

Q2 What are the consequences to the CBD of the move to out-of-town retail parks? (5 marks)

I'm gonna bore you now like some old Grandma...

There's definitely been a big change in retailing over the last 30 years or so. Back in the day, pretty much all shops were in town centres, none of them were open on Sunday, and almost none of them opened past 5.30pm (unless they were having Very Special Late Night Shopping in the run up to Christmas). Compare that with Bluewater, the Trafford Centre, and 24 hour Tescos and Asdas.

Changing Office Employment

The distribution of office employment in the UK has changed over the last few years.
*These pages are for **AQA A**, **AQA B**, and for the urban course of **Edexcel A** and **Edexcel B**.*

All Sectors of Industry Need **Office Workers**

1) **Office** workers are the **highest proportion** of all workers in the UK, over **all economic sectors**.

2) All sectors need supporting office workers in administration, finance and marketing.
Primary industries like **mining** need some office workers, **secondary** industries like **car manufacture** need them, **tertiary service industry** is largely made up of **desk jobs**, **quaternary** finance and support industry is **entirely office based** and **quinary** industry has a **high proportion** of **office workers**.

Service Employment has **Grown** in the UK since the **1960s**

1) As the UK **deindustrialised**, there was growth in **service employment**. With global interdependence, national economies have become more **specialised** within the global economy — e.g. Colombia grows coffee, the UK does services (OK, that's a very simplistic example, but you get the point).

2) With deindustrialisation comes a new **consumer economy** where most people have lots of money to spend. Both the **consumer services sector** (tertiary) and the **producer services sector** (quaternary) have grown massively to meet the demand for consumer goods.

3) Some jobs in offices are **great**, but many are **low paid**, quite **low skilled**, **temporary**, **repetitive** or **part-time**. The total of jobs created **hasn't compensated** for the job losses of deindustrialisation. Many people (especially men working in heavy industry) lost jobs during deindustrialisation and have never been re-employed.

Service Employment has **Decentralised** since the **1980s**

1) In the UK, some firms and government offices have moved away from city centres to **small towns** and **suburbs** — especially in the **south east**, the **Midlands** and **East Anglia**. This is called decentralisation. For example, Commercial Union moved from London to Basildon and Allied Dunbar moved from London to Swindon.

2) **Decentralisation** has happened because of **competition** for **office space** and **office staff** in city areas, traffic and public transport **congestion**, and lack of parking.

3) Decentralisation has **benefits** for both **businesses** and **employees**. Businesses can pay **lower office rents** and **lower wages** outside London. Employees want jobs close to their **suburban** homes where the environment is attractive and **commuting costs** are low.

4) Efficient **communications** (e.g. phone, fax, email, video conferencing, broadband internet access) have made decentralisation possible.

5) Business head offices are **major employment centres** in the regions. IBM's HQ near Portsmouth employs nearly 3 000 people. Councils near London took steps to **encourage** firms to **relocate** to their area. Croydon attracted over 30 000 jobs in 25 years.

In the 1980s, office employment was centralised — based in city centre areas.

1) **High level functions** and big decision making tend to stay in city centres, e.g. a **finance department** of a national firm, or a **bank HQ**.

2) **Routine office work** like office **admin.** and **payroll** doesn't **need** to be in the city centre, because they don't need **face to face** contact with clients. These routine functions are often called **back office** functions.

Public Service Employment has **Decentralised** As Well

1) Like all businesses, the government likes to keep costs down. Having civil servants from all government departments based in London is very **expensive** in terms of **office space** and wages.

2) Moving jobs to provincial cities helps provide **employment** in those areas. The UK government has relocated some of its offices to areas which have suffered unemployment, and even to rural areas.

- The **Department of Health** has offices in Leeds as well as London.
- The Department for **Education and Skills** has offices in **Sheffield**, **Darlington** and **Runcorn** as well as London.
- The **Inland Revenue** has regional offices **all over Britain**.
- The **Office of National Statistics** has centres in Newport (Wales) and Titchfield (a village in Hampshire).

Changing Office Employment

Call Centres are a Big New Thing in Office Employment

1) Businesses can move from **high street branches** and **face to face customer contact** to **telephone call centres**, where customer services and sales staff answer phone calls all day.

2) In 2000, there were some 10 000 call centres in the UK, employing 3% of the UK's workforce.

3) The development of new **telephone** and **computer technology** has triggered this change. Call centres couldn't operate without advances such as **Automated Call Distribution** which uses computers to set up queues of customers on the phone line for operators to respond to.

4) 14% of call centres are in **London** and 25% are in the South East — a lot of these are based at company headquarters. 21% of centres are in Northern England. Larger call centres (more than 250 phone operators) tend to be in the North and in Scotland. It has been suggested that customers like Northern and Scottish regional accents.

5) New call centre work is going **abroad**. Several UK banks have opened centres in **India**, where **staff costs** are **lower** than those in the UK. Staff are well-educated and work long hours. **Thousands of jobs** have moved out of the UK to India.

6) Critics of call centres say that call centre jobs aren't really "**new**" jobs because they replace jobs previously done in individual high street branches — e.g. **telephone banking** call centre jobs replace **bank clerk** jobs.

7) Critics also say that call centre jobs are **low quality**. Call centre staff can be under a lot of **pressure** to complete a **certain number of calls** a day. This can mean that **customer service suffers**, as well.

The following factors make a location **suitable** for call centres:
- a **large workforce** (especially if they're willing to work for low wages);
- good quality **offices**;
- **financial support** from **local authorities** or from **regional development** agencies.

Advantage to customer	Call centres offer a **24 hour service** and **up to date information**.
Disadvantage to customer	There's a **lack of face to face contact**. There may be a perceived lack of understanding with foreign call centres. **Long waiting times** to speak to a customer service person can be very, very annoying.
Advantage to business	Call centre staff are **cheap**.
Disadvantage to business	**Staff turn-over** can be **high**. **Set up costs** can also be high.
Advantage to worker	There are lots of **jobs** for young people. Hours are **flexible**, which suits **students** and **parents**.
Disadvantage to worker	The work is **low paid**. It can be a **pressurised** work environment and work is unrewarding and repetitive. Lots of jobs are going **abroad** — there's **little job security**.

Practice Questions

Q1 What is "decentralisation"?
Q2 What are "back office" functions?
Q3 What is a "call centre"?
Q4 Why has India been chosen as the site for so many call centre jobs?

Exam Questions

Q1 Assess the extent to which service industry has changed its location in recent years. (6 marks)

Q2 Describe the development and location of call centre businesses in the UK. (4 marks)

Your call is very important to us. Please stay on the line...

There are two main things going on with these two pages. First off, there's been huge growth in office employment. Secondly, office employment has moved around the country, from major city centres (especially London) to the suburbs, to the rural-urban fringe, and to towns all around the country. Some call centres didn't stay long in the UK before going to India.

Quaternary Developments

These pages are about financial services and technical research services.
*They are for **AQA A**, **AQA B**, and for the urban course of **Edexcel A** and **Edexcel B**.*

There's Been **Massive Growth** in the **Quaternary Sector** in the UK

1) All businesses need **quaternary** sector **producer services** — e.g. **financial** services, **market research**, **management consultancy**, **advertising**, and **legal** functions.

2) The growth in producer services is due to economic growth worldwide and increased global consumption.

3) Producer services tend to cluster together. Some services need to be close to clients. Similar services need to have access to similar information, and to a similar workforce. It makes sense for them to be located close to each other. This is called an **economy of agglomeration**. **Agglomeration** means **clumping together**. Economies of agglomeration are savings that businesses make by being **close** to other businesses.

Business Parks are Purpose Built Developments

1) **Business parks** are a collection of **newly built**, **low density** buildings used for producer services. Business parks can be out of town, in suburbs or even quite close to the town centre.

2) **Offices** in business parks are **ready to move into**. Photocopying, cleaning and other support services are included.

3) Firms on business parks benefit from economies of agglomeration — they **share support services** and communication links (phone infrastructure etc).

Advantages of business park locations	Disadvantages of business park locations
1) They're an **attractive work environment**.	1) They use up **greenfield** sites.
2) There's room to **expand**.	2) Parking and **congestion** can be a problem.
3) They're close to **motorways**.	3) **Housing** for workers may be very **expensive** because of high demand.
4) There are benefits from **agglomeration**.	
5) **Support services** like cleaning are **provided**.	

Case Study — Business Parks in Reading

Background: Reading is 60 km west of London, on the M4 (Junction 11). It has successfully attracted business from the rest of the UK and abroad. By 1999 there were 4000+ businesses, of which nearly 90% were service based. These new businesses have replaced manufacturing industry in Reading.

Parks: The businesses have located in purpose built parks around Reading (e.g. Green Park Business Estate, Thames Valley Business Park and Reading International Park).

Science Parks are High-Tech Developments

Science parks are for **high-tech** industry, like computer software.

1) Science parks were originally an **American** idea. Cities like Palo Alto and San Jose in the "**Silicon Valley**" area of California saw huge growth of **computer businesses** in the 1980s.

2) Having close links to nearby **universities** really helps science parks. The UK Science Park Association defines a science park as "a collection of new and low-density buildings, with operational **links** to **universities** and **higher education** institutions which **exchange information** and expertise." **Stanford University** is right by Palo Alto, and much of the technology used by computer businesses in **Silicon Valley** was originally developed at Stanford.

3) In the UK, there's "Silicon Fen" based around the Cambridge Science Park, "Silicon Glen" in Scotland, and the "Silicon Strip" along the M4 corridor. Ireland has the "Emerald Corridor" of high-tech development between Belfast and Dublin.

> Microsoft's HQ is rather like a science park all by itself in a suburb of Seattle. The HQ of Apple in California looks like a university campus.

Case Study — Cambridge Science Park.

Background: Cambridge Science Park was the first in the UK.

Why Cambridge: Good **communications** with **London** (M11) and **Stansted Airport**. There's a pool of **high quality labour**. It's a **desirable** area. There are entrepreneurs in the area ready to invest **venture capital**. Links with the **University of Cambridge** provide new ideas used by business in the park. Neighbours on the park are involved in similar activities, so you have **economies of agglomeration** and potential passing-on of ideas.

Problems: There's bad **congestion** on the **roads** around Cambridge, and little **parking**. Business development encroaches on the countryside. With high demand from workers, **house prices** are sky-high, and schools are oversubscribed.

Quaternary Developments

Business Services can Also be Located in City Centres

1) City centres have a **specialised infrastructure** that suits many producer services.
2) They have **office space**, and good **telecommunications**. **Quaternary** businesses can deliver services to clients both **face to face** and via high-tech **communication** systems.
3) Major cities have a **stock** market — it makes sense for big financial institutions to be right there where the action is.
4) **City centres** also offer the benefit of **agglomeration**.

Case Study — Financial Services in Central London

Background: London is the **financial capital** of Europe. **5.5% of the UK's producer service workforce** work in the **financial district** of London — the "City" or "Square Mile".

Why London: **English** is the **international business language**. Many international firms and financial institutions are **already** in London. London has a good **infrastructure**. There's a large and high quality **workforce**. Agglomeration makes services accessible to local clients and suppliers.

Effects: **Skyscrapers** are being built. London is becoming **busier** and **public transport** is getting **congested**.

The future: Continued service growth may cause some problems for London:

1) There **aren't enough** highly skilled **workers** to meet growing demand.
2) **Office space** is horribly **expensive**. Many companies are moving away from Central London to larger purpose-built premises at more economic rents in Docklands, the SE and East Anglia.
3) New and improved **public transport** will be needed to meet demand.

Planners Have to Decide Between Business Parks and City Centres

You can't just build a business park wherever you like. Developers need to get **planning permission** from the local authority first. Some local authorities like business parks, others prefer to keep new business development in the **CBD**.

Planners have to look at the **costs** and **benefits** of both options. On one hand, business parks can bring in a lot of jobs to an area, and boost the local economy. On the other hand, planners don't want the CBD to become run down.

Developers often employ **consultants** to **negotiate** with local authorities and **persuade** them to give planning permission.

Globalisation has Affected the Quaternary Sector

1) Now that manufacturing has been globalised, **producer services** have been **globalised** as well.
2) Some services have to be in the **big financial centres**, because they need to have face to face meetings with clients.
3) **Back office** services are "**footloose**". They can be **globally decentralised**. Deindustrialised countries like the UK specialise in "back office" producer services. The UK today is the world's second biggest **exporter of services** after the USA. Call centre jobs have been relocated to India (see p137).

Practice Questions

Q1 Give an advantage to a business of locating in business parks.
Q2 What is a "science park"?
Q3 What factors influence the location of science parks?
Q4 What kind of producer services continue to locate in city centres?

Exam Questions

Q1 Examine the advantages and disadvantages of locating new business and science parks in out-of-town locations. (7 marks)

Q2 With reference to a science park, explain why high-technology firms agglomerate. (6 marks)

But where is the duckpond? Where are the dog walkers?

For business and science parks, you need to know what they are, why they're growing, and why planners might choose to put them near town centres, in suburbs, or out on the rural-urban fringe. It's also well worth remembering that not all quaternary services can easily move to a business park. Some services still need to be in the thick of the CBD, and preferably in London.

Employment Issues

Over the last 30 years, employment patterns in the UK have changed a lot.
*These pages are for **AQA B**, and are useful for **Edexcel B**.*

There are **Gender Differences** in **Employment**

These **gender differences** have been **changing** over the last 30 years.

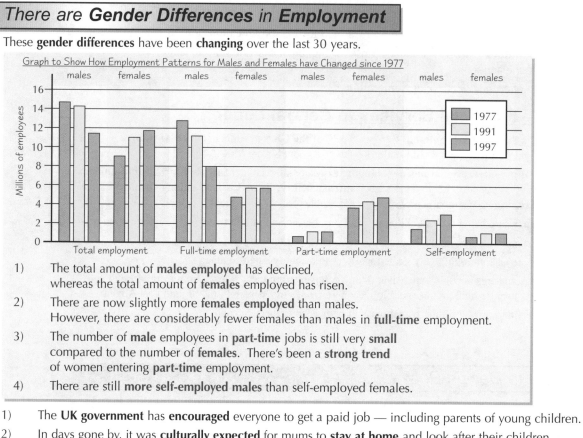

Graph to Show How Employment Patterns for Males and Females have Changed since 1977

1) The total amount of **males employed** has declined,
whereas the total amount of **females** employed has risen.

2) There are now slightly more **females employed** than males.
However, there are considerably fewer females than males in **full-time** employment.

3) The number of **male** employees in **part-time** jobs is still very **small**
compared to the number of **females**. There's been a **strong trend**
of women entering **part-time** employment.

4) There are still **more self-employed males** than self-employed females.

1) The **UK government** has **encouraged** everyone to get a paid job — including parents of young children.

2) In days gone by, it was **culturally expected** for mums to **stay at home** and look after their children.
Nowadays, it's becoming culturally expected for mothers to **go out to work**.

3) However, some **small businesses** are worried about employing women of childbearing age.
Female employees are entitled to **maternity leave**. Employers have to find a **replacement** to cover maternity
leave, and they have to **pay** the pregnant employee/new mum **maternity pay** while she's on leave.
This is all rather **expensive** — for a small business with tight cost margins it could seem too expensive.

The growth of **service** industries has had a **significant** effect on **employment patterns**.

1) There's been a **decline** in secondary sector heavy industry — this is traditionally **male** employment.
Some men who lost heavy industry jobs during deindustrialisation have never been re-employed.

2) Increasing numbers of **women** are employed in **service industries**. The **catering** and **hotel** industry and
the **retail** industry have **traditionally** employed a lot of women. The **quaternary sector** (business to business
services, e.g. finance, legal services, marketing) has employed increasing numbers of women in recent years.
Women are often perceived as being good at customer-facing jobs, e.g. customer services, call centres, retail.

3) There are a lot of **part-time jobs** in the service sector. **Mothers** often take part-time jobs to fit in with **childcare**.

There's More **Part-Time** Work **Now** Than There Was **30 Years Ago**

Some people work part-time out of choice — e.g. mothers of young children,
university students. Some work part-time because they can afford not to work full-time.

Others work part-time because they can't get a full-time job.

The biggest proportion of part-time jobs are in the hotel and restaurant industry, and in distribution.

*Part time work is
usually defined as less
than 30 hours a week.*

Temporary Work Lets Businesses Respond to **Peaks** in **Demand**

1) Service industries employ a lot of people on **short term temporary contracts**.

2) It allows firms to respond easily and cheaply to **peaks in demand**, for example
Christmas in the retail sector, or the summer holidays in the tourism sector.

3) Temporary workers are also used to cover permanent employees on holidays, on maternity leave, etc.

Employment Issues

Job Share, Flexitime and Teleworking — a Different Work/Life Balance

Work/life balance is a big **buzz phrase** in late 1990s and early 2000s employment.
The idea is that people need to have more **control** over their time, and more **free time**.
There are trends away from regular 9-5 employment and towards **flexible** working hours.

Job share is where two people share one job

1) Each person in the job share has a **permanent part-time job**. They **share** the **holiday** and **benefits** between them.
2) It's ideally suited to **working mothers** who want a working life and income as well as having time to spend at home with young children.
3) **Job sharing** is easier to carry out in some industries than others. Those that require continuity of interpersonal relationships (e.g. doctors, teachers, lawyers) find it harder than routine office workers.

Flexitime is Flexible Work Hours

1) Flexitime lets the **employee choose** when they start and finish work, within certain limits agreed with the employer.
2) Flexitime also includes **flexible leave**. The employee can work extra hours, and trade them for time off.
3) For flexitime to work, it needs **trust** between employer and employee. There needs to be a good, accurate system of recording hours worked.

For example, arrive at work between 8am and 10am, definitely be there from 10 am to 4pm, and leave between 4pm and 7pm, as long as you work 35 hours a week.

Teleworking (working from home) is increasing

1) The development of **telecommunications** technology, including **email** and the internet have made it easier for office workers to work from home. Workers can use email to communicate with colleagues and customers.
2) Industries which make use of teleworking include design-based work, journalism, advertising and call centre work.

Self-Employment has Increased in the last 30 Years

1) The rise in **self-employment** is perhaps the most significant change in employment patterns in recent years. Self-employment now accounts for **12%** of the UK workforce.
2) For many years the majority of self-employed workers were in the **construction** industry, e.g. plasterers, plumbers, painters and decorators. Today, self-employment has moved into many other economic sectors — e.g. **IT**, **sales**, the **financial** sector (financial advisers are often self-employed), **estate agency**, **design**.
3) Many self-employed people are based in their **own homes**. Self-employment has all the **benefits** of **flexitime** and **home working** — complete **control** over the structure of the working day. Self-employed people can start work at 11am if they want to (or work until 1am if they want to or have to).
4) On the other hand, self-employed workers are **totally responsible** for making sure they've got **enough work** to pay the bills. When the work dries up, there's **no income**.

Practice Questions

Q1 Why have women had an increasing role in employment in service industries?
Q2 Explain the difference between flexitime and jobshare.
Q3 What is meant by "teleworking"?
Q4 How has the role of being self-employed changed over time?

Exam Questions

Q1 Explain how the growth of the service sector has resulted in a greater number of females in employment. (5 marks)

Q2 Suggest reasons for the increase in self-employment over the last decade. (4 marks)

If Geography revision was a job, would you be a part-timer...

I suppose it makes sense that as the structure of the economy has changed from manufacturing to services, the way people work might have changed as well. There's been a trend towards parents wanting to have a job and spend time with the kids too. There's also been a trend towards everyone wanting more control over their working day. Learn the gender stuff as well.

Renewable and Non-Renewable Resources

A resource is something which people use to survive, generate wealth or enjoy. Energy is one of the most important of all the world's resources. This short section is for AQA B. Bits of it are helpful for other specifications, so feel free to give it a quick butchers even if you're not doing AQA B.

Non-Renewable Resources *Can't Be **Replaced** Once Used Up*

1) **Coal**, **oil** and **gas** are non-renewable resources. They are referred to as **fossil fuels** and were formed **underground** over millions of years, from **compressed plant or animal material**. Once they're dug up and burned that's it, for us.

2) **Coal** is **forecast** to last another **300 years** or so. Current **oil** reserves will last **50 years**, and natural gas **70 years**.

3) Coal, oil and natural gas provide **75% of the world's supply of energy**, and they're mainly used by **MEDC** countries.

Renewable Resources *Can Be Used **Again** and **Again***

Water, **wind**, **solar**, **geothermal**, **tidal** and **wave** energy can be used to generate electricity.

Solar and **geothermal** energy can also be used to **directly heat water** for domestic use.

Renewable energy resource	How it works	Advantage	Disadvantage
Hydro-electric power (HEP)	Uses **moving water** to turn a turbine and generate electricity.	Clean	**Dams** and **power stations** are **expensive** to build.
Wind power	**Wind turbines** generate electricity.	Clean	Only works when the wind's blowing. Some find wind farms **ugly** and **noisy**. May be dangerous to birds.
Solar power	Can generate **heat** or **electricity** (through photovoltaic cell).	Clean, can be cheap	Works best in **sunny**, semi-arid regions. Not so great in the UK.
Geothermal power	Energy from underground **heats water**, or turns water into steam to power **steam turbine**.	Clean, reliable	Some parts of the Earth's crust are **hotter** underground than others so it only works in some locations.
Tidal power	Tidal water flows through **turbines** to generate electricity.	Clean, reliable	Tidal barrages are **expensive**.
Wave power	Waves slosh into a chamber, displacing **air**, which turns a **turbine**.	Clean	Wave power is **difficult** to harness.

Biomass and biogas are also used as fuel

1) **Wood** is the most common source of **biomass**. Wood burning can account for up to 90% of energy use in LEDC countries.

2) **Rubbish**, **animal dung** and **crops** (e.g. sugar cane) are sources of biomass.

3) Biomass can be burned to produce **heat**, or burned in power stations to generate electricity.

4) Some biomass such as **wood** or **paper pulp** can be **burned as it is**. Other biomass products have to be **processed** to turn them into fuel.

5) Sugar cane is **fermented** to turn it into **ethanol**, which can be burned as a fuel. Bioethanol is used as a fuel for **cars** in **Brazil** — most Brazilian cars can run on ethanol.

6) **Sewage sludge**, **rubbish** and **animal dung** are **digested by bacteria** to produce **biogas**. Biogas is a mixture of **carbon dioxide** and **methane**. Biogas can be burned to produce **heat**, or burned in a power station to generate **electricity**.

Renewable energy schemes can be **expensive** — but renewable energy is **getting cheaper** compared to non-renewable energy.

Top-down projects in LEDCs such as Ghana's **Volta Dam** are paid for with foreign investment, and have **negative effects** on local communities, as people are displaced from their land. **Smaller scale**, grass roots projects can be more **sustainable**.

Renewable Resources *Can Be **Sustainable**, But they **Aren't Always***

1) All the **renewable energy sources** in the **purple table** up there are **sustainable**. The sun's always going to shine, the wind's always going to blow, the tides will always ebb and flow.

2) **Wood use isn't sustainable** in many **LEDCs**. Deforestation causes problems — see p64-65.

3) **Biomass fuels** from **crops** can be sustainable if the crops are managed properly — e.g. if more replacement crops are planted etc. There's a bit more about this on p144, in the bit about the greenhouse effect and global warming.

Renewable and Non-Renewable Resources

Oil is The Most Important Non-Renewable Resource

1) Crude oil is a mixture of **hydrocarbon** chemicals. It was formed **millions of years ago** from the remains of **marine animals** and **plants** which sank to the bottom of the sea, and got covered with sediment. As more layers of sediment piled up, huge **pressure** was put on the layers below. Over **tens of millions of years**, the sediment hardened into sandstone, and the remains of the marine organisms turned into **crude oil** and **natural gas**.

2) Crude oil is **refined** into many products. **Petrol** and **diesel** are used as **fuel** for **cars**. **Kerosene** is used as fuel for **aircraft**. Distillation of crude oil also produces **waxes**, **bitumen** and **petrochemicals**, which are used to make **plastic**.

3) Oil is the world's **main source of energy** (see pie chart below).

4) **70% of the world's oil** is found in the **Middle East** (**Saudi Arabia** in particular). There's also oil in the United States, Venezuela, Russia, Azerbaijan, Canada and the North Sea (and a few other places — oil companies are always **looking for more oil**). Very few industrialised countries have enough oil reserves to meet their needs.

5) The UK has been **self-sufficient** in oil since the discovery of North Sea oil in the 1970s. North Sea oil production is in **decline** though, and the UK has just become a net **importer** of oil.

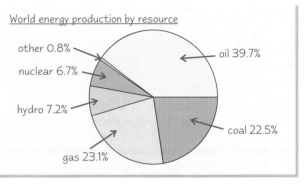

World energy production by resource

other 0.8%
nuclear 6.7%
hydro 7.2%
gas 23.1%
oil 39.7%
coal 22.5%

Advantages of oil	Oil is **efficient to burn** — you get more energy from a tonne of oil than a tonne of coal. Oil is reasonably easy to **handle** and **distribute** (in barrels or through pipelines). Oil **pollutes less** than coal (there's less sulphur in oil than in coal, on average). The world's **transport** systems (trains, planes, ships, cars) are all **set up** to run on **oil** products.
Disadvantages of oil	Reserves may only last a **few decades** unless new reserves are found. It's **difficult** and **expensive** to **discover** and exploit new oilfields. **Oil terminals** and **refineries** take up lots of **space**. There's a danger of spills and explosions. The price of oil can **change suddenly**. It's vulnerable to **political pressures**.

Wind is a Commonly Used Renewable Resource

1) The wind carries energy, which can be harnessed by windmills, or wind turbines. Wind turbines have three blades, connected to a generator, which rotate when the wind blows.

2) There are lots of **wind farms** in Germany and Denmark (where the governments are rather pro-green), and quite a few in the **UK**. **UK wind farms** produce **0.4%** of the electricity supply.

3) **Strong winds** blow out at **sea**. In the UK, **offshore wind farms** have been built off the North Wales and Northumberland coasts, and there are more on the way.

4) Wind turbines are quite **efficient** when they're generating, but they **don't** generate electricity **all the time**.

5) Although they're **clean**, wind farms aren't **popular** with everyone. Many people think they **spoil the view**, and they do make **noise**. There are **pressure groups** which try to stop wind farms being built in places like Cumbria.

Practice Questions

Q1 What is a resource?
Q2 What is the difference between "renewable" and "non-renewable" resources?
Q3 Name three countries which produce oil.
Q4 Give one advantage and one disadvantage of wind power.

Exam Questions

Q1 What are the economic problems of relying on oil for our electricity? (4 marks)

Non-Renewable Resources are running out — and they're NON-Renewable...

There's a need for renewable energy resources, even though it can be expensive and difficult to develop them. It just isn't sustainable to use up all the non-renewables until they run out — people need to come up with alternatives before the price of oil hits the roof. There are environmental issues as well, but they're on the next page.

Energy Harnessing and Pollution

Harnessing energy from fossil fuels and nuclear energy creates serious pollution problems.
*These pages are for **AQA B only**.*

Global Warming and Greenhouse Gas Emission are Linked to Fossil Fuels

1) **Global warming** is an **increase** in the **average temperature** of the world's atmosphere (well, duh...).

2) **Global warming** can be caused by an **increase in the greenhouse effect**. The greenhouse effect is the way that the Earth's atmosphere **keeps heat in**. **Greenhouse gases** such as **carbon dioxide** and **methane** allow the **Sun's radiation** to **pass through** (heating the Earth up) and stop radiation from the Earth's surface from escaping into space (not allowing it to cool down). **More greenhouse gases** = more greenhouse effect = **global warming**.

3) Burning **fossil fuels** and **wood** releases **carbon dioxide** into the atmosphere. There's a **difference** between fossil fuels and wood though — it's a **tiny bit tricky**, so make sure you follow this next bit carefully.

4) Carbon in **fossil fuels** comes from plants which were alive **millions of years ago**. The carbon in wood comes from trees which have only **just been cut down**. Trees take **carbon dioxide out of the atmosphere** while they're **alive**. So... the amount of **carbon dioxide** a tree **takes out** of the atmosphere **balances** the amount of carbon dioxide it releases when it's burnt. But fossil fuels just **release** carbon dioxide, they **don't take any out** of the atmosphere.

5) **Renewable biofuels** such as **bioethanol** (made from sugar cane) are **really neat** because they can be "**carbon dioxide neutral**". This means that the sugar cane plants take the **same amount** of carbon dioxide out of the atmosphere as the bioethanol **releases** when its burnt. Bioethanol **doesn't contribute** to the greenhouse effect.

> Global warming has various **consequences**. **Sea levels** could **rise**. Global sea currents such as the Gulf Stream could change course. Some parts of the world could get **hotter** and **drier**. Others could become **colder** and **wetter**. There's **more** about the consequences of global warming on p58.

1) The **Kyoto Protocol** is an international agreement which aims to reduce emissions of carbon dioxide into the atmosphere. It was drawn up in Kyoto, Japan in 1997.

2) The USA (and others) have **pulled out** of the agreement, causing a lot of debate whether the targets set can be met. The USA is the **world's greatest consumer of energy** and therefore creates a lot of pollution.

3) Developing **renewable energy resources** will play an important part in helping to meet the targets set by the Kyoto Protocol. The cost of **researching** and **developing** renewable energy sources is high, though. Also, many renewable sources don't generate enough energy to completely replace fossil fuels, yet.

Acid Deposition is an International Problem Caused by Fossil Fuels

1) Sulphur and nitrogen oxides are emitted when **fossil fuels** are burnt. **Sulphur** and **nitrogen** compounds are found in small amounts in **fossil fuels**, and they're turned into **oxides** when the fuels are **burnt**. **Power stations**, **industry** and **motor vehicles** are responsible for most acid pollution.

2) Some sulphur and nitrogen oxides fall directly to ground as **dry deposition**. **Wet deposition** or **acid rain** is formed in the atmosphere when SO_2 (sulphur dioxide) and NO_x (nitrogen oxides) dissolve in rain to form **sulphuric acid** and **nitric acid**.

3) The effects of acid deposition include: increased acidity in **lakes** which **kills fish**, increased acidity in **soil** which **reduces crop yields**, damage to **forests** and damage to **buildings**.

4) Sulphur and nitrogen oxides are carried **thousands of miles** by the wind before being deposited. A lot of the acid rain falling on **Scandinavia** has been caused by **pollution in Britain**.

Deforestation is a Problem in LEDCs

1) Trees are cut down for **fuel** in many LEDCs.

2) Trees are also cut down for **commercial** reasons. Timber is sold to make furniture, etc. Rainforests are cleared for agricultural and industrial development, and to build houses.

3) Vegetation **absorbs carbon dioxide** and releases oxygen — it helps clean the air of carbon dioxide released by industry. The more trees there are, the better protected the Earth is against excessive greenhouse effect. **Rainforests** have massive amounts of vegetation, so they absorb **huge quantities** of carbon dioxide.

4) **Rainforests** also contain **important plant and animal species**, which are worth preserving. There's more on rainforest destruction on p64-65.

5) **Deforestation** contributes to **soil erosion**. Deforestation reduces the amount of organic material in the soil, which makes it more likely to erode. Tree **roots** also help **anchor** soil.

6) **Deforestation** also increases **flood risk**. Trees intercept rainfall and take up water for use in photosynthesis.

Energy Harnessing and Pollution

Nuclear Power Doesn't Add to Global Warming, but has its Own Problems

Many industrialised countries which lack coal and oil reserves have turned to nuclear power —
e.g. **France**, which produces nearly **80% of its electricity** in nuclear power stations.

How it works	**Uranium 235 nuclei** are split apart. This produces colossal amounts of energy, which heats water, turning it into **steam**, which then powers **turbines** to make **electricity**.
Advantages of nuclear	It doesn't cause **acid rain** or produce **greenhouse gases**. It's **efficient** — it uses very small amounts of raw materials to produce a lot of energy.
Disadvantages of nuclear	There's **danger** from **radiation**. **Waste disposal** is a **huge problem**. It **costs** a lot to **build** a nuclear power station, and it costs a lot to "**decommission**" one (decommissioning means **taking it apart** and making it **safe**).

Nuclear Waste is Radioactive and Therefore Dangerous

1) Nuclear fuel is radioactive. Even once it's used, it's **still radioactive**, and stays radioactive for **thousands of years** — it has a long half-life (half life is the time taken for the radioactivity to decrease by half). Radiation can **kill** or cause serious **illness** and **birth defects**, so it really does need to be stored safely.

2) Nuclear waste is divided into **high level waste** (very radioactive), **intermediate level waste** and **low level waste**. 95% of the waste from a nuclear power station is low level waste, which is easily dealt with. The other 5% is a big problem — it's **very dangerous**, and will stay dangerous for thousands of years.

3) Nuclear waste has to be **contained** so that it **won't leak** — it's often blended with glass or concrete. It has to be **stored** in **lead lined steel containers** to keep the radiation in (lead blocks radiation). It has to be **transported** by **rail** in special containers that **won't break** even if there's a crash.

High level waste	This is **blended with glass** in a process called **vitrification**. It can be **stored in steel containers** and **buried deep underground** or **under the sea**.
Intermediate level waste	This isn't as radioactive. It can be contained in **cement** or **bitumen**, and stored in **steel drums**.
Low level waste	This includes protective clothing and radioactive hospital waste. It's **stored** until it loses enough radioactivity to be disposed of like **ordinary rubbish**.

In the UK, vitrification is carried out at Sellafield, Cumbria.

The Future of the Nuclear Industry Depends on Dealing With Waste

Until there are **foolproof**, long-term ways of dealing with the waste, development of nuclear power can't really proceed.

Deep storage poses problems. There's a risk of nuclear waste leaking out and seeping into **groundwater**. Most people wouldn't want a nuclear waste dump in their area — plans for a deep storage facility in the UK were ditched in 1997.

98% of the UK's high level nuclear waste is at Sellafield in Cumbria, waiting for a permanent solution.
Post 2001, the risk of terrorism seems rather threatening. If terrorists flew a plane into Sellafield, we'd be in BIG trouble.

Practice Questions

Q1 What are the causes and effects of global warming?
Q2 What are the causes and effects of acid rain?
Q3 Why is nuclear waste so dangerous to deal with?
Q4 How is high level waste treated, transported and stored?

Exam Questions

Q1 Increased concentrations of carbon dioxide in the atmosphere contribute to global warming.
(a) Describe the mechanism by which this warming takes place. (3 marks)
(b) Explain how the use of energy resources has contributed to the problem. (4 marks)

Q2 Describe the problems related to storing nuclear waste. (4 marks)

It'll take a while to clear up all this mess...

Woo hoo, what a nice note to end the book on. Global warming, acid rain, and terrorists wiping us all out (well all of us in North West England anyway) by crashing a jumbo jet into Sellafield nuclear facility. I was feeling pleased about it being the end of the book, and now I feel a bit "brrrr". Well, anyway, bear all this in mind for your exam.

Answers

Section One — River Environments

Page 3 — The Hydrological Cycle

1   Maximum of 4 marks available.
    There will be percolation of water down through the permeable rock [1 mark], reducing runoff and channel flow (river discharge) [1 mark], increasing infiltration [1 mark], increasing through flow and groundwater flow [1 mark].

2   Maximum of 4 marks available.
    Wet and dry seasons affect the availability of water from precipitation [1 mark]. Warm seasons provide more heat for evaporation and encourage vegetation growth plus transpiration. The effect is to reduce water reaching a river [1 mark]. If the heat increases convectional rainfall this could cause storms to fill the river at times [1 mark]. Cold seasons reduce plant growth and evaporation so more precipitation reaches the river [1 mark].

Page 5 — River Discharge

1   1 mark for each point up to 4 marks total.
    Construction of: impermeable surfaces such as concrete [1 mark], drainage systems [1 mark], dams [1 mark], channel straightening [1 mark], other channel modifications [1 mark] and removal or addition of water [1 mark].

2   Maximum of 4 marks available.
    Vegetation intercepts water and slows its progress to the river [1 mark]. This will have most effect during the growing season and when deciduous trees have leaves [1 mark]. Removal or dying off of vegetation will reduce interception and reduce lag time [1 mark]. The more vegetation there is, the more water is lost by transpiration and the less water flows into the river channel [1 mark].
    You need a few details. It's not enough to mention interception and leave it at that.

Page 7 — River Processes

1   Maximum of 3 marks available.
    A river's hydraulic radius is a measure of its efficiency [1 mark].
    The hydraulic radius is calculated by dividing the river's cross sectional area [1 mark] by the length of its wetted perimeter [1 mark].

2   Maximum of 3 marks available.
    Near the source, during floods or high discharges, the river has the competence to carry large particles, but they are dropped when the competence falls [1 mark]. The river has the competence to carry smaller particles further downstream [1 mark]. Also, particles are broken down by attrition, so that mean particle size decreases towards the sea. [1 mark].

Page 9 — River Landforms

1   Maximum of 4 marks available.
    Braided channels are seen when rivers split up into many smaller channels, due to the formation of islands in the bed. The channels split up and rejoin often over large areas. [1 mark for definition] The conditions needed are: 1) lots of erosion, e.g by meltwater, to provide lots of sediment [1 mark], 2) a gentle gradient (e.g. in a delta area) to slow the river down causing deposition of islands [1 mark], 3) the river becomes so over-loaded with sediment that it has to deposit the load as islands. [3 marks].

2   Maximum of 4 marks available.
    1 mark for each of four of these points, up to a maximum of 4:
    The discharge will have been reduced during the normal flooding period but regulated to supply irrigation water throughout the year [1 mark]. This makes a more constant flow in the river [1 mark]. The supply of (fertile) eroded material normally deposited on the flood plain is cut off [1 mark]. The sediment collects in the reservoir instead [1 mark]. The delta does not grow as it would have before the dam was built [1 mark].

Page 11 — Ecosystems in a River Environment

1   Maximum of 4 marks available.
    (a)   1 mark for each of four of these points, up to a maximum of 2:
          Few plants can live in the deeper, darker, open water [1 mark] and there are fewer nutrients in the open water [1 mark]. Boats disturb the water too much for plants to grow [1 mark].
    (b)   The functioning of a hydrosere ecosystem means the flows of energy within the system [1 mark] and the flows of nutrients within the system [1 mark].

2   Maximum of 4 marks available.
    You can choose two threats out of the following. Give one mark for the threat, and one mark for the explanation up to a total of 4 marks. Flood control schemes [1 mark] can turn the banks into sterile concrete walls where nothing can grow [1 mark]. Eutrophication [1 mark] is where the river becomes too rich in nutrients from fertiliser etc. Plants grow too much, and when they die their decay uses up so much oxygen that nothing else survives [1 mark]. Pollution [1 mark] can poison plants and animals or cause eutrophication [1 mark]. Wetlands are drained for farming and housing [1 mark], which removes the whole habitat [1 mark]. Peat digging [1 mark], removes the fragile peat bog [1 mark].
    It's important to give an explanation for full marks.

Page 13 — Flooding as a Hazard

1   1 mark for each of the following to a maximum of 2:
    Flooding recharges ground water supplies [1 mark]. Flooding encourages wetland ecosystems. [1 mark]. Flooding deposits fertile silt on the ground [1 mark]. Flood management systems don't prevent all floods from happening. When the river eventually floods, the flood will be extremely destructive. It's better to cope with floods as they happen [1 mark].

2   You can choose two reasons from the following:
    Give one mark for the reason and one mark for the explanation up to a maximum of 4 marks: Towns have large areas of impermeable tarmac and concrete [1 mark], so when it rains, runoff is very rapid [1 mark]. There are fewer areas of soil and vegetation [1 mark] which would allow slow interception and infiltration [1 mark]. Also gutters and drains [1 mark] quickly take runoff to the rivers [1 mark].

Page 15 — Drainage Basin Management

1   You can choose one strategy from the following. Give one mark for each effect on river processes and one mark for each effect on river ecosystems up to a maximum of 3 marks:
    Dams regulate discharge [1 mark]. Depositional processes are changed (i.e. sediment is deposited in reservoirs) [1 mark]. Wetland habitats are destroyed [1 mark]. Channelisation makes the river flow faster [1 mark]. It reduces erosion [1 mark]. The riverbanks are concreted, so they're no longer a good habitat for wildlife [1 mark]. Planting forests increases interception [1 mark], and increases lag time [1 mark]. It changes the ecosystems in the drainage basin, and may provide more habitats for wildlife [1 mark].

2   Maximum of 2 marks available.
    Water shortages [1 mark], increased levels of pollution [1 mark].

Page 17 — Drainage Basin Management

1   Maximum of 5 marks available.
    Name of general river management strategies, e.g. dams, channelisation, river restoration [1 mark]. Bare description of general river management, e.g. "channelisation straightens the river channel" [1 mark]. Named scheme, in named MEDC, e.g. Rhône basin, France [1 mark]. Economic impact, e.g. hard engineering (dams, channelisation) is very expensive, soft engineering is less expensive [1 mark]. Environmental impact, e.g. dams reduce sediment supply to deltas and coasts, wetland habitats like marshes are lost [1 mark].

2   Maximum of 5 marks available.
    Any good example can be used, probably the River Colne or River Kissimmee. River restoration returns river ecosystems to their natural state [1 mark]. Flood plains, ox-bow lakes, wetlands and marshes are restored [1 mark]. They allow the river to flood again which brings silt and nutrients to the flood plain (environmental and economic benefit) [1 mark]. It would no longer be possible to build on the flood plain [1 mark]. The direct economic cost of restoration is less than the direct economic cost of hard engineering [1 mark]. Plus named example [1 mark].
    Another example is the River Cole, Oxfordshire/Wiltshire border, UK.

Section Two — Coastal Environments

Page 19 — Introduction to Coastal Environments

1   Maximum of 3 marks available.
    A berm is a ridge of material washed up onto the beach [1 mark] by a constructive wave [1 mark]. A storm beach is the same as a berm, but it's above the highest high tide level [1 mark].

2   Maximum of 4 marks available.
    2 marks available for points on constructive waves, from any of the following points: Constructive waves are flat and gentle [1 mark]. They have a long wavelength and low frequency [1 mark]. Their swash is greater than their backwash [1 mark].
    2 marks available for points on destructive waves, from any of the following points: Destructive waves are tall and steep [1 mark]. They have a short wavelength and high frequency [1 mark]. Their backwash is greater than their swash [1 mark].

Page 21 — Coastal Landforms

1   Maximum of 3 marks available.
    Any from: Erosion [1 mark], deposition [1 mark], transportation [1 mark], weathering [1 mark], mass movement (including terms such as slipping, sliding or slumping) [1 mark].

2   Maximum of 3 marks available.
    Strata parallel to the ground form steep cliffs [1 mark]. Strata sloping away from or towards the sea form sloping cliffs [1 mark]. Rock may crack along bedding planes and slump into the sea [1 mark].

Answers

3   Maximum of 5 marks available — any 5 points from the following:
Waves erode, transport and deposit material [1 mark]. High energy surfing
breakers erode material, low energy surging breakers deposit material [1 mark].
When waves break parallel to the shore, they build a swash aligned beach, with
no longshore drift [1 mark]. When waves break at an angle, you get longshore
drift [1 mark], and spits are formed, often with recurved laterals [1 mark].
Waves refract around headlands — where they converge, they erode more,
and where they diverge they lose power and deposit more [1 mark].
Remember to mention things like longshore drift and wave refraction.

Page 23 — Changing Coastal Ecosystems

1   Maximum of 4 marks available.
3 marks for any three of these:
A good supply of sand [1 mark], large exposed area at low tide [1 mark],
prevailing onshore winds [1 mark], undisturbed backshore [1 mark].
Plus 1 mark for one of these:
plant succession [1 mark] or named plants e.g. marram grass [1 mark].

2   Maximum of 4 marks available.
The mature dunes are further along in the plant succession, so there's been
more time for more species to grow [1 mark]. The mature dunes are held in
place by plant roots, so plants aren't disturbed by sand movement [1 mark].
Mature dunes have more soil and nutrients to support a variety of plants
[1 mark]. Mature dunes are less salty, so a variety of plants can grow [1 mark].

3   Maximum of 5 marks available.
Lava from underwater volcanic eruptions forms a volcanic island [1 mark].
Coral grows around this island to form a fringing reef [1 mark]. The volcano
erodes, and sea water forms a lagoon between the reef and the island, making
a barrier reef [1 mark]. Eventually, the volcano sinks below sea level [1 mark],
and the coral carries on growing at the same rate as the island sinks, to form a
ring shaped atoll [1 mark].

Page 25 — Coastal Processes and People

1   Maximum of 6 marks available.
(sample answer based on Humber and Holderness study)
Area is the fastest eroding coastline in Europe. The local soil is clay, which
erodes quickly [1 mark]. Cliffs are literally falling into the sea [1 mark].
The area is heavily populated — 500 000 people live there [1 mark]. There are
ports and industrial developments which would be threatened by coastal
erosion [1 mark]. Wetland habitats are threatened by flood [1 mark].
Low lying land, especially around Spurn Head spit, is threatened by storm
events [1 mark].
You can get the marks if you use a good example from your reading of class lessons.
Any six points based on a named case study will do you.

2   Maximum of 4 marks available. Any of the following points, to a maximum of 4.
100 million living in coastal areas will be at risk and need re-settlement
[1 mark]. Coastal cities will be lost [1 mark]. Agricultural land will be lost
[1 mark]. Coastal industries e.g. oil refining, power stations, chemical works
will be lost [1 mark]. Low lying tropical islands will be submerged [1 mark].

Page 27 — Human Use of Coastal Areas

1   Maximum of 4 marks available.
Tourists' feet trampling on the path erode the path, which affects the landscape
[1 mark]. Footpath widening affects the look of the landscape [1 mark].
Intensity of use affects the amount of erosion [1 mark]. Wildlife habitats are
affected — the presence of tourists discourages wildlife from settling in the area
[1 mark].

2   Maximum of 4 marks available.
For industrial and urban use — Increased pollution [1 mark]. Sewage will need
to be processed and dumped into the sea [1 mark]. Appearance of coast is
altered [1 mark]. Land may need to be reclaimed for development, destroying
salt marsh habitats [1 mark].
For tourist use, any 4 from — Appearance of coast is altered [1 mark]. Issues of
waste disposal [1 mark]. Loss of ecological sites [1 mark]. Erosional and other
damage by tourists [1 mark]. Blow-outs in sand dunes [1 mark].

Page 29 Management of Coastal Systems

1   Maximum of 7 marks available.
Needs example. Answers depend on the example chosen.
For a coastline with cliff erosion (e.g. North Norfolk), the following apply:
hard engineering at the cliff foot such as curved walls [1 mark], stepped
barriers [1 mark], gabions [1 mark] and revetments [1 mark].
Hard engineering on the cliff face, e.g. steel sheets [1 mark]. These are used to
protect the cliff from waves [1 mark]. Soft engineering on cliffs includes
planting vegetation and lowering cliff slope [1 mark]. Cheap methods such as
rip raps and gabions are likely to be used where resources don't stretch to a
sea wall [1 mark].
For a coastline at risk of floods, flood defences such as earth banks can be used
[1 mark]. Tidal barriers are very expensive, and only worth it to protect big
cities, e.g. London [1 mark].
For a coastline at risk of beach erosion, groynes can be used to trap sediment
[1 mark]. Groynes can reduce deposition on downdrift coasts, which puts
downdrift coasts at risk of erosion [1 mark].

Section Three — Glacial Environments

Page 31 — Glacial Systems and The Formation of Glaciers

1   Maximum of 3 marks available.
A glacial budget is the balance between inputs and outputs [1 mark]. When the
glacial budget is positive, there's more accumulation than ablation and the
glacier moves forwards [1 mark]. When the glacial budget is negative, there's
more ablation than accumulation and the glacier retreats [1 mark].

2   Maximum of 5 marks available.
Snow settles [1 mark]. Snow freezes and thaws several times and changes into
a denser and more granular consistency called firn or névé [1 mark]. Increased
pressure causes pressure melting, which makes the snow into a structureless
mass [1 mark]. It has far less pore space so it's less permeable than fresh snow
[1 mark]. Air is squeezed out, and particles of ice fuse together. This is called
sintering [1 mark].

Page 33 — Glacial Movement and Erosion

1   Maximum of 4 marks available.
Extending flow and compressing flow make the glacial ice crack [1 mark] under
forces of tension and compression [1 mark]. The ice slips downwards in
extending flow and forwards in compressing flow [1 mark]. The cracks widen
and form crevasses [1 mark].

2   Maximum of 4 marks available.
Glaciers pick up debris by plucking [1 mark] and abrasion [1 mark]. Plucking is
when ice thaws around rocks and then refreezes. When the glacier moves
forward, it plucks the rock from the valley floor or wall [1 mark]. Abrasion is
when debris carried by the glacier scrapes material off the valley walls and floor
[1 mark].

Page 35 — The Glacial Trough and Glacial Deposition

1   Maximum of 4 marks available.
North facing slopes get least heating from the Sun [1 mark] and face the colder
winds from the north [1 mark]. This enables ice to accumulate [1 mark] and
carve out corries on north facing slopes [1 mark].

2   Maximum of 4 marks available.
A hanging valley is a tributary valley [1 mark] left at a higher level when the
main valley is deepened by the glacier [1 mark]. A fjord is the lowest part of the
over-deepened main valley [1 mark] which is then flooded by the sea [1 mark].

Page 37 — Fluvioglacial Landforms

1   Maximum of 4 marks available.
Moving ice can temporarily dam rivers, or meltwater can collect against hills
[1 mark]. This makes a proglacial lake [1 mark]. Where the lake overflows it
may erode a gorge [1 mark] which the river follows when the ice melts — so
the river follows a different course than its original course [1 mark].

2   Maximum of 4 marks available.
Layers of coarse deposits form when meltwater flows fast during rapid
summer melt, [1 mark] whereas layers of fine deposits settle out during the
cold autumn when the lake surface is frozen [1 mark]. In summer, fast
flowing meltwater carries all particles, and drops coarser ones as the velocity
decreases when the lake forms [1 mark]. The finest silts stay in suspension in
the lake and settle out slowly during the autumn and winter [1 mark].

Page 39 — Periglacial Processes and Landforms

1   Maximum of 4 marks available.
Solifluction terraces are step shaped ridges [1 mark] on slopes in areas of
permafrost [1 mark]. The active layer of permafrost thaws and becomes very
waterlogged [1 mark]. It flows in a viscous way downslope [1 mark].

2   Maximum of 4 marks available.
Ice forms a lens shape under the surface [1 mark]. It pushes the surface up
into a small hill – a pingo [1 mark]. Sand and gravel slide down the slope
round the lens of ice in the process of solifluction [1 mark]. Ice thaws, and
the hill collapses [1 mark].

Section Four — Tectonics and Weathering

Page 41 — Plate Tectonics

1   Maximum of 4 marks available.
Most activity is at or close to plate margins [1 mark]. Reasons for this are that
where rigid plates move against one another they create a lot of friction. Plate
movements create shockwaves which are called earthquakes [1 mark]. Where
crust is subducted as two plates meet heat from friction melts the crust, leading
to the formation of molten magma which escapes onto the Earth's surface as
volcanoes [1 mark].
At mid-oceanic ridges crust plates are moving apart and new magma rises from
below to create new oceanic crust with associated volcanic activity [1 mark].

Answers

2 Maximum of 5 marks available.
For destructive margins, any 5 points from the following:
Deep sea trenches are formed as denser oceanic crust sinks below the
continental crust **[1 mark]**. A subduction (Benioff) zone forms at an angle
below ground as the crust sinks and becomes subjected to extreme pressure
and heating, causing it to melt **[1 mark]**. This molten magma is less dense and
therefore tries to rise to the surface **[1 mark]**. If it reaches the surface it causes
volcanoes **[1 mark]** but if it solidifies within the crust before it reaches the
surface it forms huge batholiths **[1 mark]**. Fold mountains form along the edge
of the plate as the pressure causes sediments at the edges of the plates to
become crumpled and uplifted **[1 mark]**. If two oceanic plates meet the
subduction creates an ocean trench **[1 mark]** and a series of island arc
volcanoes **[1 mark]** along the edge of the plate. The collision of two
continental plates involves no subduction as both plates are lower in density
than the asthenosphere below. Instead intense crumpling and buckling of the
sediments occurs, forming huge fold mountains **[1 mark]**.
Remember that you only need to write about destructive plate margins here —
anything else wouldn't be relevant to the question.

For constructive margins, any 5 marks from the following:
These form as plates move away from one another **[1 mark]**. The split is
marked by a rift valley **[1 mark]** and oceanic ridges **[1 mark]** form where
magma flows upwards and spreads to form new oceanic crust **[1 mark]**.
As the magma cools it cracks to form transform faults **[1 mark]**.
You would probably not get a choice of plate margins in an exam. If you do, make
sure you state clearly at the start of your answer which option you've chosen.
You're asked to describe AND explain so try to link each thing you describe to its
explanation as you go along. It saves time.

Page 43 — Weathering Processes

1 Maximum of 7 marks available.
OK — not all drainage basins have all weathering processes going on,
so the answer you give depends on the basin you choose. For a UK basin, the
most common forms of physical weathering will be freeze-thaw, wetting-drying,
and salt crystallisation (on the coast). There'll be chemical weathering from
oxidation, carbonation, hydration, hydrolysis (of clay). Biological action
includes weathering by tree roots, chelation and bacterial action.
1 mark for each of these points up to a maximum of 7:
Freeze-thaw weathering is when water gets trapped in crevices, freezes and
expands **[1 mark]**. This puts pressure on the rock and widens the crack
[1 mark]. Wetting-drying **[1 mark]** happens when clay in rock gets wet and
swells, putting cracks in the rock **[1 mark]**. Salt crystallisation weathering
happens by the coast. Salt crystals grow in rock crevices **[1 mark]**, exert
pressure on rock and make it crack **[1 mark]**. Oxidation produces compounds
which can be softer and more easily eroded than the original rock **[1 mark]**.
They can also be bigger in size than the original compounds, causing splits and
cracks **[1 mark]**. Carbonation is when carbon dioxide mixes with rainwater to
produce carbonic acid **[1 mark]**, which attacks carbonate rocks like limestone
[1 mark]. Hydration is when a mineral absorbs water. It expands, which makes
it disintegrate **[1 mark]**. Hydrolysis is a chemical reaction between water and a
mineral to form clay, which is easily weathered **[1 mark]**. Tree roots force rock
apart **[1 mark]**. Animal burrows let water in, which facilitates other forms of
weathering **[1 mark]**. Bacteria break down some minerals **[1 mark]**. Decaying
conifer needles produce a lot of humic acids **[1 mark]**. which remove mineral
ions from soil **[1 mark]**.
Some of this depends on which basin you choose, but the basics of the answer will be
the same for most places.

2 Maximum of 5 marks available.
Climate affects weathering **[1 mark]**. Freeze-thaw and wetting-drying
need water, and freeze-thaw needs it to be cold **[1 mark if example of
weathering given]**.
Rock type affects weathering **[1 mark]**. Rocks have a variety of chemical
compositions so they react differently **[1 mark]**.
Rock structure affects weathering **[1 mark]**. Porous rocks have pore spaces,
which let water through. Permeable rocks have routes for water to pass
through them, such as along joints, bedding planes and faults **[1 mark]**.
Relief affects weathering **[1 mark]**. On steep slopes regolith is quickly removed,
exposing new rock. On gentle slopes a deep protective layer of regolith can
accumulate **[1 mark]**. Vegetation can provide a protective cover against
weathering **[1 mark]**. Human influences e.g. pollution causes acid rain which
affects weathering **[1 mark]**.

Page 45 — Mass Movement

1 Maximum of 5 marks available, from any of the following:
Quarrying reduces the stability of slopes **[1 mark]**. Building disturbs slope
equilibrium **[1 mark]**. Planting forests (afforestation) stabilises slopes
[1 mark] and deforestation destabilises them **[1 mark]**. Traffic noise and
vibration can destabilise slopes **[1 mark]**. Mining deposits can produce
unstable slopes **[1 mark]**. Ploughing loosens soil, making it more prone to mass
movement **[1 mark]**. Overgrazing removes vegetation and exposes slopes to
weathering **[1 mark]**.

2 Soil creep creates little steps (terracettes) on slopes **[1 mark]** and causes
features (walls, buildings, fences) to lean over **[1 mark]**. Solifluction creates
terraces and lobes of regolith **[1 mark]**. Mudflows are fast and can sweep away

people and buildings **[1 mark]**. Cliffs can collapse (slumping, landslides,
rock falls) **[1 mark]**. Shanty towns can be destroyed by flows and slumps
on slopes **[1 mark]**.

Section Five — Climate

Page 47 — The Global Energy Budget

1 Maximum of 4 marks available.
Some energy is absorbed by ozone **[1 mark]**. Some is absorbed by gas and
dust in the atmosphere **[1 mark]**. Some is reflected by clouds **[1 mark]**.
Some is reflected by particles in the atmosphere **[1 mark]**.
It's well worth learning that complicated energy budget diagram.

2 Maximum of 5 marks available.
Latitudes near the Equator get more energy from the Sun than they lose from
longwave radiation **[1 mark]**. Latitudes near the poles lose more energy than
they gain from the Sun **[1 mark]**. This imbalance has to be evened out
[1 mark]. Energy is transferred from the Equator to the poles **[1 mark]**.
The 0-40° region has all the excess energy — all that excess has to pass through
40° on the way to the poles **[1 mark]**.
You could explain why there's an imbalance (angle of the Sun's rays hitting the
Earth, Sun's rays passing through more atmosphere at the poles, therefore more
absorption and scattering, more reflection at the poles because of high polar albedo
and low equatorial albedo), but you don't have to. The question only says to
describe the difference in energy budgets, NOT to explain it. Explaining would
be a waste of time.

Page 49 — Energy Transfers and British Weather

1 Maximum of 5 marks available.
As the warm front approaches, it starts to rain **[1 mark]**. When the warm front
has passed, the rain stops and the temperature rises (as the warm sector passes
overhead) **[1 mark]**. The cold air behind the cold front moves faster than the
warm air, and can overtake and undercut the warm sector. This creates an
occluded front which gives a longer period of rain **[1 mark]**. Some hours on, it
gets windier and colder. Clouds build up as the cold front moves in. Heavy
rain falls **[1 mark]**. As the cold front passes, the wind changes direction (veers)
from warm southerly to cool north-westerly **[1 mark]**.
If you learn this off by heart, it's EASY.

2 Maximum of 4 marks available.
A kink in the polar front allows warm, wet tropical maritime air to push north
into cold polar air **[1 mark]**. Where warm air pushes into cold air, there's a
warm front **[1 mark]**. Where cold air pushes back into warm air, there's a cold
front. Along both the warm front and the cold front, warm air rises and then
cools. Moisture in the air condenses and forms clouds **[1 mark]**. As the
warmer, less dense air rises over the colder air it creates an area of low pressure
— a depression **[1 mark]**.

Page 51 — Cool Temperate Western Maritime Climates

1 Maximum of 4 marks available.
'Temperate' means that a climate has no temperature extremes — it is neither
very hot nor very cold. **[1 mark]**. CTWM climates are temperate because
they are in the mid latitudes — neither tropical nor polar **[1 mark]**. Areas with
a CTWM are always coastal and because sea water heats up more slowly than
land does in summer temperatures are kept cool **[1 mark]**. In winter the sea
cools more slowly than the land keeping temperatures warm **[1 mark]**.

2 Maximum of 3 marks available.
There are 3 important points to be made when you describe the distribution —
1) CTWM climates lie in the mid latitudes (about 40° -60° N and S) **[1 mark]**.
2) They are all on Western coasts **[1 mark]**. 3) Some examples are Western
Europe including UK, and Tasmania **[1 mark]**.

Page 53 — Climatic Hazards: Strong Winds

1 Maximum of 7 marks available.
In an MEDC, there are adequate warnings before a tropical revolving storm
[1 mark]. Early warning systems are expensive, so LEDCs don't have this ability
[1 mark]. In MEDCs people can afford to protect their homes, stockpile food
and evacuate when necessary **[1 mark]**. In LEDCs people are often unable to
take advantage of any warning **[1 mark]**. MEDCs have evacuation centres set
up ready in schools and gyms in safe areas away from the hurricane's path
[1 mark]. MEDCs are able to organise relief efforts quickly, and offer financial,
medical, and social support to people who have been affected by the hurricane
[1 mark]. LEDCs don't have the infrastructure or money for big relief efforts
[1 mark].
In the actual exam, it'll help to give examples, e.g. of recent tropical revolving storms.

2 Maximum 3 marks available.
Hurricanes fade away when they pass over land **[1 mark]**. This is because they
need a supply of water **[1 mark]** which condenses to provide energy to keep
them going **[1 mark]**. Hurricanes also fade away as they travel towards the
poles, away from their heat source **[1 mark]**.

Answers

Page 55 — Local Energy Budgets

1   Maximum of 3 marks available.
Ground frost only forms when the surface of the Earth is cooled to below 0°C *[1 mark]*. On cloudy nights, the surface of the Earth does not cool down as much as it does on clear nights *[1 mark]*. This is because cloud cover reflects outgoing longwave radiation back to the surface *[1 mark]*.

2   Maximum of 4 marks available.
A temperature inversion is when there's a layer where temperature increases with height (normally, air gets cooler with height) *[1 mark]*. A temperature inversion traps warm polluted air underneath it *[1 mark]*. Temperature inversions occur in anticyclonic conditions, with clear skies and no wind *[1 mark]*. The surface cools through radiation and makes the air near to the surface cooler, and the cooler lower layers don't mix with the warmer upper layers *[1 mark]*.

Page 57 — Urban Climates

1   Maximum of 4 marks available.
1 mark for description: The Urban Heat Island Effect is the fact that urban areas are usually a couple of degrees warmer than the surrounding countryside *[1 mark]*.
3 marks for explanation — 1 mark for any of these points, up to a maximum of 3: Dark coloured concrete, brick and tarmac surfaces are non-reflective (they have a low albedo), so they absorb and store heat during the day *[1 mark]*. Pollution and smog traps outgoing heat radiation *[1 mark]*. Car fumes, factories, power stations, central heating and people all release heat *[1 mark]*. Most rain runs off through the city's drainage system, so it doesn't lie around and then evaporate *[1 mark]*. There isn't much vegetation, so there's little transpiration *[1 mark]*.

2   Maximum of 4 marks available.
1 mark for each of the following points up to a maximum of 4: Lack of technology *[1 mark]*, high cost of technology *[1 mark]*, slow processes of making new legislation *[1 mark]*, difficulties enforcing legislation *[1 mark]*, reluctance of governments to make unpopular policies *[1 mark]*, reluctance of the public to change their habits and lifestyles *[1 mark]*.

Page 59 — Global Warming

1   Maximum of 5 marks available.
There's a financial risk in taking unilateral action *[1 mark]* — if one country spends money on reducing greenhouse gases, and all its international competitors don't, then the country will lose money *[1 mark]*. It's best if countries can arrange to take action at the same time *[1 mark]*. All countries will be affected by global warming to some extent *[1 mark]*. Even countries which get a nice climate will be indirectly affected by economic damage to trading partners *[1 mark]*. Therefore all countries need to take action to protect themselves in the long run.

2   1 mark for each of the following to a maximum of 4:
Natural light through roof lights replaces the need for artificial light during the day *[1 mark]*, double or triple glazing *[1 mark]*, solar panels to provide heat and generate electricity *[1 mark]*, roof insulation to reduce heat loss to air *[1 mark]*, cavity wall insulation to reduce heat loss through walls *[1 mark]*, no windows on north facing wall to minimise heat loss *[1 mark]*, the most energy efficient central heating system possible *[1 mark]*.

Section Six — Energy and Life

Page 61 — Systems, Flows and Cycles

1   Maximum of 5 marks available.
A food chain is a simple series of steps showing feeding levels (trophic levels) in an ecosystem *[1 mark]* starting with a plant, then a herbivore, then a carnivore *[1 mark]*. A food web is more realistic, being a more complex, interlinking diagram showing for example, that carnivores can eat several different herbivores *[1 mark]*.
Energy is lost at each stage because 1) animals use up a lot of energy in respiration and moving and 2) energy is lost as not all of a creature may be eaten *[2 marks]*.

2   Maximum of 4 marks available.
There are two ways that nutrients can enter the soil: via decomposition by microorganisms *[1 mark]* and via weathering of rocks *[1 mark]*. Once the nutrients are in the soil they are lost in two ways: via uptake by plants through their root systems *[1 mark]*, and through leaching where nutrients are washed out of the soil by rain *[1 mark]*.

Page 63 — Plant Succession

1   Maximum of 4 marks available.
Lack of sufficient fertile soil *[1 mark]*, waterlogged conditions *[1 mark]*, fire caused by lightning *[1 mark]*, volcanic activity *[1 mark]*.

2   Maximum of 6 marks available.
Vegetation cleared *[1 mark]*; non-native plants introduced *[1 mark]*; trees felled for firewood, house, furniture and ship construction, farmland, industrialisation *[1 mark]*; cultivating crops *[1 mark]* and over-grazing by too many animals *[1 mark]*; pollution damaged forests *[1 mark]*.

Page 65 — Rainforest Destruction

1   Maximum of 4 marks available.
Most nutrients are in the trees and vegetation. If trees or vegetation are destroyed the nutrients are removed *[1 mark]*. This leaves little for crops and pasture to use *[1 mark]*. This can also cause leaching and soil erosion *[1 mark]*. It is important to conserve nutrients taking only a small amount of produce each year and not destroying the forest *[1 mark]*.

2   1 mark for each point up to a maximum of 4.
Biodiversity should be preserved — once gone, extinct species cannot be replaced *[1 mark]*. All species have a right to exist *[1 mark]*. The majority of medicines are based on chemicals from plants, trees and animals, at least a third of them from tropical rainforest *[1 mark]*. Keeping and using biodiverse ecosystems is part of the sustainable way forward (e.g. one brazil nut tree can produce more protein than cattle on the same area of land) *[1 mark]*.

Page 67 — Soil Characteristics

1   Maximum of 6 marks available.
2 marks for water: Water transfers nutrients down into the soil *[1 mark]*. It moves particles down the profile, creating horizons of different colours *[1 mark]*.
2 marks for organic matter: Organic matter is decomposed to form the O horizons *[1 mark]*. It can be acidic and help in leaching *[1 mark]*.
2 marks for inorganic matter: Inorganic matter is regolith, which affects the texture, e.g. sandstone makes sandy soils *[1 mark]*. Inorganic particles affect the rate of movement of water through the soil *[1 mark]*.

2   1 mark for each of these points, up to a maximum of 7.
Good soil for farming should drain well, but not too fast *[1 mark]*. It should have air spaces *[1 mark]*, and it should have nutrients. Sandy soil has large particles and drains too quickly *[1 mark]*. Clay soil has small particles and drains too slowly *[1 mark]*. Sand has large air spaces *[1 mark]*. Clay and silty soils have small air spaces *[1 mark]*. Nutrients stick to clay particles *[1 mark]*. The ideal texture for farming combines clay, silt and sand — it's called loam *[1 mark]*. The ideal structure for farming is crumb. It has small peds with plenty of pore spaces *[1 mark]*.

Page 69 — Types of Soil

1   Maximum of 4 marks available.
Podsol has clear horizons formed by leaching *[1 mark]*. Organic acids remove iron and aluminium oxides from the A horizon, leaving behind grey silica *[1 mark]*. The oxides are deposited in the B horizon, which has a brownish look *[1 mark]*. Some oxides may cement together into a solid reddish iron pan in the B horizon *[1 mark]*.

2   Maximum of 4 marks available.
On steep slopes mass movement may remove soil as it is formed *[1 mark]*. On less steep slopes soil is carried away before it has the chance to form horizons, so it's shallow and azonal *[1 mark]*. A catena may form on a slope *[1 mark]*. This is a sequence of different soils down a slope caused by the slope rather than differences in climate or rock type *[1 mark]*. Waterlogged gley soils often form at the foot of the slope *[1 mark]*.

Section Seven — The Rural Environment

Page 71 — Introducing Rural Areas

1   Maximum of 2 marks available.
The rural-urban continuum is all the land between extreme urban and extreme rural *[2 marks]*. 1 mark for "outskirts of a city" or similar.

2   Maximum of 7 marks available.
Answer depends on the regions chosen, but there are some basic common points. 1 mark for each point below, to a maximum of 7.
At least 2 marks must be similarities, and 2 must be differences.
Similarities: Low population in settlements *[1 mark]*, low population density, employment in agriculture *[1 mark]*, land use mainly agricultural *[1 mark]*, villages have a sense of community *[1 mark]*.
Differences: UK village has lower % involved in farming *[1 mark]*. In UK village more people work outside the village *[1 mark]*. In UK village, there's more tourism and other service activity *[1 mark]*. UK village has more services (e.g. shop, public transport, school, doctor) *[1 mark]*. Urban amenities are more accessible from UK village *[1 mark]*. UK village more likely to be suburbanised *[1 mark]*.

Page 73 — Changes in Rural Areas

1   Maximum of 8 marks available.
Mechanisation means that there are fewer jobs in farming *[1 mark]*. Farm labourers tend to work part time rather than full time *[1 mark]*, and some labourers work seasonally *[1 mark]*. This means that alternative employment is needed in rural areas *[1 mark]*. The average field size has increased *[1 mark]*, because it's more efficient to run a tractor or combine harvester over one big field than two small fields — less time wasted turning around *[1 mark]*.

Answers

Farms have got a lot bigger *[1 mark]*, as farming has become dominated by large agribusinesses instead of small family farms *[1 mark]*.

2   Maximum of 8 marks available.
5 marks for points on the inefficiency of the open field system.
The open field system wasted land *[1 mark]*. 1 out of its 3 fields was left fallow, and produced nothing *[1 mark]*. Land was wasted on paths between each strip *[1 mark]*. The system wasted labour. The fallow field had to be ploughed even though it wasn't producing anything *[1 mark]*. The system wasted time — families had to travel between strips *[1 mark]*.
3 marks for arguments about the 1700s:
In the 1700s, the population was growing *[1 mark]* and urban settlements started to expand. The three field system couldn't produce enough food to feed urban dwellers as well as rural people *[1 mark]*. However, improvements in agriculture actually had to come before the Industrial Revolution — there had to be enough food available before people could move to cities *[1 mark]*.

3   Maximum of 14 marks available.
Answer depends on area chosen. Some common points (1 mark each to a maximum of 13), plus 1 mark for a good named case study.
Land use changes from agriculture to tourism *[1 mark]*. Services reflect needs of visitors rather than inhabitants *[1 mark]*. Tea shops and restaurants open *[1 mark]*. Gift shops and shops selling equipment for recreational activities open (mountain clothing in a mountainous area, e.g. Lake District or Snowdonia, beach kit in coastal area, e.g. Devon and Cornwall coast) *[1 mark]*. Car parks are needed, which puts pressure on land use *[1 mark]*. Footpaths are eroded. Wildlife habitats and vegetation are damaged by tourists' feet and bikes *[1 mark]*, and by pollution from the large number of visitors' cars etc *[1 mark]*. Holiday traffic causes congestion *[1 mark]*. More holiday homes, so prices rise beyond reach of locals *[1 mark]*. Noise pollution *[1 mark]*. With houses being sold off as holiday homes, village can end up empty in winter, which is bad news for local businesses *[1 mark]*. Jobs are created for local people *[1 mark]*. More wealth in the local economy *[1 mark]*.

Page 75 — Changes in Rural Areas

1   Maximum of 7 marks available.
1 mark for definition of rural depopulation: Rural depopulation is a serious decline in the population of a rural area *[1 mark]*.
1 mark for each factor: Lack of job opportunities in rural area *[1 mark]*. Low paid, low status jobs in rural area *[1 mark]*. Poor housing *[1 mark]*. Poor service provision *[1 mark]*. Perceived opportunities in cities *[1 mark]*. 1 mark for a named area *[1 mark]*.

2   Maximum of 8 marks available.
The economically active age group are most likely to get HIV/AIDS *[1 mark]* because they are the sexually active age group *[1 mark]*. The local economy loses their labour *[1 mark]*. People sell possessions to pay for healthcare and funerals *[1 mark]*. Poverty makes people more likely to migrate to urban areas *[1 mark]*. Young men are the most likely to migrate, and may use prostitutes in the city, increasing the rate of HIV infection *[1 mark]*. Poor women are more likely to become prostitutes *[1 mark]*. This creates a multiplier effect — more HIV leads to more poverty, which leads to more HIV *[1 mark]*.

Page 77 — Challenges Facing Rural Areas

1   Maximum of 11 marks available.
Rural deprivation means the extent to which a rural area lacks services or amenities *[1 mark]*.
Maximum of 5 marks available for explaining how rural deprivation has been managed in an MEDC — the following sample answer uses the Llangurig example from p76:
Local school had few pupils and was at risk of closure *[1 mark]*. Local housing agency advertised *[1 mark]* for Welsh speaking families to live in their properties at reduced rent *[1 mark]*. Tenants were found, and their children attended the primary school *[1 mark]*, saving it from closure *[1 mark]*
Maximum of 5 marks available for explaining how rural deprivation has been managed in an LEDC — the following sample answer uses the Malawi example from p82:
Rural households had no access to financial services *[1 mark]*, and therefore could not run businesses *[1 mark]* and get out of poverty *[1 mark]*. United Nations Rural Development Programme provided loans to poor Malawians *[1 mark]*, allowing them to set up small businesses *[1 mark]*.

2   Maximum of 8 marks available.
Tourism brings money to an LEDC rural area *[1 mark]*. The area will need to change to accommodate the wishes of visitors (e.g. hotels, discos) *[1 mark]*. People who work in tourism may be better paid than other locals, which causes conflict *[1 mark]*. Mass tourism impacts on the environment, e.g. by creating rubbish and by contributing to erosion *[1 mark]*. Communities need to manage conflict between farmers preserving their livelihood, and locals wanting to make money from tourism developments *[1 mark]*. They can do this by making sure that everyone in the community can share in the success of tourism *[1 mark]*. Ecotourism aims to conserve environments and local culture and make money at the same time *[1 mark]*. It can offer a compromise to resolve the conflicts between development and conservation *[1 mark]*.

Page 79 — Rural Futures

1   Maximum of 7 marks available.
Integrated development means trying to meet different needs with one piece of development *[1 mark]*. In the UK countryside, there are several problems *[1 mark]*, e.g. lack of services *[1 mark]*, poor public transport *[1 mark]* and lack of jobs *[1 mark]*. The UK has an integrated rural development agency, the Countryside Agency *[1 mark]*. They aim to improve the quality of life of people in the countryside through integrated development *[1 mark]*.

2   Maximum of 7 marks available.
Top-down development is planned on a national scale *[1 mark]*, and imposed on rural communities *[1 mark]*. Bottom-up development is planned on a local scale *[1 mark]*. It is tailor made with the local community's needs in mind *[1 mark]*. Local people are more likely to make a project work if their interests are represented *[1 mark]*. Large scale top-down developments like the Aswan Dam have unintended negative consequences for rural people, e.g. the decreased fertility of delta land *[1 mark]*. The bottom-up micro-hydro projects in Nepal have been much more successful *[1 mark]*.
You'll also get marks for different examples, as long as they're good ones.

Section Eight — The Urban Environment

Page 81 — Urban Areas and Urbanisation

1   (a)   Rural-urban migration in the Industrial Revolution *[1 mark]* as people sought jobs in urban areas *[1 mark]*.
    (b)   Current rural-urban migration *[1 mark]* and population growth *[1 mark]*.

2   Maximum of 2 marks available.
There's been a lot of urbanisation in the LEDCs *[1 mark]*. Urbanisation in the LEDCs is happening faster than in the MEDCs *[1 mark]*.

Page 83 — Settlement Hierarchies

1   Answer should give reasons why the actual sphere of influence may differ from the theoretical one. Maximum of 6 marks from the following: Traffic problems *[1 mark]* and expensive parking may make the actual sphere of influence smaller than the theoretical one *[1 mark]*. Good quality shops in peripheral towns *[1 mark]* or poor quality shops in the central place may make the actual sphere of influence smaller than the theoretical one *[1 mark]*. Positive or negative perceptions of a centre may make the actual sphere of influence differ from the theoretical one *[1 mark]*. The actual sphere of influence may be stretched out beyond the theoretical one in the direction of a good road *[1 mark]*. Hills and rivers act as a barrier, so the actual sphere of influence may be squashed so that it is smaller than the theoretical one *[1 mark]*. Settlements on the coast have semicircular spheres of influence making them a different shape from the theoretical one *[1 mark]*.

Page 85 — Cycle of Urbanisation

1   1 mark for each point below to a maximum of 8.
4 points must be about MEDCs, 4 points must be about LEDCs.
In MEDCs urban growth and suburbanisation started in the early 20th century *[1 mark]*. Early growth was along transport routes, and areas in between were infilled later *[1 mark]*. Suburbs were carefully planned *[1 mark]*. Suburbs are mainly middle class residential *[1 mark]*. In the late 20th century there's been urban sprawl characterised by sprawling suburbs *[1 mark]*, and widespread car use *[1 mark]*.
In LEDCs, urban growth has been fastest in the late 20th century *[1 mark]*. Suburbs were unplanned *[1 mark]*. Suburbs have industrial land use as well as residential *[1 mark]*. Urban sprawl has caused more serious pollution and quality of life problems than in MEDCs *[1 mark]*.

2   Maximum of 7 marks available.
Reurbanisation is the move back to the city centre *[1 mark]*. Young professionals move back into luxury accommodation *[1 mark]* in "trendy" areas of the city, where they can be close to the cultural activities of the city centre *[1 mark]*. The time and money saved by not commuting can be used on leisure *[1 mark]*. Former factory units and warehouses are converted into luxury flats *[1 mark]*. In Manchester, warehouses in Castlefields have been converted into apartments *[1 mark]*. Council flats in Manchester and Salford have been replaced by low density housing *[1 mark]*.

Page 87 — British Cities Through History

1   Maximum of 5 marks available. 1 mark for each point up to a maximum of 5.
Depends what town you studied — could be York, Leicester, Nottingham, Ludlow, Worcester, etc... Sample answer is for York.
Towers on town walls are evidence of Roman town *[1 mark]*. Town walls are medieval *[1 mark]*. York Minster is medieval *[1 mark]*. Narrow winding streets also date from Middle Ages *[1 mark]*. The Shambles are medieval *[1 mark]*. Half timbered buildings remain from Tudor times, e.g. Merchant Adventurers Hall *[1 mark]*. Mansion House dates from Georgian times *[1 mark]*. New Earswick is a garden village built in the early 1900s *[1 mark]*. New estates on the outskirts of the city date from the late 20th century *[1 mark]*.

Answers

2 Maximum of 7 marks available.
People living in urban slums had poor health *[1 mark]*. Cholera and typhoid were common and killed many *[1 mark]*. The terraces were back to back around tiny courtyards *[1 mark]*, so there was little fresh air *[1 mark]*. There was no clean water supply *[1 mark]*. There was no refuse disposal *[1 mark]*. There were no sewers, so human waste seeped into the water supply, spreading disease *[1 mark]*.

Page 89 — New Towns, Building Materials and Techniques

1 Maximum of 7 marks available.
3 marks for reasons, 3 for description, 1 for named example.
Reasons: To prevent urban sprawl *[1 mark]*. To relieve overcrowding in towns *[1 mark]*. To provide new housing to allow slum clearance to go ahead *[1 mark]* and to provide housing as part of the post-war rebuilding of war-damaged houses *[1 mark]*. To act as growth poles in regions of high unemployment *[1 mark]*.
Description: Low and high density housing mixed *[1 mark]*. Neighbourhood communities *[1 mark]*. Each neighbourhood with its own schools, churches, shopping and social facilities *[1 mark]*. Housing separated from industry *[1 mark]*. Factories built on the edges of the town *[1 mark]*. Separation of traffic and pedestrians *[1 mark]*.
You could choose any New Town — Stevenage, Hemel Hempstead, etc.

2 1 mark for each point up to a maximum of 7.
Successes: spacious well-equipped homes *[1 mark]*; semi-rural surroundings *[1 mark]*; jobs *[1 mark]*.
Failures: not self-sufficient *[1 mark]*; not always enough new jobs *[1 mark]*; inadequate services *[1 mark]*; some see architecture as ugly *[1 mark]*; desired social mixing not achieved *[1 mark]*.

3 Maximum of 6 marks available.
Describe 3 technologies — 1 mark for naming the technology, 1 for describing the impact. Reinforced concrete *[1 mark]* has allowed large concrete structures to be built *[1 mark]*. Cladding *[1 mark]* has been used to give attractive finishes to exteriors *[1 mark]*. The invention of the lift *[1 mark]* makes it possible to build high rise blocks *[1 mark]*. Steel girders and curtain wall construction *[1 mark]* make it possible to build high buildings *[1 mark]*.

Page 91 — Urban Land Use

1 Maximum of 5 marks available.
Answer depends on the land model chosen — up to 2 marks for an accurate drawing of the model and up to 3 marks for a correct description of what the different sectors of the model are.

Page 93 — Urban Land Use

1 Maximum of 7 marks available.
LEDC land use models usually incorporate unplanned shanty town or squatter development *[1 mark]*. LEDC land use models have elite housing near the CBD *[1 mark]* and poor housing in the outskirts. It's the opposite way around in MEDCs *[1 mark]*. In pre-industrial cities, most transport is still on foot *[1 mark]*. Many LEDCs were at some point colonial *[1 mark]*. LEDC cities would have zones which were originally used by colonial administrators and now used by government elites *[1 mark]*. In their colonial past, LEDC cities would have been ethnically segregated, with a white European district and a "native" district *[1 mark]*. Neither of these apply to MEDCs.

Page 95 — Changing Urban Structure

1 Maximum of 7 marks available.
3 marks for description points, 3 marks for explanation points, 1 mark for relating it all to named city. Answer depends on which city you've chosen, but these are common points:
Decreasing population density *[1 mark]* because of movement to suburbs *[1 mark]*. Improvements in traffic congestion *[1 mark]* because of improved public transport *[1 mark]*. Recent increase in population *[1 mark]* because of reurbanisation *[1 mark]*. Fewer shops *[1 mark]* because of growth in retail parks *[1 mark]*. Fewer jobs *[1 mark]* because of growth of out of town business parks *[1 mark]*. More attractive *[1 mark]* because of gentrification *[1 mark]*. More trendy bars and restaurants *[1 mark]* because of gentrification *[1 mark]*.

2 Maximum of 7 marks available.
Answer depends on which city you choose. Sample answer is for Ancoats, Manchester.
Regeneration projects to stop crime and improve quality of life include home security programme *[1 mark]*, neighbourhood watch *[1 mark]* and car crime education project *[1 mark]*. Public private partnerships between Urban Village project and local Italian community *[1 mark]* set up to redevelop buildings *[1 mark]*, recreating the Little Italy district with shops, bars *[1 mark]*. English Heritage have contributed money *[1 mark]*.

Page 97 — Conflict on the Rural-Urban Fringe

1 Sample answer (for Ashwell, Hertfordshire). 1 mark for each point up to a maximum of 5: The population has grown considerably in recent years *[1 mark]*, by over 20% in the last 30 years *[1 mark]*. This is because improvements in transport allow people to commute from there *[1 mark]*. The age structure has changed so there are more retired people *[1 mark]*. Now over 20% of the population are retired people *[1 mark]*. This is because many urban dwellers prefer the peace and quiet of the countryside once they retire from work *[1 mark]*. Many old barns have been converted into houses *[1 mark]*. These barn conversions are popular because they look more traditional than newly built houses *[1 mark]*. Modern housing is of different styles to the original village houses *[1 mark]*. Incomers need houses so several new estates have been added to the village *[1 mark]*.

2 Maximum of 7 marks available.
Don't forget specific examples or you won't score more than 4 marks.
Pressure for the green belt to be used for building land, because of housing shortage in SE *[1 mark]*. Townspeople need areas for recreation and leisure and this puts pressure on the green belt *[1 mark]*. Proposals for golf courses often cause conflict in the green belt area *[1 mark]*. Since land is often cheaper in green belt areas than in city centres, businesses see it as an ideal place for new premises *[1 mark]* and several retail parks have been built there, despite opposition from town centre traders *[1 mark]*.
You could use the example of cheap land on the outskirts of London and large retail parks such as Bluewater in Kent and Lakeside in Essex.
The rural land contained within the green belts is an asset which many people think should be conserved *[1 mark]*. or Many people think that all development in rural areas destroys the local ecology *[1 mark]*. There are many areas of ancient woodland around English towns which, once destroyed for development, would be lost forever. This causes conflict *[2 marks]*. Wetland areas in the Lea Valley contain endangered species *[1 mark]* which many people think should not be threatened by housing and industrial development *[1 mark]*. They think the area should be left as natural as possible and serve as an area for recreation *[1 mark]*.
You aren't tied to one specific case study here so you can write about the urban fringe round any city or a bunch of different cities. Choose whichever places give you the best examples.

Page 99 — Urban Quality of Life

1 Any four points from the following, to a maximum of 4 marks.
There are high levels of unemployment *[1 mark]*, because industries have moved elsewhere *[1 mark]*. There's poor housing *[1 mark]* and overcrowding *[1 mark]*. There is a higher risk of crime *[1 mark]*. There is social exclusion caused by factors such as unemployment, low income, poor housing and poor access to healthcare *[1 mark]*.

2 Maximum of 7 marks available.
For the first part, give causes of squatter settlements — push and pull factors leading to rapid urbanisation in LEDCs. There are 3 marks available here. You won't get credit for giving a pull factor and its exact opposite as a push factor. You should give at least one pull factor and at least one push factor.
Push factors: Rural poverty *[1 mark]*. Few jobs in rural areas *[1 mark]*. Poor crop yields in rural areas, so not enough food to feed growing families *[1 mark]*. Pull factors: Perceived job opportunities (in formal and informal sectors) in city *[1 mark]*. Perceived improvements in accessibility of services such as schools and doctors *[1 mark]*.
For the second part, describe conditions in a squatter settlement. The actual details you give will depend on your chosen example, obviously. There are a maximum of 4 marks available here. Your description of the conditions should include facts such as the location, rough population density *[1 mark]*, size of the settlement *[1 mark]*, endemic diseases *[1 mark]*, local employment *[1 mark]* etc. You could also mention any improvement schemes that you know about.

Page 101 — Urban Ecosystems

1 Maximum of 5 marks available.
The answer you give depends on the urban environments you choose to describe (almost all UK cities have parks, allotments, playing fields, cemeteries, railway embankments, etc). You're best off choosing about 3 environments and giving a spot of detail for each — like this example answer: Leicester has large urban parks (e.g. Abbey Park, Victoria Park). In urban parks there is a maintained plagiosere community *[1 mark]* of grass, flowers and trees *[1 mark]*. These are deliberately introduced, and mostly aren't native species *[1 mark]*. Houses have gardens which are cultivated with introduced exotic plants *[1 mark]*. Grass lawns are a relatively barren environment — they don't support a lot of wildlife *[1 mark]*. Railway embankments provide a good environment for wildlife, e.g. birds, foxes and butterflies *[1 mark]*. Buddleia bushes growing on embankments are attractive to butterflies *[1 mark]*.

2 Maximum of 5 marks available.
Stage 1: Mosses and lichens develop on bare concrete *[1 mark]*. They weather the concrete, and leave organic matter and regolith, which provides a soil for other plants to grow in *[1 mark]*. Stage 2: Seeds of flowering plants such as Oxford Ragwort blow in on the wind and germinate in cracks *[1 mark]*. Stage 3: As plants die, they rot down to produce humus, which

Answers

enriches the new soil. Bigger plants like Rosebay Willowherb can grow *[1 mark]*. Stage 4: After a few years, herbs and grass are replaced by shrubs and trees such as Sycamore and Rowan *[1 mark]*.

Page 103 — Managing Urban Housing

1 Maximum of 7 marks available.
The exact details you give depend on the examples you choose.
To get the marks you need to mention the following: whether it's a greenfield or brownfield site *[1 mark]*; where it is in relation to the town centre (city centre, suburb, rural-urban fringe) *[1 mark]*; the size of housing (2 bedroom, 3 bedroom etc) *[1 mark]*; the type of housing (flats, semi-detached houses, detached houses) *[1 mark]*; whether they're all new build or conversions of barns or warehouses *[1 mark]*; the style of architecture (designed to look like cottages and blend in with a village, modern block of flats, etc) *[1 mark]*; if it's part of an inner city generation scheme *[1 mark]*.

2 Maximum of 7 marks available.
The actual details will depend on your specific examples, but likely attempted solutions will probably include:
Self help housing schemes *[1 mark]*, including site and services *[1 mark]*, where the local authority provides plots of land *[1 mark]* with water and sewerage *[1 mark]*, and incomers build their own houses on the plots, using low cost basic building materials *[1 mark]*. Authorities also build satellite towns to try to get people out of overcrowded squatter settlements *[1 mark]*. 1 mark for a named example.

Page 105 — Managing Urban Transport

1 Maximum of 3 marks available.
As car ownership increases the provision of public transport decreases *[1 mark]*. This is a negative relationship *[1 mark]*. Either one of the following points for the third mark: With more cars people use less public transport and it becomes uneconomic *[1 mark]*. Services are withdrawn so fewer people can use them creating a downward spiral *[1 mark]*.

2 Maximum of 7 marks available.
6 marks for descriptions and explanations, 1 mark for example.
1 mark for each of these points to a maximum of 6: Park and ride schemes *[1 mark]*, which reduce the number of private cars driving into the city centre *[1 mark]*. Bus and cycle lanes *[1 mark]* make it more convenient to travel by bus or bike, as you're not stuck in car traffic *[1 mark]*. High parking fees *[1 mark]* discourage people from driving into town *[1 mark]*. "Tidal flows" give a road more lanes in the direction where most traffic is going *[1 mark]*, which eases congestion *[1 mark]*. Congestion charging costs people money whenever they drive into the city centre *[1 mark]*, deterring them from travelling to the CBD by private car *[1 mark]*. Improved public transport e.g. tube/trams/local rail *[1 mark]* give people a valid alternative to the car *[1 mark]* for your named example — London, Manchester, Newcastle, or wherever.
Try to link the effect of each solution to its description – this saves you having to write things twice. London is a good bet for an example if you can't think of another one. It's got congestion charging, there are improvements being made to bus and riverboat services, it costs shed-loads to park and there are bus lanes aplenty.

3. Maximum of 9 marks available. (Maximum of 3 marks for causes, 3 marks for effects and 3 marks for attempted solutions) The actual details will depend on your specific example, but will be similar to the following:
Causes — Urbanisation means a larger urban population need to travel around *[1 mark]*. Rapid increase in car ownership leads to more cars on the roads *[1 mark]*. Rapid unplanned growth of the city means there is no management of transport systems *[1 mark]*. Effects — Traffic is chaotic, especially at rush hour *[1 mark]*. Large volume of poorly managed traffic leads to many accidents *[1 mark]*. Poor quality vehicles cause large volumes of air pollution *[1 mark]*. Emissions can have an adverse effect on people's respiratory health *[1 mark]*. Solutions — Elevated roadways /skytrains are built as alternative / additional routeways *[1 mark]*. Tram systems built for use by commuters *[1 mark]*. Building an underground system to relieve congestion *[1 mark]*. Use of catalytic converters and unleaded fuel to cut down on emissions *[1 mark]*.

Page 107 — Urban Environmental Problems

1 Any of these points to a maximum of 7 marks.
Toxic gases given out from industries (e.g. in Mexico City) cause and aggravate respiratory problems *[1 mark]*. Photochemical smog during summer anticyclones, e.g. in Los Angeles or Kuala Lumpur *[1 mark]* (or any other valid example) increases the dangers to people with respiratory problems *[1 mark]*. Vehicles contribute to air pollution *[1 mark]* and also to deaths from road accidents *[1 mark]*. Lack of adequate clean drinking water supplies (only in LEDC cities such as Kolkata) spreads water-borne diseases *[1 mark]*. Inadequate sewage disposal (again, in LEDC cities) contaminates water supplies and spreads disease *[1 mark]*. Toxic discharges into rivers and water systems have an effect on food chains and eventually on food that humans eat *[1 mark]*.
You can use any examples you like, just as long as you're sure that they illustrate your point.

2 Maximum of 7 marks available.
You can use any example, but the Los Angeles case study is a good bet. Any of these points to a maximum of 7 — BUT if you don't say if any of the measures did well or badly, you won't get more than 5 marks.
Most of Los Angeles' smog comes from car pollution *[1 mark]*. Los Angeles has a public transport system of buses and metro *[1 mark]*, but it isn't particularly successful (only 5% of people commute to work on public transport) *[1 mark]*. There's a rigorous programme of emissions tests for all cars *[1 mark]*. Cars which fail have to be fixed and retested, by law *[1 mark]*. This has been successful in cutting emissions *[1 mark]*. LPG or electricity fuelled cars are allowed to use the "carpool" lane, which encourages people to switch to low emission fuels *[1 mark]*. This has been quite effective *[1 mark]*, but the USA is lagging behind countries like Brazil, which has a higher proportion of low emission vehicles *[1 mark]*.

Page 109 — Managing Urban Social Problems

1 Any of the following points up to a maximum of 6 marks.
Authorities can put more police on the streets *[1 mark]*. Zero tolerance policing is where all offences are prosecuted, including littering and minor vandalism *[1 mark]*. The idea is that people will not commit crime if they see that no crime is tolerated *[1 mark]*. Zero tolerance has been used in New York, and in Middlesbrough *[1 mark]*. Private individuals and businesses install burglar alarms *[1 mark]*. Businesses use security guards *[1 mark]* (any decent example for *1 mark*). People set up neighbourhood watch schemes *[1 mark]*.
You don't have to do any evaluation for this question.

2 Maximum of 7 marks available.
2 marks for definition of the term "ghetto" and 5 marks for the reasons for their formation. Make sure you include both parts. You must give both positive and negative reasons for the formation of ghettos.
Definition: An area in a city occupied by a minority group *[1 mark]*. Ghetto areas are usually disadvantaged *[1 mark]*. Reasons for formation of ghettos (to maximum of 5): sharing a common language *[1 mark]*; sharing religious traditions *[1 mark]*; sharing cultural traditions *[1 mark]*; discrimination in housing market (e.g. some landlords unwilling to let to ethnic minority people) *[1 mark]*; defence against racism *[1 mark]*; unemployment which leads to people being concentrated in areas of cheapest housing *[1 mark]*.

Page 111 — Urban Futures

1 Maximum of 4 marks available. 3 marks for description, 1 mark for example.
Urban areas regenerate by converting disused industrial buildings *[1 mark]* into high quality housing *[1 mark]*, offices *[1 mark]* and leisure facilites *[1 mark]*. For example London's Docklands, Salford Quays, Liverpool's Albert Dock *[1 mark]*.

2 Maximum of 7 marks available.
This answer is about Curitiba. 1 mark for each of these sustainability measures to a maximum of 6: Integrated transport system encourages public transport use *[1 mark]*. Green areas are a priority for town planners *[1 mark]*. Lakes are used as flood control reservoirs *[1 mark]*. There is a waste exchange scheme *[1 mark]* where people bring in recyclable waste in exchange for food, books and toys *[1 mark]*. Water quality is monitored regularly, and schoolchildren are involved in this *[1 mark]*. 1 mark for evaluation: Curitiba's sustainability measures have been very successful, and the city has won international awards for them *[1 mark]*.

Section Nine — Population Dynamics

Page 113 — Population Distribution and Density

1 Maximum of 4 marks available.
1 mark each for 3 of the following ideas: River valleys have rich alluvial soils for growing crops and for grazing land *[1 mark]*. They provide water supplies *[1 mark]*. The valley is a natural transport route *[1 mark]*. The land is flatter for building on *[1 mark]*. 1 mark for naming an example, e.g. The Rhone, Rhine, Hwang-he or other river *[1 mark]*.

2 Maximum of 4 marks available. You can choose any LEDC, but Brazil's the one in the book...
1 mark for each of these points to a maximum of 4: Most of Brazil's population live near the coast *[1 mark]*, with large numbers along the SE coast, e.g. at Sao Paulo *[1 mark]*. As you go inland to the West and North, there are fewer people *[1 mark]*. Some parts of the interior are virtually uninhabited (e.g. Amazonia) *[1 mark]*. An exception is the Brasilia area, where there is a local concentration of people *[1 mark]*.

Page 115 — Population Terms and Definitions

1 Maximum of 4 marks available.
Name your area (e.g. NE Brazil) *[1 mark]*. (Other areas are possible, e.g. Bangladesh, Ethiopia, China in 1949.)
1 mark for each of these points to a maximum of 3: Poverty *[1 mark]*, poor housing *[1 mark]*, job shortages *[1 mark]*, low literacy levels *[1 mark]*, poor farming *[1 mark]*, poor industry *[1 mark]*, poor health *[1 mark]*, low life expectancy *[1 mark]*.

Answers

2 Maximum of 5 marks available.
E.g. A one child policy in China combined with the fact that people in rural China prefer to have boy babies has meant that many girl babies have been killed *[1 mark]*. This has also made the population become unbalanced (more males than females) which will cause future problems *[1 mark]*. In Singapore, strict birth control policies have led to the possibility of a falling population, which will lead to future problems (elderly population) *[1 mark]*, or will lead to future economic decline with a shortage of middle aged working people *[1 mark]*. Plus 1 mark for giving names of examples *[1 mark]*.

Page 117 — Population Change

1 Maximum of 4 marks available.
2 marks for a social factor and explanation. 1 mark for any social factor, and 1 mark for the explanation to go with it, from: Medical advances, e.g. vaccinations *[1 mark]* make people healthier, so fewer die. Better diet *[1 mark]* improves health *[1 mark]*. Improved sanitation *[1 mark]* means that fewer people die from illnesses related to polluted water or bacteria from sewage *[1 mark]*.
2 marks for economic factor and explanation — any economic factor from: Improved farming *[1 mark]* means there's less starvation *[1 mark]*. Improvements in transport also improve food supplies *[1 mark]*, so fewer people starve *[1 mark]*. Increased wealth (due to industry) provides money for education and health care *[1 mark]*, so people learn how to improve their health *[1 mark]*.

2 Maximum of 4 marks available.
2 marks for each factor and each explanation. Maximum 2 factors.
Birth control is increasingly used *[1 mark]* because women and families want to delay having children *[1 mark]*. A falling death rate means that more babies survive and grow up *[1 mark]*, so there is no need to have lots of children to replace those who die *[1 mark]*. More women are educated and work *[1 mark]*, and no longer wish to stay at home bearing children *[1 mark]*. Large numbers of children are no longer needed as workers *[1 mark]* when mechanisation starts *[1 mark]*. People start to want wealth *[1 mark]*, so they choose to have fewer children *[1 mark]*.

Page 119 — Applying the DTM

1 Maximum of 3 marks available. 1 mark for named example and 2 for 2 reasons.
In the case of France *[1 mark]*, the reasons for wanting to increase the birth rate are: it will prevent population decline *[1 mark]*; it will provide more young people who will become a future workforce *[1 mark]*; an increase in births will eventually provide workers and money to support the elderly *[1 mark]*; the country doesn't want to rely too much on immigrant workers *[1 mark]*.

2 Maximum of 4 marks available. Write about 4 problems, 1 mark for each.
Low birth rates mean there'll be fewer workers in the future, and possible economic decline *[1 mark]*. Low birth rates and few children lead to school closures *[1 mark]*. More people become elderly but a smaller working population means there is less money provided for them *[1 mark]*. Increasing numbers of elderly need more care (e.g. hospital care, nursing homes) *[1 mark]*. The population will fall *[1 mark]*.

Page 121 — Types and Theories of Migration

1 Maximum of 4 marks available.
1 mark for reason, 1 for explanation, for maximum of 2 reasons.
Moving to take up a new job *[1 mark]* which is too far away to commute to *[1 mark]*. Moving to look for a job *[1 mark]* in an area with more employment prospects *[1 mark]*. Moving to retire to the countryside where it's quieter *[1 mark]*.
You could have other reasons and answers, for either an LEDC or an MEDC.

2 Maximum of 3 marks available.
The distance decay principle states that as distance increases, the volume of movement decreases *[1 mark]*. This is true of migration because the longer the distance, the greater the cost of moving so many can't afford it *[1 mark]*. People find it easier to move a short distance so they won't be far from relatives *[1 mark]*. Distant moves are harder if there's a different language/customs *[1 mark]*.

Page 123 — Causes of Migration

1 Maximum of 5 marks available.
Negative attitudes are the problems or 'push factors', which make people want to migrate away *[1 mark]*.
3 marks for examples of negative feelings — 1 mark for each of these to a maximum of 3: farming problems caused by poor soils and soil erosion *[1 mark]*; worries about low rural wages *[1 mark]*; job shortages *[1 mark]*; poor services, e.g. schools *[1 mark]*; worries about droughts or other disasters *[1 mark]*.
1 mark for named example, e.g. This makes people move from villages in Mexico to Mexico City *[1 mark]*.

2 Maximum of 4 marks available. It'd be best to have 2 economic push factors for 2 marks each and 2 economic pull factors for 2 marks each.
Economic push factors — Closure of older industries (e.g. shipbuilding, textiles, port jobs) in the North *[1 mark]*, and the lower standard of living in the North compared to the South *[1 mark]*. Many jobs in the North are lower paid *[1 mark]*.
Economic pull factors —Higher paid jobs, e.g. in offices in London *[1 mark]*, and higher standard of living *[1 mark]*. Growth of high-tech industries in the South has attracted workers *[1 mark]*.
Make your push and pull factors different, not straight opposites.

Page 125 — Government Migration Policy and Effects of Migration

1 Maximum of 5 marks available.
1 mark for definition: Guest workers are workers from abroad who are invited and encouraged to come and work in another country by its government *[1 mark]*.
4 marks for explanation of problems — any of the following points to a maximum of 4: Turkish guest workers in Germany have become a problem because of conflict and tension between Turks and Germans *[1 mark]*; unemployment has risen in Germany, and some feel that the Turks are no longer needed and should be sent home *[1 mark]*; but the original Turks and their grown up children see Germany as their home now *[1 mark]*; the former West Germany has received East Germans since the unification, and they need jobs; some feel that the Turks' jobs should go to East Germans *[1 mark]*. Other case studies could be used here, e.g. Algerian and Moroccan workers in Paris, France; or West Indian people in UK.

2 Maximum of 4 marks available.
Describe 4 negative impacts, with 1 mark for each. For example: cities, e.g. Mexico City and São Paulo, have grown enormously (urban sprawl) with the growth of squatter settlements *[1 mark]*; squatter settlements have problems of disease, e.g. cholera and dysentery *[1 mark]*; the city can't afford to provide services, e.g. clean water and sanitation, for all the immigrants *[1 mark]*; there aren't enough jobs for all the immigrants *[1 mark]*; there's overcrowding *[1 mark]*; rivers are polluted by sewage *[1 mark]*; health services and schools are overstretched *[1 mark]*.

Page 127 — Population Structure

1 Maximum of 6 marks available.
Hint – many students find it difficult to describe the shape of a pyramid. You need to imagine it divided into 3 horizontal parts – the young, the middle-aged and the elderly, and describe each of these, like this:
The base is wide, and almost half the population is aged under 15 *[1 mark]*. This is because the birth rate is high (there is little birth control, and people need to replace children who die) *[1 mark]*. In the middle years the pyramid narrows rapidly *[1 mark]*, as many die in all age groups because of poor diet and disease *[1 mark]*. There are very few elderly people (and there are more women than men) and almost no-one over 80 *[1 mark]*, because of poor health and diet *[1 mark]*.

2 Maximum of 3 marks available.
1 mark for each effect of war on a pyramid, up to a total of 3. Deaths during a war shown by indentation in the bars of a pyramid *[1 mark]*. There's also an indentation in age groups born during the war, showing that birth rate during war was lower than usual *[1 mark]*. Longer bars in an age group born just after the war can be the result of an increased birth rate as peace returns — this is the "baby boom" *[1 mark]*. Large indentations could be the result of emigration or refugee movements due to war *[1 mark]*.

Section Ten — Economic Activity

Page 129 — Sectors of Economic Activity

1 Maximum of 5 marks available from the following.
Primary industry needs to be situated right where the resources are *[1 mark]*. Secondary industry needs to be located near to transport facilities, e.g. a sea port, so that raw materials can be brought in *[1 mark]* and finished goods sent out easily *[1 mark]*. It needs to be close to a suitable workforce *[1 mark]*. Quaternary industry doesn't need raw materials but needs to be close to an educated and skilled workforce *[1 mark]* or close to client businesses *[1 mark]*.

Page 131 — Secondary Activity in MEDCs

1 Maximum of 8 marks available.
There has been deindustrialisation in traditional manufacturing areas *[1 mark]* such as South Wales, the North East, and Yorkshire *[1 mark]*. Heavy industry declined *[1 mark]* from the mid 1970s to mid 1980s *[1 mark]*. Light industry grew in the 1990s *[1 mark]*. New "sunrise" industries have developed, e.g. computers, pharmaceuticals *[1 mark]*. These tend to be in areas like the M4 corridor around Reading *[1 mark]*, not the same places where heavy industry jobs were lost *[1 mark]*.

2 Maximum of 18 marks available.
Competition from abroad has caused the decline of European manufacturing industry *[1 mark]*. Countries like Japan, Taiwan and Malaysia could sell things

Answers

more cheaply than European manufacturers *[1 mark]* partly because their labour costs were lower *[1 mark]* and they didn't have to follow strict health and safety laws *[1 mark]*. Some industries in the EU didn't keep up with changes in technology, and didn't modernise their working practices *[1 mark]*. During the 1970s, trade unions actively resisted modernisation *[1 mark]*, particularly in the UK. "Smokestack" industries such as steel, textiles, shipbuilding and pottery have suffered most *[1 mark]*. Heavy industries used to be near coalfields, because they relied on coal as a source of electricity *[1 mark]*. Nowadays, heavy industry doesn't need to be near the coalfields any more *[1 mark]*. This has resulted in deindustrialisation of the Rhine/Ruhr *[1 mark]*, and North East England *[1 mark]*. The coal industry declined because of a lack of demand for coal, and because areas elsewhere produced coal more efficiently *[1 mark]*. Deindustrialisation is also linked to increased demand for services — as economies grow, incomes rise, and there's demand for consumer durables and services *[1 mark]*.
Newly industrialised countries make consumer goods more cheaply than the EU *[1 mark]*. Iron ore in the UK and in Germany isn't as good as iron ore from outside the EU, so the steel industry suffered *[1 mark]*. There was some lack of government support in the UK *[1 mark]*. There was a world economic recession in the 1970s/80s which lowered demand for EU products *[1 mark]*. The UK £ is "strong" (has a high value) so UK made goods are expensive to buy abroad *[1 mark]*.

Page 133 — Newly Industrialised Countries

1   Maximum of 8 marks available.
Manufacturing industry in NICs is near to raw materials *[1 mark]*, ports (for exporting finished goods) *[1 mark]* and near to a source of cheap labour *[1 mark]*. Industry therefore tends to be on coastal locations close to primate cities *[1 mark]*. Food processing, ore processing and textiles in particular need to be near to raw materials or near to transport facilities where raw materials are brought in *[1 mark]*. High tech industry needs to have plenty of educated and skilled workers *[1 mark]*. As NICs develop, their industry can move from coastal locations to locations near universities *[1 mark]*. Multinationals choose to locate where there's cheap labour *[1 mark]*.

2   Maximum of 6 marks available.
Environmental — rapid growth leads to pollution *[1 mark]* and deforestation *[1 mark]*. **Economic** — Investment of capital leads to development *[1 mark]*. Average incomes rise *[1 mark]*. Dependence on selling primary goods is reduced *[1 mark]*. There's a wage gap between people working for big companies and people still doing agriculture *[1 mark]*. **Social** — workers exploited *[1 mark]*. Rural-urban migration causes overcrowding *[1 mark]*.

Page 135 — Changes in the Retail Industry

1   Maximum of 7 marks available (any 7 points from the following).
Advantages — convenient for customers *[1 mark]*. Provide a good shopping experience so customers spend lots of money *[1 mark]*. Have leisure facilities, e.g. cinemas and restaurants *[1 mark]*. Land is cheaper on rural-urban fringe *[1 mark]*.
Disadvantages — Roads around retail park become congested *[1 mark]*. There aren't any independent stores *[1 mark]*. Retailers in town centres suffer, as customers go to the retail park instead *[1 mark]*. This can cause a multiplier effect (i.e. it keeps making itself worse) — as shops close down they leave behind boarded up buildings, and no other retailers want to rent a unit in a run-down looking area *[1 mark]*.

2   Maximum of 5 marks available.
Retailers in town centres have lost custom *[1 mark]*, as customers go to the retail park instead *[1 mark]*. There's a multiplier effect as other retailers don't want to rent a unit in a run-down looking area *[1 mark]*. The risk of crime increases in run-down town centres *[1 mark]*. The CBD has to respond by creating new indoor malls (e.g. Birmingham's Bull Ring) and pedestrianisation *[1 mark]*.

Page 137 — Changing Office Employment

1   Maximum of 6 marks available.
Service employment has been decentralising in recent years *[1 mark]*. This means it's moving away from London to regional towns *[1 mark]*, and from city centres out to small towns and villages *[1 mark]*. However, high level functions tend to stay in city centres, and in London *[1 mark]*, because they need face to face contact with clients *[1 mark]*. Back office functions like admin. and payroll can be easily decentralised *[1 mark]*.
Notice how there's nothing about why decentralisation happens, the high price of office space, the hassle of commuting, the technological advances that make decentralisation possible. That's because the question only asks about the extent of decentralisation. It wants you to mention the difference between high level functions and back office functions.

2   Maximum of 4 marks available.
The call centre industry was originally based in company head offices, usually in the SE of England *[1 mark]*. To some extent, there was a move to the regions, especially Scotland and the North East *[1 mark]*. This was partly because market research showed that people liked the sound of Scottish and Geordie accents *[1 mark]*. There was also a pool of suitable labour in Scotland and the North of England *[1 mark]*. In the early 2000s, there was a big move of call centre jobs to India *[1 mark]*. However, there's been a perception that some

Indian workers don't have the cultural knowledge necessary to solve UK-centric problems quickly, so some call centre jobs have moved back to the UK *[1 mark]*.

Page 139 — Quaternary Developments

1   Maximum of 7 marks available.
Advantages — attractive work environment *[1 mark]*; close to transport links *[1 mark]*; benefits of agglomeration *[1 mark]*; support services provided *[1 mark]*.
Disadvantages — use greenfield sites *[1 mark]*; traffic congestion *[1 mark]*. Housing may be expensive because of high demand *[1 mark]*.

2   Maximum of 6 marks available.
Agglomeration means clumping together *[1 mark]*. By being close to similar businesses, a business can have access to the same information *[1 mark]* and workforce *[1 mark]*. This is useful for businesses on a science park, which need specialised information *[1 mark]*, and highly qualified workers *[1 mark]*. They usually cluster around universities *[1 mark]*.

Page 141 — Employment Issues

1   Maximum of 5 marks available.
Service industries like hotel/catering and retail have traditionally employed a lot of women *[1 mark]*. The quaternary sector has employed increasing numbers of women in recent years *[1 mark]*. Women are often perceived as being good at customer-facing jobs, e.g. customer services, call centres, retail *[1 mark]*. There are a lot of part-time jobs in the service sector *[1 mark]*, and mothers often take these to fit in with childcare *[1 mark]*.

2   Maximum of 4 marks available.
People are attracted to self-employment because it means they can be their own boss *[1 mark]*. There's been a focus on work/life balance in recent years, so being self-employed has become more attractive *[1 mark]*. Employers may lay workers off (especially IT workers) and then re-engage them as self-employed consultants *[1 mark]*. Some service sectors, e.g. financial advisors and plumbers, are traditionally self-employed, and there's been growth in those sectors *[1 mark]*.

Section 11 — Resources

Page 143 — Renewable and Non-Renewable Resources

1   Maximum of 4 marks available.
Oil might not last very long — maybe only 50 years. When it gets scarce, the price will rise a lot *[1 mark]*. New oil is difficult and expensive to discover *[1 mark]*. The price of oil is vulnerable to political pressures — if a country doesn't like us, they can stop selling us their oil *[1 mark]*. When the price of oil goes up, the price of electricity generated by burning oil also goes up *[1 mark]*.

Page 145 — Energy Harnessing and Pollution

1 a) Maximum of 3 marks available. Global warming is caused by an increased greenhouse effect *[1 mark]*. The Sun's radiation passes through most of the gases in the atmosphere, warming the Earth, but CO_2 and some other gases prevent much of the outgoing radiation from the Earth from escaping into space *[1 mark]*. Increased levels of CO_2 (due to things like deforestation and fossil fuel burning) have increased this effect, causing temperatures to rise *[1 mark]*.
  b) Maximum of 4 marks available. Burning wood for fuel releases more CO_2 into the atmosphere, adding to the greenhouse effect *[1 mark]*. Vehicles burning fossil fuels do the same *[1 mark]*. Industries using coal, oil or gas as fuels also release CO_2, adding to global warming *[1 mark]*. Power stations burning fossil fuels for electricity also add to the problem *[1 mark]*.

2   Maximum of 4 marks available.
Nuclear waste is radioactive *[1 mark]* and can cause cancers and birth defects *[1 mark]*. High level radioactive waste is particularly dangerous and stays radioactive for thousands of years *[1 mark]*. Nuclear waste can spill and contaminate earth or groundwater *[1 mark]*.

Index

Index

Index

Index